Practical Public Speaking

EUGENE E. WHITE
The Pennsylvania State University

Practical Public Speaking

FOURTH EDITION

Macmillan Publishing Co., Inc.
New York
Collier Macmillan Publishers
London

Printed in the United States of America

Macmillan Publishing Co., Inc.
866 Third Avenue, New York, New York 10022

Collier Macmillan Canada, Inc.

Library of Congress Cataloging in Publication Data

White, Eugene Edmond, (date)
Practical public speaking.

Bibliography: p.
Includes index.
1. Public speaking. I. Title.
PN4121.W372 1982 808.5'1 81-8446
ISBN 0-02-427050-4 AACR2

Printing: 3 4 5 6 7 8 Year: 3 4 5 6 7 8

ISBN 0-02-427050-4

Preface

In preparing the fourth edition of this book, I have sought to preserve the philosophy and approach that carried the first three editions to more than a score of printings. This edition, as were the earlier ones, is designed to be a practical, relatively complete guide to the preparation and presentation of public speeches.

What is different about this edition? Among the more obvious changes, I have added a chapter (Chapter 2, "Understanding Basic Communicative Concepts") that focuses on what I believe are the most important pragmatic concepts involved in public speaking. I have grouped slightly differently the early chapters in order to emphasize the interaction between the demands (needs or requirements) exerted upon the speech by the audience, speaking occasion, the speaker, and the speech purpose (Chapters 3 and 4) and the answering of those demands by the strategies of speech development, rehearsal, and delivery (Chapters 5–16). I have also divided the treatment of developing the Body of the speech into three chapters, instead of the two found in the third edition. My reason for doing this is to improve the focus, to make clearer the critical concepts inherent in developing ideas clearly, interestingly, and persuasively.

Among the somewhat less obvious changes, I have updated illustrative materials; tried to incorporate advances in psychology, sociology, and related disciplines; attempted to sharpen the explication of the various concepts and their application, expanding explanation here and reducing it there; and sought to improve the capacity of the text to engage the reader in an ongoing dialogue concerning speech preparation and delivery—in essentially the same way that the effective speaker promotes a cyclical interrelationship between himself and the listeners, which continues throughout the speech.

Those who have used and liked the third edition will be pleased that this edition contains no sharp divergence in matter or form. In Chapter 1, as in previous editions, I have attempted to engage the serious beginning speakers' concerns and understanding. In subsequent chapters, by supplying answers to their felt—if unexpressed—questions, I have sought to help them grow, to extend themselves toward greater confidence and capability in speech preparation and delivery. Instead of ready-made formulas that tend to stultify original thought, I have tried to give the kind of specific guidance that will sensitize the readers, first, to a greater awareness of the influences that may limit or extend their freedoms as a communicator in a given set of circumstances and, second, to the range of options that are available to them in responding to the various rhetorical demands with which they are confronted.

My intention in this edition, as in previous ones, has been to treat concisely yet comprehensively those principles that are basic to proper perspectives concerning public speaking and to effective speech preparation and delivery. With the student-reader foremost in my mind, my goals have been ready understandability, practicality, friendly and informal style, and brevity. To achieve a cumulative effect, principles are stated, explained, summarized, looked at from different points of view, and integrated—until they become a natural part of the reader's thinking. As each element of effective speaking is studied, the reader is constantly reminded of the ancient origins and honorable continuum of rhetorical theory and of the social and ethical responsibilities that must be assumed by the speaker.

Like the earlier editions, this one is primarily designed for use in the beginning undergraduate course and the adult public-speaking course in extension divisions or in industry. However, this edition will also provide self-help for individuals who are not enrolled in a formal course but who wish to improve their skills in speechmaking.

As in the previous editions, I have followed each chapter with exercises and problems that are intended to aid the teacher in planning assignments and to aid the student in putting principles into practice. The sequence and grouping of chapters have been designed to provide maximum utility and flexibility in usage. To enable the student to prepare and deliver a speech before reading large segments of the book, the fundamentals of public speaking are introduced in Chapter 1. A study of the detailed treatment of these principles in later chapters may follow several different approaches. For example, some instructors may apply the existing sequence of chapters; others who prefer to begin with a study of the techniques of delivery may assign Chapters 1 and 12–15 before Chapters 4–11; and still others may wish to consider one of the special types of speeches in Chapter 16 prior to a careful examination of speech preparation and delivery.

Regretfully I cannot thank individually here all those who contributed directly or indirectly to the preparation of this edition. However, I do wish to express my special appreciation to Lloyd C. Chilton, executive editor of Macmillan Publishing Co., Inc., for sharing generously of his time and wisdom and to my wife, Roberta Fluitt White, for providing—as always—wise counsel, encouragement, and, best of all, sprightly good humor. I am, of course, solely responsible for any shortcomings this book may possess.

University Park, Pennsylvania Eugene E. White

Contents

SECTION I

Developing the Proper Perspectives

Essential Purpose of Section I: to enable the reader to adopt proper perspectives about public speaking by approaching speechmaking positively and by understanding certain basic communicative concepts

CHAPTER 1

Approaching Public Speaking Positively

So you're going to make a speech! That entails facing an audience, something you may not have done since a childhood performance in a school play. You may recall the anxious faces of your parents as their lips moved with your words and their relief when your lines came out letter-perfect. Possibly your last speaking appearance was the giving of an oral book report or the reading aloud of a theme in a freshman English class. Very likely you are beginning the study of public speaking with mixed feelings: although possibly disturbed at the prospect of speechmaking, you value the opportunity to develop speech skills and want to do well.

Why are you enrolled in a course in public speaking? If you are a typical college student beginning a regular college course, you probably recognize the need for effective oral communication in almost any career you may pursue. As you move upward from your initial job experience to greater responsibility, increased opportunity to help others, and higher pay, your professional growth will be tied to your ability to communicate with others. Of more immediate concern, you may wish to understand and solve communicative problems you now have as a student. Perhaps you have been elected fraternity president and you need to energize the fellows to cooperate for the benefit of the order; member of the student senate and you have to propose and defend pieces of legislation; secretary of the Cavers Club and you must read the minutes and give reports. Maybe you have been appointed resident counselor and you are required to hold weekly meetings with the girls on your floor. Your curriculum, say in architecture, may necessitate your giving frequent oral reports and you feel that you don't represent yourself or your ideas as well as you would like. Or, possibly you have wanted occasionally to ask questions in large lecture-classes, but have had the nerve to do it only once—and then someone tittered as your tongue got twisted up.

Common to thousands of persons who each year enter the beginning course in public speaking is the knowledge that man is a talking animal and that speaking is our most prevalent form of communication. For every word we write, we speak thousands. It has been suggested that the American people utter some seven trillion words daily! And each time we talk—on the street, in a neighbor's home, across the conference table, before an audience—we are judged not only by *what we say* but also by *how effectively we say it.* In increasing numbers, people are realizing that the ability to communicate well may mean greater economic efficiency in a highly competitive world, more rewarding social relationships, increased personal satisfaction, and more responsible citizenship.

Misconceptions About the Study of Public Speaking

Before a positive philosophy for the beginning speaker can be presented and methods for achieving it suggested, several erroneous conceptions should be examined.

"You Either Have It Or You Don't"

Without remembered effort, most of us learn to talk early in childhood. Persons who speak volubly and effortlessly are labeled "born with the knack." Those who have less verbal facility may be tabbed "the quiet type." Like blue eyes or curly hair, the ability or inability to talk fluently is accepted by many as a hereditary trait. Subscribers to this theory point to Bill Jackson, who can always say "a few well-chosen words" at any time, before any audience, on any subject. In contrast, Professor Ellsworth Fox drones ineffectually to his classes and to women's clubs on his specialty, medieval art. Fox has lectured for fifteen years, is highly educated, and once took a course in public speaking. Jackson, on the other hand, has had no formal speech training, little education, and, until his "talent" was discovered, had had almost no public speaking experience.

Indeed, cases such as these exist. Possibly you can cite similar examples. Without training and apparently without conscious effort, some persons become adequate and, occasionally, exceptional speakers. Corresponding aptitudes, of course, occur in other endeavors—in music, art, drama, and athletics, for instance. Nevertheless, those with high aptitudes in these arts nearly always profit from study. Evidence refutes the claim of some people that speaking ability is easily acquired as a by-product of conversation, committee leadership, or recitation. To develop into skilled public speakers, most of us need concentrated effort, preferably under skilled supervision.

"You Can't Trust an Effective Speaker"

Since the time of Socrates, and possibly before, some persons have been skeptical of speech training, attacking it upon ethical and moral grounds. Perhaps because they have been deceived by a "high-pressure" salesman or a "slick operator," the skeptics distrust an individual who is articulate and persuasive, and believe that a stumbling, halting speaker is more sincere and trustworthy. Many years ago, however, Aristotle pointed out the absurdity of assuming that the misuse of speaking skills by some speakers constitutes an indictment of the skills themselves: "If it is urged that an abuse of the rhetorical faculty can work great mischief, the same charge can be brought against all good things (save virtue itself), and especially against the most useful things such as strength, health, wealth, and military skills. Rightly employed, they work the greatest blessings; and wrongly employed, they work the utmost harm."

Although in the *Rhetoric* Aristotle deplored both the chicanery sometimes employed by speakers and the susceptibility of some persons to dishonest persuasion, he stated categorically that the way to prevent the triumph of fraud and injustice was to *increase* speech training, not to abandon it: "The art of rhetoric . . . is valuable, first, because truth and justice are by nature more powerful than their opposites; so that, when decisions are not made as they should be, the speakers with the right on their side have only themselves to thank for the outcome. Their neglect of the art needs correction." The only way to combat fraudulent advocates is for honorable persons to develop ability in speaking and in analytical-evaluative listening.

Golden Voices and Silver Tongues

The studied, oratorical kind of speaking that was common some generations ago is as outdated today as tickets to last year's World Series. Effective speaking is not a "performance" staged to display the ability of the speaker; it is a communicative process designed to stir up desired responses from a particular audience assembled at a specific time and place. To secure these responses, you must learn to recognize the freedoms and restraints that characterize the particular speaking situation. You must develop the ability to identify the rhetorical needs with which you are confronted and to select and apply the rhetorical means that will satisfy, as well as possible, those needs. You must acquire the faculty of encouraging listeners to engage in a creative sharing with you concerning items under discussion; facility in linking your ideas to values, wants, and interests of listeners; proficiency in organizing and developing your ideas in the most effective logical and psychological manner; as well as the ability to speak clearly, precisely, and fluently.

Instead of flowery language, gestures on cue, pompous posing, and other trappings of the old-fashioned orator "out on display," your study will concentrate on those principles and skills that will promote the effective sharing of your ideas and feelings with your listeners.

A New Personality?

Obviously a single public-speaking course is not capable of satisfying all student needs. For instance, a student occasionally enrolls in a speech course with the hope that it will cure some personality or adjustment problem. A deep-seated emotional problem will not be solved by limited training in public speaking. Although the increased confidence and poise resulting from improvement in self-expression may alter a person's typical behavior patterns, it would be unrealistic to anticipate a personality metamorphosis as a consequence of a semester course in public speaking.

A Philosophy for the Beginning Speaker

As you approach the preparation of your first speeches, many thoughts may enter your mind. If you have had little or no previous public-speaking experience, you may ask yourself, "What can I talk about? How shall I prepare? Shall I write out the speech and read it, commit it to memory, try to talk from an outline, or what? Shall I rehearse? Where? How often? Should I begin with a joke? Could I get away with using last week's English theme? Should I drop the course?" These questions are typical. If you experience any of these feelings, you may be comforted to know that many beginning speakers share your uncertainty.

Of course, if you have had some successful speaking experience, you are probably more positively oriented. You may be thinking, "I'm beginning to enjoy this. I'm looking forward to giving my speech."

To secure maximum benefit from your speech training, you should minimize uncertainty or apprehension by adopting appropriate attitudes.

Confidence Can Be Acquired

A common initial reaction of the beginning speaker is that of apprehension, commonly termed "stage fright." Some students let trembling hands and knees, perspiring palms, dry mouths, tremulous voices, breathlessness, loss of memory, and "butterflies in the stomach" serve as stubborn roadblocks to improvement. Further elaboration of the symptoms of stage fright is probably unnecessary. A student once confessed that until his high school teacher described in vivid detail the symptoms of stage fright he had felt reasonably confident about speaking. Upon hearing of the panic felt by some at the prospect of facing an audience, he became fearful that a barrage of similar reactions might attack him. This apprehension triggered a fear reaction each time he spoke thereafter. Before you tend to react similarly, let us leave the symptoms of stage fright and look for its causes and remedies.

The primary prerequisite to recovery from emotional stress, psychologists tell us, is to understand its nature and what brings it upon us. What is the cause of this tension felt in some degree by nearly all of us when arising to speak—and by some when merely thinking about making a speech? Why are we afraid? We are in no physical danger. Audiences rarely shoot or lynch speakers, we tell ourselves. A little introspection will remind us, however, that there are many kinds of fear that are not the result of imminent danger to one's physical person. When we begin to speak, and perhaps even for some time before a performance, we may feel *social fear*. If this happens to you it may remind you vaguely of your first school dance, when you were so concerned about your appearance and so anxious to please your date that you didn't have much fun—at least during the early part of the evening. Perhaps you looked forward to the party with some eagerness; yet you feared the possible disapproval of others who would attend. Similarly, when we face an audience, we may experience uneasiness or anxiety in being the focus of attention; we may fear a negative response from our listeners and, hence, lowered self and group status. Most of us apparently are victims of a strange paradox: we desire audiences and yet fear them. Part of the tension we feel may result from the conflict of these antagonistic forces. We may not fear the process of speaking as such—but rather the consequences of it, particularly the possibility of a negative reaction from the audience.

Although the causes of speech fright are varied, complex, and inadequately understood, effective treatment can be offered. However, do not expect to receive advice that will make public speaking entirely "risk free." No interaction among individuals is totally without risk to one's ego or group status. You would not want it otherwise. If all elements of chance, or uncertainty, were removed from life, we would lead a boring existence indeed. Nevertheless, the following section contains suggestions that have proved helpful to students in reducing emotional stress. After applying these guides, if you think that your degree of tension is unusually severe, talk over your problems with your speech instructor. He, or she, will be pleased to help you help yourself.

First, Choose Subjects that You Strongly Wish to Discuss with Your Listeners. Do not summarize an article that catches your eye in the latest magazine digest or Sunday supplement. Instead, by following the advice given in Chapter 4, "Analyzing Demands: The Speech Purpose," you should be able to discover a variety of topics that *excite you*—that have *vivid personal meaning to you.* Now, from among these possibilities select those topics that should be *keenly interesting and meaningful to your listeners.* Chapter 3, "Analyzing Demands: The Specific Speech Situation," and Chapter 4 contain advice that should help you adjust your speaking purpose to the interests, desires, and experiences of the auditors so that you can encourage them to be continuing, creative, active—though silent—participants. A final screening process: out of the potential topics that are meaningful and interesting to both you and your listeners, settle upon the one that you most strongly wish to share with the audience. If you are eager to communicate a particular message, negative tension is much less likely to build up.

Second, Prepare Thoroughly. To slight preparation is to invite tension. Chapters 5–11 contain detailed advice for organizing and developing the speech in the most effective logical and psychological manner. Chapter 13 contains suggestions for rehearsing the speech. If you have earned the right to talk by acquiring a thorough understanding of the subject, by carefully organizing and developing the speech, and by rehearsing until you know the sequence of the ideas you will present, you will possess the solid comfort of knowing that you have done everything possible to prepare yourself intellectually for the speaking assignment.

Third, Prepare Yourself Psychologically. Practice good mental hygiene by giving yourself psychological "shots in the arm" such as the following.

Your speech will do something for your listeners. If you have followed the advice offered above, your subject will be interesting and meaningful to your hearers. It will do something *for them.* Your concern to be helpful to your listeners—to provide them with a service—to do something for them will help divert your attention from negative apprehensions.

You know more about the subject than your audience does. This is so because of your strong interest in the subject and your long-term and immediate preparation for the speech—as described. In "real-life" speaking situations, a person is rarely asked to speak unless it is believed that he has special knowledge or experience, or represents an important viewpoint. In the classroom, if you possess keen interest in your subject and have prepared thoroughly, you are probably better informed on the subject than most of the listeners. Confidence born of enthusiasm and solid preparation is a basic bulwark of poise.

You appear more confident than you feel. It is a truism that we do not see ourselves exactly as others see us. Such is the case when we face audiences. Upon finishing his first speech, a student who had appeared poised and confident told the class with a sigh of relief that he was "glad that was over." He confessed to extreme stage fright and admitted that he had doubted he would be able to complete the speech. Although initially reluctant to believe that he had appeared in control of himself and the situation, he was finally convinced. His attitude then became, "If I can feel that terrible and look that good, I suppose I can put up with tension and fear." He no longer had to "put up with" agonizing apprehensions, however; once he realized that his nervousness was not conspicuous and that the audience had accepted him as a poised, efficiently functioning speaker, the major cause of his tension was eliminated.

Not all instances are as striking as this one, but be assured that "butterflies" are usually undetectable, muscle tremor is so minute it is unnoticeable in most cases, and only a surgeon sees a racing heart. If you recognize that you may appear more confident than you feel, you may quickly experience a diminution of fear reaction.

Others share your misgivings. It is said that misery loves company because company reduces misery. To be singled out as the only youngster in the block to come down with measles may be an excruciating experience; but if an epidemic strikes and no one can romp and play, a child may not be quite as unhappy at the prospect of being quarantined.

You may be relieved to discover not only that many of your classmates are as uncomfortable as you but also that many distinguished and successful actors, musicians, lecturers, and athletes are chronic sufferers of stage fright. Some of them testify that they have never been without nervous tension in public appearances. In an interview with the author, the renowned minister Norman Vincent Peale explained that his problems with stage fright stimulated him to want to become a public speaker. "I doubt that anyone was ever less likely to become an effective speaker than I," he said. "I definitely was not endowed with superior linguistic skill. In fact, as a boy in Ohio, I was exceedingly shy and inarticulate. One of my most important early battles was to acquire adequate poise in ordinary social situations." In describing his fears during his first public speech, Dr. Peale said, "When I stood up, I became literally stiff with fear. I couldn't get the first words out. In the embarrassed silence, a little girl in the front row giggled to her mother, 'Gosh, look at his knees shake.' That made me so angry that I found my voice and gave a spirited speech."

When asked if he still experienced nervousness, Dr. Peale replied, "Occasionally I get a little apprehensive before speaking. Last Sunday, for example, I fidgeted with my outline while the hymn was being sung, and then I thought how foolish I was being. If I didn't know what I was going to say by then, I never would know."

Harry S. Truman once told the author that he always experienced some nervousness before a speech and that in his early career this had caused him concern. As he acquired experience he learned to control tension. "My first speech was a complete failure," he admitted. "It took a lot of appearances after that before I felt at home on the platform and could put my ideas across the way I wanted."

A complete list of performers who have suffered to some extent from tensions before performances would include virtually all persons who speak, act, sing, play, or compete in public. When you are convinced that you do not differ significantly from a host of others who appear publicly, many of them successful and famous, you have given yourself one of the best antidotes for excessive apprehension.

Audiences are friendly. Inasmuch as the novice may be more apprehensive about the possibility of unfavorable listener reaction than about the act of speaking itself, the audience may be the focal point of his fear. Students sometimes think that listeners look bored and "poker-faced," seem to smirk, and in other ways noticeably indicate their disapproval. Such negative judgments often represent errors in interpreting the feedback from the audience. Unless hearers are actively hostile to you or to your subject, they are unlikely to show overt signs of disapproval. This is especially true in the public-speaking class; since everyone in the audience has to speak repeatedly during the term, he is motivated to follow Artemus Ward's quid pro quo, "You scratch my back and I'll scratch yourn"—"You listen positively to me and I'll do the same for you."

Heightened feeling is essential to effective speaking. When it is controlled and utilized, nervous energy is a friend to be welcomed—not an enemy to be feared and resisted. Heightened feeling is essential in toning the neuromuscular system for maximum efficiency. Just as the successful athlete is "keyed up" before a game, so the effective speaker is emotionally charged to meet the requisites of the speaking situation. Your goal should not be to eliminate tension, but so to temper and regulate it that it works for you rather than against you. If at first you have excessive amounts of nervous energy, you should recognize that this is nature's way of preparing you for an emergency. If you are typical, your tension will decrease with successful experience.

Tension usually decreases with experience. The majority of students steadily and rapidly acquire poise throughout a course in speech. By the end of the term they are vastly more at ease—a comforting thought for the nervous beginner. Even better news: experimental evidence indicates that this acquired poise is retained by the student in speaking to other groups after the completion of the course. If your initial tension causes you discomfort, face up to it and determine to live with it. As you learn to "handle" tension and to translate it into heightened awareness of the situation and increased vocal and physical animation, your anxiety will probably soon diminish and, perhaps, even disappear. As a rule, the progress of the typical student in conquering stage fright is proportional to the extensiveness and frequency of his successful public-speaking experiences.

Fourth, in Delivering the Speech, Promote Confidence by Following these Guides. From the time you enter the room before your speech until you have concluded your remarks, try to "accentuate the positive" and "eliminate the negative." DON'TS: Don't focus inwardly, that is, avoid being overly concerned about how you look, sound, or feel. Don't concentrate on how well you are doing or on whether the listeners like you personally, think you are nervous, or consider you to be an ineffectual speaker. DO'S: Concentrate upon the process of communicating your ideas to the listeners. Think affirmatively. If you act as if you are confident, you may begin to feel more confident. Meet squarely the gaze of your listeners. Talk directly to them. Consider them receptive persons who are pulling for you to do well. Remind yourself that your task as a speaker is to engage them in a meaningful "dialogue" on your topic. Attempt to convert nervous energy into appropriate outlets of animated vocal and physical delivery. *Without going to extremes,* engage in sufficient activity to release the tension in antagonistic muscle groups. Be vigorous. If you feel like doing so, try some gestures. Turn toward one section of the audience and speak directly to it; then turn toward another section. Occasionally change position on the platform. Use a pointer to direct attention to some element of a visual aid. Try to maintain the lively, flexible vocal and physical delivery of forceful conversation—expanded to meet the needs of public speaking.

What is your prognosis? If you follow the simple principles outlined in this section, your chances of avoiding excessive nervous tension are excellent.

Anybody Can Talk—But Effective Public Speaking Must Be Learned by Experience and Discipline

A professor, who is himself a notoriously inarticulate lecturer, once asked, "Why do colleges offer courses in public speaking? Except for the rehabilitation of speech defects, I see no reason for speech training. Anyone can talk!" Although most persons probably speak with sufficient volume and distinctness to be understood in most social situations, it is doubtful that they are adequately skilled even in ordinary social and business communication.

Even if we were to agree, which we do not, that "anyone can talk" with adequate facility in social and business communications, this would not mean that such competency automatically extends to public speaking. Substantive differences exist between the communicative skills needed in the give and take exchanges of social and business conversations and those required in public speaking to provide the sole continuous verbal input over an extended period to a body of listeners. Many persons who function adequately in conversation lack the "know-how" necessary to make a satisfactory speech. They are ineffectual public speakers for a variety of reasons, some of which are inadequate projection, awkward physical delivery, inability adequately to structure and develop an extended message, ill-chosen language, deficiency in maintaining attention, misdirected psychological appeals, and failure to adapt to the constraints of the speaking occasion. To limit speech training to the correction of speech defects is as irrational as limiting training in writing to the correction of grammatical errors and then assuming that anyone can write.

Although almost "anyone can talk," anyone who is unseasoned or inexpert in public speaking can profit by studying the principles of effective speaking as set forth in this book and by acquiring successful speaking experiences under the guidance of a trained expert.

So! You Don't Want to Be an Orator

At the conclusion of the first class meeting a student asked if completing the course would qualify him for employment as a professional public speaker. He was advised that in the vast majority of cases, public speaking is a supplementary—not the primary—source of a speaker's reputation and income. The professional public speaker is an established person with a message. No lecture bureau would consider attempting to book a speaker for a series of engagements—regardless of his possible skill in speaking—unless he could attract audiences by virtue of his unusual knowledge, experience, or special distinction. Few who read this book will become professional public speakers. Your speech course is not designed to produce professional speakers. Its purpose is to help you to improve your overall capabilities in public speaking, thereby enabling you to achieve greater self-realization, improve social relationships, increase professional and economic opportunities, and serve more effectively your community and nation.

"I'm Eager to Learn"

Neither the author of *Practical Public Speaking* nor any legitimate speech instructor will guarantee your success as a speaker. There are no shortcuts to effective speaking. You have to earn your way. As you begin your program of speech training, adopt the attitude of being eager to learn. Conscious application of the principles in this book, under the guidance of your instructor, should help you to achieve maximum results in minimum time. Prepare each assignment with care, and attempt to profit from the suggestions of your instructor and classmates.

The Ladder To an Effective First Speech

The ladder to giving an effective speech has seven steps and two handrails. A brief explanation of the ladder will guide you in preparing initial speeches without first reading the entire book. In later chapters we shall ask you to linger with us for a more careful and thorough study of each part of the ladder.

The Handrails Hold the Ladder Together

The Left Handrail on the Ladder to Effectiveness Represents YOUR Audience and the Speech Occasion. Before choosing and developing a subject, it is necessary to analyze those who will listen and the situational circumstances under which you will speak. What potential subjects would be interesting and meaningful to your listeners? To answer this query you need to probe the nature of your listeners by asking additional questions, such as these: What do the persons in class know about the topic I am considering and how do they feel about it? Why is it that they feel and think this way? If I select this topic can I develop it in a way that will do something for the listeners? How will the listeners view me as the speaker on this topic? Will they consider me to be sufficiently knowledgeable and experienced? Adequately objective? In answering these questions, and others like them, you should study as closely as you can the individual members of the class. Probably you already know something about them, because you have met them once or twice previously in class and have associated with students roughly similiar to them since the beginning of school. If, however, the extent of your knowledge about the audience is limited to an understanding of its general composition, you can gain some helpful clues to the listeners' opinions, values, interests, and behaviors by

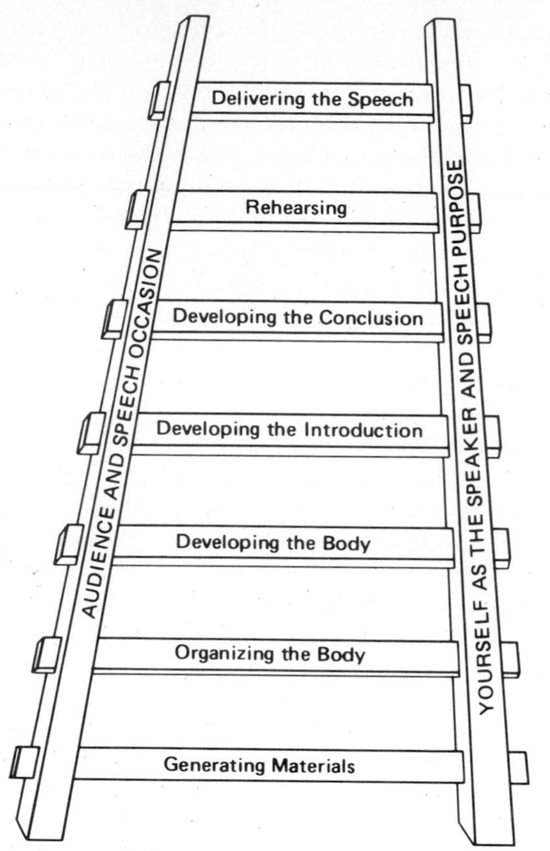

Fig. 1. The Ladder to an Effective First Speech

studying the listeners in relation to their age and sex grouping, their educational backgrounds, occupational interests, and so on.

Both you and your listeners will be affected by the speaking occasion. Therefore think about how your choice of subject will be influenced by the purpose of the meeting and by the physical and psychological environment, that is, by the basic nature of the meeting—the time, location, and mood—what else is included in the program—and how much time is allotted to you.

The Right Handrail on the Ladder to Effectiveness Represents YOU and YOUR PURPOSE IN SPEAKING. Is your potential subject within your field of interest? Is it within your range of experiences, either firsthand or vicarious? Are you eager to share with your listeners your ideas and feelings on this topic? Do you believe that by the time of your speech you will have earned the right to talk on the subject? Does the topic conform reasonably well to the image your listeners have concerning your reputation, status, maturity, appearance? If you can answer each of these questions affirmatively, you are ready to work on focusing your subject.

Probably your initial assignment is to give a speech to inform (because speeches to inform are generally considered to be easier for beginners than speeches to persuade). This means that your general purpose in speaking is to enable the listeners to acquire knowledge, information, understanding. So far in your thinking you no doubt have been concerned with general subject areas, such as jogging, inflation, campus activities, or cars. Obviously, however, you can't inform the listeners about, say, cars. Such an area is almost infinitely broad. You need to particularize the general subject area, bringing it into a limited field of focus. Conceivably you might decide that your Specific Speech Purpose is "to have my audience understand that the BMW 320i is an extremely high-performance car" or "to inform my audience that Japanese automobile manufacturing plants are much more automated than are U.S. plants." As you can see from these examples, the Specific Speech Purpose is a definite, concise statement of exactly what you want to accomplish in your speech.

Because the handrails (that is, "you as the speaker," "the purpose," "the audience," and "the occasion") are fundamental to each step in the ladder to effectiveness, you should keep them constantly in mind as you proceed. Maintaining a firm grip on each handrail, let us climb the first step. (See Chapters 3 and 4, if you wish, for an extensive discussion of the handrails.)

The Steps Lead to Effectiveness

The First Step on the Ladder to Effectiveness is Generating Materials. Fortify yourself with an abundance of material, much more than you will have time to use in the speech. If this is done, you will be able to select from this supply the most effective illustrations, quotations, facts, comparisons, and statistics. The first means of securing materials is to *think*. Make a systematic inventory of the ideas, beliefs, and feelings you have concerning the subject. Then try to estimate *what* additional materials you still need to acquire in order to accomplish your speech purpose and *how* the materials can be secured. Second, *observe*. An extremely valuable means of securing opinions and facts is personally to observe matters relating to your subject. Determine whether you can secure helpful information by making an on-the-site inspection of, let us say, a session of juvenile court, the behavior of pickets during a strike, or the testing of fire-resistant shingles. After considering the factors of time, cost, and availability of the thing to be observed, settle upon your investigative goals and procedures. Your observation should be as complete as your purpose warrants; also, it should be accurate and objective. Third, *communicate with others.* Draw upon the information, experience, and wisdom of persons who are knowledgeable on your topic. By engaging others in conversation, by interviewing experts, by attending public discussions on the topic or by listening to them on television, and by writing letters of inquiry, you can see secure valuable ideas and information. Fourth, *read.* Much of the accumulated knowledge of man is accessible to you in your library or by means of interlibrary loan. Read selectively, objectively, and analytically. To facilitate retention, record specific data on note cards (Chapter 5).

The Second Step on the Ladder to Effectiveness Is Organizing the Body of the Speech. Like nearly all speeches your first talk should be divided into three parts: Introduction, Body, and Conclusion. The major import of your speech will be accomplished in the Body, which may comprise 80 to 85 per cent of the total speech. Because of its relative length and importance, the Body should be prepared before the Introduction or Conclusion.

From the materials you have accumulated in STEP ONE, jot down the various points you might wish to use in your speech. After studying this list carefully, evolve two to five principal ideas which enable you to accomplish your Specific Speech Purpose and under which you can later group supporting points. Now arrange the main ideas according to one of four patterns or sequences of thought. (In Chapter 6 you will become acquainted with other patterns, but for your first speech you probably should use one of these simpler patterns): *Time* pattern (chronological units of time or steps in a process); *Space* pattern (areas in a geographical sequence); *Topical* pattern (natural, traditional, or convenient categories—as "students, faculty, administration" or "offensive and defensive formations"); *Problem-Solution* pattern (a problem-solving sequence).

The Third Step on the Ladder to Effectiveness Is Developing the Body of the Speech. Your main points must be explained, clarified, and made interesting. Choose any of the following methods to support each of your main headings: examples, statistics, comparisons, testimony, explanation, and visual aids. To help maintain audience attention, plan your supporting materials so that they utilize *proximity* (your material has personalized meaning to your listeners, that is, it directly concerns their immediate wants, interests, and desires), *vivid concreteness* (your language evokes images in the minds of your listeners), *significance* (your material deals with genuinely important matters or with appeals to significant human wants), *variety* (your discussion has diversity of kinds of supporting materials, motive appeals, imagery, and so on), and perhaps *humor* (your attempts to amuse possess freshness, relevance, and appropriateness) Chapters 7 and 8.

The Fourth Step on the Ladder to Effectiveness Is Developing the Introduction. The Introduction, which may perhaps be about 10 per cent of the length of the speech, serves as a bridge between the initial reaction of the audience and your major ideas, as represented in the Body. The Introduction may serve two functions: to stimulate favorable interest in you as the speaker and in your message, and to orient the audience to the nature and purpose of the Body.

Although in Chapter 10 you will learn additional ways to encourage favorable attention, you will probably want to begin your first speech by referring to the significance of the subject, telling an illustrative story, using a stimulating quotation, or mentioning common bonds, such as associations, experiences, ideals, beliefs, desires, interests, or attitudes which you share with the listeners. To help orient the hearers to the subject, you may state the POINT in a terse sentence or two (If your Specific Speech Purpose were "to have my listeners understand that the BMW 320i is an extremely high-performance car," your statement of the POINT might be something like this: "In the next few minutes I should like to explain why automotive experts consider the BMW 320i an extremely high-performance car."); explain how you plan to develop the Body, by summarizing its contents or listing the main ideas; and provide necessary background explanations or definitions. Avoid apologizing, being long-winded, antagonizing, or using irrelevant material.

The Fifth Step on the Ladder to Effectiveness Is Developing the Conclusion. A speech should conclude rather than just come to an end. Although the nature and length of the Conclusion depend upon the particular speech and speaking situation, the typical Conclusion may possibly be about 5 per cent of the total speech length and ordinarily it should crystallize the thought and promote the proper mood.

To accomplish the functions of the Conclusion you could restate the POINT of the speech, list or review concisely the main ideas of the Body, and/or summarize indirectly by means of a quotation, comparison, or example. Avoid making apologies, being distractingly abrupt or long-winded, introducing important undeveloped new points of view, including irrelevant material, or drastically altering the mood established throughout the speech.

The Sixth Step on the Ladder to Effectiveness Is Rehearsing the Speech. Musicians, actors, and athletes are unlikely to appear before the public without having practiced sufficiently to ensure a high-quality performance. For the same reason, you probably should rehearse your speeches, either in isolation or in the presence of competent critics. Very likely you should not begin your rehearsal until your outline is finished, and you should complete the rehearsal before the beginning of the class period at which the speech is to be delivered. After the meeting starts, you probably should put your speech out of mind and concentrate on the proceedings; in this way you will become more thoroughly in tune with the mood and tempo of the meeting and may be less inclined to build up prespeech tensions. In rehearsing, the first stage is to fix firmly in mind the sequence of ideas you wish to present; this will involve memorizing the outline structure prepared in climbing the second, third, fourth, and fifth steps of the ladder. The second stage is to work to improve the effectiveness of your vocal and physical delivery. How many times should you rehearse a class speech? One or two complete rehearsals may be enough for some students; others, however, will perhaps need additional rehearsals for maximum effectiveness. Caution: in your eagerness, do not practice to the point that you lose your zest for the speech or that your delivery becomes stilted or mechanical (Chapter 13).

The Seventh Step on the Ladder to Effectiveness Is Delivering the Speech. While presenting your speech, think constantly of your ideas and the process of communicating with your listeners. If your mind is filled with your message and with the process of stimulating a continuing interaction with your listeners, there will be little opportunity for the intrusion of excessive concern about how well you are doing. Attempt to read the feedback supplied by the nonverbal responses of your listeners and attempt to adjust your content and delivery accordingly. Speak extemporaneously—beginners rarely are effective when they memorize or read their speeches. Except for necessary references to notes or visual aids, keep your eyes on your listeners. Adjust your volume to the acoustics of the room and to the size of the audience. Gesture when you feel like doing so. Occasionally change your position on the platform, if you wish. Not only should you *be* eager to share your ideas with the listeners, but you should also *appear to be.* Therefore, project your friendliness, sincerity, and enthusiasm in the way you speak. Be lively and vibrant. (Chapters 12, 14, and 15)

Evaluations and Your Development as a Speaker

When you have finished your first speech don't just sit down with a sigh of relief, thinking "Well, that's done!" To derive maximum benefit from the speech as a learning experience—and from all other speeches you will give during the term—you should welcome evaluations from class members and the instructor. Study all such suggestions carefully in terms of your own analysis of your performance. In this review do not concentrate on finding "mistakes" that you can "correct." Seek, instead, to acquire insights enabling you to develop better skills in analyzing listeners and speech situations and in formulating, organizing, developing, and expressing ideas. Also, do not accept uncritically all suggestions. As in any other subjective evaluation, speech critics sometimes offer conflicting opinions, and sometimes they are partially or even completely inaccurate. Therefore, you need to weigh each suggestion before incorporating it into your program of personal growth as a speaker.

Summary

Approach public speaking positively! Accept the possibility that you may experience some emotional stress but that such tension will decrease with successful experience. Reject misconceptions about the study of public speaking and develop a positive philosophy that will enable you rapidly to acquire effectiveness.

As you approach the ladder to giving a successful first speech, notice that the handrails hold the ladder together and that seven steps lead to effectiveness. As you ascend the ladder keep a firm grip on the handrails: the audience and the speech occasion; yourself as the speaker, and your purpose in speaking. Also, give careful attention to each of the steps: generating materials; organizing the Body; developing the Body; developing the Introduction; developing the Conclusion; rehearsing the speech; delivering the speech.

After you have given your first speech—and, of course, after all subsequent speeches—welcome evaluations from class members and your instructor. Weigh such suggestions in terms of your own evaluation of your performance. Incorporate all useful insights into your program of personal development as a speaker.

Exercises and Assignments

1. What are your present attitudes toward the study of speech? How did you acquire them? Are they desirable or undesirable in your opinion? Write an analysis of your attitudes to hand to your instructor. Be ready to discuss them in class.
2. What misconceptions about the study of speech did you bring to this course? How did you acquire them? Do you anticipate difficulty in eliminating these attitudes? If so, why?
3. What examples of speaking for dishonorable causes are you able to list from your knowledge of history and current events? Did effective speech combat them successfully? If not, why not?

4. Write an inventory of your assets and liabilities as a speaker. Save it, and note at the conclusion of the course whether the list should be altered. How does your list compare with your instructor's evaluation of your assets and liabilities?

5. Interview another member of the class. Then introduce him to your classmates in a two- or three-minute speech. Possibly include his name, age, family status (single, married, parenthood), national origin, educational background, professional objectives, work experiences, present job, interest group affiliations, religious preference, political preference, major likes and dislikes, travel, hobbies, and so on.

6. Listen carefully to the speeches assigned in Exercise 5 to discover the nature of the audience you will be addressing during the remainder of the course. On the basis of these speeches, prepare a brief statement for each member of the class in which you include information concerning his predominant interests and predilections—anything that you think might help you to understand the person better as a potential listener. During the passage of the term make an effort to become better acquainted with each classmate and as a result of your increased knowledge and improved insights, add to your initial analysis of him as an audience member. The better you understand the audience the better you should be able to promote and reinforce listener identification in your choice and development of topics.

7. Using the steps on the ladder to effectiveness, prepare a four-minute speech, which may be (1) A persuasive speech on any subject on which you have definite personal convictions. State your convictions tersely in a sentence or two and give three or four important reasons for your beliefs. (2) An informative speech describing your present job, your reasons for attending college, or an interesting personal experience. (3) A process-inquiry speech, in which you explain how to do something or how something is produced or how it operates. During the talk the audience may interrupt at any time to ask questions. Answer each question and then continue your speech until the next question is asked.

8. An unusually good means of integrating the ideas introduced in this chapter is to analyze an advertisement in a short speech.

Purpose of Speech: Your assignment is to analyze the rhetorical merit and rhetorical strategies of a particularly "good" or particularly "bad" printed advertisement, in an uninterrupted presentation of approximately four minutes. Note: your aim is not to "sell" the product but to analyze how well you think the advertiser met his apparent rhetorical needs.

Rationale: The assignment provides an easy-to-effect introductory public-speaking experience. It offers a model guiding the speaker to a selection of suitable rhetorical goals, to the designing of an appropriate structure for his speech, and to the securing of relevant ideas and supportive materials. It also provides experience in the process of problem solving and practice in the presentation of visual aids. This exercise also illustrates the universal applicability of basic rhetorical principles and practices. In your advertisement, the advertiser is making an exceedingly terse attempt to induce the reader to adopt desired patterns of thought and behavior. In a sense it is a miniaturized "speech" to persuade. It uses the "same" rhetorical strategies that are available to the public speaker. Your presentation is therefore a kind of rhetorical analysis.

Procedure: In a brief *Introduction,* you might present necessary clarifying materials and possibly those that will stimulate the favorable interest of the listener. Perhaps explain where your advertisement was published, the nature of the readers of that publication, the character of other ads in that publication, the purpose of the ad (that is, to introduce a new product, to prompt immediate sales of an established product, to foster goodwill, to promote recognition, and the like), and so on.

The *Body* of your presentation can be directed to the answering of five questions about the ad. The following suggestions are intended to spark your thinking, rather than to direct it.

I. *Is the ad well planned to capture favorable ATTENTION?* Keeping in mind the nature of the readers and the purpose of the advertiser, explain why you believe that the qualities of the ad possess good, or poor, attention-getting potential. Among the many characteristics that you might consider are size, placement in the publication, colors, contrast, kinds of print, use of pictures, focus, unusualness, familiarity, and human interest appeals.

II. *Does the ad encourage the reader to experience a feeling of NEED or WANT?* To what extent, if any, does the ad attempt to create in the reader an unsatisfied state, dissonance, or desire? How is this done? For example, in its pictures or in its written continuity does the ad explain that protracted illness may bring crushing financial problems? In your estimation, is the "need appeal" (if there is one) sufficiently clear and striking? Is it overdone?

III. *Does the ad suggest to the reader that the advertised product will SATISFY the need or want?* With what degree of explicitness does the ad explain how the product will satisfy the alleged need? How is this done? For instance, does the ad point out that the advertised health insurance policy will pay a particular sum for living expenses over a particular number of months, provide other specified benefits, cost so much, and so on? Is the ad less specific than this in its "satisfaction appeal"? Does it provide any overt claims that the product will answer alleged needs? In terms of the apparent purpose of the ad and the nature of the readers, does the "satisfaction" character of the ad seem well planned?

IV. *Does the ad PERSONALIZE its message so that the reader tends to identify with the message and, hence, the product?* What qualities of the ad encourage, or discourage, empathy? In this regard, you might consider the style of the written matter, the use of personal pronouns, the presence or absence of pictures, the incorporation of human interest values, and so on.

V. *Does the ad attempt to impel the reader to ACTION?* What kind of action does the ad seek to effect? That is, does the ad try to prompt immediate sales? Delayed purchases after thought? A feeling of goodwill toward the product or the advertiser? A recognition of product or company name or identifying symbol? And so on.

In a brief *Conclusion,* you probably should recapitulate the essence of the message you have presented. Offer, perhaps, a capsule judgment of the rhetorical merit or possible effectiveness of the ad.

9. Inasmuch as an exchange of ideas through discussion is frequently helpful in establishing positive attitudes toward the study of speech, the class might be divided into panels of four to seven persons. Each panel could select a subject concerning oral communication and present a discussion on that topic before the

class. Following each panel's presentation, the other class members may wish to ask questions and offer observations. Possible subjects include: (1) What should a student expect to realize from his speech training? (2) In what ways can skill in speaking and listening enable one to enjoy a fuller, more useful life? (3) How can one analyze tactfully and constructively the speech presentation of a classmate? (4) How can a person estimate accurately his own assets and liabilities as a speaker? As a person? (5) How can the consumer of oral communication protect himself/herself from fraudulent advocates who are effective speakers?

CHAPTER 2

Understanding Basic Communicative Concepts

Let us assume that by following the suggestions in Chapter 1 you have rejected misconceptions about the study of public speaking, adopted a positive philosophy that will help you develop oral effectiveness rapidly, and acquired a working understanding of the ladder to effective speaking. Now we should consider certain communicative principles that are fundamental to any attempt to influence others.

The Function of Speechmaking: Closure

What is it that any speaker seeks in giving a speech? EFFECT. Effect means that the speaker wants to cause the listeners to experience CHANGE in some specific way in which they view their world. Change, of course, involves MOVEMENT from an initial position to a new one. The INITIAL POSITION of the listeners is the status of their sense of involvement-knowledge-beliefs-values-attitudes-behaviors concerning the subject matter—when the speaker begins the talk. The END POSITION toward which the speaker wishes the listener to move is the residual message, or the configuration of knowledge-beliefs-values-attitudes-behaviors held by the speaker in this particular matter—or, in other words, the SPEAKER'S POSITION. With these basic assumptions in mind, we are now better prepared to understand the meaning of effect.

When we think of effect in speechmaking we are really concerned with CLOSURE. The function of the speaker is to promote closure, that is, to encourage the maximum amount of movement possible under the circumstances away from the listener's initial position and toward the speaker's position. Thus to promote closure means to narrow the gap—to reduce the distance—between listener and speaker. Complete closure, of course, would be complete intellectual-emotional concurrence with the speaker's position. Although such complete closure is theoretically impossible, the speaker tries to get the listener to move as close to complete closure as conditions permit.

You remember that the top of our ladder in Chapter 1 leads to effective speaking. And now you should understand that the base of the ladder rests upon this fundamental premise: always in purposeful speaking your basic task as a speaker is to move the listeners as far as possible under the circumstances from their initial position toward closure with your own position.

The Medium for Achieving Closure: Continuing Cyclical Interaction

If the function of speechmaking is to promote closure, when and by what medium does movement toward closure come about? Sometimes after the speech—as a result of their thinking about the topic, recalling some points made by the speaker, hearing reinforcing opinions from others they respect, and so on—the listeners may experience some of the change desired by the speaker and, thus, move closer to the speaker's position. However, for our purposes the basic thrust toward closure occurs during, and by means of, the cyclical interrelationship between the speaker and the listeners that continues throughout the speech. Too often the beginner conceives of speechmaking as a unidirectional flow. He believes that, much like the process of writing on the chalkboard, the speaker imposes a message upon a passive audience: the self-identity, as well as the response, of the listener is held in abeyance until the close of the speech; if the speaker has done a good job, he or she has imprinted upon the listener's mind some new understanding, or, perhaps, some new attitude; the hearer, like the chalkboard, has been acted upon. This, however, is not at all the way the speaker-listener relationship works, as the following items illustrate.

First, the speaker does not determine unilaterally the standards that prevail. By and large, the listeners—under the demands of the situation—determine what are, and are not, acceptable modes of thought and behavior. The listeners, if their attendance is voluntary, accept as legitimate the speaker's attempt to influence them; but, except in the most unusual circumstances, the listeners remain "free agents," reserving the right and the power to accept or reject anything the speaker says, or even the speaker himself.

Second, the speaker does not inform or persuade the listeners. No one can inform or persuade someone else. All the speaker can do is to supply the listeners with the informational and motivational means—the climate—that will enable them to teach or convince themselves. As we shall see in the following section, learning or believing is an active creative process in which the person actually grows, changes, extends his own self in some way. This involves more than thinking. It includes the functioning of the whole self, the entire constellation of memories, experiences, knowledge, beliefs, values, attitudes, feelings, goals, desires, and behaviors.

Third, the only means the speaker has of influencing the listeners is through their own selves, by so impinging upon their immediate perceptions, cognitions, and behaviors that the speech touches off "inner springs of response." Much of our attention in *Practical Public Speaking* is addressed to the satisfaction of this rhetorical need.

Fourth, speechmaking involves a sharing of risk. It is not only the listener who may be changed as a result of the speech. The speaker must accept an even broader spectrum of risk. As a result of the response accorded the message, the speaker may acquire more—or less—confidence in his ideas, greater—or lesser—self and group status, augmentation—or diminishment—of his career possibilities, and so on.

Fifth, the listener shares as an equal participant with the speaker in the interrelationship that begins as soon as the speaker and audience are mutually aware of each other and that continues as long as the speech lasts. In a limited sense the two are engaged in a circular dialogue. The speaker supplies verbal and nonverbal symbols to the listeners who receive and interpret them in terms of their own experiences, beliefs, knowledge, interests, and needs. The listeners do more than this, however. In the action of turning over in their minds what the speaker is saying, the listeners make judgments about what they hear. To some extent these judgments are reflected in their subconscious manner—whether they look animatedly at the speaker, chuckle in the appropriate places, yawn, shift frequently in their seats, and so on—which may be read, or misread, by the speaker.

This process of affirmative or negative response to the way the speaker looks and to what he/she says and how he/she says it will last as long as the speaker-listener relationship exists. Throughout the speech the speaker picks up clues concerning the way the listeners are responding, and modifies, or fails to modify, his/her content and delivery accordingly. Changes in the speaker are received and interpreted by the listeners, who may evince their internal response by some external behavior. The speaker interprets these behaviors, and thus a cyclical interrelationship occurs. When speechmaking is at its best, this continuous intercommunication amounts to a kind of dialogue between the speaker and the listeners, with the listeners participating actively and creatively in the development of thought-feeling. Although they may receive and process the speaker's message silently, the listeners contribute significantly to the ongoing communicative flow.

The Agency for Achieving Closure: Identification

We are now ready to see how the speaker may encourage a continuing dialogue with the listeners—thereby fostering closure with his/her position. Our first step in this regard is to appreciate the active nature of the listeners' movement toward closure.

Why Is the Movement Toward Closure an Active Process for the Listener?

Because the speaker cannot make that transition for the listeners. All the speaker can do is to facilitate this movement by offering resources to the listeners that may make it possible for them, if they wish, to change themselves. Our cognitions and behaviors are largely the consequences of our past. Altering the knowledge-belief-value systems of the individual requires an EXTENSION or modification of the existing systems. Learning and believing represent a stretching, an extending, of what one presently knows or believes.

This stretching or extending of one's self cannot take place unless what the speaker is saying seems sufficiently *like* what the listener knows or believes to provide a *basis* for initial understanding and/or acceptance. Otherwise the listener cannot, or will not, integrate the matter with his currently held cognitions, affections, and behaviors. One learns only by *analogy*. That is, one learns only by linking the new to familiar experiences and thinking. If the material is too strange, too different, too complex, no analogy exists for the individual—hence the desired learning does not take place. Similarly, one secures new beliefs, or intensifies old ones, only by *analogy,* that is, by consolidating the new with existing belief and value structures, which, themselves, condition the acceptability of the new belief or attitude. Thus the listener must contribute an initial status of knowledge-understanding-feeling-belief.

Furthermore, to make the communicative transaction work—from the perspective of the speaker—the listeners must be able and willing to extend, or change, their own selves toward that status of thought-feeling desired by the speaker. Extension of one's self in this way takes cooperative, productive effort. If for any reason the listeners cannot make, or do not wish to make, the necessary exertion, they can simply "tune out" the speaker.

We have now seen that listeners can change only by means of an extension of their own selves, that a new idea-belief-feeling cannot be understood or accepted unless the listeners can assimilate it into their existing selves and integrate it with what they already know-believe-feel, and that for the listeners to grow, to extend themselves in this way involves an active, creative process.

What Do the Concepts of "Self-System" and "Identification" Mean? How Do They Relate to the Active Process of Closure?

To encourage the listeners to extend themselves—from their initial position (of knowledge, beliefs, values, attitudes, and behaviors concerning the subject) toward closure with the position (of knowledge, beliefs, values, attitudes, and behaviors concerning the subject) that you wish them to have when you have finished your speech—requires that you help them to perceive analogous relationships with what you are saying, that is, to link the new with the familiar and the accepted. In order to help the listeners perceive the analogy you must estimate their state of receptivity and then adjust your materials to that receptivity. The key to estimating listener receptivity is the concept of "self-system," and the key to adjusting materials is the concept of "identification."

What Is the "Self-System"? It is the complex of functionally interrelated anchors—or patterns—that give continuity and being to an individual. These patterns provide the way we perceive, judge, decide, remember, imagine, and react. The self-system includes all our social learning, all the internal factors that at a particular moment influence the psychological functioning of the individual. Given a particular stimulus situation, the self-system determines the way that we size up the world and respond to it. It is, however, much more than the porthole through which we see and make contact with the external world. It directionalizes what we see in a particular situation, how we interpret and judge what we see, how we respond internally and externally to our cognitions, and how we remember and act upon the experience. The self-system, then, is one's sense of identity of who one is—along with one's remembered past and imagined future, one's habits of observing and of making assumptions and inferences, one's enduring and passing motives, and one's complex of sometimes contradictory beliefs, values, attitudes, and behaviors.

It is critically important to recognize that the self-system can and does change. In fact it is locked in the constant process of incremental change and development. Obviously the self-system possesses a psychologically necessary consistency and stability over time. Otherwise, one's personality, character, goals, behavior would always be in flux, and one would lose one's sense of identity and one's ability to cope with the environment. Thus the self-system is not so much an entity, or being, as it is a becoming.

With these definitions in mind it is easy to see how the nature of the listeners—that is, their self-systems—necessarily constrain the approach of the speaker. The listeners' self-systems determine whether they are able, or willing, to perceive analogous relationships between what the speaker is saying and their own familiar and accepted patterns of thinking/behaving. Further, it basically determines how much and what kind of movement the listeners can, or will, experience toward closure with the speaker's position.

What Is "Identification"? For our purpose it is the perceiving by an individual of analogous relationships between a cognitive-affective-behavioral aspect of his/her self-system and something said or done by the speaker. Each of us possesses the predisposition to screen incoming stimuli for connections and patterns that are relevant to our own selves. The act of establishing such relevancies—such sense of sameness, unity, or oneness—is called *identification.* The concept of identification is central to the entire process of influencing others. In his *Rhetoric of Motives,* Kenneth Burke suggests, "You persuade a man only insofar as you can talk his language by speech, gesture, tonality, order, image, attitude, idea, *identifying* your ways with his." Burke's major contribution to speech theory perhaps lies in his insistence upon identification as the *sole* avenue of persuasion, thus supplying new dimensions to the age-old axiom: effective speechmaking is audience centered. According to Burke, you can hope to "talk the language" of another only after you understand his conscious, and, as far as possible, his unconscious motivations and needs. Only by clearly fusing "your ways with his" will you reach him; when such identification fades, so will your rapport. Unfortunately most speakers are so self-oriented they lack sufficiently sensitive perception of the individual and collective wants of an audience. They fail to appreciate the depth of meaning in Atticus' statement in *To Kill a Mockingbird:* "You never really understand a person . . . until you climb into his skin and walk around in it."

How Is "Identification" Applied to the "Self-System" of the Listener to Promote Closure? We have seen that one acquires new knowledge or new belief only through analogy, that one's perception of analogous relationships between some aspect of one's self-system and what the speaker says or does depends basically upon one's self-system, and that we can consider the action of perceiving analogous relationships under the term "identification." Now let us take an introductory look at the way you apply identification to the self-system of the listeners to facilitate their movement toward your speaker's position.

To speak effectively you must meet the listeners where they are. You must recognize as well as you can their starting position of knowledge, belief, understanding, feeling, and degree of commitment toward your position. Your earliest words should encourage at least a tentative union between the listeners and yourself and your speech. This means that you must provide the listeners with the means within their relevant complex of knowledge-belief-values-attitudes-behavior to relate as closely as possible with your message. Then, on the basis of your analysis of the listener's readiness to be influenced, you should supply him with the means of reinforcing and expanding his initial identification.

In a sense, then, your speech must provide, first, the means by which the listeners can perceive the existence of analogous relationships—or areas of identification—that link them with you and your message. Second, during the course of your remarks you should supply the resources that will enable them to perceive the gradual consolidation, expansion, and coalescence of these analogous relationships—these beachheads of identification. In this way the listeners are enabled to secure new insights, understanding, and awareness that may cause them to extend themselves, change themselves, move themselves toward closure with your position.

The Process for Achieving Closure: Matching Demands with Satisfactions

The process by which you help the listener to establish and extend analogous relationships—that is, beachheads of identification—with you and your speech can be conceptualized as matching demands (that is, needs or requirements) with satisfactions. Inasmuch as the remainder of this book is directed to this purpose, it is enough here merely to introduce the concept.

What are "demands"? They are the elements in the speaking situation that influence—in other words, that constrain—the speaker's choice of strategies in his/her effort to help the listener perceive and expand beachheads of identification, thereby moving toward closure. Demands include both "restraints" and "freedoms." The amount of influence that a demand, or cluster of demands, in a particular situation may exert upon your selection of options may range from "absolute" prescription to gentle direction. In a specific instance, demands may prescribe what you must and must not do to promote analogous relationships, leaving no realistic choice in that particular aspect of your speaking. (As an obvious example, if you wished to encourage partisan supporters of one political candidate to vote for another candidate, you would impair the establishment of beachheads of identification by blaming your listeners for holding their present views.) On the other hand, demands ordinarily suggest a range of acceptable options from which the speaker may select the most promising. Thus demands not only prescribe communicative necessities (restraints) but also can describe communicative possibilities (freedoms).

What are communicative satisfactions—options—strategies? They are the means that the speaker may employ in the speech in response, or in answer, to impinging demands. It is the task of the remainder of this book to help you anticipate both the demands upon your speech and the communicative choices at your disposal to meet those constraints.

For our present purposes we need to note here only that the basic kinds of demands are represented by the "handrails" of the ladder to effective speaking, discussed in Chapter 1: the audience, speech occasion, you as the speaker, and your purpose in speaking. Section II of this text contains explanations of these demands. All of the basic demands are interrelated and all influence every aspect of speech development and delivery. And, of course, the basic kinds of communication strategies, or satisfactions, are represented by the "steps" of the ladder, each step possessing a range of possible options from which you may choose the most promising: generating materials; organizing the Body; developing the Body; developing the Introduction; developing the Conclusion; rehearsing the speech; delivering the speech. Sections III and IV explicate these strategies. As you give more speeches and study more about communication, you will develop greater appreciation that effectiveness (that is, the successful promotion of closure) depends upon your selecting appropriate strategies to meet the demands on your speech.

We begin our study of matching demands with satisfactions in the next chapter, "Analyzing Demands: The Specific Speech Situation." Before we do that, however, we should examine the procedure by which you should evaluate your speechmaking.

The Evaluation of Speechmaking: Closure Versus Demands

After each of your speeches you should assess the merits and deficiencies of your presentation in order to gain insights and understandings that will help you be more effective in your following speeches.

To help you make such an inventory, we should address the questions, "What is a good speech?" "What is an effective speech?" You may be thinking, "If the listeners learned, believed, or did what I wanted them to do, I gave a good speech; and if they didn't, I gave a poor one." This simplistic answer is more wrong than right. One reason it is wrong is that its yardstick of merit is the measurement of how skillful the speaker was in telling the listeners what they wanted to hear. Such a standard assumes that all speechmaking is pandering and demagoguery. As an ethical persuader you are not free to tell your listeners *just anything* that will promote identification and reinforcement. Your sense of ethics constrains you to speak only what you consider to be true, beneficial, and moral—even if that may not promote analogous relationships between your listeners and you as the speaker and your speech.

A second reason the simplistic answer above is wrong is that it ignores the relative difficulty of your communicative task. Perhaps what you wanted to accomplish in your speech (Specific Speech Purpose) is counter to (or reinforces) the beliefs, values, or behaviors of the listeners. Perhaps the listeners are tired, or bored (or fresh, eager to listen). Perhaps the acoustics were bad (or very good), or distracting noises—such as a lawn mower or trucks being unloaded—have interrupted your speech (or the room was so quiet that the proverbial dropped pin would make a noise).

Any estimation of communicative effectiveness must consider the demands upon the speech. Remember, in the beginning of this chapter I stated that the base of the ladder to effective speaking rests upon the fundamental premise: always in purposeful speaking your basic task as a speaker is to move the listeners *as far as possible under the circumstances* from their initial position toward closure with your position. Therefore, the merit of your performance (that is, how well you did, or how effective you were, in your particular speech) is determined by how close you came to promoting the maximum movement possible on the part of your listeners—considering the demands upon your speech—toward closure.

You will soon discover how difficult it is to estimate the amount of movement your listeners have experienced. Your best ways of making this estimation are your observations of listener-behavior during the speech; the amount and kind of questions asked in the forum following the speech; the oral/written observations by classmates about your speech, if this method of analysis is used by your instructor; direct feedback to specific follow-up questions you ask the listeners (see Exercises 5 and 8 at the end of this chapter); and your instructor's observations. Despite the necessarily subjective nature of this procedure, after each of your speeches estimate as well as you can the amount of audience movement that occurred and how closely this degree of movement approached the maximum amount possible, keeping in mind the constraints upon your speech.

In addition to this basic assessment of merit, review the individual basic demands upon your speech and estimate how well your responding strategies answered, or matched, these demands. For example, consider the demands imposed by your particular listeners. If they were uninterested in hearing your speech—perhaps because it was late in the class period—how well did your materials stimulate and sustain interest? If they questioned your credibility in speaking on your topic, how well did you construct a positive speaker image? If they found the information difficult to assimilate, how well did you help them to establish analogies between what they already knew and the new data? Later chapters and Exercises 6, 7, 9, and 10 at the end of this one should help you to evaluate how well your strategies matched the impinging constraints.

Summary

In this chapter we have considered several basic communicative concepts. The *function* of speechmaking is to promote closure. This means that in purposeful speaking your basic task as a speaker is to move the listeners as far as possible under the circumstances from their initial position (complex of knowledge-beliefs-values-attitudes-behaviors concerning the subject) toward your position (your configuration of knowledge-beliefs-values-attitudes-behaviors on this particular matter).

The *medium* for achieving closure is the cylical interrelationship between speaker and listeners that begins as soon as the speaker and audience are mutually aware of each other and continues as long as the speech lasts.

The *agency,* or means, by which the cyclical interrelationship may encourage the listener to move toward closure is identification. The listeners can acquire new understanding or belief only by establishing and maintaining analogous relationships between what they already know and believe and what the speaker is saying. The action of perceiving such analogies, or linkages, is called identification. If the speech enables the listeners to establish beachheads of identification and to maintain identification with your unfolding speech, the listeners will experience an expansion of the original beachheads, thus actively extending themselves (changing themselves, moving themselves) toward closure. The listeners' ability and willingness to establish analogous relationships is basically determined by their self-systems.

The *process* by which you help the listeners establish analogous relationships with you as the speaker and your speech can be considered the matching of demands (needs or requirements) with satisfactions. You should attempt to determine from the demands of the total situation the nature of the communicative needs with which you are confronted. Then you should select from the available communicative strategies those that you believe will best answer, or satisfy, these needs.

To ensure that each of your speeches affords the most beneficial learning experience, after each performance *evaluate* your presentation for its merits and deficiencies. Estimate how closely you came to promoting the maximum movement possible on the part of the listeners—considering the demands upon your speech—toward closure. Reinforce this basic assessment by reviewing the individual basic demands upon your speech and estimating how well your responding strategies answered, or matched, these demands.

Exercises and Assignments

1. If the speaker's basic task in purposeful speaking is to move the listeners as far as possible under the circumstances toward closure with his/her position, can you evaluate the speaker's performance without estimating his/her intentions—that is, his/her position, his/her Specific Speech Purpose? What are some of the problems inherent in assessing a speaker's purpose? How would you go about making such an estimation?

2. In listening to classroom lectures, speeches in the community, advertisements on radio/television, and the like, select one or more examples that seemed to encourage a cyclical interrelationship. That seemed to be directed to a passive audience. In a short speech, explain how the selected communications seemed to encourage (discourage) cyclical interaction.

3. Keep a diary for several class periods in which you record specific behaviors of classmates during speeches. Interview each speaker soon after his/her presentation to determine whether the speaker was aware of these responses to the speech and, if the speaker was aware, what adjustments—if any—he/she made in content and delivery. Prepare a written statement of your findings.

4. Listen to a lecture or read a passage from a textbook employing the minimum degree of attention that permits you to follow what is being said. Estimate how deeply involved you became and how much you learned. Then listen or read a similar communication making the maximum effort to gain as much from the experience as possible. Comparing the second experience to the first one, did you gain significantly more knowledge and undestanding (that is, did you move closer toward closure with the communicator's position)? Did you become more actively involved? Did you sense that you were establishing and extending analogous relationships with the material?

5 (6, 7). To estimate how much movement your first informative speech encouraged in the listeners, prepare and give to five classmates just before and immediately after the speech a short list of explicitly phrased questions that test whether the listener possesses the desired knowledge and understanding. Prepare a short written statement of your findings.

6 (5, 7). Interview each of the five listeners in Exercise 5 to ascertain in what ways your speech helped (or failed to help) them establish and extend analogous relationships. In preparation for your interviews you may wish to preview later

chapters. This should help you do a better job of estimating how well your communicative strategies met the constraints impinging on your speech. Prepare a short essay concerning the results of your interview.

7 (5, 6). Using the information secured in Exercises 5 and 6, prepare a written analysis of your speech, including specific ways in which the speech might be improved.

8 (9, 10). To assay how much movement your listeners made toward closure in your first persuasive speech, duplicate a sufficient number of copies of Figure 2, page 81. Before your speech ask each person to indicate by an "X" on the diagram his degree of agreement or disagreement with your proposal, and collect ths signed papers. Immediately after your speech ask each listener to indicate his current position. Note the difference in each case. Prepare a chart indicating the relative amount of movement made by the various listeners.

9 (8, 10). Interview five listeners to determine how well your strategies helped them perceive that you had answered their reservations and expectations.

10 (8, 9). On the basis of the feedback you secured in Exercises 8 and 9, make a written analysis of the merits and deficiencies of your persuasive speech, including an explicit explanation of what changes might have made your persuasion more effective.

SECTION II

Analyzing the Basic Demands Upon the Speech

Essential Purpose of Section II: to enable you to estimate the basic demands (needs or requirements) exerted upon your speech by the audience, occasion, yourself as the speaker, and your purpose in speaking

The agenda of the program (pp. 60)
Time limitations (pp. 61)

Demands: yourself as the speaker

The speaker should be a morally responsible person (pp. 62)
The speaker should possess desirable qualities of personality and character (pp. 62)

Goodwill
Sincerity and honesty
Emotional maturity
Animation and enthusiasm
Objectivity
Sense of humor

The speaker should be intellectually prepared (pp. 65)
The speaker should be skilled in applying the principles of speech preparation and delivery (pp. 66)
The speaker should dress and conduct himself appropriately (pp. 66)

Chapter 4: Analyzing Demands: The Speech Purpose

Determining the subject area

Examine your personal resources to discover potential subjects that will meet the needs of the audience, speaking occasion, and yourself as the speaker (pp. 72)

"Life" experiences
Professional or occupational experiences
Beliefs
Hobbies, special interests, special skills
Reading
Courses of study
Listening

Examine external resources to discover suitable subjects (pp. 74)

Current events
Recent inventions and discoveries
Scheduled events
Controversial issues
Standard subject areas

Determining the general and specific speech purposes

Do you want to inform your audience? (pp. 77)

Lectures
Reports and briefings
Directions

Do you want to entertain your audience? (pp. 79)
Do you want to persuade your audience? (pp. 80)

The general purposes to convince and to stimulate (reinforce or impress) as applied to controversial issues
The general purpose to stimulate (reinforce or impress) as applied to noncontroversial topics
The general purpose to actuate

Evaluating the Specific Speech Purpose

CHAPTER 3

Analyzing Demands: The Specific Speech Situation

As you will remember from Chapter 1, the handrails of the ladder to effective speaking are labeled the audience, occasion, yourself as the speaker, and your purpose in speaking. These labels are affixed to the handrails because—much as handrails hold a ladder together—the *demands* represented by the audience, occasion, yourself as the speaker, and your speech purpose "hold" your speech "together," that is, they constitute needs or requirements the speaker must consider in climbing each step of the ladder. We shall take up these demands in Section II, with Chapter 3, considering the audience, occasion, and yourself as the speaker and with Chapter 4, considering your speech purpose. How you go about the task of answering these demands (that is, of climbing the steps of the ladder to effective speaking) is the subject of Section III: "Developing the Speech" and Section IV: "Delivering the Speech."

A student once said that an effective speech is "fourthright": It is the "right" speaker delivering the "right" speech to the "right" audience at the "right" time and place. Unknowingly this would-be humorist echoed a basic principle that has been expressed in writings on speechmaking from the earliest systematic treatment by the Sicilian Corax in the fifth century B.C. to the present text: Successful oral communication is dependent upon an appropriate fusing of speaker, speech, audience, and occasion. Each of these basic elements of the speech situation interacts with the others. In order for you to select, develop, and deliver a message that will promote maximum movement of the listeners from their original position toward closure with your position, as represented in your Specific Speech Purpose, you must carefully analyze the demands (needs or requirements) imposed upon the message by the other elements and must adapt your message accordingly. Only by analyzing the freedoms and restraints projected by the audience, speaking occasion, and yourself as the speaker can you competently assess the rhetorical problems confronting your speech. Only by estimating the nature and intensity of your rhetorical needs can you calculate which of the various rhetorical choices available to you will most effectively satisfy, or answer, these needs.

Demands: The Audience

The most careful analysis of the demands (requirements and needs) imposed by the audience does not guarantee success in choosing or developing a speech, but the following analysis should be helpful to you in estimating the rhetorical problems you will encounter and in finding answers to them. Perhaps the best way of getting at the relevant concepts is to engage the reader in a kind of Socratic dialogue.

Why Analyze the Audience to Determine Its Constraining Influences?

So that you can secure some grounds for estimating the readiness of the listeners to be influenced on your topic, by you as the speaker, under the circumstances of the situation. To discover, and respond appropriately to, the nature of the audience's influence-readiness is perhaps your most important problem in speaking.

Why Should the Speaker Be Concerned Constantly at All Stages of Speech Preparation and Delivery with the Readiness of the Listeners to Be Influenced?

As we discussed in Chapter 1, your purpose in speaking is to secure a desired effect. You wish to promote *closure,* to attain, under the existing circumstances, the greatest amount of movement, or change, in the listeners from their original position toward closure with your position (what you know-believe-feel about the topic *and* want your listeners to know-believe-feel about it), as represented in your Specific Speech Purpose. To accomplish this desired movement—as explained in Chapter 2—your earliest words should encourage at least a tentative union between the listeners and yourself as the speaker and your speech. Then, on the basis of your analysis of the readiness of the listeners to be influenced, what you say and do in the course of the speech should supply the listeners with the means of reinforcing and expanding their initial identification. The consolidation, expansion, and coalescence of the areas of identification constitute a movement or extention of the listeners toward closure with your position. Such a securing of new insightfulness, of new relationships by your listeners requires their active involvement. They must not only be *able* but also *willing* to extend, or change, their own selves toward the complex of knowledge-beliefs-values-attitudes-behaviors you want them to have. Each aspect of developing, rehearsing, and delivering the speech must be carefully adjusted to the readiness of the listeners to be influenced.

To Estimate the Influence-Readiness of the Listeners, What Basic Areas Does the Speaker Probe?

In estimating the readiness of your listeners to be influenced you are essentially concerned with their relationship to the message, to you as the speaker, and to the speaking occasion.

Relation of the Audience Toward Your Potential Subject and Developmental Materials. As you will see in the following chapters, you should carefully consider the potential responsiveness of your listeners not only to your speech topic but also to each contention and each piece of supporting evidence. Ask yourself: What do my listeners know about, and how do they feel about, my potential subject and developmental materials? What are the reasons or causes that might account for the status of their belief-feeling? In order to find answers to these primary questions, you might explore subsidiary queries such as these: What commonalities and differences probably exist within the audience concerning my proposals? What values, desires (basic psychological anchorages of the self-system) are served by the listeners' adhering to their existing belief-feeling patterns? What do the listeners consider to be the logical and psychological requirements of the subject that I must meet in order to induce them to move the maximum distance toward closure with my position, as indicated in my Specific Speech Purpose?

If you wish to inform your listeners, naturally you should pick a subject within the range of their interest and understanding. What is the status of their knowledge? How much can you assume they already know? How much background information must you provide? How easily can they assimilate the new information? What will be their attitudes toward acquiring the new knowledge? Resistance? Apathy? Curiosity? Active interest? What characteristics of their educational, life, or job experiences can you utilize as associational beachheads into the unknown? Do hidden emotional attitudes block the way to understanding? If you were exactly in their position, how would you wish to be informed on this topic? What would you consider the easiest, most direct, and most pleasant route to understanding?

If you wish to persuade your listeners, consider their probable attitudes toward your proposition. Are they primarily favorable? Neutral? Uninterested? Uninformed? Mildly opposed? Openly hostile? What logical commonalities relevant to your proposals do you share with your listeners that you can build upon to promote further agreement? What logical objections do you need to remove? What is the minimum burden of documentation and explanation that they will probably require? What and how much do you have to prove? Are there superordinate goals and values you might evoke in order to link favorably you and your topic with dissident hearers? What psychological needs do the listeners have in relation to the subject that you must meet in order to induce them to move toward closure with your position? What salient psychological agreement already exists between the listeners and your proposal? What salient psychological barriers exist? How intense are they? How pervasive are these barriers among the listeners? What underlying motivations might you ethically tap? What built-in biases and subconscious pockets of resistance might interfere with a rational examination of your ideas? Putting yourself in the position of the probable listeners, how would you wish to be approached on this subject? What will it cost your hearers to move toward your position? What changes will they need to make in their self-systems, that is, in the way they perceive, interpret, judge, and respond to their internal and external worlds?

Relation of the Audience to You as the Speaker. Sometimes the degree to which your listeners identify with you, feel a union of sameness with you, will be more important than what you actually say. To determine your personal potential to influence the listeners, ask yourself: What is the listeners' image of me, and how do they respond to that image? That is, what do my listeners know about me, and how do they feel about me? What reasons might account for their image of me?

Considerable recent experimental research has documented redundantly what was taught by the ancients on the basis of observation and common sense: one of the most important factors that condition audience response is the attitude of the listeners toward the speaker, or the speaker's influence potential. Reported studies are in substantive agreement with researchers Charles E. Osgood and Percy Tannenbaum, who noted that "the more favorable the attitude toward a source, the greater the effect of a positive assertion on raising attitude toward the concept and the greater the effect of a negative assertion upon lowering attitude toward the concept. Strongly unfavorable sources have just the opposite effect." For example, the success of John F. Kennedy's speaking depended in part upon the image he projected. The reaction to his speaking mirrored the reaction to him as a person, that is, his physical appearance, age, personality, socioeconomic-religious background, political views, apparent wisdom and judgment, and so on. Those who responded with suspicion and hostility to this image were not converted easily by his persuasion; those who were attracted by this image tended to respond enthusiastically to his speaking. Can anyone doubt that the persons described in the following analysis by Joseph Alsop would respond noncritically to Kennedy's persuasive appeals?[1]

> A lot of people in these Kennedy crowds would turn out for any Democrat. More would turn out for any passing show. Yet you cannot doubt, all the same, that Kennedy has somehow captured the imaginations of enormous numbers of the American people.
>
> The "jumpers," as the reporters on the safari call the young girls who leap up and down in groups at Kennedy's approach, are an odd phenomenon in themselves. More remarkable still are the "touchers," the very considerable numbers of people, grown-up, hard-working people, who long to touch the candidate, as though he were imbued with some sort of valuable, transferable personal magic or private electricity.
>
> One outwardly serious, sensible-looking old lady was even heard shrieking to a friend, "I can't get near enough. I'll touch you and you touch him for me"—as though a current would flow from Kennedy through her friend to herself.

As Aristotle pointed out in his *Rhetoric,* the *ethos* of a speaker is dependent upon his identifiability with the listeners—the image that the listeners have concerning his character, sagacity, and goodwill. Considering these three aspects as representing the dimensions of your personal proof, you should ask yourself questions such as the following. What is the opinion of my audience concerning me? Do my hearers admire, respect, dislike, or distrust me? Are they indifferent toward me? What do they know about me? What is their attitude toward my occupation or profession? If they consider me a representative of some organization, concern, or agency, will this condition their attitude toward me? If so, how? Is there anything about my age, physical appearance, dress, grooming, personality, voice, or deportment that might influence their initial reaction? How can I improve upon a favorable initial reaction? Minimize an unfavorable one? What commonality apparently exists between my life, job, and academic experiences and those of my listeners? What dissimilarities apparently exist? Will they come to the meeting to hear my speech or something else on the program?

[1]Joseph Alsop syndicated column, release date: October 6, 1960.

If you are regarded as an expert in a particular area, you may have relatively high persuasiveness when speaking on this subject, but may suffer a loss of persuasiveness when discussing subjects other than your specialty. A personnel manager will enjoy higher status when speaking on problems associated with his occupation than on almost any other subject. The audience knows that he knows what he is talking about. Sometimes the ability to say "I was there" or "In my twenty years at Blenders Tube Company" will be worth a notebookful of statistics.

If you are an "authority" brought in from out of the city or out of the state, you may enjoy somewhat higher status than would a local "authority." It is sometimes easier to impress strangers than our friends. As the Bible says, a prophet is not without honor save in his own country. If you are a last-minute substitute, you possibly will experience a diminution of prestige in the eyes of the audience. Your auditors may be more receptive if they know that you have been selected in advance of the occasion and if you have received considerable publicity.

If you have reason to believe that the audience may react negatively to certain of your physical, mental, moral, or "personality" characteristics, you may wish to adjust your topic, supporting materials, and approach accordingly. For instance, some time ago one of the members of a country club urged that organization to support a particular project. Ordinarily, this man is a very effective speaker. On this particular occasion, however, he got little response. A person sitting in the back row summarized the situation in these words: "It's probably a worthy cause, but I can't get very enthusiastic about it with——sponsoring it." In the past the speaker had been notoriously uncooperative in supporting other club activities, and members did not like to have such an individual pressure them to contribute their time generously to his project.

Relation of the Audience to the Occasion. Inasmuch as we cover the demands of the occasion later in this chapter, perhaps it is enough here to point out the considerable importance of estimating the nature of the influence that the situation has upon the readiness of your listeners to be influenced. The physical and psychological circumstances of the occasion, along with the purpose, or urgency, that caused the meeting to occur, all tend to have an effect upon the listeners. As a speaker, one of your tasks is to estimate to what extent, and in what ways, the potential responsiveness of the listeners may be conditioned by the occasion.

What Specific Procedures Does One Follow in Analyzing an Audience?

We have already seen that your purpose, or goal, in audience analysis is to determine as well as you can the way your listeners will respond to you and your message, under the conditioning influences of the situation. You want to know how their minds work, how they feel, what interests them, what repels them, and so on, in relation to your message. By analyzing the goals, values, beliefs, attitudinal predispositions, experiences, personal characteristics, and so on of the listeners, you anticipate that you can interpret better their rhetorical needs. To some extent we have considered *what* kinds of questions you should ask in order to secure insights concerning the audience influence-readiness. We turn now to a consideration of *how* you should apply such questions to your listeners.

In probing the natures of your listeners, you should keep in mind the admonition of Professor Hadley Cantrail, "We are constantly seeing things not as they are but as we are. . . . Man sees what he wants or expects to see in people as well as things." For us this assertion has two applications. In the first place, you should be alert to avoid self-projection when examining your listeners. Avoid the mirror fault! In the second place, you should anticipate, however, that every auditor is like you in that he looks at the world through the porthole provided by his self-system. He interprets all impingements in relation to himself. Thus, he possesses attitudinal reflexes concerning anything that is significant to him.

Your analysis of the audience should begin immediately upon receiving the invitation to speak and—please note—should continue throughout the delivery of the speech. You should secure from the person or committee extending the invitation as complete a briefing as possible concerning the relation of your listeners to your message, to you as the speaker, and to the occasion. In addition, you might consult other members, or officers, of the sponsoring organization.

When you know personally the individual members of your audience, as in the case of the classroom speech, you can apply the questions we have been discussing directly to the persons involved. Engage various auditors in conversations that directly or peripherally concern your subject. Go back over your experience with the listeners and what you know about them. After acquiring useful estimations of their relevant thinking-feeling patterns, probe behind these patterns (reason backward from this data) to calculate the source, or reason, for their knowledge and attitudes.

When you do not know the individual members of the audience, you might find these suggestions helpful. If the meeting is to be a closed one, with the audience restricted to the members of the organization and invited guests, study carefully the nature and reputation of the organization. Since people of similar character tend to band together, the identity of the organization should provide useful clues as to the nature of the members. If feasible, join one or more members of the organization in conversation on the topic you propose to use. Sound out the thinking and emotions of persons who belong to similar organizations, or talk with persons who seem to be similar to your potential auditors in their backgrounds and interests. For example, if you are going to talk to a meeting of the "Over Sixty-five Club," you might discuss your ideas with several of your older neighbors or relatives.

If you are speaking at an open meeting, consider all of the circumstances that might influence the types of persons who will be attracted to the meeting. Will the character of the sponsoring organization appeal to particular types of persons, as in the case of a public rally arranged by the Young Democrats Club, or a protest meeting by the WEAL? (See the analysis of the demands of the occasion later in this chapter.) By questioning appropriate persons, you should be able to discover the general composition of audiences that have attended similar meetings in the past; by making adjustments for dissimilarities between the two meetings, you should arrive at tenable conclusions concerning the general nature of your potential audience.

Also, significant insights into the possible receptivity of your listeners may sometimes be obtained by considering their age, sex, educational backgrounds, occupations, and special interest group affiliations, and the number of persons present in the audience.

Age of Listeners. Although our basic interests may change little throughout life, our attitudes toward those basic interests do alter considerably. To some extent, as we get older, we acquire a greater number and variety of life experiences and an increased maturity of understanding. Sometimes the maturing influence of experience is vividly evidenced, as in the case of the engineer who acquires practical experience in the field. Along with increased maturity, added years may bring a hardening of the attitudes and a growing "conservatism." The *status quo,* like a pair of well-worn house slippers, may become comfortable and natural as we become accustomed to it.

Every age has its particular strains and stresses, ambitions, and disappointments. As drill work in audience analysis, think for a moment of the problems confronting these individuals of different age groups. Mary, a high school sophomore, is concerned over her pug nose and myriad freckles. She wants poise and self-assurance. She wants her "ideal" boy in the junior class to ask her for a date, but he is too busy flirting with other, better-looking girls. She is ashamed of her family because she thinks that Mom looks a little dowdy and Dad "really ancient," much older than the fathers of her friends. She wishes Dad would get rid of his 1978 Chevy Caprice and buy a new Mercedes like the one Helen's dad bought. She feels frustrated because some of her class friends have a video-disk player but her family cannot afford one. Mary's problems of self-adjustment are very vivid to her.

Contrast her problems with those confronting her brother Bill, who is about to complete the requirements for a master's degree in chemistry. Bill, twenty-nine, taught high school for five years before starting graduate work. Married, and the father of two little boys, Bill finds that the income from his teaching assistantship and from his Saturday job at a car wash is inadequate to cover the rent and other essentials. Because his wife has had to take a secretarial job on campus in order to supplement the family income, Bill has had to assume many of her household duties. He does not complain, but is silently irked at having to sacrifice so much study time to the drudgery of washing dishes, vacuuming the house, feeding the baby, and supervising the children's play. He is devoted to his family and enjoys his graduate work, but he gets insufficient sleep, drinks too much coffee, and works too consistently and too hard. The closer the time comes for his M.S. examination, the more jittery he becomes. Several apparently competent candidates failed the examination last semester. If Bill should fail his examination, all his efforts and those of his wife will have been in vain. In addition, the job market seems unusually tight at this time. Even if Bill completes his degree, there may be no immediate opening for him. When he thinks of a recent *Newsweek* report on "a new class—the under employed college graduates," he becomes more apprehensive. The report stated that "each year from 1969 to 1978, according to the Bureau of Labor Statistics, an average of 400,000 new college graduates could not find jobs commensurate with their education" and that from 1981 until 1990, almost one fourth of college graduates who were born in the baby boom years of 1946-1961 "will be overeducated for the jobs they get." Bill is somewhat relieved, however, when he reflects that job opportunities for persons in his academic field are much more promising than in some other fields. He remembers with sympathy the plight of his wife's close friend Jennifer who received an M.A. in anthropology three years ago from the University and has had to find work driving a school bus.

One of the firms at which Bill has applied for a job is the Johnstone Chemical Corporation in his hometown. If he is hired, Bill's immediate boss will be Mr. Clark, an executive in his mid-forties. Mr. Clark is pleasant in a dynamic bustling sort of way. Increasing years have given him new status, along with additional problems. He feels deeply that labor is attempting to exert too much influence over the management of the plant. Honors are beginning to come to him. He has served as president of the country club for the past two years and is president-elect of the city's Chamber of Commerce. Despite his successes, Mr. Clark has a variety of "hidden" problems. He is vaguely concerned about the blackish pouches under his eyes and a duodenal ulcer that he needs to humor. His wife is a confirmed club woman who has insufficient time for her home and family. His twelve-year-old daughter is given to tantrums and lying and cannot get along with her classmates. His son, recently expelled from his freshman class at an Ivy League university, has not only rejected most middle-class values but also occasionally uses cocaine. Because the son's views are well known in the home community, Mr. Clark feels that he must speak up sharply, often, and clearly in defense of conservative American values. He is afraid that the possibility of his being selected Republican National Committeeman is being reduced by his son's excesses. Also, he has feelings of inadequacy. Because his wife's family has for many years been the majority shareholder in the company, he suspects that his success is the result of his family connections, rather than his own ability. In short, Mr. Clark is a busy, efficient businessman with varied interests and responsibilities, as well as "hidden" problems and relatively set attitudes.

Mary and Bill's father is nearing retirement. His company will supplement his social security payments with a limited, though fairly adequate, pension as long as he lives. He is grateful that he is more fortunate than most senior citizens. Although he is pleased that much of the bitterness and competition of life is now behind him, he views retirement with apprehension, as well as anticipation. He has been doing some reading on the subject and knows, for example, that inflation will steadily reduce the purchasing power of his retirement income and that the social security system is endangered, that many older persons suffer from feelings of rejection and loneliness, that his age group has the highest suicide rate, and that some experts fear that the incipient discontent of older persons may cause them to fuse into a power block, demanding greater largesses. He is intrigued by the statistic that of all the persons who have attained the age of sixty-five since the beginning of time, more than one third are alive today. When the negative features of retirement disturb him, he remembers that actuaries give him better than two chances out of three to reach the age of seventy-five and one out of four to reach eighty-five and that psychologists agree the level of family satisfaction is as high for couples celebrating their fiftieth anniversary as for those in their first two years of marriage. Then, he lights his pipe and opens a Florida real estate brochure that promises gracious living in the twilight years—quiet days, tropical sun, deep-sea fishing, patio lazing, and year-round gardening.

Although these are only suggestive samplings, perhaps they illustrate the problems, interests, and attitudes that are representative of different age groups. As a speaker you should be interested concerning the range of ages that will be represented in your audience and the age group that will predominate. This knowledge may help you to identify better your speech purpose and developmental approach with the influence-readiness of your listeners.

Sex of Listeners. Because tremendous changes have occurred in recent years in the status of women—the way they view themselves and their roles in society and the way the rest of society views them—generalizations concerning similarities and differences between men and women tend to be hazardous. Nevertheless, if there is a dominant trend in the position of women it is toward a similarity with men. Let us look briefly at this trend and then at some continuing differences between the sexes that may concern the public speaker.

One way that women have become more like men is in sexual attitudes and behaviors. For instance, some universities—reflecting this general movement toward the emancipation of women—have removed the "burglar-proof," "kiss-proof" wire fences that encircled the girls' dormitories and have instituted coed dorms. Women are apparently freer in sexual expression, or at least in talking about sex, than during the Kinsey generation. In one recent survey of 2,000 adults, 5 per cent of married couples under age 35 admitted to swinging at least once; and in a group of 20,000 readers of *Psychology Today,* one third of the married respondents asserted that they were considering mate-swapping in the future, "if an attractive opportunity occurred." In the past it was almost universally agreed that women did not become sexually aroused as quickly as men and were not as stimulated by erotica. Some recent research, however, suggests that there is little if any difference between the sexes in these regards. It is possible, however, that openness and liberality in sexual expression by both men and women has reached its furthest extension for the time being and may be receding somewhat in accord with the present general inclination toward conservatism.

A second way that women are becoming closer to men is in their addiction to serious crime. In recent years, according to the FBI, the arrest rate for females has increased about three times faster than that for males, and the arrest rate for girls under eighteen is especially high. The increase in female arrests is especially noteworthy because considerable evidence indicates that male police officers are less likely to arrest women than men for similar offenses and that the court system also discriminates in favor of women. If brought to trial, women are less likely to be convicted than men; and if convicted, they are only half as likely to be sent to prison. If convicted for a serious offense, confinement for women is "almost always less harsh than it is for men."

A third way in which the gap between men and women has narrowed is in education. Whereas in 1950 the ratio of persons completing four years of college was 66 women for every 100 men, in 1980 the ratio was about 80 for every 100 men. In 1950 women received about 10 per cent of the Ph.D. degrees awarded. By 1980 this percentage had about doubled. On the one hand, most women college students, who still tend to adhere to a narrow career focus, study for traditional female occupations in which positions are scarce and relatively low-paid. On the other hand, women have been moving with dramatic speed into some academic fields that were formerly dominated by men, such as engineering and law where the proportion of women majors is now around 10 per cent and 30 percent.

Still another way in which women are moving toward greater similarity with men is in employment. Women took 60 per cent of the new jobs created during the 1970s. Today about 42 million women, more than half of all women over sixteen years old, work outside the home. Three-fourths of women under thirty-five hold jobs. Even in the thirty-five to forty-five-year-old age group, 66 percent of married-couple families have both members working. Furthermore, about four of every ten women with preschool youngsters and six of every ten with school-age children are part of the work force. According to Sheila Rule, "employers are hiring women in fields of higher status and earnings that they would not have considered them for a few decades ago. And as the world grows every more dependent on people trained in the technically sophisticated fields where there tend to be fewer women, special attention will be given to qualified female candidates who not only provide expertise but also help to satisfy affirmative-action goals." At the present, however, 80 per cent of working women are concentrated in traditional "female" jobs—in clerical, sales, operative, plant-factory, or service jobs—and the median salary of women workers is only 59 per cent that of men. Few women have attained the inner circles of elite professions. They hold less than 1 per cent of top-management posts and about 6 per cent of top-level positions in the federal government. According to market researcher Douglas Hoffer, working has caused considerable change in the way women perceive themselves and their role function. For instance, he says that working "makes an essential difference in priorities, in emphasis, most of all in available time to perform home tasks with care [and] even shop with care for food." Among other things, working has also contributed to the dramatic increase in women's assertiveness. For example, according to one study, whereas 66 per cent of the women surveyed in 1962 believed that major family decisions should be made by the husband, only 28 per cent of the same women believed this way in 1980.

Despite striking, continuing change in the status and perception of women—and in perceptions about women—some observations can be offered concerning similarities between the sexes. For instance, it seems probable that, as the similarities between men and women increase in the various ways just mentioned, the values, attitudes, and behaviors of men and women will also tend to become more similar. That is, as women's responsibilities, work experiences, recreation, habits, and so on approximate more closely those of men, the distance between the sexes in the way they view these aspects of living will lessen. For another instance, home and family continue to constitute the chief focal points for both men and women. The proportion of persons who are married, or expect to marry, is higher than ever before. Although this is much less true for college graduates, most working women seem to consider their employment a means of supplementing the family income—not a career opportunity. Men are moving toward the position of women in that they are more home-oriented than ever before and share more than their fathers did in the actual operation of the home. Regardless of age, income, or educational level, the large majority of both men and women say that they are "very happy" with their home life and a similar proportion would "probably" or "certainly" marry the same person again. In various polls nearly everyone has indicated family relationships as providing them the most satisfaction in life. This contrasts sharply with the belief of Alva Myrdal and Norma Klein that "housewives in our time have become a discontented class." Perhaps a more accurate assessment than Myrdal and Klein's would be that increasing numbers of women have become less willing to dedicate their full lives to the drudgery of housework, but that for both sexes planning the future mainly concerns home and family.

Although the interests of men seem to be similar to those of women in comparable occupations and status in life, significant differences probably still remain. Psychologists say that in general women are more conservative than men, more religious, more readily disciplined, healthier, (although women are somewhat more subject to acute illnesses) longer-lived, and possibly more easily persuaded. Experimental studies indicate that men may tend to be somewhat less self-centered, less emotional, less subject to periods of depression, and less sensitive than women; also, they seem to complain somewhat less and to have fewer absences on the job. In general, men possibly are more tolerant of moral, religious, and political nonconformity, probably are more interested in politics and more likely to vote, are more "liberal" politically, and are more knowledgeable concerning science, business, industry, international relations, and sports. Women seem to be more interested than men in the activities of the elite social set, in television and movie personalities, in the lives of famous persons, in people in general, in fashions, in art, in the legitimate theater, in the ballet, in literature, in classical music, in the style and appointments of automobiles rather than in their mechanical efficiency, and so on. For further discussion of male-female contrasts, see Diane McGuinness' and Karla H. Pribram's "The Origins of Sensory Bias in the Development of Gender Differences in Perception and Cognition" in *Cognitive Growth and Development—Essays in Memory of Herbert G. Birch,* Morton Bortner, ed (New York: Brunner/Mazel, 1979), pp. 3–56.

Size of the Audience. Admittedly the number of listeners is not a major concern for one learning to speak in the college or continuing-ed classroom. You should recognize, however, that when you do become a practicing public speaker you will need to consider the demands represented by the size of your audience.

Although it may be difficult, even impossible at times, to estimate the size of the audience that will attend a particular meeting, a consideration of the following principles may be helpful in choosing and developing a subject. Despite available research findings that indicate the contrary, some speakers believe that it is more difficult for a large audience to attend to a sustained hard line of thought than it is for a small group and that it is easier to win overt mass response from a large audience. Testifying on this controversial point, Jawaharlal Nehru, an effective speaker before groups of all sizes, found that winning rapport was much easier with the large, tightly packed audience. In an interview with Norman Cousins, he said, "The place where I function with the greatest ease is before a large crowd. . . . I can give myself to the crowd because the crowd gives itself to me. I find myself revitalized by the crowd." Benito Mussolini, the first political leader fully to use the electronic means of voice amplification, admitted that he considered as "wax," or "molding clay," or "sheep" the great throngs that were herded into the Piazza Venezia and other great squares. Such crowds were so easily mesmerized that the Duce considered his speaking on such occasions to be of utmost significance to the Italian war effort. "Today," he once said, "I spoke only a few words to those in the Piazza. Tomorrow millions will read them, but those who actually stood there have a livelier faith in what they heard with their ears and, if I may say so, heard with their eyes. . . . That is why speeches made to the people are essential to the arousing of enthusiasm for a war."

A correlation may exist sometimes between the size of the audience and the prestige of the speaker. If only a handful of people appears at an open meeting, a person in the audience may reason that the speaker must not be "much good" or more people would have attended. On the other hand, a large assemblage may be considered to be a vote of confidence in the worth of the speaker. As we have already seen, a person with high prestige can expect to accomplish more with his audience than can one with lower prestige.

Although some exploratory experimental research does not reinforce this point, some experienced public speakers consider that the number of people in the audience in relation to the size of the room may affect the speaker-audience relationship. Their reasoning is that large vacant patches in an audience may make the speaker's task of securing rapport more difficult. The ingroup feeling may possibly be fostered by having the room filled or overflowing. An aggregation of one hundred auditors may appear to be much "larger" in an auditorium designed for that number than the same audience in a hall large enough to accommodate five hundred.

Educational Background of Listeners. Even if you are a student speaking to other students in a college public-speaking class, the educational background of your listeners presents important demands you should consider in selecting and developing your topic. In speaking to groups outside the classroom, this consideration becomes even more important. Here are some points you may wish to think about in estimating how the educational background of your listeners may influence your attempts to encourage identification-extension-closure.

Many listeners—especially if they have had college training—have been conditioned to accept that education is the most important requisite for "success in life," more important even than hard work. Several years ago the Census Bureau estimated that a man who completed four years of college should earn approximately $200,000 more during his working life than a man with only a high school diploma. More recently Sylvia Porter has said that "a college education is among the very best investments you can make in your entire life," and the president of Temple University, Marvin Wachman, has insisted that "despite steep rises in tuition rates, higher education is still the best investment in the future of American men and women." As these pages were being written, education researcher Ron Wolk argued that although many college graduates during the 1970s "had difficulty getting jobs commensurate with their education" such a condition is not likely to be true in the 1980s. "As society becomes more complex and more advanced, and as more and more people are involved in providing services rather than manufacturing products, education and skills will be in greater demand" and "the need for trained people will grow." Furthermore, Wolk points out, "people with more education tend to get the best jobs available, even if these jobs are below the level they were trained for. It is the unskilled and the untrained who wind up in menial jobs or out of work altogether." Probably most Americans believe that higher education ensures upward mobility, despite a widening criticism of the assumption that "a college degree is a necessary (and perhaps even a sufficient) precondition for success." The positive attitude of society toward education is exemplified by two striking facts: at present one of six American workers has had at least four years of college education; and in spite of soaring costs enrollment is still increasing—though the rate of growth has slowed—with about half of the high school graduates going on to college, in contrast to the 30 per cent that attended in 1939.

The amount and kind of a person's formal education may provide a very rough index of the way he looks at his world. Evidence indicates that to some extent the educational experience does influence the self-systems of students. An example of "positive" influence is that a higher per cent of college students than nonstudents seem to believe that casual premarital sexual relations are morally wrong, that religion and patriotism are very important, and that hard work pays off. An example of negative influence is that college students apparently suffer more from depression than do nonstudents of the same age, and their suicide rate is 50 per cent higher. Further differences between college students and nonstudents are suggested in the following inset.[2]

[2]Jerald G. Bachman and Lloyd Johnson, "The Freshmen, 1979," *Psychology Today* (September 1979), p. 80. Reprinted from *Psychology Today Magazine,* Copyright © 1979, Ziff-Davis Publishing Company.

THE IMPORTANT THINGS IN LIFE

What college freshmen rate "extremely important":

	College	Noncollege
A good marriage and family life	79%	76%
Strong friendships	69%	57%
Finding purpose and meaning in my life	66%	62%
Finding steady work	65%	67%
Being successful in my work	63%	52%
Making a contribution to society	23%	10%
Having lots of money	16%	19%
Being a leader in my community	10%	4%

Considerable evidence also suggests that some effects of education are enduring. Better-educated persons tend to read more books and quality magazines, to be more active in community affairs, to earn more money, to be more interested in global concerns and in political and cultural matters, and to be more liberal toward nonconformists. If you are to address an audience of college alumni, you know that they have attained at least a minimum standard of intellectual achievement (this is true, even though many of the brightest high school graduates do not continue on to college). If you have been asked to speak to the local chapter of the American Association of University Women, you will be reaching minds that should be sharper and better informed than average.

In addition to estimating the amount of formal education your listeners in a "real life" audience possess, you should attempt to ascertain whether special fields of educational experience will be represented. That is, will the gathering include significant numbers of engineers, lawyers, schoolteachers, ministers, physicians, dentists, and so forth? The reason for this concern is that the minds of these people will be especially keen in their specific and related fields. Their specialized educational training has helped shape their self-systems (that is, their knowledge-beliefs-values-attitudes-behaviors), thereby possibly conditioning their ability and willingness to identify with what you are saying and to extend themselves toward closure with your position.

A final point about the educational backgrounds of the audience is that "life" education of the listeners may be more important in shaping their self-systems than is their formal education. The "life" education of your classmates influences how they will respond to your efforts to promote identification-extension-closure. Later when you address audiences outside the classroom you will find the listeners' "life" education even more important in conditioning what you say in your speech. A marine sergeant, a night clerk in a large hotel, a crane operator, a beautician, or a nightclub entertainer has had wide "life" experiences of considerable educational value. Even rustic migrant workers can be extremely shrewd judges of human nature and of appeals to their emotions and intellect. You would be extremely unwise in a particular case to assume that, in itself, limited academic training means limited native intelligence.

Occupations of Listeners. Space does not permit a detailed examination of the probable influences exerted upon individuals by their occupations. Literally thousands of experimental studies have probed the minds and spirits of skilled, semiskilled, and unskilled workers, service employees, white-collar workers, small-shop owners, members of lower, middle, and top management, lawyers, doctors, teachers, preachers, salesmen, reporters, professional athletes, armed service personnel, postal employees, farmers, *ad infinitum.*

Perhaps the best capsule advice that can be offered to you in analyzing a "real life" audience is this: First, recognize that one's occupation does influence the nature of one's self-system. Hence, the occupations represented in your audience are important considerations in selecting and developing your subject. The occupation of an individual is frequently a fairly reliable indication of his social contacts, economic backgrounds, interests, habits, and attitudes. One manifestation of this point is that, according to Lillian B. Rubin, the work a man does "effectively defines his family's social class" and "influences family life well beyond immediate economic realities." "The social class into which we were born," she states, "shapes not only our experiences and our view of the world, but what we expect from it. . . . Thus does work performed outside the home touch the core of life inside. Whether in child-rearing practices, in educational philosophy, even in relations among family members." Second, attempt to determine the various occupations that will be represented and the approximate proportion of the listeners that falls into each occupation. Third, study carefully the occupations involved, that is, the intellectual and educational requirements for one to enter that field; the type of work done, with its broadening or limiting influence upon the worker; the personality characteristics commonly associated with persons in that occupation; the public positions on matters pertinent to your subject that have been taken in the past by organizations representing that occupation. Ask yourself questions such as these: If I were a member of this occupation, what kind of person would I be? What would interest me? Offend me?

What would be the nature of my prejudices? My attention span? My extent of knowledge? My ability to think rationally?

As drill in occupation analysis (admitting the very elemental nature of the inquiry), let us consider the reaction that a "liberal" political candidate might anticipate from two contrasting audiences. If invited to address a meeting of the county medical association, the politician may have reason to expect opposition to his left-wing position. Because of their high prestige and income, physicians as a group are well-satisfied with the *status quo*. Most are conservative on political matters. Although physicians possess superior native intelligence and have received an arduous, if not broad, education, they cannot be expected to consider the speaker's proposals with complete objectivity. In fact, their built-in biases suggest their likely negative reception. If the same "liberal" candidate should speak to an audience of unskilled workers, he could expect a considerably different reception from that accorded by the doctors. Unskilled workers represent a low-status, low-culture, low-income group and, as a rule, would rank far lower on IQ scales than would physicians. (This is not to say, of course, that a particular individual would fit this description; we are considering here group characteristics. Any large occupational group will necessarily embrace a spectrum of differing constituents.) As a group, unskilled workers are less informed and less interested concerning political matters than skilled workers and much less so than the average professional, managerial, or "general" white-collar workers. If the unskilled workers are union members, they may be more likely to vote, and to vote Democratic, than if they are nonunion workers—but they are probably less likely to go to the polls than are skilled workers or persons of higher economic, social, and educational status. Despite the limitations of unskilled workers, the candidate should recognize that they know what they want—or know what they think they want—and will be receptive to measures that seem to represent their social and economic betterment.

Special Interest Groups Represented in the Audience. In view of the advice already given in this chapter, perhaps it is necessary here merely to mention that valuable insights into the beliefs, interests, desires, values, attitudes, and behaviors of your listeners may sometimes be obtained by ascertaining their group affiliations: social, economic, religious, business, race, nationality, and so on. Will most of the people present be members of the Ipswich Country Club? Will perhaps a fourth of your auditors be delegates to the National Presbyterian Youth Conference, which is meeting in your town? Will significant numbers belong to the Elks, Civil Liberties Union, Junior Chamber of Commerce, Kennel Club, Downtown Athletic Club, Library Reading Club, or Masons?

We live in a group-oriented environment. We are a nation of joiners. Most of our living is done in groups. And, by and large, we subscribe to the objectives of the groups to which we belong. Nevertheless, the group memberships of a particular person are imperfect indicators of the knowledge that he may have concerning your subject or his attitudes toward it. Many complex variables exist, including contradictions in purposes among the groups to which he may belong and the differing degrees of loyalty and personal identification that he feels toward the groups involved. Furthermore, in any loosely constituted group—as a social or economic class, political party, or religious denomination—the general characteristics of the group provide only tentative clues concerning the individual members. Nevertheless, if you were asked to speak to the PTA in the country club district, you know that the parents would represent a superior economic and social position. In contrast to persons of low income and low status, these parents should be better dressed, better groomed, better educated, more cultured, better informed, better read, more traveled, possibly somewhat more tolerant of different ideas, more active in the running of their community, more inclined toward political conservatism, more likely to attend cultural affairs, and more interested in reading—a difference that is especially great when considering books and quality magazines. If you were to speak at a PTA meeting in the decaying tenement district, you could expect that the reverse of these characteristics of the country club district might be true.

A person's religious affiliation, or lack of it, may also afford helpful indications. If a significant number of Jews will be present in your audience, it might be helpful to you to know that Jews, in contrast to the general public, tend to possess superior education and income, have a higher proportion of professional, business, and white-collar workers, and lower incidence of crime and delinquency. Jews are preponderantly members of the Democratic party and are strong supporters of liberal social legislation. Also, Christian church affiliations may provide clues to the members' attitudes on some social, religious, and political matters. However, you should not expect church policy necessarily to predict the beliefs and behaviors of individual members of that faith. For example, despite the inflexible stand of the Roman Catholic Church against birth control and abortion, polls suggest that the birth control practices of Catholics are "virtually indistinguishable" from non-Catholics and that only 25 per cent of Catholics believe abortion should be illegal under all circumstances, "indicating that a cross-section of Catholics feel no different about the subject than does the American public as a whole." Also, you should not assume that church-goers differ widely in religious beliefs from those who do not attend church. In this connection, one poll reported that among church-goers 93 per cent said they believed in the resurrection of Jesus, 89 per cent in Jesus being the son of God, and 83 per cent in life after death and that among nonchurch-goers the corresponding figures were 68 per cent, 64 per cent, and 57 per cent. Only 3 per cent of the unchurched, according to this poll, said they never prayed and about 25 per cent—

versus 43 per cent of church-goers—reported a "born-again" experience. Finally, if Evangelical Christians are present in your audience, you should not assume that such persons think alike on all social and political questions. One recent poll found that 20 per cent of evangelicals think of themselves as being left of center, 31 per cent as middle of the road, and 37 per cent as right of center (corresponding groupings of the general public are 22 per cent, 37 per cent, and 31 per cent). Three basic characteristics define evangelicals: they feel that they have had a "born-again" experience; they have encouraged other persons to believe in Jesus Christ; they accept the literal interpretation of the Bible, or the absolute authority of the Bible. These characteristics do cause major differences between them and nonevangelicals on issues related to morality and religion (as, rights of homosexuals, abortion, and prayer in the public schools) but not on other issues, such as gun registration, the death penalty for murder, construction of additional nuclear power plants, and government social programs.

If space permitted, we could look closely at various special interest groups. However, you yourself can do much of this analysis. Remember, if significant portions of your audience will be members of particular interest groups, consider the influence of these groups upon their members—before selecting your subject and speech materials.

Demands: The Occasion

Just as there are guides to assist us in our choice of wearing apparel for the social occasion, there are guides to help the speaker adjust his speech preparation and delivery to meet the needs of the particular speaking occasion. In analyzing the demands exerted by the rhetorical situation, consider these items: the basic nature of the meeting, the circumstances of time, location, and mood, the remainder of the program, and time limitations.

The Basic Nature of the Meeting

Many times the purpose of the gathering will determine the character of your speech. Your initial concern should be to determine why the meeting is being held. What urgency, that is, what condition of affairs, has created a need for the meeting? What relationship do the listeners have to the provoking state of affairs? What do the listeners need to acquire from you in order to share appropriately in the modification of the urgency? If they are unaware, or insufficiently appreciative, of the urgencies, what problems does this present to your efforts to bring them to a proper conceptualization of the urgency?

Is the meeting a regular assembly of some particular organization, such as the weekly luncheon of the Kiwanis? If so, perhaps you were asked to talk because you are an assistant scoutmaster in charge of the local jamboree, or because you are chairman of the university committee to investigate conditions of off-campus student housing. Even if you were told that you could "speak on anything," you were probably invited because your current activities or your background appeared interesting. You will be expected to choose and develop your subject accordingly.

Is the occasion to be a special assemblage devoted to a specific purpose, that is, to the response to a specific provoking urgency or condition of affairs? If so, that purpose will largely determine your choice of subject. Is one of the men at the office leaving, and the meeting is a farewell celebration in his honor? Is the meeting a ceremony attending the opening of a new department store, a political barbecue, or a "kickoff" luncheon for the Community Fund? Is the occasion a unit in a planned campaign or sequence of programs? Is it a commencement program at a high school or university? Is it the annual stockholders' conference of your corporation? Is it a ceremony commemorating the birthday of Abraham Lincoln? Has the meeting been arranged specifically for fellow detectives to hear your report concerning your attendance at an FBI seminar on antiwiretapping devices? On any occasion having the purpose of responding to a specific provoking urgency, your subject and speech materials must conform to the object or intent of the meeting.

Consider also the relation of the sponsor to the basic purpose of the meeting. Who are the sponsors? Why have they assumed the task of arranging the meeting? What benefit to themselves do they expect to receive from their efforts? What is their status in the community? How closely identified will you be with the sponsors? Will this relationship aid or hinder your effectiveness? How can you capitalize upon a favorable relationship, or minimize the effects of an unfavorable one? In what ways will the nature of the sponsoring organization influence the purpose, development, or general tone of your speech?

Circumstances of Time, Location, and Mood

In addition to the purpose of the meeting, consider how the time, place, and mood may affect the receptivity of the listeners. As most students can appreciate, at a breakfast or early morning meeting many persons may still be sleepy; at a meeting just prior to lunch, auditors may be more concerned with the thought of food than with your ideas; at a late afternoon meeting, listeners may be tired and somewhat irritable; at an evening meeting, audience members may consider the occasion more important than a similar meeting in the morning or afternoon and may expect more from the speaker. Also, the date may warrant some recognition in your speech preparation. Is the date historically important, or does it have special local significance? Is it the day before spring vacation? Is it Mother's Day? Yom Kippur? Labor Day? The opening day of the Interfraternity Carnival? Good Friday? The third anniversary of the disastrous fire at the neighborhood elementary school?

The location of the meeting may influence the psychological state of your listeners. In his *Mark Twain on the Lecture Circuit,* Paul Fatout observed that Twain disliked lecturing in a church because he found that people were "afraid to laugh there" and he was inclined to press too hard to dispel what he considered to be a "sanctimonious pall." Where will your speech be given? What will be the nature of the physical surroundings, the acoustics, the ventilation, the lighting, and the physical comfort of the audience? What will be the size of the hall and its size in relation to the number of people expected? Will decorations, symbols, ornaments, pictures, bunting, and so on be present? If so, what psychological effect will these objects exert upon the audience? Will you be expected to speak from a raised platform (an influence toward formality) or from a position directly in front of the first row of seats (an influence toward informality). If the speech is to be delivered outdoors, what protection from the elements will be afforded you and your auditors? Will adequate seating be available? Will there be probable distractions such as the noise of traffic, of nearby construction work, or of children on their way home from school? Notice how any of the following settings would condition the nature and tone of a speech: a campfire site in the woods; a local baseball park; a cemetery; a union hiring hall; the auditorium of a noted art gallery; the garage headquarters of the volunteer fire department; a university planetarium; ground-breaking ceremonies for a new children's clinic.

As further guides for anticipating the mood of the occasion, ask yourself such questions as these: Will the general mood be extremely informal, as at the ceremonies opening a policemen's benefit ball, or at a stag party? Will people come to the meeting expecting an evening of hearty laughter? Will they expect to heckle playfully the speaker? Will the general mood be relatively informal, yet serious? Will the auditors expect to interrogate, or—if they so desire—to argue with, the speaker? Will the atmosphere be formal and somewhat stilted, as at a dedication ceremony? Will there be open or cloaked resentment, or boredom and apathy—as at some university lectures series with compulsory attendance. Along somewhat different lines of inquiry, you should consider the amount of publicity that you and the meeting have received, as well as the importance of the meeting. Naturally, the degree of impressiveness will help to determine the mood of the occasion and your prestige. The weekly meeting of a lodge may not afford the same receptive mental state on the part of the listeners as would a formal banquet celebrating the fiftieth anniversary of that organization's founding. Naturally, the basic mood or psychological set of the audience influences its attention span and partly determines its patterns of thought and behavior.

The Agenda of the Program

The selection of the particular response that you wish to win from the listeners, as well as your speech materials and speech delivery, should be conditioned by what precedes and follows your speech.

Will you be the only speaker? If there are other speakers, what will be the subjects and basic mood of their talks? Imagine your consternation if a preceding speaker should talk on your topic, leaving you without a speech? A light, humorous approach may be inappropriate if the other speeches are serious attempts to grapple with pressing problems. Ordinarily, you and the other speakers will be expected to present a unified program. Is your talk an incidental item on the program, or is it one of the main features? Usually the major address is the last presentation. If your contribution is supposed to be a minor part of the proceedings, endeavor to supplement rather than compete with the main address. Secure from the chairman a clear understanding of what is expected from you in the way of speech purpose, development, mood, and style of composition.

Will nonspeaking events, such as musical numbers, sports exhibitions, contests, or games appear on the program? Will the audience participate directly, as in singing, responsive reading, pledging allegiance, reciting rituals, or, as mentioned earlier, interrupting, ribbing, or interrogating the speaker? If so, what may be the influence upon the psychological set of the audience? Obviously, you cannot expect a sustained intellectual effort from your audience if your speech is sandwiched between the halves of an exciting football game, or between a magician's act and a dart-throwing contest at a club social.

What is your position on the program? If you are the initial speaker, your presentation will do much to set the tone for the entire meeting. If your position is later, your speech should possess sufficient flexibility, especially in the Introduction, for you to adjust smoothly to the preceding speeches. Unfortunately, speakers often exceed their time limits and the speaking part of the program may stretch exhaustingly into the night or intrude into the time planned for the serving of refreshments, social mixing, or the presentation of awards. If your position is near the end of a long program including considerable speechmaking, your auditors may be restless when you begin your speech, and very likely will appreciate a lighter touch—perhaps, even a telescoped speech.

Time Limitations

Many inexperienced speakers select subjects that cannot be treated adequately in the time at their disposal. In such cases, the speaker either handles his subject superficially or exceeds his time limit. To overstep time boundaries is discourteous to other speakers and to the audience. If given time restrictions, you should narrow the subject to a specific area that can be covered within the time available.

Do not use a blunderbuss, scatter-gun approach. Avoid broad themes such as Russia, Eastern philosophies, government spending, prejudice, crime, the merchant marine, the history of the South, or modern man. Most of these subjects would require at least a book for a complete discussion. Instead of speaking on poverty, limit the scope of your talk to, for example, the necessity of community support for the urban renewal project in your home community. Avoid the error committed by the student speaker who endeavored to describe in twenty minutes all of the improper practices in business and the professions. How mistaken the speaker was to believe that in such a short time he could present adequately the illegitimate procedures sometimes followed in the repairing of watches, automobiles, radios, television sets, and power mowers, as well as those occurring in the canning industry, the drug business, and the professions of osteopathy, medicine, dentistry, and law! Any one of these topics would have been more than ample for a full-length address. The speaker would have been much more effective if, for example, he had selected the problem of unnecessary surgery. Such a topic, adequately developed, might have made a genuine contribution.

Demands: Yourself as the Speaker

Earlier in this chapter we observed that the attitudes the listeners have toward you as the speaker may be exceedingly important in determining the success of your speech. One of your tasks, therefore, is to project an image of your true self that will foster acceptance of your ideas.

To accomplish this, you must first learn what constitutes an appropriate public speaker image; second, evaluate yourself in terms of these criteria; and, third, attempt to improve the distinctiveness and suitability of the image you project. This point should be clearly understood: your image as a speaker tends to mirror your qualities as a person. Your image is the total impression that you make as a speaker and as a human being. As Ben Jonson once said, "Speak that I may know you; for speech most shows the man."

The following paragraphs offer no legerdemain, no artful tricks by which one can camouflage one's motivations or inner nature and, thereby, deceive the unwary listener. Instead this text indicates that typical audiences want the speaker to evidence high intellectual, moral, emotional, and social qualities and will respond best to speakers who possess these qualities. The desires of the audience are not answered merely by the speaker's possession of the requisite qualities; the listeners must recognize that the speaker does possess these qualities. Therefore, the speaker must be concerned that he project the appropriate image to the listeners. He must reveal to the listeners that he has the qualities they want him to possess.

In a sense, the public speaker image represents identification in reverse. The listeners tend to respond favorably to the speaker who they think possesses qualities that they admire. Naturally, considerable individual differences exist among auditors as to what they consider the most important characteristics of a speaker. The following considerations, however, are basic to acceptance by representative audiences.

The Speaker Should Be a Morally Responsible Person

Long before the Watergate scandal, Cato characterized the effective speaker as a "good man skilled in speaking." Moral responsibility is the foundation of a suitable speaker image. All other qualities depend upon this basic one. To be a morally responsible person demands a positive, personal commitment. A speaker is believed because he is "believable." That is, the image of morality he projects meets the requirements of his listeners —he seems trustworthy; he appears to be a person in whom the listeners can have faith; his motives appear above suspicion; he shows respect for the aspirations and the intrinsic worth of his fellowmen; he evidences recognition of his moral obligations and responsibilities as a speaker. Of course, upon occasion the slick salesman, the contriving politician, or the crafty agitator may successfully simulate moral responsibility; but over the long pull, there is no substitute for genuine moral responsibility.

The Speaker Should Possess Desirable Qualities of Personality and Character

Desirable qualities of character and personality, which are close correlatives of morality, include goodwill, sincerity and honesty, emotional maturity, animation and enthusiasm, objectivity, and a sense of humor.

Goodwill. Goodwill is "catching." If you exude goodwill, your listeners will probably respond similarly, and good rapport will follow. Unfortunately, many beginning speakers are grievously self-centered. They seem indifferent to, and sometimes even unaware of, their listeners. Occasionally, even experienced speakers display arrogance or hostility toward their listeners. Although there are numerous ways to fail as a speaker, this is perhaps the surest. You should have more than an abstract interest in your auditors; you should have warm personal regard for them and genuine sympathy for their problems. Furthermore, you should demonstrate by your manner and approach that you appreciate and understand their points of view, and that—when ethically permissible and when consistent with your speaking purposes—you have identified yourself and your message with their interests and wants. If you have little concern for the well-being of others, the chances are that your listeners will sense this deficiency. Become genuinely interested in others. Want to do something *for* your listeners. Sensitize yourself to their emotional and intellectual needs. Consider that as a speaker you are your brother's keeper and that each speech is an opportunity to win friends and to serve the best interests of your hearers.

Sincerity and Honesty. In an experimental study of audience attitudes, W. K. Clark found that "sincerity" was considered the most important characteristic of a speaker. Some experts believe that many undecided voters were persuaded to cast their ballots for Ronald Reagan in the 1980 election because in his televised debates with Jimmy Carter he had demonstrated to their satisfaction that he was a good and kindly man, one who was honest and could be trusted. The sincere and honest speaker advocates only those causes in which he believes. Because the audience accepts that he believes what he says, his delivery may acquire a sharper edge of impressiveness. Honestly compels this speaker to recognize the many aspects of any significant problem and to arrive at judgments only after a careful analysis of all the evidence. Honesty compels him to reject the Machiavellian concept that the end justifies the means and to abstain from deliberate distortion of the facts, specious reasoning, and improper emotional appeals. He does not consider speechmaking to be a technique, a "bag of tricks." In a speech to the House of Commons, Winston Churchill once asserted, "The only guide to a man is his conscience; the only shield . . . the rectitude and sincerity of his actions." This statement might well serve as your guide to ethical-effective speechmaking.

Emotional Maturity. Listeners expect the effective speaker to have a well-integrated personality with good attitudes toward himself, his speech, and his audience. The emotionally mature speaker evinces an appropriate balance between *assurance* and *modesty*. During the time you are addressing an audience, you are a leader. To lead others you must first have confidence in your competency as a person and as a speaker. Assurance grows out of the realization that because of research or personal experience you have earned the right to speak on your topic and that as a result of careful analysis of the speaking situation your speech has been calibrated to meet the intellectual and emotional needs of the listeners. Assurance comes from confidence in the intrinsic worth of the listeners and confidence that they will respond favorably to you and your message. If you wish to be successful, you must expect to be! Nothing is a greater encouragement of failure than the anticipation of defeat. In the well-integrated person, self-assurance does not foster arrogance. The emotionally mature person possesses the humility necessary to recognize his own limitations and to respect the opinions and attitudes of his listeners. Only such a person can establish intimate rapport with another and "talk his language by speech, gesture, tonality, order, image, attitude, idea," thereby identifying one's "ways with his."

In his manner and approach, the emotionally mature speaker employs moderation, tact, common sense, and good taste. He perceives what is appropriate to say to his particular audience and what should remain unsaid. He is reasonable rather than abrasively extreme in subject matter, style of composition, or methods of delivery. In brief, the emotionally mature speaker is poised, considerate, and sensitive to the standards of behavior that are acceptable to the audience.

Animation and Enthusiasm. Listeners want a speaker to be spirited and forceful. They want him to be obviously eager to share his ideas with them. Perhaps this concept is covered best by the umbrellalike terms—animation and enthusiasm. Nevertheless, the catalog of similar terms is extensive, including pep, vitality, life, verve, sparkle, optimism, dash, vigor, freshness, and buoyancy. Such qualities are attractive to the typical auditor and, therefore, he tends to respond positively to them. In contrast, negative qualities in the speaker, such as weakness, flatness, and dullness, are unattractive to the average listener, who will react apathetically to the speaker. Few other qualities in the speaker are mirrored so faithfully in audience response as animation and enthusiasm. To be a dynamic speaker, you must be a vital, alert person with an absorbing interest in your subject, a sympathetic awareness of your audience, and a keen eagerness to communicate your message to your particular audience.

Objectivity. Psychologists say that complete objectivity is probably impossible and, if it were possible, undesirable. If the emotional envelope were peeled from all our convictions, we would become neurotically confused. Our subjective, predetermined judgments give substance, dimensions, and direction to our lives. (Review the discussion concerning the "self-system" earlier in this chapter. The concept of self-system is central to any analysis of yourself as the speaker or of your listeners.) No reasonable listener expects the persuasive speaker to be a dispassionate neutralist. The reasonable listener knows that the "will to believe" affects the speaker as well as the audience and that the speaker possesses his full share of built-in biases and is motivated by conscious and subconscious drives. Despite such recognition of the speaker's subjective nature, listeners expect the speaker to be intellectually honest, to respect the opinions and attitudes that differ from his own, and to be fair in his treatment of the evidence. To expect more from a speaker may be unrealistic; to expect less is to debase speechmaking.

Sense of Humor. Admittedly, some successful speakers evince scant ability to appreciate or to exploit the funny, amusing, or the ludicrous. Nevertheless, a well-developed and discriminating sense of humor is a valuable asset. It helps the speaker project the image of a genial, likeable, and interesting person. It provides a flexibility and perception denied the deadly serious person. As one textbook writer has suggested, "Humor, insight, and language skill are the aspects of intelligence most significant to speech development." A sense of humor enables the speaker to view in perspective his speaking efforts and to avoid magnifying the importance of his successes and failures. It helps him to detect and to turn to account the incongruent and the incompatible, the pompous and the pretentious, the sanctimonious and the saccharine, and the oleaginous and the bland. Humor offers an unexcelled means of securing and maintaining close rapport with one's listeners. It can provide a lightness of touch and a freshness of approach. It can bring to the listeners welcome relief from the task of assimilating and evaluating an assembly line flow of statistics, examples, arguments, and so on. Unremitting pressure upon listeners to learn or to believe may produce resistance, conscious or unconscious. Listeners may feel that they are being pushed or herded. By providing disarming and pleasurable outlets, humor may dissipate these tensions.

The Speaker Should Be Intellectually Prepared

As the eighteenth-century rhetorician Hugh Blair pointed out, "Next to moral qualifications, what, in the second place, is most necessary to an orator is a fund of knowledge." The effective speaker must seem to be an intelligent, knowledgeable person who is especially competent in the subject area of his speech. Throughout the text you will find advice to help you utilize as effectively as possible your present store of information and intellectual abilities. You will learn how to select speech topics within the scope of your personal or acquired experience, how to gather additional materials, how to evaluate the reliability and applicability of available evidence, how to assess the cogency of your reasoning, and so on. You will soon appreciate, if you do not already, the wisdom of Cicero's assertion:

"Excellence in speaking cannot be made manifest unless the speaker justly comprehends the matter he speaks about."

Outside the limitations of this text, but exceedingly important to your development in speaking, is your general acquisition of a liberal education. By developing interests in, and knowledge about, a wide latitude of subjects, you will improve the sensitivity of your awareness and discernments, you will become better rounded and more mature, and you will accumulate a reservoir of information and attitudes that can be tapped in the preparation of individual speeches. This concept of liberal education for the speaker is not new. Many generations ago, François Fénelon echoed the ancients when he wrote in his *Dialogues on Eloquence* this passage:

> There is not time to give yourself three months of preparation before making a public speech; these immediate preparations, however laborious they may be, are necessarily very incomplete. . . . You must spend many years in getting abundant resources. After this sort of general preparation, immediate preparations cost little. But if you have only applied yourself to the preparation of particular subjects, you treat only commonplaces . . . you sew up rags not made for each other . . . you are restricted to superficial and often false arguments; you are incapable of showing the full extent of truth, because all general truths have necessary interconnections. . . .

The Speaker Should Be Skilled in Applying the Principles of Speech Preparation and Delivery

When making an airline reservation, submitting to a dental examination, discussing the blueprints of a new home, or listening to a public speaker, we expect the person involved to be a competent craftsman—to know his business. Likewise, we want the speaker to possess adequate poise, to know precisely what he wishes to accomplish in his speech, to structure and develop adequately his basic ideas, to present his contentions clearly and with dispatch, and to make effective use of the elements of vocal and physical delivery—in short, to use skillfully the principles of speech preparation and delivery discussed in this text.

The Speaker Should Dress and Conduct Himself Appropriately

Some experimental evidence seems to indicate that superior height and weight may make a man's appearance more impressive and, hence, increase somewhat his leadership qualities. Other studies suggest that attributes such as attractiveness of face and figure are also advantageous to the speaker. There is no point, however, in wishing that one were taller, had more hair, or were more handsome. One should do the best one can with the physical characteristics that one possesses. Under ordinary circumstances, cleanliness, neatness, attention to grooming, suitable dress and platform deportment are minimal requirements of the public speaker image. Details concerning dress and behavior are presented in Chapter 12, therefore, it is sufficient here to direct your attention to the necessity of your looking and acting the part of the public speaker.

Summary

This chapter explains how you may analyze the demands of the rhetorical situation so that you can estimate better the rhetorical needs facing you in the preparation and delivery of your speech. A proper understanding of your rhetorical problems, or needs, is critically important to you in calculating which of the various rhetorical choices available to you will most effectively satisfy, or answer, these needs.

The first section concerns the constraints provided by the audience. An essential part of this analysis is to appraise the relation of the audience to your message, to yourself as the speaker, and to the occasion. The analysis of the audience should begin immediately upon your receiving the invitation to speak and should continue until the speech has been delivered. Specific advice was offered in this section about *what* kinds of questions you should ask in order to secure insights concerning the audience's influence-readiness and about *how* you could apply such questions to your listeners.

The second section concerns the demands exerted by the speaking occasion. In this connection, consider the purpose of the meeting, the circumstances of time, space, and mood, the remainder of the program, and the time limitations.

The third section concerns the constraints involving the speaker. Listeners tend to respond favorably to the speaker who possesses qualities that they admire. Although considerable variation exists among audiences, a representative audience wants the speaker to be a morally responsible person; to possess the personality and character qualities of goodwill, sincerity, honesty, emotional maturity, animation and enthusiasm, objectivity, and a sense of humor; to be intellectually prepared; to be skilled in applying the principles of speech preparation and delivery; and to dress and conduct himself appropriately.

Exercises and Assignments

1. In the Appendix of this book you will find many possible speech subjects representing a wide variety of fields of interest and of types of purposes. Select a representative list of twenty of these topics, and prepare for class discussion a brief analysis of the characteristics of the audiences and occasions for which the individual topics would be especially appropriate. Which of the topics would be most suitable for your class?

2. Become better acquainted with the syndicated public opinion polls. (If you need assistance, your instructor or librarian will be glad to help.) Sometimes the polls record the reactions of different age groups to various social and political questions. At times they indicate differences in beliefs of persons of different levels of education and of different types of employment. In each case try to reason why these people believe as they do.

3. Analyze your own thinking to discover biases and prejudgements. If you are "neutral" toward some social, political, religious, or moral issue that possesses significance for you, is it because you have no attitude toward it? Or is it because a conflict between attitudes of relatively equal intensity has left you undecided?

4. Can analyzing an audience before a speech ever ensure complete success in choosing a Specific Speech Purpose? In developing the content of a speech? Why, or why not?

5. Some psychologists say that education tends to reduce the differences in thinking and in attitudes between the sexes. Do you agree? If true, does this concept have meaning for the speaker?

6. Is it logically sound for an audience to permit the reputation of a speaker (for learning, character, accuracy of judgment, and so on) to influence its willingness to accept the speaker's message?

7. Can the speaker who is a partisan ever be completely objective in his thinking?

8. Can you define explicitly the words "will to believe"? Could this drive operate upon the speaker as well as upon the audience? What is the connection between the "will to believe" and the demagogue? The statesman?

CHAPTER 4

Analyzing Demands: The Speech Purpose

In Chapter 3 we considered three of the basic demands (needs or requirements) upon the speech: the audience, speaking occasion, and the speaker. In this chapter we examine the fourth basic demand, the speech purpose.

As we have seen, effective speechmaking attempts to promote maximum change in the listeners. Under the constraining influences of the total situation the speaker seeks to move the auditors the greatest extent possible from their original status of knowledge-belief-feeling toward closure with his/her position. The speaker's position is the status of knowledge-belief-feeling that the speaker possesses on this topic and would like the listeners to acquire as a result of the speech. The speaker's position provides the basic thrust—the basic thesis of the speech. For our needs we can refer to this speaker's position as the Specific Speech Purpose.

The Specific Speech Purpose is a basic demand because it, in conjunction with the other demands, influences what strategies the speaker may choose to encourage listeners to perceive and expand areas of identification, thereby moving toward closure. The Specific Speech Purpose helps determine both what possibly *may* be said and what should *not* be said in the speech. Sections III and IV of this book concern the communicative options available to the speaker that may be used to answer, or satisfy, the demands of the Specific Speech Purpose—and the other basic demands. The procedures for selecting the Specific Speech Purpose provide the focus of this chapter.

To select a suitable Specific Speech Purpose you must carefully analyze the demands exerted by the audience, occasion, and yourself as the speaker. In the following discussion, which assumes you have made such an analysis, you will find suggestions for selecting the subject areas of your first speeches and for applying to the subject areas the concept of the General Speech Purpose and the Specific Speech Purpose. These procedures should help you to choose an appropriate response that you have a reasonable chance of achieving from your listeners under the existing situational circumstances.

In determining the focus of your speech, you could employ three distinct stages or steps: (1) select the general subject area; (2) choose your general purpose in speaking, that is, to inform, entertain, or persuade your auditors; (3) particularize the subject area and the speaking purpose to an explicit statement of the exact response you wish to receive from your listeners by the time you finish your speech. This explicit statement is your Specific Speech Purpose; that is, it is the position, or condition, toward which you want to move your listeners from their initial status of knowledge-belief-feeling. The inset illustrates that, depending upon your point of departure, either stage one or stage two could be the initial step.

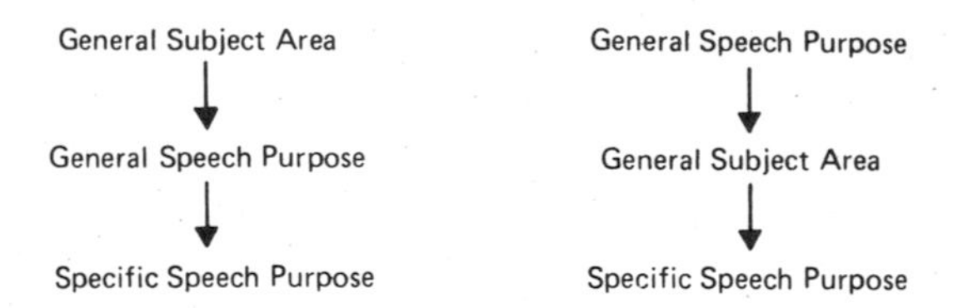

To understand this procedure, let us assume that your instructor has assigned you to make an informative speech; thus, your first step—the General Speech Purpose—has been determined. Because "art" is your academic major and because several persons in class have evidenced an interest in learning how to express themselves in simple art forms, you decide upon "creative art" as your subject area. Obviously, however, you cannot inform an audience concerning "creative art"; such a subject has almost no dimensions, no focus. Therefore, you must select a facet of "creative art" that can be covered adequately in your short speech. To particularize the subject area and the General Speech Purpose, your reasoning might follow these lines: Because I want to encourage the listeners to learn how to engage in simple, creative art expression, because I want to teach a creative art process that is relatively easy to explain and to demonstrate, because I want to use a form of art expression that suits my special talents and interests, and because I want to illustrate my explanations with a number of suitable models in various stages of completion—without preparing them especially for my speech—I, therefore, shall teach the class how to use a burning tool to create pictures on wood.

Or, let us assume that your instructor has asked you to prepare a speech lasting, say, five or ten minutes. In this case, you might first decide that you would like to talk about "creative art"; then, elect to inform the listeners rather than to persuade or entertain them; finally, settle on explaining how to use a wood-burning tool to create pictures.

Both processes are illustrated in the following schema.

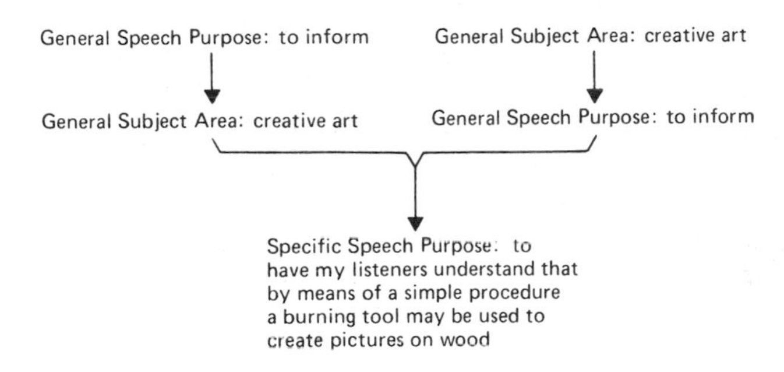

Thus, in this example, what you would be trying to do *to* or *for* the audience is this: by the time you are through speaking you want the listeners to have acquired a clear comprehension that through the application of a simple procedure—described in the speech—one can use a burning tool to produce pictures on wood.

Determining the Subject Area

In "real life" situations speakers customarily draw their topics from circumstances that provoked the speech occasion—in conjunction with their special areas of competency: their public interests and responsibilities, their hobbies, their jobs, their experiences, and so on. Unfortunately, because of inexperience and because of the artificial nature of the classroom environment, the selection of an appropriate speech subject can be a harrowing task for the beginning student. In the following pages we discuss how to select subject areas that are appropriate to the audience, speaking occasion, and yourself as the speaker.

Examine Your Personal Resources to Discover Potential Subjects That Will Meet the Needs of the Audience, Speaking Occasion, and Yourself as the Speaker

Do not permit yourself to be so blindfolded by the immediacy of your personal world that you fail to see topics beneath your nose. Before turning to external sources, concentrate on your present and past environment, your interests, beliefs, feelings, desires, and attitudes. See through any negative and false defenses, such as "I'm not well informed on anything," "I'm not really interested in anything," "Nothing that I know anything about would concern anyone else." Such rationalizations are palpably false; if true, you would have lived the life of a vegetable, not that of an alert, intelligent person in a marvelously challenging and constantly changing world.

"Life" Experiences. Perhaps you have had unusual experiences, such as helping to rescue a drowning youngster at the city pool last summer when you were working as a lifeguard (This might suggest a speech on safety in the water or on the need for better community programs to teach children how to swim); being manhandled by a gang of young toughs late one night when you were returning home from a meeting at the university (This might suggest a speech on curbing juvenile delinquency in the community or on establishing a national works program for young people); as a reporter for the school paper, interviewing recently a distinguished campus visitor (This might suggest a speech on the man's life or his professional contributions). You may have visited interesting places, a description of which would be meaningful, such as the Nile Valley, the Smithsonian Institution, the control center of a missile base, a national park, or backstage at a Broadway musical comedy. You may have witnessed interesting processes that could be explained in a speech, such as the excavating of a cliff dwelling, the treatment of a cardiac arrest case by the staff of a hospital emergency room, the conditioning of a race horse, or the preparation of a dinner for the passengers and crew of a cruise ship. Your home community or region may afford numerous interesting and meaningful subjects. Do some of the inhabitants maintain quaint customs, dress, manners, traditions? Is your region especially noted for its hospitality, tall buildings, good fishing, beauty contests, successful race relations, progress in solving traffic problems? Could topics be drawn from landmarks of your region, such as internationally known institutions (as the American Antiquarian Society in Worcester, Massachusetts), parks (as the Everglades National Park in Florida), farms or ranches (as the King Ranch in Texas), homes of famous persons (as the former residence of Ernest Hemingway in Sun Valley, Idaho), historic shrines (as the Gettysburg National Cemetery in Pennsylvania)?

Professional or Occupational Experiences. Out of your employment last summer as pick-off man at the capping machine of a bottling company might come a protest against the dehumanizing tyranny of the machine. Out of a part-time job as a dairy store soda fountain clerk might come a warning against unsanitary conditions in eating establishments. Out of experience as an encyclopedia salesman might come a speech urging others to seek such employment. Out of a career as a hygienist might come an instructive speech concerning oral hygiene.

Beliefs. Probably a little probing of your attitudinal reflexes would demonstrate that you care deeply about a number of social, economic, political, or religious matters—deeply enough to want to bring them to the attention of others, possibly for the purpose of enabling them to understand your point of view, of converting them to your beliefs, or of intensifying the emotional acceptance of those who share your beliefs. Are you an animal lover? Perhaps the local SPCA organization needs funds for a larger staff, enlarged quarters, or improved care of injured or ill animals—if so, in a class speech seek support for the organization. Are you an enlisted man in the Air National Guard? Perhaps you are irritated by widely published charges that certain officers have arranged pleasure flights for themselves or their families—if so, in your next speech defend the officers or castigate the practice.

Hobbies, Special Interests, Special Skills. Rewarding subjects can be drawn from hobbies, such as listening to foreign shortwave broadcasts, collecting rocks, studying Civil War battles, collecting medieval armor, and bird-watching. Also, suitable subjects may be evolved from areas of your special skills and interests, such as golf, opera, folk music, drama, ice-skating, camping, canoeing, archery, wrestling, dancing, gymnastics, choral singing, arranging orchestrations, designing hats, making dresses, woodworking, cooking, gardening, making automobile repairs, racing hot rods, or composing poetry.

Reading. Review your memory of recent reading in newspapers, magazines, and books. If you have been reading with interest and comprehension, numerous possible topics will soon begin to come into focus. For instance, you might remember how deeply stirred you were when you read an article in the *Washington Post* concerning the high levels of carcinogenic agents permitted in peanut butter by the FDA. As a result, you might decide to speak on the "permissive" nature of the FDA in such matters. Of course, the article in the *Washington Post* would provide only an introduction to your subject; you would need to research the subject carefully before facing an audience.

Courses of Study. The information and viewpoints acquired in college and high school courses of study should provide the nuclei for many successful speech topics. Example: As required reading in a course in government, a student read *The Changing American Voter* by Norman H. Nie, Sidney Verba, and John R. Petrocik. The volume so stimulated him that he prepared for his term paper an analysis of recent changes in the campaigning of presidential candidates. By combining this background with the knowledge acquired in a course in social psychology and one in radio-television, he delivered a splendid speech on the importance of television in presidential campaigning.

Listening. Another rich source of speech subjects is your recollection of talks, group discussions, interviews, plays, documentaries, and news-in-depth reports that you have heard in person or on radio or television. Perhaps a suitable subject could be drawn from the lecture concerning cosmic geography that you heard last week on the university lecture program.

Examine External Resources to Discover Suitable Subjects

By listening to radio and television and by reading you can discover potentially rich sources for subjects for your speeches. Apply the checklists later in this chapter to determine whether those sources will be fruitful or not.

Current Events. You may be able to provide a genuine service for your listeners by interpreting the meaning and significance of some occurrence in the news. To think of current events as being limited to front-page political happenings is to constrict inaccurately the meaning of the term. Any topic that is presently newsworthy is a "current event." Spend several hours with last Sunday's edition of a metropolitan newspaper. Go through it carefully, section by section. As you do so, note the gamut from advertisements, art, and architecture to vacation travel and weather. Ideas for speech topics should leap up at you from each column.

Recent Inventions and Discoveries. As Roger Burlingame pointed out, "The history of the United States is fundamentally a history of invention." Significant new inventions and discoveries are being made constantly in major areas from the auto industry and bacteriology to drugs, plastics, X-ray equipment, and wood products. In this era of the research scientist, today's inventive breakthroughs provide the means for further extensions of the frontiers of discovery. To learn of interesting and meaningful developments, you can interview professors in various fields, thumb through journals in different areas, check major papers such as the *New York Times, St. Louis Post-Dispatch,* or the *Milwaukee Journal,* and examine in newsmagazines like *Time* such departments as Business, Education, Science, Medicine, and Transportation.

Scheduled Events. By consulting the university calendar, the public relations office of the university, and the city desk of the local paper, and by being alert to announcements in the press and on radio or television, you should discover numerous coming events that could be called to the attention of your audience. Perhaps a renowned Russian gymnastic troupe is coming to the campus. Perhaps a debate historically important to the state or nation is to be re-enacted at the state capitol as part of a civic celebration. Perhaps in the near future a Vienna world congress of distinguished scientists is scheduled to discuss the ethical considerations of genetic alterations.

Controversial Issues. Speech subjects can be drawn from the numerous persistent problems that confront the university, community, state, nation, or the world at large. Do you believe that some condition needs to be improved, that some new program or policy should supplant an outmoded or unsatisfactory one, that certain laws or traditions should be abolished, that existing institutions or values need to be critically reexamined? Or, instead of supporting some reform, you might wish to defend or justify some institution or program, or merely to direct attention to some controversial issue—to explain the agreements and disagreements concerning the nature, severity, and causes of the alleged problem and the various "solutions" that have been proposed.

Standard Subject Areas. When all else fails, consult the following list of standard general subject fields. If you apply your personal interests and store of knowledge to each item, you should come up with a variety of acceptable subjects.

- agriculture
- anthropology
- architecture
- art
- biology
- business
- chemistry
- communications
- crime
- drama
- economics
- education
- geology
- geography
- government
- health
- history
- industry
- international relations
- journalism
- labor
- language
- law
- literature
- military
- music
- national security
- nature
- philosophy
- politics
- psychology
- radio-television
- religion
- safety
- science
- sociology
- sports
- technology
- theater
- transportation

Determining the General and Specific Speech Purposes

When the skilled archer draws back his bow and sights along the shaft of his arrow, he does not aim merely for the large straw-stuffed circular target; he aims for the bull's-eye. He has narrowed his sights from a generalized target to a specific, restricted goal. Every field agent of the Federal Bureau of Investigation spends one full day each month on the firing range, practicing shooting with a variety of weapons. His target is a silhouette of a man, on which various zones are carefully indicated, and his score depends upon the percentage of hits in the vital zones. To apply this analogy to speechmaking, the speaker has located his *general target* when he determines which of the general speech purposes will best fit his subject, audience, and occasion: (1) to inform; (2) to entertain; or (3) to persuade. The final step in focusing the speech is to narrow the general purpose and subject area to the *specific target,* the bull's-eye of the talk, which is the *Specific Speech Purpose.* We already know that the Specific Speech Purpose is a concise, definite statement of what the speaker wishes to accomplish in the speech, that is, the response the speaker hopes to secure from the hearers. To accomplish this purpose the speaker must be able to move the listeners from their initial states of knowledge-belief-feeling, in the course of the speech, to the status of knowledge-belief-feeling indicated in his Specific Speech Purpose. Obviously the speech goal should be one the speaker can *reasonably expect* to achieve in addressing the *particular listeners* under the *existing situational circumstances.*

Before we look at each of the general speech purposes to see how the specific purpose is evolved for each type, we should recognize that the cataloging of speeches into informative, entertaining, and persuasive types is essentially a matter of pedagogic convenience. In reality, the speaker's thrust is invariably to effect the maximum possible change in the listeners—to move them the greatest distance possible, under the situational circumstances, toward closure with his position, as represented by the Specific Speech Purpose. By the time he has finished speaking, he wants the hearers to share some aspect of his system of knowledge-belief-feeling. The response he seeks from the listeners is for them to extend their existing state of knowledge-belief-feeling toward that of the speaker, as identified in his Specific Speech Purpose. This is the essence of communication. To promote this extension of the listener, the speaker must influence the listener to attend to the language stimuli he is presenting—to evoke images in his mind that are similar to those in the mind of the speaker, keep him agreeably occupied or interested, and, by supplying knowledge, enable him to find form and character in what is being said. Thus, to evoke movement on the part of the listener requires elements of informing, entertaining, and persuading. It is basically for instructional purposes that this process is considered as constituting three somewhat different, somewhat overlapping subtypes: to inform, to entertain, and to persuade.

Do You Want to Inform Your Audience?

The major, ultimate goals of the speech to inform are understanding and retention by the audience. Although nearly all speeches contain informational materials, only the speech to inform has as its primary purpose to give knowledge, to make things clear, and to secure understanding. And, in no other form of speaking is retention of what the speaker says as important as it is in the speech to inform. Although it is highly desirable that the listeners remember the signal ideas of any speech, such retention is the basic purpose of only the informative speech. The speaker who wishes to entertain his listeners accomplishes his principal purpose if he successfully diverts them. The speaker who wishes to persuade accomplishes his primary purpose if his listeners believe, feel, or act as he requests them to. On the other hand, the speech to inform cannot be considered a success unless the listeners remember enough of the more important information to enable them to make closure with the speaker's position, that is, to accomplish the response desired in the Specific Speech Purpose. In informative speaking you are not concerned principally with proving points, changing emotional attitudes, or evoking specific action. Such aims, when they are necessarily elements in a speech to inform, are means to the end of enabling the listeners to "see" what you want them to "see." Ordinarily, you are a "salesman" only in the limited sense of identifying your materials with the interests, desires, and needs of the listeners so that you encourage them to want to learn and to remember the information you present.

Informative speeches may be conveniently divided into several categories.

Lectures. As a student you do not need a detailed description of the lecture as a type of informative speaking. You have been attending lectures almost daily since your matriculation. Other examples of lectures include Robert Penn Warren speaking on "The Modern Novel" to aspiring writers at the Breadloaf School of English summer program, and a scientist telling the visitors assembled in the Smithsonian lecture hall about the contributions to astronomy of the world's largest telescope at Arecibo, Puerto Rico.

Reports and Briefings. When an official of a corporation presents the results of a sales campaign to a board of directors' meeting he is giving a *report*. When the mayor returns from a national conference on problems of the city, he is expected to *report* at the next city council meeting concerning the activities of the convention. The student, after reading an assigned reference, stands in front of the class and makes a *report*. At the beginning of the school year, the dean of students *briefs* the resident assistants about their duties and responsibilities. The chairman of the homecoming parade, when he meets with representatives of the various organizations entering floats, *briefs* them concerning details of the parade.

Directions. Men and women who have served in the army realize the important role that oral directions played from the time they formed in queues to take their physical examinations until their service terminations. A major league coach is using informative speech when he assembles his rookies around the slide pits during spring training and describes the art of stealing bases. An expert at cooking school is giving directions when she explains how to make quiche Lorraine, as does a forest ranger when he tells his crew how to plant seedlings, or a supervisor at a large department store when she informs a corps of new salespersons about their duties.

In the particularizing of your general subject area and general purpose to inform, avoid selecting as your Specific Speech Purpose one that is too technical or too complex for your audience, one that is too broad for the time limitations, or one that covers well-known materials. Obviously in such cases you could not provide a suitable learning experience for your listeners.

Whether you are giving a lecture, report, or directions, your subject will probably be drawn from one of several somewhat overlapping sources: descriptions, criticisms, definitions, explanations, demonstrations, reviews, interpretations, or narrations. Notice that the following sample Specific Speech Purposes represent specific, limited targets rather than generalized goals.

Description By the time I have finished my speech I want my listeners to understand that nature's most successful design may be exemplified by the beetle

Criticism To have my audience understand that William Faulkner possessed a distinctive literary style

Definition To have my listeners understand that the scanning electron microscope is unique in that it uses electronic methods to interpose an elaborate sequence of events between the object and the receiver

Explanation To have my audience understand that controlled hunting can be an effective means of game management

Demonstration To have my audience understand that bleeding can be stopped by the application of simple first aid procedures

Review To have my listeners understand that the plot of John le Carre's *The Honorable Schoolboy* consists of many subplots that come together at the end with ironic implications exceeding those of *The Spy Who Came in from the Cold*

Interpretation To have my audience understand that the battle of Antietam was a turning point in the Civil War

Narration To have my listeners understand that Custer's last stand concluded a comedy of errors on the part of Custer

Do You Want to Entertain Your Audience?

Sometimes the major intent of the speaker is to get the listeners to *enjoy* the address, rather than principally to acquire knowledge or to change some aspect of their beliefs-feelings-behaviors. The entertaining speech may be completely without serious purpose, such as the telling of a series of risqué stories at a convivial banquet. Because of the great volume of readily available professional entertainment, the purely diverting speech is probably not as frequently presented as it once was. As a rule, the entertaining speech of today has a secondary purpose of conveying information or fostering persuasion. (Conversely, most successful public lectures are at least as much entertaining as they are informative or persuasive.) Naturally the more significant this secondary function is, the more important is its shaping influence upon the content, organization, and delivery of the speech. The best-known speech for entertainment is the after-dinner speech (see Chapter 16 for an analysis of this type of speech), although some after-dinner speeches are designed principally to inform or to persuade. Occasions at which entertaining speeches are sometimes presented include special meetings for recreation sponsored by various clubs and organizations, and social gatherings of various types, such as fun nights, club meetings, and parties.

It is easy to see that the speech basically to entertain may be directed at a wide range of possible responses. For several decades Auguste Piccard and his son Jacques thrilled juveniles and adults with their stories of adventures in exploring the ocean depths. Today, Jacques Cousteau carries on the tradition of explorer and raconteur. A Harvard archeologist might entertain his listeners by telling them how he and his party explored the inner recesses of a newly discovered Egyptian tomb. A Detroit jeweler might amuse a Thursday evening "fun fest" meeting of the Junior Chamber of Commerce by describing some of his unusual customers. A woman just returned from traversing the Inter-American highway from the American border at Juarez to Guatemala might tell of her experiences at an AAUW travel interest group meeting.

Now let us look at some examples of the Specific Speech Purpose for the speech to entertain.

- To entertain my audience with a description of the antics of Botto, the baby chimpanzee at the zoo.
- To divert my audience with a narration of my boat trip down the Amazon.
- To amuse my audience with a demonstration of some sleight-of-hand card tricks.
- To amuse my listeners with a description of some of my professors at the university.
- To amuse my listeners with a discussion of the humorous implications of "robot medicine," the new development of ergometrics.
- To entertain my audience by relating some of my lighter experiences as a director at Scout camp.
- To divert my audience with predictions concerning family life one hundred years from now.

Do You Want to Persuade Your Audience?

The persuasive speaker aims at inducing the audience to think, feel, or act in the manner he desires. By supplying goals, evidence, and reasoning with which the listener may identify, he hopes to engage the listener in a cyclical interaction that will cause him to move the maximum distance possible under the circumstances toward closure with his position—that is, toward the status of believing-feeling-behaving that is represented in his Specific Speech Purpose. Although the speech to persuade may contain much informational material, the function of such content is to supply the means to the end—persuasion. Although speeches to persuade may contain streaks or pockets of entertainment, the function of this diverting material is to harness the attention and capture the goodwill of the listeners, thereby furthering the persuasive aims of the speaker.

For purposes of convenience, persuasive speeches may be divided into three types: those that *convince*; those that *stimulate* (*reinforce* or *impress*); and those that *arouse action.* In later chapters we discuss the psychological and logical means of persuasion and the structuring of the persuasive speech; in the immediately following discussion we consider basic concepts concerning the selection of the Specific Speech Purpose.

First, Let Us See How the General Purposes to Convince and to Stimulate (Reinforce or Impress) May Be Applied to Controversial Issues. A careful study of the following diagram is the starting point for an understanding of how to motivate others to think, feel, or act as you desire. Whenever you present a controversial issue, the mental attitude of everyone in the audience toward your argument will fall somewhere on this diagram.

As a result of your analysis of the potential audience and the speaking occasion, you have acquired some understanding of the knowledge of your listeners concerning the subject, as well as their probable beliefs, values, and attitudes. When the speaker's point of view falls within the latitude, or range, of acceptance of the audience, basic agreement already exists between the speaker and his hearers. The favorably disposed audience—especially if the members personally feel strongly involved—is sympathetic toward the speaker's position.

Because this is so, the speaker should have little difficulty in enabling the listeners to perceive analogous relationships between their self-systems (that is, their relevant complex of knowledge-beliefs-values-attitudes-behaviors concerning the topic) and the speaker's basic thesis, arguments, and developmental materials. When an instructor tells you that your hard work and high test scores in his course warrant an "A," are you inclined to question him? Of course not! He is telling you what you want to hear, what you readily accept as a correct perception of reality.

The *moderately* favorable audience would like to agree with the speaker. It is not as critical of the speaker's logical development as the neutral audience, but probably will refuse to be swayed as easily as the definitely or extremely favorable one. The *definitely* favorable audience is eager to believe, but is more analytical than the *extremely* favorable audience—such as a group of militant right-wingers listening to a speaker advocating military preparedness—which may be almost completely noncritical of assertions reinforcing their core beliefs. (This does not mean, of course, that logical development can be entirely lacking, even in the speech to an extremely favorable audience. The most ardent of listeners wants to believe that his judgments rest on sound logical and moral bases.)

To summarize this point, if a preponderance of the audience is receptive to the speaker's recommendations, his basic task is to buttress, to justify existing beliefs-values-attitudes-behaviors, to impress or stimulate the listeners so that they acquire a greater appreciation, stronger commitment, more ardent conviction, deeper devotion, more intense dislike, and so forth. In other words, his purpose is to so *stimulate* (*reinforce*

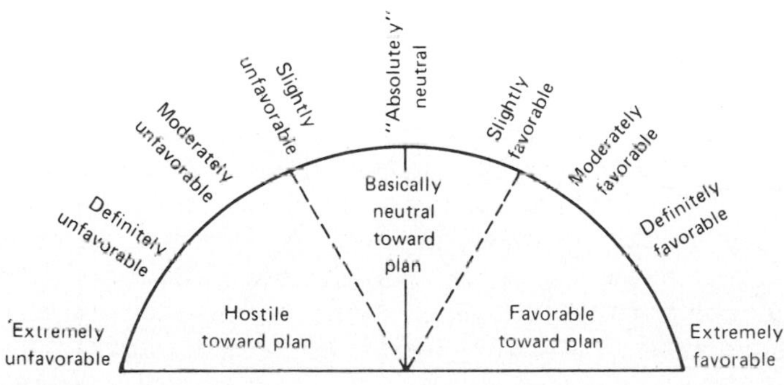

Fig. 2

or *impress*) the listeners that they will move significantly toward closure with his speaker's position of belief-feeling.

When the speaker's point of view falls within the latitude or range of *noncommitment* of the audience, the speaker encounters a *basically neutral* group, one that probably has a more open mind on the topic than either the audience that is favorable to his position or the audience that is opposed to it. Listeners may be noncommitted because of insufficient information or interest or because of a clash of conflicting beliefs-values-interests. Although perhaps not as easily affected by emotive appeals as the favorable audience, the neutral audience will not be emotionally hostile to the speaker's case. When speaking to a basically neutral audience upon a controversial issue, the speaker's General Speech Purpose is to *convince* the listeners that they should abandon their position of indecision, doubt, or neutrality, and move toward acceptance of his views.

When the speaker's point of view falls within the latitude, or range, of *rejection* of the audience—especially if the matter is important to the listeners, if they feel a deep sense of involvement, if they have identified with the opposing views—the speaker encounters an exceedingly difficult, perhaps impossible, task of persuasion. The *hostile* audience does not want to believe; it is intellectually and, probably, emotionally conditioned against the speaker's arguments. As discussed in Chapters 7, 8, and 9, the speaker can select certain rhetorical options to encourage a somewhat

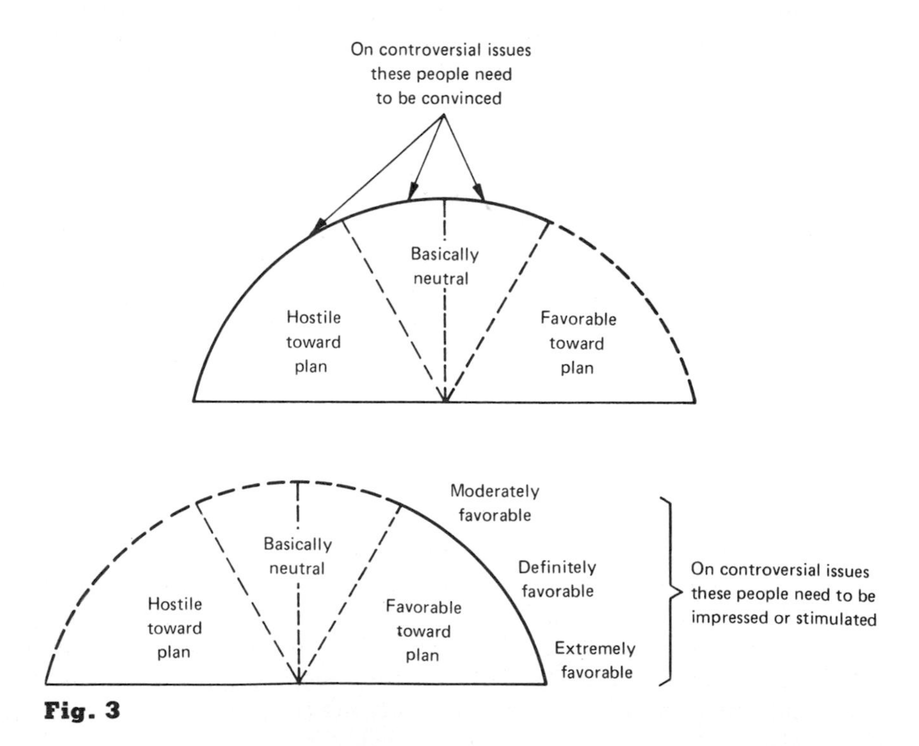

Fig. 3

more favorable reception toward himself and toward his speech. The spectrum of moderate, definite, and extreme hostility presents a sliding scale of increasing subjectivity on the part of the audience concerning the point at issue. In facing an audience located anywhere on this spectrum, the speaker must seek to *alleviate opposition* and—to the extent possible—to *convince* the listeners that they should move toward accepting his views.

An accurate understanding of the distinctions between the general purposes to convince and to stimulate (reinforce or impress) is essential. Each type of purpose demands a different kind of speech—different in objectives, in the selection and organization of materials, and perhaps also in vocal and physical delivery. The hinge of the matter is that on controversial issues the basic opinion of the audience determines the type of speech purpose.

The following speech situations are designed to illustrate the influence exerted by the initial position of the audience upon the formulation of the Specific Speech Purpose.

Speech situation no. 1. If an advocate of the decriminalization of marijuana were to address a group of "liberal" students on the subject, he would find that his position was within the listeners' latitude of agreement; they would be sympathetic to his proposal. Therefore, his purpose would be to reinforce existing intellectual and emotional agreement, to stimulate or impress the listeners so that they acquired a deeper appreciation, a stronger commitment. His Specific Speech Purpose might be phrased something like this: By the time I am through speaking I want my listeners to believe and feel more strongly that marijuana should be decriminalized. If the advocate were to speak to a basically neutral fact-finding panel appointed by the governor, he would try to influence the members to move away from their position of noncommitment and toward his views. His Specific Speech Purpose, then, might be: To convince my listeners that marijuana should be decriminalized. If the advocate were to confront a hostile group of, say, legislators and law enforcement officers, he knows that they would actively resist his attempts at persuasion. Therefore, his Specific Speech Purpose might be: To have my listeners be less opposed to the decriminalization of marijuana and, to the extent that it can be accomplished under the circumstances, have them move toward accepting its decriminalization.

Speech situation no. 2. If a speaker should address liberal Democrats on the need to maintain current funding for the school breakfast and lunch programs, he would face a very favorable audience. His Specific Speech Purpose might be: To have my listeners believe more deeply, feel more intensely, that the federal government should maintain current funding for the school breakfast and lunch programs. If he were to speak to a group of uncommitted voters, his Specific Speech Purpose could be: To convince my hearers that they should move toward the belief that the federal government should maintain current funding for the school breakfast and lunch programs. If he were to address an audience of conservative Democrats, his Specific Speech Purpose might be: To have my listeners be less opposed to a federal program to maintain current funding for the school breakfast and lunch programs and to move as far as possible toward accepting such a program.

A consideration of three additional points is necessary to provide an accurate understanding of the relationship to controversial issues of the general purposes to convince and to stimulate (reinforce or impress). For the sake of simplicity we have considered audiences that fall completely within the range of being favorable, neutral, or opposed to the policies of the speaker. Many audiences are not so easily categorized. Frequently, for instance, some individuals in the audience will be strongly in favor of your views, others less favorably predisposed, some more or less hostile, and a large proportion essentially noncommitted. Ordinarily, although in such cases you should attempt to gratify the favorable wing and conciliate the hostile wing, you should concentrate major attention on the undecided auditors—especially if they constitute a majority.

Second, even though you follow the advice in Chapter 3 for analyzing your potential listeners, it is not always possible to ascertain in advance the attitudes you will encounter. In such situations, you probably should anticipate a "normal distribution curve" of reactions with most persons being basically neutral or undecided, some being more or less favorable, and some being more or less opposed. For this sort of audience you would prepare a speech to convince. Such preparation, however, is akin to feeling one's way in a dark, unfamiliar room; so, it is especially important in this kind of speech to retain enough flexibility in speech composition to make on-the-spot adaptations to the feedback you receive from your listeners.

Third, in the preceding analysis of the speech to convince we have been concerned solely with long-range influence. The convincing speech is directed toward the future; it tries to instill beliefs and concepts that will withstand any subsequent doubts of the persuadees and any counterarguments they may hear. To influence "permanently" the neutral or hostile auditors, you must enable them to identify with your proposal, partly by removing the cause for their objections through logical and psychological means. Admittedly, short-range or transitory influence sometimes may be secured by using humor, vivid human interest stories, or personal charm to so stimulate neutral or negative listeners that they "forget" their objections. But listeners who are so persuaded soon "remember" their objections, and revert to their original patterns of thinking-feeling. They have not been convinced, merely temporarily diverted. Their identification with the counterposition remains unaltered. Thus, the salesman who knows that he should spend the afternoon making calls may be persuaded by a friend to attend a baseball game. His enjoyment of the game may be ruined, however, by feelings of guilt that soon crowd into his consciousness—he is shirking his job and letting his family down. Many a silver-tongued politician, such as presidential candidate William Jennings Bryan, has charmed his or her audience at the hustings only to find that such persuasion failed to last until Election Day.

Let Us See How the General Purpose to Stimulate (Reinforce or Impress) May Be Applied to Noncontroversial Topics. Speakers sometimes seek to stimulate listeners on noncontroversial matters, that is, on topics or themes that do not provoke conflicting opinions, for or against. Nearly everyone would agree on such matters—but they may not think about them very often or very deeply. A speech of this type is usually concerned with stirring those persons who are relatively indifferent or unimpressed. It attempts to arouse listeners in some way, such as these:

- To render heartfelt devotion in place of lip service.
- To substitute active apprehension for jaded complacency.
- To acquire a more sensitive awareness of accepted but neglected values.
- To reaffirm one's feelings of fidelity, trust, or reverence.
- To awaken curiosity, respect, or even wonderment.

Sources for noncontroversial topics may represent a wide spectrum, as suggested by the following.

- patriotic, religious, and moral themes
- significant and revered events of the past or present
- interesting and important philosophies, movements, institutions, and organizations
- outstanding personages
- heroes, or role models, especially those who have made selfless sacrifices
- acts of devotion, valor, fortitude

The following Specific Speech Purposes demonstrate the application to noncontroversial subjects of the general purpose to stimulate (reinforce or impress).

- To have my audience acquire greater respect for the wonders of nature.
- To have my listeners feel a stronger devotion to their families.
- To have my listeners experience feelings of pride in the achievements of the women's intercollegiate sports program at our university.
- To have my listeners be impressed with the role played by the barbed wire fence in the winning of the West.
- To have my listeners acquire a more active sense of involvement in the race problems of the community.

- To have my listeners appreciate more fully the contributions made by the public libraries of the state.
- To have my listeners become more concerned about the rising cost of hospital care.
- To have my audience develop a more active apprehension concerning the dangers of inflation.
- To have my listeners acquire a more sensitive awareness that genetic engineering poses problems as well as promises benefits.
- To have my audience become curious about how LSI (large-scale integration of circuitry) may soon change Americans' life-style.
- To have my listeners develop stronger feelings of social consciousness.
- To have my listeners be impressed with the role ACS (alternating current synthesizer) may play in helping alleviate the energy problem.

Now, Let Us Look at the Third Type of Persuasive Speech, the Speech to Actuate. Unlike the other types of speeches we have studied, the actuating speech attempts to produce direct, observable action on the part of the audience. According to their basic function, informative speeches give knowledge; entertaining speeches provide enjoyment; convincing and stimulating (reinforcing or impressing) speeches produce intellectual agreement and emotional feeling. None of these specifically requests action in the near future. Naturally, any speaker with a serious theme hopes that he will affect the thinking and attitudinal reactions of his listeners—thereby indirectly influencing their behavior. Such potential action is delayed and unpredictable. If it does result, it may occur at times, in places, and in forms that are unforeseen by the speaker. In contrast, the speech to actuate aims at more than intellectual and emotional agreement—the audience is requested to engage in some observable action within the near future, that is, to *buy, join, sign, vote, rent, make, sell, enroll, depart, enlist, contribute, give, attend,* and so forth.

Although the selection of the Specific Speech Purpose is of critical importance in all types of speeches, perhaps for the actuating speech it poses somewhat greater problems and requires somewhat greater care in formulation. The specific action requested must be activity that can reasonably be expected from the persuadees: It must be congruent with their present or potential willingness, abilities, resources, limitations, and

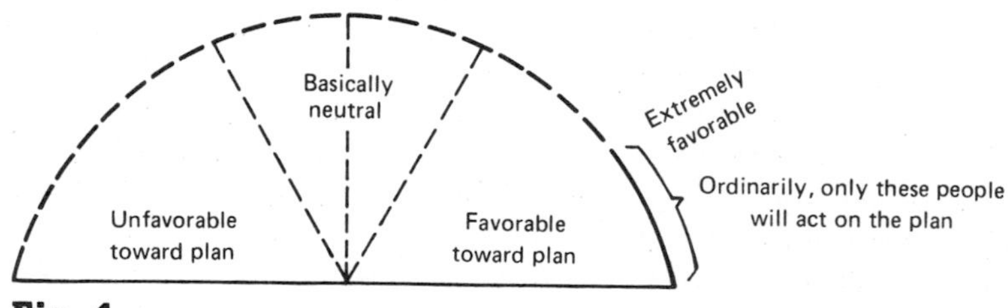

Fig. 4

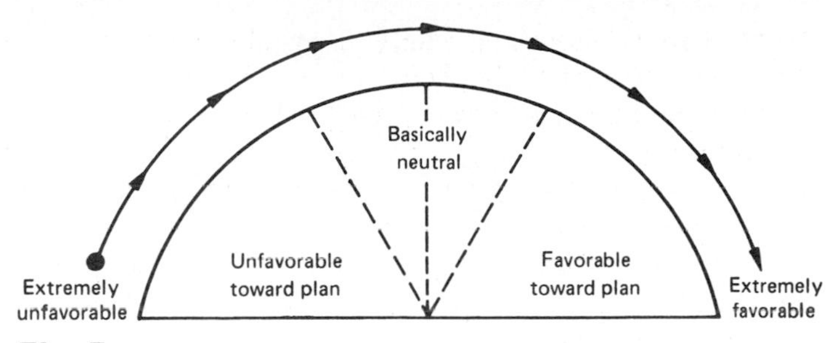

Fig. 5

motivations. A real-estate salesman should attempt to sell property within his client's price range and suitable to his aesthetic and family needs. A YMCA physical education instructor should seek to enroll an audience of middle-aged businessmen in a "Y" program that is tailored to their special needs for reconditioning. Do not press the members of your audience to do something that they cannot or will not do; the requested activity should be within the anticipated capabilities and inclinations of the listeners.

Does this mean that a speaker may address actuating appeals only to audiences that initially are favorable to his proposals? Not at all—assuming that the listeners have the capabilities to act and lack only desire. It does mean that in general the probability of success varies inversely with the intensity of initial resistance. If listeners in the beginning are opposed to his plan, the speaker must first remove the cause for their negative thinking and feeling, convince them that the evidence and, if possible, their personal interests impel them to accept the "rightness" of his course, and stimulate them to becoming extremely favorable to his proposal. Ordinarily, when persons have freedom of choice—to do or not to do—only those who are strongly motivated will act. Figure 5 illustrates that to evoke hostile auditors to action the speaker must move them from the left side (opposition) all the distance to the extreme right side (strong affirmation).

If his audience is neutral, his chances of inciting it to action will be better than if it were initially opposed. And, naturally, if the group is favorably disposed, the speaker's task is much easier. Think of the master diagram as being a hill with a sharp ascent at the beginning that gradually tapers off at the crest. At first the hill falls away gradually, then more steeply. If circumstances forced you to push a stalled automobile, where would you want the car to be located in relation to the slope of this hill? Wouldn't it be easier to push the vehicle on the relatively level ground at the top of the hill than to try to move it up the side? Wouldn't it be still more satisfactory if the motor stopped when the vehicle was going downhill? Compare the following diagram, Figure 6, with the master diagram, Figure 2.

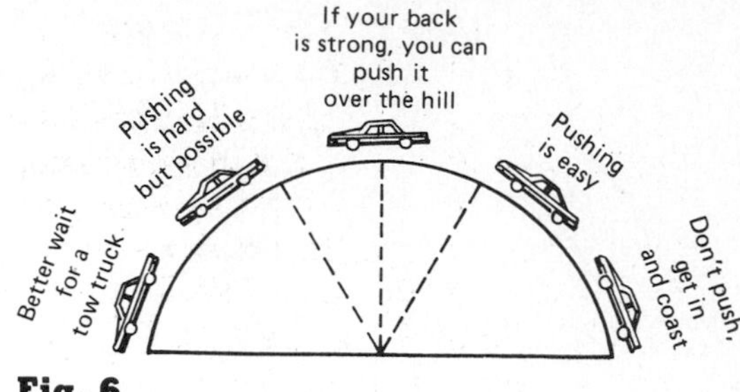

Fig. 6

Here are some examples of the Specific Speech Purpose of the speech to actuate.

- To have my listeners sign a petition demanding the resignation of the football coach.
- To have my listeners contribute to the United Fund.
- To have my listeners attend the science club lecture this evening.
- To have the members of my audience contribute blood to the campus blood bank.
- To have my listeners come to prayer meeting on Wednesday night.
- To have my listeners buy copies of the current issue of the campus literary magazine.
- To have the members of my audience join the debate squad.
- To have the members of my audience enroll for the summer term.
- To have my listeners quit smoking.
- To have my listeners initiate a self-help program to increase their vocabularies.

Evaluating the Specific Speech Purpose

Once you have tentatively selected a Specific Speech Purpose, gauge its suitability by means of the following checklists.

Speaker Checklist

1. Have I, through personal or vicarious experience, earned the right to select this Specific Speech Purpose?
2. If I am not thoroughly informed in the area intrinsic to the Specific Speech Purpose, does sufficient, readily-available material exist and adequate time remain for me to develop competency?

3. Am I enthusiastically interested in the subject?
4. Do I strongly wish to communicate it to the listeners?
5. Can I make an original contribution to the topic?
6. Will the time and effort spent in the preparation, rehearsal, and delivery of a speech with this Specific Speech Purpose provide a worthwhile experience for me?
7. In consideration of the knowledge my listeners have of me and their attitudes concerning me, do I have sufficient personal proof to speak to this Specific Speech Purpose?
8. Will this Specific Speech Purpose permit me to capitalize upon my outstanding personal assets, such as wide travels, knowledge of business operations, or skill in the preparation of visual aids?

Audience Checklist

1. Is the Specific Speech Purpose well adjusted to the centrality of wants, interests, and needs represented in the audience?
2. Is the Specific Speech Purpose suited to the intelligence and background knowledge of the listeners?
3. Will specific aspects of the audience, such as sex or age or educational backgrounds, compromise the appropriateness of my Specific Speech Purpose, or reduce the probability of achieving the desired listener response?
4. Are the listeners in a position to take my advice concerning the acceptance of a belief or the adoption of a course of action?
5. Is the Specific Speech Purpose well suited to the initial receptivity of the listeners? If not, what is the nature and cause of their resistance? Prejudice? Conviction? Apathy? Probable existence of hidden pockets of repugnance? Can this resistance be overcome under the conditions imposed by the speech occasion?
6. Will the topic offend the moral or religious sensibilities of any reasonable person (an important consideration when addressing a captive audience)?
7. Will a speech with this Specific Speech Purpose result in solid benefits to the listeners? Provide them a needed service? Make them better persons? Equip them better to answer some personal or societal problem? Enable them to live richer, more satisfying lives?

Occasion Checklist

1. Is the Specific Speech Purpose suited to the purpose of the meeting?
2. To the psychological mood of the occasion?
3. To the remainder of the program?

4. To the particular circumstances of the meeting, as the time, place, physical conditions, or the nature of the sponsoring organization?
5. To the time limitations?

Miscellaneous Checklist

1. Is the Specific Speech Purpose suitable for oral presentation? Is it too complicated? Too involved? Too technical? Too abstract? Too personal in orientation for public airing?
2. Is the Specific Speech Purpose ethically worthy?
3. Is the Specific Speech Purpose intellectually worthy?
4. Is the Specific Speech Purpose socially acceptable? Will it help strengthen basic human values, rights, and liberties—or debase them?
5. Is the Specific Speech Purpose timely?

Summary

It is important that the student recognize the correlative association between this chapter and Chapter 3. Chapter 3 concerned the demands imposed by the audience, occasion, and speaker upon both the selection of the speech purpose and the speech itself. The Specific Speech Purpose is the fourth basic demand upon the speech. The demands represented by the Specific Speech Purpose, audience, occasion, and yourself as the speaker constitute the major communicative problems (requirements, needs) that you must answer or satisfy in your speech.

In this chapter we have considered the three distinct stages, or steps, you necessarily follow in determining your Specific Speech Purpose: (1) select the general subject area; (2) determine your general purpose in speaking, that is, to inform, entertain, or persuade; (3) particularize the subject area and the speaking purpose to a specific, definite statement of your position, that is, the exact response you want from your listeners: your Specific Speech Purpose. Depending upon your point of departure, either stage one or stage two could serve as the initial step.

To determine appropriate subjects, or subject areas, for your beginning speeches, (1) consult your personal resources, such as "life" experiences, professional or occupational experiences, beliefs, hobbies, special interests, special skills, reading, and courses of study; (2) examine external resources, such as current events, recent inventions and discoveries, scheduled events, controversial issues, and standard subject areas.

You have located your general target when you determine which of the general speech purposes will best fit the constraints of your subject, audience, occasion, and yourself as the speaker. *Informative* speeches basically promote understanding and knowledge. *Entertaining* speeches essentially provide enjoyment. *Persuasive* speeches seek to convince, stimulate (reinforce or impress), or actuate: *convincing* speeches attempt to move the neutral auditor toward the speaker's view and/or to remove or lessen the opposition of the hostile listeners and, to the extent possible under the circumstances, to move these once hostile listeners toward the speaker's beliefs; *stimulating* (reinforcing or impressing) ones try to reinforce, justify, and make vividly meaningful those beliefs and attitudes already held by the listeners; *actuating* ones attempt to impel the auditors to engage in some specific, observable action in the near future.

The final step in focusing the speech is to narrow the general speech purpose and the subject area to the *specific target* of the talk, the Specific Speech Purpose. This precise statement of your position is the exact response you wish to achieve from your listeners. All speechmaking is an attempt on the part of the speaker to move the listeners the maximum distance possible, under the constraints of the total situation, toward closure with his position. Intelligent criticism of your speech centers upon the amount of audience movement toward closure induced by your speech in relation to the demands imposed by the total situation.

To evaluate the suitability of the Specific Speech Purpose, match it against the checklists supplied in the chapter: Speaker Checklist; Audience Checklist; Occasion Checklist; Miscellaneous Checklist.

Exercises and Assignments

1. If the audience fails to retain the main ideas of an informative speech, despite the speaker's having presented information in a logical manner, has the talk been effective? Why, or why not?

2. In a short speech to the class, elaborate on this sentence from the Summary of this chapter: "Intelligent criticism of your speech centers upon the amount of audience movement toward closure induced by your speech in relation to the constraints imposed by the total situation."

3. Explain to the class the importance of audience retention in speeches promoting long-range influence as compared with that in speeches designed to produce immediate action.

4. In five minutes explain to the class the basic differences between an "audience-centered" speech and one that is "subject-centered."

5. Which of the three basic types of speeches do you think would be the most difficult (the easiest) for you to prepare and deliver? Compose your answer to this question in the form of a short talk and give it to the class.

6. Listen to a major speech on television and estimate how well its basic thrust is adjusted to the demands of the audience, occasion, and the speaker himself.

7. Use the following form as a basis for estimating the suitability of the Specific Speech Purpose of a speaker at some public speaking situation off the campus, such as a Rotary luncheon, a church service, a political rally, or a PTA meeting.

Specific Speech Purpose: identify in one sentence the purpose of the speech.

Suitability of the Specific Speech Purpose to the Audience

I. Identify the audience (example: parents and teachers of the Roosevelt Junior High School PTA).
II. Estimate the relation of the audience to the subject.
III. Estimate the relation of the audience to the speaker.
IV. Estimate the relation of the audience to the occasion.
V. What in your opinion was the initial readiness of the audience to be influenced by the speaker on his topic?
VI. Explain the specific procedures you followed in analyzing the audience. In assaying the readiness of the listeners to be influenced, what use—if any—did you make of the age, sex, educational backgrounds, occupations, and special interest group affiliations of the listeners? Of the number of persons present in the audience?

Suitability of the Specific Speech Purpose to the Occasion

I. Identify the occasion (example: the monthly meeting of the Roosevelt Junior High School PTA; location, the school auditorium; date, October 31, 1983).
II. Did the S.S.P. fit the basic nature of the meeting?
III. Did the S.S.P. fit the circumstances of time, location, and mood?
IV. Did the S.S.P. fit the remainder of the program?
V. Did the S.S.P. fit the time limitations?

Suitability of the Specific Speech Purpose to the Speaker

I. Was the speaker obviously vitally interested in his subject?
II. Was he apparently eager to communicate his message to the audience?
III. Was he obviously well informed on the topic?
IV. Was the speech well suited to the speaker's personality?

8. After your next talk in class, use the form given in number 7 to analyze the suitability of your Specific Speech Purpose.

SECTION III

Developing the Speech

Essential Purpose of Section III: to enable the reader to select rhetorical strategies in developing the speech that will answer the basic demands (needs or requirements) imposed by the audience, occasion, the speaker himself, and the speech purpose

Chapter 6: Organizing the Body of the Speech

Chapter 7: Developing the Body of the Speech: Understanding Kinds of Content

Chapter 8: Developing the Body: Understanding Methods of Development

Inference (pp. 188)
Intensification
- **The nature of attention (pp. 189)**
- **Factors of Interest (Factors of Intensification) (pp. 190)**
  - Proximity
  - Vividness
  - Significance
  - Variety
  - Humor

Chapter 9: Developing the Body: Applying Principles to Speeches of Basic Types

Developing the Body of the informative speech
- **The supporting materials should encourage the listeners to engage with you in a continuing dialogue (pp. 208)**
- **The supporting materials should demonstrate that you possess proper attitudes as a speaker (pp. 209)**
- **The supporting materials should facilitate interest-understanding-retention (pp. 210)**

Developing the Body of the entertaining speech (pp. 212)
Developing the Body of the persuasive speech
- **The speech to convince (pp. 215)**
  - Identification and the speech to convince
  - Inference and the speech to convince
  - Emotions and the speech to convince
  - Additional suggestions for the speech to convince
- **The speech to stimulate (reinforce or impress) (pp. 223)**
  - Polarity and the speech to stimulate
  - Logic-ethics and the speech to stimulate
  - Unethical artifices and strategems and the speech to stimulate
  - Ethically "gray areas" and the speech to stimulate
  - Additional suggestions for the speech to stimulate
- **The speech to actuate (pp. 230)**

Chapter 10: Developing the Introduction of the Speech

Understanding the principles of development
- **Stimulating favorable attention (pp. 233)**
  - Refer to the significance of the subject
  - Use humor
  - Tell an illustrative story
  - Use a stimulating quotation
  - Ask the audience a striking question
  - Make a pithy, provocative statement
  - Refer to the audience, occasion, or purpose of the meeting
  - Compliment the audience

Preparing the audience for the Body of the speech (pp. 243)
State the POINT of the speech
Explain how you plan to develop the Body
Provide necessary background explanations
Avoiding common faults of the Introduction
Applying principles to speeches of basic types
Planning the Introduction of the speech to inform (pp. 250)
Planning the Introduction of the speech to entertain (pp. 251)
Planning the Introduction of the speech to persuade (pp. 252)
The favorable audience
The primarily neutral audience
The hostile audience

Chapter 11: Developing the Conclusion of the Speech

Understanding principles of development
Clarify the thought and promote the proper mood of the speech (pp. 262)
State the POINT of the speech
List the main ideas of the speech
Review informally
Review indirectly by means of quotations, comparison, or example
Avoiding common faults of the Conclusion (pp. 270)
Applying principles to speeches of basic types
Planning the Conclusion of the speech to inform (pp. 270)
Planning the Conclusion of the speech to entertain (pp. 272)
Planning the Conclusion of the speech to persuade (pp. 273)
Speech to convince
Speech to stimulate (reinforce or impress)
Speech to actuate

CHAPTER 5

Generating the Speech Materials

Digging is usually a difficult and time-consuming job. Ask the gardener or the farmer. Nevertheless, before food can be eaten the ground must be turned, the seed must be planted, and the food sometimes taken from the soil; before water will flow, a ditch must be dug; before engines can turn, coal or oil for fuel must be extracted from the ground; before the blueprint becomes a house, the foundation upon which the house is to rest must be imbedded and the construction materials secured. Similarly, before a Specific Speech Purpose becomes a speech, you must search for those ideas and information with which to build the speech.

Accomplished speakers spare neither energy nor effort in persistently searching for ideas and information. Woodrow Wilson had been a college professor for a number of years before he made his first public pronouncements on educational philosophy; he had studied politics and international relations most of his life prior to attempting to persuade the world to accept the League of Nations. Listeners who marveled at Daniel Webster's profound grasp of national affairs in the Webster-Hayne debate were perhaps reminded that the famous orator had been grappling for years with the very ideas he expounded so effectively in the Senate. The thorough understanding of America upon which Edmund Burke based his Taxation and Conciliation speeches was the result of persevering close-range study of the Colonies. Albert J. Beveridge's maiden speech in the

Senate on the subject of the Philippines was successful partly because he had spent six months in the Orient methodically gathering material. Franklin D. Roosevelt prepared himself with "painstaking precision" for each speaking engagement. For instance, during his flight to the Teheran Conference he spent most of his waking hours studying the summaries prepared for him by various branches of the federal government. He gave particular attention to a special report, prepared under the direction of Henry Field, which contained answers to anticipated "supercharged diversionary" questions by Stalin and "ammunition" to be used as "friendly ploys" at crucial moments in the discussion. The effective speaking of Harry S. Truman on his campaign tour in 1948, a trip which many—including Mr. Truman himself[1]—believed turned the tide in his favor, was aided by a carefully prepared notebook of salient facts about the audiences, towns, regions, and cultural groups he would encounter. Better than almost any other President, John F. Kennedy kept on top of significant matters by extremely wide general reading and by an endless stream of daily memoranda and conferences. Nevertheless, a sizable staff of special assistants was required to help him prepare for speaking appointments. For instance, on the day before the live televised presidential press conference, White House Press Secretary Pierre Salinger held a meeting with a small group of the top informational people in the federal government. At this meeting a list of anticipated questions and tentative answers was drawn up. On the day of the conference, Salinger and a smaller group of key advisers had breakfast with the President and, depending upon the news developments, consulted with him at various times during the day, prior to a final meeting just before President Kennedy departed for the New State Department Building where the conference was televised.[2] Presidents Nixon, Ford, and Carter have likewise been attentive to the need for careful preparation. Ronald Reagan became more careful in his speech preparation after his alleged carelessness became a campaign issue in the 1980 election.

Established and successful speakers, almost without exception, recognize the importance of painstaking preparation. Can you afford to slight research in your speech preparation?

Before beginning your quest for materials, it is necessary to know what to look for and how to find it. What are these materials? They include facts, opinions, observations, factual and hypothetical examples, literal and figurative comparisons, definitions, descriptions, visual aids, and statistics that concern your subject. (For a discussion of these items, see Chapter 7, the section on Forms of Support.) How are these materials to be found? Follow these four steps in your search for ideas and information: think; observe; communicate with others; read.

[1]Based upon the author's interview with Mr. Truman in the summer of 1954.
[2]Based upon interviews of the author with Pierre Salinger, February 7 and 8, 1963.

Securing Materials by Thinking

In Chapter 4 you learned that the starting point in selecting a speech subject that will meet the demands of the audience, occasion, and yourself as the speaker, is to examine your personal resources. Ideally, you should select only those subjects on which you have "earned the right to speak": the more extensive, varied, and significant your experiences and knowledge concerning the subject, ordinarily the better qualified you are to speak on it. Even for subjects on which you lack thorough competency, however, you are not completely without personal resources: although you may not possess much specific data on the topic, you should have some relevant background knowledge and beliefs. Therefore, once the topic has been determined, your first step in gathering materials is to exploit thoroughly your personal resources. *Make a systematic inventory of what you already know and believe concerning the subject and what additional information and ideas you perhaps will need to accomplish your Specific Speech Purpose.*

A student who decided to talk on West Germany's problems with contract foreign workers delivered a speech that was taken almost verbatim from *Newsweek.* Although he had spent much of his life in various countries of Europe where his father, an army officer, had been stationed, it did not occur to him to make use of his experiences in preparing the speech. Topics such as "Critical Needs of Higher Education" or "Better Traffic Enforcement" or "How to Improve Local Charities" are sometimes expounded in student speeches without a single reference to the speaker's personal opinions or experiences. These are examples of speakers who neglected to *think,* the first step in finding materials.

Plato wrote, "Knowledge is but to remember." Examine your present and past environment, your interests, knowledge, beliefs, feelings, desires, and attitudes. What *life experiences* have you had which relate to the topic? In what ways, if any, can your daily use of the Fleet Street bus, or your observations of public transportation systems in other communities, supplement your analysis of the City Transit System? Have your experiences as a baby-sitter or counselor at a summer camp furnished you with additional ideas for a speech on child care? Can you draw illustrative materials from your hobbies (as stamp collecting), special interests (as primitive art), or special skill (as hand balancing)? In writing this book, the author attempted to interpret the principles of effective speaking in the light of his particular experiences, backgrounds, and training.

What ideas, beliefs, or feelings, do you have concerning the subject? Does the topic impinge upon *convictions, values, attitudes,* or *behaviors* that are significant to you? If so, by probing your thinking-feeling can you come up with ideas-evidence-reasoning-feeling to support your speech purpose? Examine your memories of the *reading* you have done. Review *courses of study*. Here is an opportunity to put your academic experiences to practical use. Dust off the acquired knowledge that you have relegated to storage on some neglected intellectual shelf. What do you remember from lectures in ROTC that could be applied to your topic on the deployment of missiles? What did you learn in Forestry 374 that relates to your topic on the "Wilderness" law? Reflect on what you have *heard* pertaining to the subject on newscasts—in speeches—at public discussions—in television dramas or movies—from friends, associates, or family members.

Also, you may find it worthwhile to employ free association. Find a quiet, secluded place and, putting aside the haste and pressures of your daily schedule, let your mind roam freely among your memories. Place no demands of productivity upon yourself—just meander, or leap, in the track and at the speed that impulse directs. Can you link your subject to childhood memories of farm life, Fourth of July parades, worship of some athletic star? To your attitudes toward organized religion? To your experiences of living, or visiting, in different parts of the country? To experiences as a union worker? To your first impressions of college life? To the fear and pain you suffered in an automobile accident? The full value of experiences, former study, backgrounds, and training can be realized only if you *think*.

A somewhat different kind of mental probing from that of free association is the method that was universally used by the ancients—to run a standard set of categories or topics through the mind in relation to key concerns of the speech. The intent of this procedure is to prod the mind systematically to generate ideas and associations that it might not produce otherwise. The way this procedure works is to apply individually the topics in a list such as the following to the major thrusts of your speech. Use each topic as a kind of fulcrum to pry open your thinking. To illustrate the application of this method, let us assume that you are in the process of developing a speech advocating the establishment of a national system of health insurance for all citizens (see pages 143–145 for the outline of such a speech). After the entry of each topic, we offer sample questions that you might use to start your exploiting of that topic. Remember that the application of this list of topics[3] is meant to be merely suggestive, not prescriptive.

Existence-nonexistence (Is there a concerted undercover effort in the medical profession to prevent the establishment of a program

[3]For this list of topics I am indebted to the *Speech Communication 200 Student's Manual* (University Park: The Pennsylvania State University, n.d.), 3rd ed. Also, see John F. Wilson and Carroll C. Arnold, *Public Speaking as a Liberal Art* (Boston: Allyn and Bacon, Inc., 1978), 4th ed.

of compulsory health insurance? Is there a shortage of medical facilities in this country? ETC.)

Degree or Quality (To what extent do rural areas fall behind other areas in the number of doctors? How does the United States compare with other countries in the quality of its medical care: ETC.)

Space (What is the distribution of doctors throughout the country? Are clinics largely clustered in urban areas? ETC.)

Time (How long would it take to put into operation a program of compulsory health insurance? Over the past three decades what has been the record concerning hospital charges? Office visits? ETC.)

Motion or Activity (Has the drive to enact socialized medicine accelerated in recent years? How actively and consistently are unions pushing for it? ETC.)

Physical or Abstract Form (Is the support for socialized medicine hardening? Softening? Is it clear (vague) who supports and opposes? What form will the campaign for adoption take? What kind of diseases are increased by inadequate national health care? ETC.)

Substance (How real, unreal, are the dangers involved in establishing a program of compulsory health insurance? How solid is the opposition in the medical profession? ETC.)

Capacity to Change (Does the present fee-for-service system have the capability to expand medical facilities and improve research? Is the American Medical Association a static organization? Progressive? Regressive? ETC.)

Potency (How much power do right-wing conservatives have in obstructing the establishment of a program of compulsory health insurance? The liberal elements in fostering the program? How much energy will the administration devote to this task? ETC.)

Desirability (What desirable results does compulsory health insurance promise? What unfortunate consequences does its adoption threaten? ETC.)

Feasibility (Can a program of compulsory health insurance be practically administered? Financed? Can sufficient medical personnel be provided? Have similar programs worked in other countries? ETC.)

Causality (Can we attribute the [effect] inadequacies of our present system primarily to the fee-for-service method of payment [cause]? Would compulsory health insurance [cause] result in regimenting the medical profession [effect]? ETC.)

Correlation (Is compulsory health insurance compatible with our democratic system? Can free enterprise coexist with state planning of this magnitude? ETC.)

Genus-Species Relationship (Is the effort to promote compulsory health insurance part of a socialistic conspiracy? Part of a major social movement toward equality? ETC.)

Similarity-Dissimilarity (What are the similarities and differences between the proposal for compulsory health insurance and the

British system of medicine? Under compulsory health insurance, in what ways would the doctor-patient relationship be the same as it now is? In what ways different? ETC.)

In making a systematic inventory of what you already know and believe about the subject and of what additional information and ideas you may still need to acquire, two cautions are perhaps in order. First, try not to be dogmatic about your initial ideas: consider your opinions tentative, withholding final judgment until preparation is more nearly complete. Second, unless you are an expert on the subject at hand, do not rely exclusively upon what you already know. To meet the logical-psychological needs of the subject, audience, and occasion, you will undoubtedly need to secure additional ideas and information.

By thinking about the matter, try to pin down the nature of the materials you still need to discover. Although such preliminary thinking may not provide an exact research design, it should provide direction to the remaining steps in your preparation: it should help you locate gaps in your background knowledge and theory; weaknesses in particular areas of the topic; salient questions to which you have inadequate answers; problems that you cannot resolve at this stage; needs for graphic illustrations, verifying statistics, and impelling testimony to make your ideas clear, interesting, and persuasive.

Upon completing the preliminary stage of thinking, as just described, you should move to the next steps in gathering materials (observing—communicating with others—reading). These subsequent steps will, of course, demand effectual thinking: analysis, synthesis, meditation. Critical and imaginative evaluation of materials is essential if you are to meet the constraining influences of the total speech situation.

Securing Materials by Observing

The saying, "a picture is worth a thousand words," applies in one sense to the speaker in search of materials. As used in this way, the maxim does not refer to the photograph or sketch that you may use as a visual aid in your speech, but to the continuous flow of pictures registered upon the retina of the eye—the things you see. Careful observation of matters relating to your subject can be an invaluable means of speech preparation. However, we should recognize the distinction between "seeing" and "observing." When our eyes are open, all of us with the power of sight *see;* but, we do not necessarily *observe.* To observe means to examine or inspect in order to learn something. The "see-er" retains only a few unsystematized visual memories. The "observer," on the other hand, sorts, interprets, evaluates, organizes, and retains his visual impressions so that he can make efficient future use of them.

What are the characteristics of good observation? How does one use observation to secure speech materials? The principles that the speaker should follow in using observation are pretty much the same as those recommended for any investigator—be he a chemist, FBI agent, CAB crash investigator, or physician. Effective observation is *directed, complete, accurate,* and *objective.*

Directed observation has focus. Like a speech, theme, or business letter, it has a specific purpose or goal. By means of preliminary thinking and study, you should determine the nature of the information you wish to secure and the research design most likely to produce the information, with a minimum expenditure of time, effort, and expense. Before you attempt to observe, know *what* you are looking for and *how* you expect to get it. After you have analyzed your speech needs in relation to factors, such as time, cost, and availability of the thing to be observed, you should carefully settle on your observational goals and procedures. Thereafter, you should adhere to your research design—unless unforeseen circumstances necessitate change. If your speech is a report on conditions at the local jail, you first should determine what "conditions" to investigate. Perhaps you should select these: food, recreational opportunities, sanitary arrangements, visitation arrangements, custodial treatment. Next, you should determine how to gain the cooperation of the mayor, sheriff, guards, and prisoners and how to observe so as to secure reliable judgments concerning each of the conditions.

Make your observations as *complete* as your purpose warrants—no more and no less. Although an afternoon spent visiting the jail may provide sufficient evidence that the facilities are overcrowded and/or outmoded and/or unsanitary, it probably would not provide adequate means to determine whether inmates are humanely treated, discrimination is practiced, food is monotonous or of poor quality, a serious effort is being made to rehabilitate prisoners, and so on. To ascertain other information, such as the mental, moral, and emotional effect of existing conditions upon the prisoners, would be far more difficult and might require much more time, money, and planning than is necessary to answer the practical needs of your speech.

In addition to discovering all necessary information, your observation should be planned and executed so that the secured data is *reliable*—true-to-fact. Most of us are neither completely accurate nor objective in interpreting what we see. Court records abound with the testimony of witnesses later proved to be inaccurate. Understandably, chance "seeings," which are unexpected and perhaps startling, may be inaccurate. On the other hand, a controlled, systematic investigation should reveal what exists, or what happened—the facts, undistorted by faulty research design or emotion.

Finally, your observations should be *objective*. Do not permit biases to color your findings. Recognize that if you are a partisan you may be inclined to see what you want to see—or expect to see. What happens when the senator who has for years condemned the "wasteful squandering of foreign aid funds" goes abroad to see conditions firsthand? He returns with his prejudices confirmed by the "wasteful squandering of foreign aid funds" he has seen in the countries visited. Likewise, when the senator on the opposite side of this issue goes abroad, he returns with prejudgments vindicated. A student once underscored this point by saying, "Don't close your eyes to avoid seeing facts and don't look cross-eyed at facts in order to distort them. Even a demagogue should know what the facts are—otherwise, how will he know how much he is doctoring them?"

Securing Materials by Communicating with Others

Often the inexperienced speaker makes no attempt to tap the wealth of information, experience, and wisdom which can be derived by communicating with others. Consider whether you can secure useful information from persons in the college and local community. Your classmates come from different environments and, perhaps, different parts of the country. Some may come from abroad. They possess varied experiences, interests, and skills. Can you enlist their help? If your college is a large one, its faculty includes specialists in almost every area of human wisdom and achievement. Experts on your subject may be available in local business or industrial concerns or in government offices or agencies. Also, you may be able to secure information and opinions from experts living in other parts of the state or nation. Communicating with others can be an extremely valuable means of securing speech materials.

Three methods are available to you for securing information from others: (1) conversation and discussion, (2) interviews, and (3) letters.

Conversation and Discussion

Participation in conversational and discussional groups can be an excellent means of speech preparation. Although "bull sessions" usually have little intellectual value, they can be directed into meaningful, provocative channels. You might engage associates, instructors, businessmen, and so on, in conversation and direct the talk to your speech topic. As John C. Calhoun, Theodore Roosevelt, and Jimmy Carter have done, you can test your ideas and arguments in various conversational situations. In doing so, notice the reactions of your listeners, their questions and rebuttals. Try to acquire information, fresh insights, new points of view.

Also, you can attend forums and discussion programs that concern subjects related to your speech topic. For maximum benefit, participate as well as listen, when the opportunity is presented.

Interviews

If an authority on your subject is available, perhaps you should try to arrange an interview with him. A student was aided immeasurably in his preparation for a speech on "Political Campaigning" by interviewing an instructor in political science who at that time was running for the United States Senate. A second student secured material for a speech on the "Use of Public Speaking in Community Fund Drives" by spending a day at Fund headquarters interviewing officials who direct the speaking campaigns. Another student acquired information and ideas on "Downtown Traffic Congestion" by interviewing the directors of the Departments of Streets and Sewers, Maintenance, and Public Safety, the Assistant Police Chief, and a score of policemen, truckers, cabdrivers, bus operators, and motorists.

Here are some principles to help you conduct a satisfactory interview:

(1) *Prepare yourself on the subject before the interview.* You will waste your time and that of the expert unless your research is sufficient to enable you to ask meaningful questions and to understand and evaluate the answers.

(2) *Learn about the expert.* Brief yourself concerning the expert: his position, background, training, special competency on the subject, biases, and so forth. This knowledge may help you ask better questions, avoid embarrassing ones, and be alert for possibly prejudiced replies.

(3) *Schedule the interview in advance.* A casual or impromptu meeting may not be productive. Very probably the expert's tight schedule will prevent his giving adequate attention to your problem.

(4) *Plan your interview.* Frame a series of specific, pertinent questions concerning areas in which the expert is especially qualified and which cannot be answered easily by other means. Do not ask vague, generalized questions, such as "What can you tell me about defense contracts?" Do not expect your host to expound at great length upon the general topic. During the interview, your tentative questions can serve as a basis. As the opportunity offers, you may select from among these pre-

pared questions or may evolve new ones out of the conversation. Ask for particular data, ideas, judgments, but do not expect him to develop your speech for you.

(5) *Conduct yourself with alertness, poise, friendliness, and respect.* Remember that your host is giving you his time, possibly at some personal sacrifice. Treat him with respect and consideration. If you disagree with him, do so silently. Your purpose is to "pick his mind," not to contradict him. Listen alertly for his points of view, significant data, and sources for securing additional information. You may wish to write down certain specific information, such as statistics, important value judgments, and so on. Otherwise, take only skeleton notes; these may be expanded after the interview is concluded.

(6) *Be time conscious.* The person you interview is busier than he may appear. To avoid imposing upon him, be on time for the meeting and stay no longer than the previously agreed upon time. If no time limits were mentioned, be alert for signals that he wishes to terminate the interview. Unless definitely encouraged to do so, stay no longer than fifteen minutes. For a busy person, fifteen minutes represents a sizable loss from the workday. Do not overstay your welcome.

(7) *Follow-up with a letter of appreciation.* Although this is sometimes unnecessary, almost everyone welcomes such a letter. Probably the more "important" the interviewee is and/or the more he has gone out of his way to be helpful to you, the greater becomes the need for a follow-up letter.

A serviceable method of securing information and ideas is to use the telephone. Libraries, information bureaus, and public relations offices are usually willing to supply a caller with information that they have readily available. Also, experts may be reached by telephone. The principles just discussed for face-to-face interviewing should be applied when using the telephone, with this particular emphasis: be especially time conscious. Inasmuch as your call interrupts what the person is doing, perhaps you should ask if he has time to talk briefly with you. Probably you should plan to ask no more than two or three questions, and these should be explicit, requiring in reply only a few terse sentences.

To derive maximum information and understanding from your conversations, discussions, and interviews, you should strive to be a good *listener.* Instead of taking listening for granted, consciously apply the principles of effective listening:

(1) *Concentrate.* Resist strongly the temptation to let your mind wander. Minimize distractions. Recognize that the process of analysis, evaluation, and synthesis demands your best thinking. If the speaker is worth hearing, he deserves your alert, complete attention.

(2) *Be open-minded.* Many of us listen eagerly to ideas that reinforce our own opinions. When opposing views are aired we are prone to

concentrate on mentally answering the speaker rather than on listening to his arguments. Nearly always you can profit by listening carefully to arguments and attitudes different from your own—you might even be persuaded to change your mind! At least, by understanding the opposing ideas you should be better prepared to expound your own point of view. If the speaker is worth hearing, he deserves open-minded consideration.

(3) *Be analytical.* Your listening will be more meaningful if you apply your critical and evaluative faculties. Is the speaker defining his terms? Is he proving his point? Is his evidence sufficient? Is his reasoning valid? Does he seem reasonably objective? Is he omitting, or perhaps purposely avoiding, an important consideration? If the speech is followed by a question period, or if you are participating in a conversation or discussion, you may have the opportunity to voice some of these queries.

(4) *Remember.* Retaining what you hear can be facilitated by employing the first three principles—concentrating, listening with an open mind, and analyzing. Taking notes will also help. Make a practice of taking a pencil and note pad with you wherever you go. Jot down facts, figures, and other pertinent material for future reference. Jonathan Edwards, the foremost preacher of the Colonial period, carried quill and ink when horseback riding and pinned his notes to his clothes to make certain that he would remember them. If inconvenient to write down ideas at the moment you hear them, do so at your first opportunity.

Letters

When individuals or information services cannot be contacted either personally or by telephone, a letter may bring the needed information. Talking with others about your subject, or consulting, say, the *World Almanac* or *Trade and Professional Associations of the United States* should uncover the names and addresses of persons, bureaus, and organizations that can be contacted by letter. In preparing a letter of inquiry, consider these suggestions:

(1) Think before you write and organize your thoughts.

(2) Be specific. State clearly what information or judgments you need. Do not ramble or stray from the point. Do not ask for information that is readily available elsewhere.

(3) Be brief. Write what is necessary and no more.

(4) Be businesslike, but try to personalize your letter. Shun the chatty style of the personal letter, but also avoid being overly formal.

(5) Enclose a stamped, self-addressed envelope.

(6) Mail your letter well in advance of the time you need the material. Anticipate that a reply will take at least a week, exclusive of travel time each way.

Securing Material by Reading

One of the results of the information explosion now taking place is that each year an unbelievably large amount of newly printed matter is added to the astronomical quantities already filed away for your use. Much of the accumulated knowledge and wisdom of man is available to you in your local or college library, or can be secured through interlibrary loan. In your search for speech materials, your problem usually is not whether anything has been written on the topic; you can assume that probably much relevant material has been published. Your problems are procedural: How to find sources? Determine what to read? Read it effectively? Retain what has been read?

Before considering some answers to these questions, perhaps we should pause for a word of caution. You may be strongly tempted to try what appears to be an easy shortcut in your search for materials. "Why bother with the laborious process of thinking, observing, communicating with others, and wide reading? Let someone else do the legwork and headwork. Find a magazine article which you can parrot, passing it off as your own production!" Like many miracle "work-savers," this one is infeasible. Shun it for a number of reasons: First, it is thoroughly dishonest. Stealing the composition of another for a speech is as clearly plagiarism as stealing it for an English theme. Stealing is stealing, whether it be a composition or a wallet. Second, if you summarize an article from one of the widely read digests or popular magazines, some of your listeners—including your instructor—will probably have also read it. Your embarrassment may be excruciating if someone points out pertinent omissions, or questions your interpretations of the author. Third, it is unfair to your listeners to ask them to attend to a regurgitated version of a work; if they were interested, they could read it in the form intended by the author. Fourth, plagiaristic speaking does not represent you at your full capacity. Each speech you give should be a personal creation. It should carry the stamp of your personality, judgment, evaluation, and interpretation. Although the author of a reference on your subject may be more of an authority than you, his work should only *contribute* to your speech, along with other sources. If you hope for success as a speaker, avoid plagiarism; it is likely a shortcut to failure.

Many speakers slight research in the library, because of either insufficient interest or ignorance of how to use the library's services. If you are unaccustomed to using the library, you may wish to request assistance from the librarian. Much in the library may be easily secured without help if you understand basic procedures. Such understanding can easily be secured from guides such as Constance M. Winchell's *Guide to Reference Books* and Jean Key Gates' *Guide to the Use of Books and Libraries.*

How to Read Effectively

Some students believe that the measure of effective reading is an impressive bibliography of sources consulted and a staggering number of pages read. Quantity and variety in reading are important; more significant, however, are the quality and relevance of the ideas and information derived.

The application of these four principles may help you to read more efficiently:

(1) *Choose the most pertinent materials.* You will not have time to read indiscriminately; therefore, become skilled in determining which references should be disregarded and which should receive closer attention. Often the reference's title or the index description of the contents, date of publication, author, or publisher will give reliable clues as to its potential usefulness. If the reference passes this screen, a rapid scanning of its contents should be adequate to estimate its merit. You may wish to prepare a flexible bibliography on note cards, arranging the cards into two separate files: (1) items providing a general background orientation to the topic, and (2) items offering specialized treatment of the topic or a facet of the topic. Begin your reading with the potentially most valuable—and more simply written—entries in the general background file and continue until you have a good grasp of the scope and dimensions of the subject. Then, as time permits, read the "specific" treatments in the second file, feeling free—of course—to continue reading for background interpretation.

(2) *Approach each source with an open mind.* Do not slight an article or book which appears to disagree with your thinking, particularly in the early stages of your research. To attain a good background for your subject, you should examine all points of view. Abraham Lincoln made a practice of "studying up" the other side of his law cases before he constructed his own presentation.

(3) *Adjust your reading habits to your material.* General background material should be read with the purpose of acquiring broad understanding. Specific facts in such reading may not be as important as basic theories, principles, and conclusions. Read general material rapidly, particularly if it is clearly organized. If your purpose is to acquire facts, statistics, and quotable testimony, read more slowly in order to test their validity and application to your purpose.

(4) *Read critically.* Some students tend to worship authority and the printed word. If something has been written by a prominent person and published, they are inclined to believe that it must be true. Be skeptical in your reading. Consider whether the author has an axe to grind. Test his reasoning. Examine his evidence. Question his sources. Evaluate carefully his conclusions, not only for their validity but also for their relevance to your purpose. In short, do not be gullible.

How to Retain What You Read

As you read, try to remember ideas, points of view, and attitudes, rather than detailed facts and figures. It is better not to depend upon memory if you wish to retain particulars. A quotation that seems unforgettable may elude you ten minutes later. Therefore, when exact recall is desired, take notes.

As a generally applicable suggestion, notes should be taken on cards of uniform size (recommended size: 3″×5″ or 4″×6″) for the same reason that playing cards are identical in size and shape—note cards also need to be shuffled and arranged into sequences as desired by the user. Later when you are organizing your speech, you may wish to spread the note cards on the table and group them under their appropriate outline headings. The flexible use of notes will be facilitated if you record only one fact or idea on each card. Saving room at the top of each card for eventual more precise labeling, identify each card according to the tentative subject division or topic under which the material falls. Make all notes as complete as your purpose warrants and *be accurate:* all quotations should be exactly what the author wrote; all paraphrases should represent with fidelity the intent of the author. Each card should contain a complete identification of the source, so as to permit easy resort to the reference. Include the full name of the author(s), title, publisher, date of publication, and page number.

Summary

When you have settled on your Specific Speech Purpose, your next procedures are to generate speech materials and to prepare the speech outline. In this chapter we have been concerned with the four means of securing materials:

(1) *Thinking.* The starting point in gathering material is to exploit thoroughly your personal resources. Make a systematic inventory of what you already know and believe concerning the subject and what additional information and ideas you perhaps will need to accomplish your speaking purpose.

(2) *Observing.* Careful observation of matters relating to your subject can be an invaluable means of speech preparation. Effective observation is directed, complete, accurate, and objective.

(3) *Communicating with others.* Tap the information, experience, and wisdom of others by means of conversation and discussion, interviews, and letters.

(4) *Reading.* Make use of the facilities of the library. Become skilled in discovering appropriate material in books, reference works, magazines, newspapers, and documents. Read selectively, objectively, and analytically. Retain what you read by concentrating on remembering general concepts and by recording specific data on note cards.

Exercises and Assignments

1. Read carefully the text of a speech from *Vital Speeches* (published biweekly by the City News Publishing Company, New York) or from some other collection of speeches. What evidence of the sources of the speaker's materials appears in the text? Did the speaker use (1) personal experience, (2) observation, (3) ideas gleaned from consulting others, (4) printed sources? Prepare a written report of the speaker's sources as evidenced from reading the speech.

2. Upon choosing the subject for your next classroom speech, prepare a written or oral report consisting of (1) a summary of what you already know about the subject, (2) an estimation of the kind and amount of information you will need to discover in the course of your preparation, (3) projects in observation that might be of value, (4) persons you might interview for ideas and information, and pertinent questions you might ask, and (5) a preliminary bibliography. Ask your classmates for their ideas, opinions, and experiences relative to the topic, as well as their suggestions of persons to interview and written sources to consult.

3. Arrange to interview a well-known speaker in your community on his methods of gathering materials. Your questions might include (1) "How much do you depend upon your background and personal experiences in your speech preparation?" (2) "Has observation been of particular value? In what instances?" (3) "Do you frequently consult others personally or by letter for information and ideas?" (4) "Do you keep a file of quotations, jokes, epigrams, and illustrations for possible use in future speeches?" (5) "Does your preparation for a particular speech usually include some specific reading, or do you rely predominantly upon the general reading you have done and the knowledge you already possess?" Report to the class the results of this interview.

4. Listen carefully to the speech of a classmate for evidence of the sources of the ideas. Does the speech draw upon a variety of sources? What are they? Either write a report or be prepared to evaluate orally his preparation.

5. Arrange and conduct an interview with an authority on a topic you intend to use for a speech. Report to the class on the material you gathered, what difficulties you encountered, how your interview might have been improved, and so on.

6. Station yourself for fifteen minutes at a busy intersection, the corner lunchroom, the college administration building, or some other spot that bustles with activity. Another member of the class should station himself at approximately the same vantage point. Without consulting one another or collaborating in any

way, each should observe what goes on and prepare to report on that observation to the class. In class check one another as to the completeness, accuracy, and objectivity of observation. If your reports are at variance, attempt to discover why, with the aid of the class.

7. Attend a speech given in the community or tune in one that is broadcast or telecast. Make every attempt to be a good listener. Present to the class a critical report on the content and delivery. Compare your report with those made by other students for accuracy, completeness, and objectivity.

CHAPTER 6

Organizing the Body of the Speech

The speaker's job of plotting the course of his talk to encourage the maximum amount of movement on the part of the listeners toward closure with his position that is possible under the circumstances (Chapters 3 and 4) is probably as complex as the task confronting the navigator of a large cruise ship. Even the most careful speaker has sometimes realized at the close of his talk that somehow his speech has "gone aground"—that he would have been more effective if he had structured his communication in a different manner. Almost all outstanding speakers of the past and present have found that for maximum effectiveness one must be diligent in planning speeches. The beginning speaker should be extremely careful to chart the speech so that the destination, the Specific Speech Purpose, can be achieved.

During, or following, the process of gathering the raw materials for the speech (Chapter 5), you should prepare the basic framework of the major segment of the speech: the Body. The necessity for good organization in the Body is apparent when one considers that it constitutes the bulk of the message, occupying possibly 80 to 85 per cent of the total length, whereas the Introduction (the beginning) may perhaps average about 10 per cent and the Conclusion (the ending) about 5 per cent. Initial and final impressions that the audience receives from the speaker and his speech are critically important: the successful Introduction prepares the audience for the Body by fostering receptive attitudes and providing necessary orienting materials; the successful Conclusion focuses final attention on the message contained in the Body, promotes the proper mood, and, if appropriate, attempts to energize the listeners to act upon the speaker's proposals. Nevertheless, the major import of the speech is usually accomplished in the Body. Most modern speech teachers agree with Cicero's suggestion that the speaker prepare the Body before the Introduction or Conclusion.

Understanding Principles of Organization

The American Automobile Association annually distributes millions of maps and booklets on accommodations. Why? Because no intelligent motorist would embark on an extended trip without knowledge of where he is going and how he intends to get there. No contractor would attempt to construct a house without the guidance of an architect's blueprint. The map is to the tourist and the blueprint is to the contractor what the speech outline is to the public speaker. Almost every speaker makes some sort of outline on paper, because that is the most practical method of organizing one's thinking. The outline helps the speaker to arrange his ideas in the most effective logical and psychological manner, to test the merit of supporting materials, to gauge more accurately the length of the speech, and to ensure that the address has unity, coherence, and emphasis.

The organization of the Body consists of main heads and subheads that are arranged to the best logical and psychological advantage. The most effective selection and disposition of major points depend basically upon the nature of the material and upon the audience's knowledge of and attitude toward the subject. In structuring the Body, constantly ask yourself: "How can I organize and develop my thoughts so they will best suit my particular audience?" Not infrequently, the inexperienced speaker throws his ideas together with little attention to their most effective presentation. What would happen if a cook should dump the ingredients for an angel food cake into a pan with no semblance of orderly sequence? Would the cake come out of the oven a delicious dessert or a wad of ill-textured dough?

When it has been completed, the outline contains the essence of the speech; it has very much the same relationship to a speech that the skeleton of beams and girders has to a building, or that the framework of ribs and keel has to a ship. Although the amount of detail incorporated in the outline varies considerably, according to the individual speaker's needs and inclinations, the outline always represents an abbreviated charting of the course of the message—it is not designed to be a manuscript verbatim copy of what the speaker will say to the audience.

In the remainder of this chapter, we are concerned with determining the basic thought development—the skeletal structure—of the Body. In Chapters 7, 8, and 9, we consider how to develop this basic structure by means of supporting devices, such as illustrations, comparisons, and statistics.

Employing a Standard System of Outlining

The primary function of an outline is to show thought relationships. To indicate clearly and accurately the relationships that each entry bears to the remainder of the outline and to the Specific Speech Purpose, you should employ a standard system of symbols and indentations, such as the one that follows.

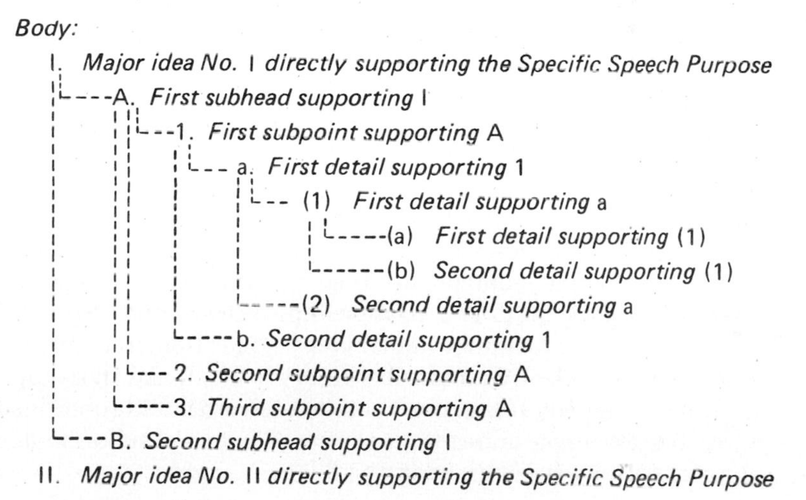

Points that possess approximately the same degree of importance, that are independent of each other, and that are logically subordinate to the same superior heading, are called *coordinate points*. If this definition seems confusing, think of how the legs of a table answer the requirements for coordinate points. Note that each leg is of approximately the same value, each leg is basically independent of the other legs, and each leg bears a similar subordinate relationship to the top of the table. Coordinate heads are placed in a perpendicular order.

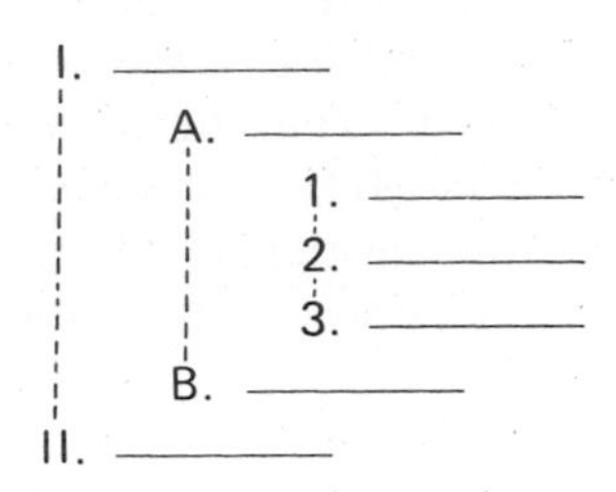

Points that support other headings are called *subordinate points* and are indented to the right and placed immediately under the heading so reinforced. This results in the staircase effect as follows.

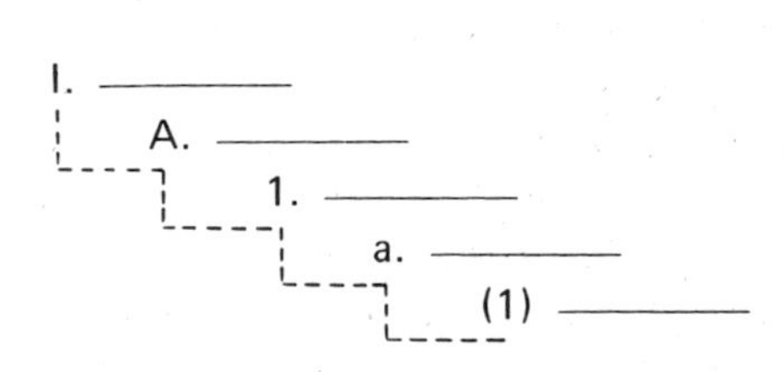

As is demonstrated in the following inset, each entry in a tightly structured outline possesses both coordinate and subordinate relationships. The Roman numeral headings are coordinate to each other and share a similar subordinate relationship to the Specific Speech Purpose. The capital letter headings immediately under Roman numeral No. I are coordinate to each other and subordinate to No. I, and those capital letter headings under No. II are coordinate to each other and subordinate to No. II. As practice in outlining, trace the coordinate and subordinate relationships of each item contained in the following inset.

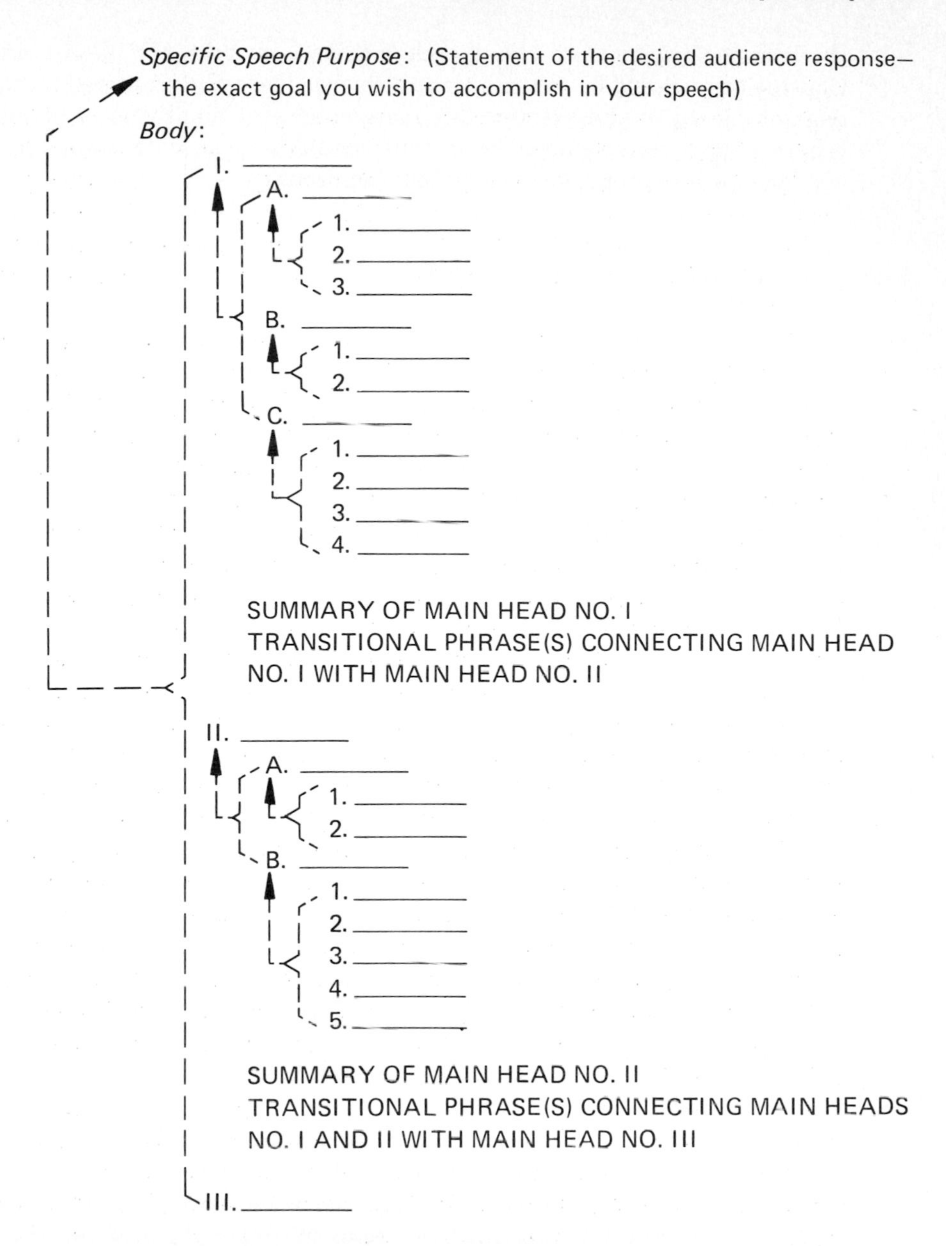

The minor mechanics of good outlining are illustrated in the sample outlines contained in this book. It is sufficient here to direct your attention to the following general guides. The Specific Speech Purpose should be labeled as such and stated tersely at the top of the outline sheet. The three major segments of the speech outline—Introduction, Body, and Conclusion—should be so identified, with the label either centered on the page or placed at the extreme left margin; several blank spaces should separate the three sections. The outline should be neat, with ample margins and with appropriate spacing between items.

Selecting the Main Heads of the Body

As a result of thinking, observing, communicating, and reading (Chapter 5), you have gathered considerable information on your subject. At this point, however, such material is analogous to a pile of boards in a cabinetmaker's shop: the carpenter must select the pieces to be used and must plan their arrangement before constructing an article of furniture. Out of the materials you have amassed and out of the thinking you have done you will develop an organizational structure that will enable you to accomplish the Specific Speech Purpose.

Your first task in organizing the Body is to determine the major ideas you wish to communicate. Ordinarily all of these first-degree headings should be at least tentatively secured before supporting ideas are grouped under any particular main heading.

The First Step in Choosing the Main Heads of the Body Is to Jot Down (During or After the Process of Gathering the Materials for the Speech) the Different Points You Might Want to Present in the Talk. Although the experienced speaker can frequently do this in his mind, the beginner probably should write these ideas on paper. Such a list might number twenty, forty, or more separate items. For the sake of convenience, we can call this group of potential points the *Analysis List.* Perhaps you remember when you received your first jigsaw puzzle how you spread all the pieces on the living room table. Your task was then to fit the individual pieces together to complete the intended picture. In a sense, your Analysis List represents possible "pieces" of your outline; by the process of synthesis, you must select the appropriate pieces, evolve new ones if necessary, and fit the pieces together in their appropriate positions.

The Second Step in Choosing the Main Heads of the Body Is to Evolve from the Analysis List a Tentative Group of Two to Five Major Ideas, Under Which Can Be Arranged Pertinent Supporting Points. As you carefully study the completed Analysis List, it should gradually lose its jumbled, shapeless, jigsaw appearance and a meaningful pattern of thought should begin to emerge. The ideas that seem most important to the securing of your Specific Speech Purpose will be the tentative main heads of the Body. It is important for you to recognize that although these basic ideas are *inherent* in the Analysis List they may not appear among the listed items, but must be evolved from one or more of the ideas contained in the series. Thus, several points in the Analysis List may be consolidated under a more general topic that is not present in the original list. When planning the section in Chapter 10 concerning the development of the Introduction, the author composed a mental Analysis List something like the following.

1. The Introduction should secure audience attention.
2. Humor is a good attention step.
3. The Introduction should clarify the purpose of the speech.
4. Tell an interesting story about yourself.
5. Tell an imaginary story.
6. Tell an interesting experience that happened to someone else.
7. Do not use stale humor.
8. Do not poke embarrassing fun at any persons or minority groups.
9. Give necessary definitions.
10. Use a striking quotation.
11. Use a striking question.
12. Do not antagonize.
13. Do not be long-winded.
14. Avoid off-color humor.
15. Make humor brief.
16. Do not let humor get away from you.
17. Use only relevant humor.
18. Use other types of humor in addition to stories, puns, and anecdotes.
19. State the main heads or arguments of the Body.
20. Give necessary background materials.
21. Bring the audience up-to-date on the subject.
22. Refer to the significance of the subject.
23. Mention common relationships, beliefs, interests, and feelings.
24. Refer to the speech occasion or purpose of the meeting.
25. State the POINT of the speech.
26. Use a pithy statement.
27. Compliment the audience.
28. Do not use irrelevant material.
29. Do not apologize.

All of these topics are connected with the speech Introduction, just as the pieces of a jigsaw puzzle are parts of a picture. As listed above, however, this Analysis List presents a conglomeration of ideas, without apparent purpose or unity. A speech, essay, or even a brick wall, for that matter, must have coherence. The cohesive force, the mortar of the speech, is the logical arrangement binding the main heads and the subheads. In the following outline the twenty-nine points have been arranged under three main topics. Notice that the first two major heads are drawn from the original Analysis List (with the phrasing being altered somewhat). The third represents a consolidation of several of the original points. In parentheses following each heading we have recorded the number of that entry in the preceding Analysis List.

I. The Favorable Attention Step secures the interest of the audience by means of: (1)
  A. Reference to the significance of the subject (22)
  B. Humor (2)
    1. Do not poke embarrassing fun at any persons or minority groups present in the audience (8)
    2. Do not use stale humor (7)
    3. Avoid off-color humor (14)
    4. Be brief (15)
    5. Be careful that the use of humor does not make it difficult or impossible to secure a serious hearing from the audience (16)
    6. Use only relevant humor (17)
    7. Use other types of humor besides stories, puns, and anecdotes (18)
  C. Illustrative story—(*evolved from* 4, 5, *and* 6)
    1. True experience (*evolved from* 4 *and* 6)
      a. Your own experience (4)
      b. Someone else's experience (6)
    2. Hypothetical experience (5)
  D. Stimulating quotation (10)
  E. Mention of common relationships, beliefs, interests, and feelings (23)
  F. Stimulating question (11)
  G. Pithy statement (26)
  H. Reference to the speech occasion or purpose of the meeting (24)
  I. Complimentary remarks (27)

II. The Clarification Step prepares the audience for the Body by: (3)
  A. Stating the POINT (that is, the basic thesis) of the speech (25)
  B. Stating the main heads or arguments of the Body (19)
  C. Providing necessary background explanations (*evolved from* 9, 20, *and* 21)
    1. Definitions (9)
    2. Historical explanations (21)
    3. General background information (20)

III. The four most common "sins" of the Introduction are: (*evolved from* 12, 13, 28 *and* 29)
  A. To apologize (29)
  B. To be long-winded (13)
  C. To antagonize or offend (12)
  D. To use irrelevant material (28)

In selecting first-degree headings, beginning students often err in choosing only one primary head or in choosing too many. When the outline of the Body contains only one major heading, no division of the Specific Speech Purpose has taken place—the heading is merely a restatement of the speech theme. As you know, each significant point in the outline of the Body must have both coordinate and subordinate relationships; however, because it includes the scope of the entire Body, the solitary primary heading has neither of these relationships. If you wish to include in the outline a statement of the basic theme or purpose of the speech, place it in the Introduction as part of the Clarification Step (Chapter 10).

An excessive number of main heads makes understanding and retention more difficult for the audience and frequently indicates muddled thinking on the part of the speaker. One of the precursors of modern rhetoricians Joseph Glanvill pointed out in the seventeenth century that "the main things to be said may be reduced to a small number of heads, which being thoroughly spoken to, will signify more than a multitude slightly touched." The number of major ideas, steps, or reasons ordinarily should not exceed five; and, if possible, the material should be consolidated into a fewer number of heads. You may be surprised to learn that for a given speech purpose the number of first-degree heads is not proportional to the length of the speech, but is determined exclusively by the characteristics of the subject area, audience, and occasion. Even Castro-length speeches probably should not exceed five major ideas. The principle that almost any subject can be divided into a few basic parts is demonstrated by Joseph P. Lash's division of the 1020-page *Eleanor and Franklin* into four parts (I. "Childhood and Youth"; II. "Wife and Mother"; III. "The Emergence of Eleanor Roosevelt"; and IV. "The White House Years"); and by the division of *Practical Public Speaking* into five parts.

The Third Step in Selecting the Main Heads of the Body Is to Apply Certain Criteria to the Tentative Major Ideas. Now that you have evolved from the Analysis List a group of two to five tentative primary ideas, your next task is to ensure that this structure not only possesses unity, emphasis, coherence, and adequate scope but that it also constitutes a strategically influential sequence of thought-feeling that will encourage the listeners to identify with what you are saying and to move—to extend themselves—toward closure with your position.

To test the suitability of your basic organizational flow, submit the tentative divisions to questions such as these: (1) Does the "territory" represented by the first-degree heads equate with that inherent in the Specific Speech Purpose? (2) Is each heading a direct division of the basic theme or Specific Speech Purpose? (3) Is each a single, separate, and independent thought unit? (4) Does each possess substantially the same degree of importance as the others? (5) Is each phrased in parallel grammatical structure with the others? (6) Do strong bonds of logical and psychological association unite the headings and provide the listeners with a progression of thought that will enable them to extend themselves toward closure with your position?

Adequate coverage. The Specific Speech Purpose relates to the Body in somewhat the same way that a map relates to the actual territory. The "territory" encompassed by the basic theme or Specific Speech Purpose should equate with the "territory" presented in the Body. Naturally, you could not exhaust all relevant considerations of a topic, even if time and the patience of your audience permitted the attempt. Nevertheless, the Body must contain all points essential to the accomplishment of the Specific Speech Purpose. If the time limitations for the speech or the availability of materials does not permit such coverage, the Specific Speech Purpose should be constricted accordingly. For example, a student failed to demonstrate that "steel strikes are harmful to all concerned" because the Body of his speech did not contain the following italicized heading.

I. Steel strikes are harmful to the workers
II. Steel strikes are harmful to the steel companies
III. *Steel strikes are harmful to the nation*

Direct division. Now that it has been established that the "territory" contained in the Body should equate with the "territory" encompassed in the Specific Speech Purpose, we can more readily see that the first-degree headings of the Body must be direct divisions of the Specific Speech Purpose. As a rather obvious example, a map of, or a speech on, the main land mass of the Western Hemisphere may be conveniently partitioned into three major segments: North America, Central America, and South America. Any topics such as Africa or Europe would not be direct divisions of this map area.

Single, independent thought units. Each first-degree heading represents a thought unit or "territory" that is contiguous with, but independent from, other primary thought "territories." Because each is a separate and distinct element, no basic overlapping should exist. In the following outline, main head No. IV overlaps No. II and, therefore, should be eliminated.

Wrong

Specific Speech Purpose: To persuade my listeners to stop smoking
Body:
I. Stop smoking to live longer
II. *Stop smoking to feel better*
III. Stop smoking to improve your physical appearance

IV. *Stop smoking to avoid smoker's cough*
V. Stop smoking to save money

Each primary heading should indicate a single basic idea, not compound ideas. Therefore, in the following inset the two contentions contained in heading No. II should be separated and each given the status of a Roman numeral head.

Wrong

Specific Speech Purpose: To convince my audience that in the case of another oil shortage the United States should not seize foreign oil fields
Body:
I. Such a seizure would be a repudiation of American traditions
II. *Such a seizure would be a crime against humanity and would alienate friendly nations*
III. Such a seizure would risk triggering a global war of terrifying destructiveness

Relatively the same importance. Although some first-degree headings may be of greater importance than others to the achieving of the Specific Speech Purpose, a coordinate relationship cannot exist among the headings if the disparity in their signification is too great. All primary headings must share the status of relatively equal partnership. In a speech describing the political parties of the United States, a speaker would not give major heading status to any of the dozen or so splinter political groups. If it seemed desirable to include a coverage of dissident factions that could not find a home within the major parties, he could employ the following divisions: I. The Democratic Party; II. The Republican Party; III. The minor parties.

Parallel sentence structure. By casting the potential first-degree headings in parallel grammatical structure, you could bring the inherent thought relationships into better focus. Also, parallel phrasing will make memorization of the outline easier for you and comprehension easier and quicker for your audience. Although skilled speakers frequently employ *key words* or incomplete sentences, as a beginning speaker you probably should write out your first-degree heads as full, definite, declarative sentences. This *full content* method of stating the primary ideas will afford both you and your instructor a better grasp of the intended thought. Compare the effectiveness of the following two outlines.

Wrong

Specific Speech Purpose: To have my listeners be motivated to buy Blue Boy cleaner
Body:
I. It is economical to buy Blue Boy cleaner
II. Little work involved

III. No harm done to hands
IV. Does an effective job

Right

Specific Speech Purpose: To have my listeners be motivated to buy Blue Boy cleaner
Body:
I. Blue Boy cleaner is economical
II. Blue Boy cleaner is easy to apply
III. Blue Boy cleaner is gentle on the hands
IV. Blue Boy cleaner is effective

Logical and psychological association. The first-degree headings of the Body should be disposed in such an order that the listener is conveyed smoothly, with a minimum of conflict or effort on his part, from his initial status of belief or knowledge toward closure with your position, that is, toward the response you are seeking—your Specific Speech Purpose. In order that the listener be moved from his original position to the desired new one, you must direct strong logical and psychological currents into appropriate channels of thought and feeling. When engaged in serious thought, people tend to think in sequences, or "channels," especially those involving time, space, topical development, cause-and-effect, problem-solution, or criteria-matching. Therefore, arrange the first-degree heads of the Body so that they follow one of these sequences of thought development (or, under unusual circumstances, the implicative pattern). By glancing ahead in this chapter, you can preview the explanation of the nature and application of each pattern.

Selecting the Headings of Second Degree

After finalizing the selection and order of the first-degree points, you should then turn to the selection of headings of second degree. You could start by analyzing carefully the logical and psychological "territory" inherent in Roman numeral No. I. Then divide this "territory" into at least two but, as a general rule, not more than five A, B, C headings. The next step could be either to develop these A, B, C headings with supporting heads of third, fourth, and so on, degree or to proceed immediately to the selection of second-degree headings in support of Roman numeral No. II, and so on.

You should recognize that the headings of first and second degree indicate the basic thought framework of the Body. The A, B, C headings represent a refinement or elaboration of the concepts inherent in the primary ideas. Further clarification and development is accomplished by means of subheads of third and, if necessary, increasingly inferior degrees; such items may be disjunctions or refinements of the immediately superior thought or may be supporting details such as illustrations, comparisons, statistics, quotations, explanations, visual aids, logical reasoning, and appeals to involuntary attention (see Chapter 8).

Since A, B, C headings represent partitions of their immediately superior Roman numeral heads—in much the same fashion that the Roman numeral heads themselves are partitions of the Specific Speech Purpose—they should be subjected to the same tests of suitability that earlier in this chapter were applied to first-degree heads. Therefore, you should determine that each set of coordinate second-degree headings covers adequately the "territory" indicated by its immediately superior head, that each second-degree heading is a direct division of its immediately superior first-degree head, that each heading is a separate thought unit possessing approximately the same value as its coordinate headings, that each is cast in the same grammatical structure as its coordinates, and that strong ties of logical and psychological association link together each set of A, B, C headings under their immediately superior Roman numeral heading.

Applying Principles of Organization to Speeches of Basic Types

Now that we have considered the principles of organizing the Body our next task is to apply these concepts to informative, entertaining, and persuasive speeches.

Organizing the Body of the Speech to Inform

Most informative speeches are probably structured according to either a Temporal or Topical sequence of main heads, with Spatial, Cause-and-Effect, and Problem-Solution being less frequently employed. A discussion of each of these types of patterns follows.

Time Pattern. In examining the Analysis List that you have prepared for an informative speech, determine if the items fall into a chronological sequence. If so, the most effective means of organizing the speech may be to let Roman numeral heading No. I represent an initial unit or period of time and to let the other Roman numeral headings move chronologically either forward or backward from the starting period. The Time Pattern is a natural method for describing a "process" or giving directions—in such speeches you are explaining an operation which in "real life" follows a time order. If describing the proposed life cycle of nuclear fuel, you could trace the stages in the cycle from the fuel conversion plant to the reactor, to the storage basin, to the reprocessing plant, and to the storage of radioactive wastes and the transfer of extracted uranium and plutonium to the fuel conversion plant—completing the cycle. If teaching a group of homeowners how to lay a concrete floor, you could start with the natural first step, followed by the second step, the third, and so on. Obviously, concrete could not be poured before the ground is leveled, before the supporting wire network has been inserted into the wooden frame, or before the frame is constructed. If you were a sergeant giving preliminary instructions to a group of recruits who had just arrived for induction examination, you would probably employ a Time Pattern. These inductees must be told (1) to take off their clothes; (2) to put their clothes in a canvas bag; (3) to check their valuables and their canvas bags; (4) to wait in a certain area for their names to be called; (5) when summoned, to fall into line in a designated place; (6) to keep in order as the line goes through the various stages of the physical examination; and (7) when their examination is completed, to redress and assemble in a particular area. By arranging his directions in accordance with the chronological sequence of events, the sergeant will give his charges a clear conception of what is expected of them.

By employing the following format for the Time Pattern, you may be assured of presenting a well-organized speech. *This format, as well as those that follow in this chapter, is intended to be suggestive, however, and should not be considered prescriptive.* As you gain experience, you may wish in a particular speaking situation to modify or ignore this training format.

Suggestive Format for the Time Pattern

Body:

I. Time period or step number one
   A. First aspect of the time period or step
   B. Second aspect of the time period or step
   C., D., and so on
II. Time period or step number two
   A. First aspect of the time period or step
   B. Second aspect of the time period or step
   C., D., and so on
III. Time period or step number three
   A. First aspect of the time period or step
   B. Second aspect of the time period or step
   C., D., and so on

Sample Abridged Outlines

(1) *Specific Speech Purpose:* To have my audience understand that the reaction to the loss of a loved one by death usually follows a predictable pattern, in the course of which the bereaved person makes real inside himself a situation that is already an established reality outside himself

Body:

I. The immediate reaction to death is shock or numbness
   A. Nature of this stage
   B. Duration of this stage
   C. Psychological function of this stage
II. Numbness is followed by pining
   A. Nature of this stage
   B. Duration of this stage
   C. Psychological function of this stage
III. Pining passes into dejection
   A. Nature of this stage
   B. Duration of this stage
   C. Psychological function of this stage
IV. Dejection slowly yields to acceptance or recovery
   A. Nature of this stage
   B. Duration of this stage
   C. Psychological function of this stage

(2) *Specific Speech Purpose:* To have my audience understand that according to some scientists the sun will die a lingering death

Body:

I. Perhaps three to ten billion years from now the sun's supply of hydrogen will begin to decrease
II. The sun will gradually swell into a monstrous "red giant"
III. The sun will then contract until its fires go out about fifty billion years from now
IV. The sun will exist indefinitely as a huge cinder

(3) *Specific Speech Purpose:* To have my audience understand that in order to produce a good crop of apples the fruit grower conducts a continuous cycle of activity

Body:

I. Maintaining the orchard following the harvest and prior to the growing season
II. Caring for the orchard during the growing season
III. Harvesting the crop

Space Pattern. You continuously encounter spatial or geographical sequences in the process of daily living. Every action, every movement has spatial as well as temporal dimensions. Your home is divided into spatial areas, as is your campus and the local community. When you attend a concert or musical comedy, the price you pay for tickets depends upon the geographical location of the seats—the more desirable the location, the higher is the price. Your college is probably accredited by a regional association of colleges and secondary schools—for example, the New England Association, the Middle States Association, the North Central Association, the Southern Association, or the Northwest Association. Carried to the ultimate, spatial dimensions exist even in the reaches beyond our galaxy.

A woman directing her husband in the rearrangement of furniture is using a "spatial pattern": "Try the sofa against the west wall; the lamp and occasional chair go in the corner; place the piano along the east wall; put the coffee table in front of the sofa." An architect explaining to his clients the floor arrangements of a new warehouse will use a spatial sequence: "The first floor will look like this," he might say as he spreads out the blueprints, "with the right wing . . . the central storage area. . . . The second floor will contain. . . . The third floor will have. . . .

In applying the Space Pattern to informative speeches, you must actually use a *sequence*. The disposition of main heads may move sequentially from the northernmost geographical entity to the most southern, or from sea level down to the ocean bottom, or from the bark of a tree to the heart wood, or from the right flank of a battle line through the middle to the left flank, or from near to far, and so on.

Suggestive Format for the Space Pattern

Body:

I. Spatial area number one
  A. First aspect of this spatial area
  B. Second aspect of this spatial area
  C., D., and so on
II. Spatial area number two
  A. First aspect of this spatial area
  B. Second aspect of this spatial area
  C., D., and so on
III. Spatial area number three
  A. First aspect of this spatial area
  B. Second aspect of this spatial area
  C., D., and so on

Sample Abridged Outlines

(1) *Specific Speech Purpose:* To have my audience understand that the structure of the earth consists of a core, mantle, and crust
Body:
  I. The core of the earth is a ball of molten iron
    A. Theories concerning the size of the core
    B. Theories concerning the physical properties of the core

II. Surrounding the core is a mantle
  A. The probable thickness of the mantle
  B. The probable makeup of the mantle
III. Enveloping the mantle is the earth's crust
  A. The bottom layer consists of basalt
  B. The surface layer consists primarily of folded granite

(2) *Specific Speech Purpose:* To have my audience understand that the earth is enveloped by five concentric layers of atmosphere
Body:
I. Troposphere
II. Tropopause
III. Stratosphere
IV. Mesosphere
V. Ionosphere

Topical Pattern. If the items on your Analysis List do not seem to fall into a temporal or spatial sequence, determine whether they tend to cluster naturally and easily into from two to five traditional or conventional categories, such as spring, summer, fall, winter; men, women, children; administration, faculty, student body; physical, mental, moral; hitting, fielding, pitching. If the list resists such facile partitioning, study carefully again the idea, institution, process, or thing about which you wish to inform your listeners. Now, ascertain if your subject matter can be contained within—and partitioned according to—one of the following, somewhat overlapping, areas or themes: (1) *Nature*—can your subject be divided so that the main heads of the Body will represent characteristics, peculiarities, properties, talents, faculties, capabilities, accomplishments, or qualities? (2) *Purpose* or *Function*—can your subject be divided so that the primary headings represent objectives, commitments, responsibilities, goals, or values? (3) *Signification*—can the major headings represent results, benefits, harmful effects, implications, or persons or areas affected? (4) *Liabilities*—can the major points represent defects, omissions, errors, or weaknesses? (5) *Parts*—can the primary heads represent structural, organizational, or organic parts of the entity you are discussing?

Suggestive Format for the Topical Pattern

Body:
I. Topic or category number one
  A. First aspect of this topic or category
  B. Second aspect of this topic or category
  C., D., and so on
II. Topic or category number two
  A. First aspect of this topic or category
  B. Second aspect of this topic or category
  C., D., and so on

III. Topic or category number three
  A. First aspect of this topic or category
  B. Second aspect of this topic or category
  C., D., and so on

Sample Abridged Outlines

(1) *Specific Speech Purpose:* To have my listeners understand that the chemical industry is actively attempting to improve its waste-disposal methods
Body:
  I. The chemical industry is attempting to eliminate wasteful practices
    A. It is redesigning manufacturing processes that improve efficiency
    B. It is adding on-line treatment systems that neutralize, reduce, or change the nature of waste by-products
    C. It is using recovery techniques that recycle wastes back into the production process
  II. The chemical industry is building secure landfills
    A. Landfills are properly designed
    B. Landfills are properly operated
    C. Landfills are properly monitored
  III. The chemical industry is sharing knowledge of new waste-disposal technology and remedial techniques
    A. It shares knowledge with industry
    B. It shares knowledge with the government
    C. It shares knowledge with the public
  IV. The chemical industry is encouraging solid-waste exchanges
    A. Sometimes the wastes of one company can become the raw material of another company
    B. The chemical industry is promoting the development of waste-exchange organizations

(2) *Specific Speech Purpose:* To have my audience understand that protection can be secured against lightning
Body:
  I. Protection of man
  II. Protection of structures
  III. Protection of power transmission lines
  IV. Protection of electrical apparatus

(3) *Specific Speech Purpose:* To have my listeners understand that most power-lifting competition consists of three different types of lifts
Body:
  I. The bench-press
  II. The dead-weight lift
  III. The deep-knee bend

Under ordinary circumstances you probably should arrange your major headings so that the strongest, most interesting topics are placed first and last, with the weakest, least interesting ones in between. Psychologists tell us that if a series of numbers is presented to an audience, the first and last numerals mentioned will be remembered more often than any others. Hence, begin and close the Body with your most important ideas. By means of your analysis of the audience and occasion, you may be able to determine which of your topics will be most significant and interesting to your listeners. If at a meeting of union men you are delivering a speech concerning recent changes in unemployment insurance, you might arrange the main heads in this manner:

I. How the changes will affect the employees
II. How the changes will affect the employers
III. How the changes will affect the general public

Being union men and members of the general public, the listeners may be primarily concerned about the effect upon these segments and least concerned about the effect upon the employers. Therefore, the explanation about the employers should be placed in the middle between the more "interesting" headings.

When speaking on a technical or involved subject, you may wish to arrange the main headings in an order of understandability, proceeding from the simplest to the most complex. Think how unsuccessful a university course in statistics would be if the professor began the semester with difficult problems of skew distribution, correlation coefficients, and complicated formulas that the class should normally encounter after several weeks of preliminary instruction. The accepted procedure in technical courses, such as statistics, is for the instructor to follow René Descartes' theory of method: "to conduct my thoughts in such order that, by commencing with objects the simplest and easiest to know," one "might ascend by little and little, and, as it were, step by step, to the knowledge of the more complex; assigning in thought a certain order even to those objects which in their own nature do not stand in a relation of antecedence and sequence." In other words, the teacher will begin with material which the students should have mastered prior to enrolling and, as the students acquire greater competency, he will introduce problems of increasing complexity. Also, a golf professional, instructing beginners in approved methods of gripping a club, will not begin with a description of those grips designed to cause deliberate hooking or slicing. Although tournament golfers are able to curve the ball around obstacles partly by varying the handgrip on the club, novices would become confused if exposed to the more difficult grips before understanding thoroughly the normal, standard grip.

An engineer instructing a class in the various uses of the slide rule might arrange his "topics" in the following simple-to-complex sequence.

I. Using the slide rule to multiply
II. Using the slide rule to divide
III. Using the slide rule to secure roots
IV. Using the slide rule to secure logarithms
V. Using the slide rule to find the functions of angles

Cause-and-Effect Pattern. Occasionally in informative speaking the most effective method of arranging the main heads of the Body is to use a causal relationship. Such a pattern may proceed from the *cause* to the *effect* (result), or from the *effect* to the *cause.* In using this sequence, be sure that the incidents, events, or factors which you allege to have produced a particular result have actually exerted a causal influence—thus avoiding the fallacy of *false cause.* Avoid committing the familiar fallacy *post hoc ergo propter hoc* (after this, therefore because of this). You must not assume that merely because one thing follows another in time, the preceding happening causes the latter. The fact that World Wars I and II and the Korean and Vietnamese conflicts occurred during the administrations of Wilson, Roosevelt, Truman, Kennedy, and Johnson, all members of the Democratic party, is not demonstrative proof that the election of these Democrats *caused* the wars. Also, avoid the fallacy of *false simplicity.* Do not oversimplify the cause by ignoring elements that have exerted significant influence in producing the given phenomenon or effect. It is fallacious to assert that the desire for religious self-determination was the sole factor in causing the Puritans to seek homes in the American wilderness.

Suggestive Format for the Cause-and-Effect Pattern

Body:

I. The causative influences
  A. The first causative factor
  B. The second causative factor
  C., D., and so on
II. The resulting effects
  A. The first resulting effect
  B. The second resulting effect
  C., D., and so on

Sample Abridged Outline

Specific Speech Purpose: To have my listeners understand that the Colonial religious revival of 1739 to 1745 (called the Great Awakening) was a major social movement with recognizable causes.

Body:

I. *(Cause)* Various factors prepared Colonial America for an outburst of religious zeal

A. The basic predisposing causes of the revival
(Under this heading the speaker would discuss the primary theological, economic, social, and political factors which over an extended time span motivated the revival.)
B. The immediate, precipitating causes of the revival
(Under this heading the speaker would analyze the events that gave immediate rise to the revival, such as Jonathan Edwards' revival at Northampton, Massachusetts, and the arrival in America of the famed English evangelist George Whitefield.)

II. *(Effect)* The Great Awakening was the major social movement in the Colonies prior to the Revolutionary War
A. The nature of the Great Awakening
B. The influence of the Great Awakening upon Colonial America
C. The long-range influence of the Great Awakening upon American institutions

Problem-Solution Pattern. Every day we are confronted with problem-solution situations. We must determine what to buy at the supermarket for Sunday dinner, which tie to select to go with a new spring suit, how to get the office force to work more efficiently, what to do about the couple next door who have noisy, late parties, how best to invest the $5,000 Uncle Harry left in his will, and so forth.

As a public speaker you may wish to inform an audience about a problem and how that problem *was* solved, *is* being solved, or *possibly could be* solved. A weather bureau official might explain how modern methods of storm detection and protection have minimized the destructiveness of hurricanes. The personnel manager of a large industrial concern might tell a meeting of the board of directors about a problem in labor relations encountered recently in the plant and how his department handled the situation successfully. An instructor at the National War College might pose a problem of logistics and suggest possible ways in which the problem could be solved. A news commentator might discuss a problem of local government and the various remedial procedures that have been proposed by civic leaders.

Suggestive Format, Problem-Solution Pattern Explaining How a Problem Was Solved

Body:

I. This was the problem
A. Importance of the problem
(Explain the significance of the problem to the listeners as well as to other persons who were directly or indirectly affected; perhaps hypothesize what might have happened if the problem had not been solved.
Notice: We see in Chapter 10 that one of the most effective means of securing the initial favorable attention of an audience is to demonstrate

the significance of the topic. Therefore, even though this heading is a logical part of the complete thought process involved in the Problem-Solution Pattern, it may be placed in the Introduction as part of the Favorable Attention Step. In this connection, it might be added that, in addition to employing this particular heading as a means of alerting the listeners to the importance of the topic, the speaker should weave into the matrix of the entire speech the thread of significance.)

B. Nature of the problem
(Explain what the problem was: the aspects, phases, or characteristics that constituted the problem; the severity, scope, and extent of the problem.)

C. Cause(s) of the problem
(Explain why the problem arose: the causative factors that produced the problem.)

II. This program solved the problem

A. Nature of the program
(Explain the characteristics of the plan that was devised to solve the problem.)

B. How the program solved the problem
(Explain what happened when the plan was put into operation: tell how the program was able to remedy the problem; perhaps trace the course of events that transpired; perhaps discuss the exigencies, difficulties, and surprises that were encountered; perhaps note various modifications in the original plan that were made necessary by the developing circumstances.)

C. Estimation of the results of the program
(Explain what were the results of the program: estimate the total effects, balancing the beneficial against the harmful. On this point, as for each of the others, you should recognize the existence of any significant divergence of opinion among competent observers.
Notice: We see in Chapter 11 that such an estimation may serve as a suitable recapitulation of the entire speech and thereby may be placed in the Conclusion as part of the Summary Step. It is included here because it illustrates the logical culmination of the complete thought process.)

If controversy exists concerning any of the items in this format, you should report the disagreements candidly. If you take sides and attempt to shape the attitudes of your listeners, you have ceased being an informative speaker and have become an advocate. In such a case, you should not hide behind the facade of an objective dispenser of facts—both you and your listeners should recognize that you are indeed a persuader.

Sample Abridged Outline

Specific Speech Purpose: To have my audience understand that the State University's evaluation program has provided the information necessary to identify problems and to solve them

Body:

I. Two years ago President Patterson stated that neither he nor anyone else had an accurate knowledge of the strengths and shortcomings of our university
   A. Effective planning for improvement was impossible without an accurate understanding of State's needs
   B. The administration feared that, like an iceberg, the unseen problems of the university would be far more numerous than those discoverable by a surface inspection
   C. This lack of accurate knowledge was the inevitable product of the major changes sustained by the university during the previous decade
II. To secure an accurate assessment of State University, President Patterson initiated a self-evaluation program
   A. The self-evaluation program was carefully planned
   B. The self-evaluation program took two years of concentrated effort
   C. In estimation of the recently completed program, President Patterson and the members of the Board of Control have agreed that the self-evaluation program has provided the self-knowledge necessary to enable the university to develop into a fine institution

Suggestive Format, Problem-Solution Pattern Explaining Proposals for Solving an Existing Problem

Body:

I. This is the problem
   A. Importance of the problem
      (Explain the consensus of informed opinion concerning the significance of the problem; if divergent views exist, you probably should mention them. Unobtrusively link the topic to the interests and well-being of your listeners, and show the relationship to other persons directly or indirectly affected. Perhaps hypothesize what might happen if the problem is not solved. As was explained in the previous Problem-Solution format, this topic is included to illustrate the total thought sequence; however, because it could serve as an effective springboard for the speech, it may be placed in the Introduction as part of the Favorable Attention Step.)
   B. Nature of the problem
      (Explain what seems to be general agreement concerning the severity, extent, and scope of the problem. Recognize any significant dissenting versions. Before an undesirable situation or condition can be remedied, a clear understanding of its character must exist. Therefore, explain the nature of the problem as lucidly and as objectively as possible.)
   C. Cause(s) of the problem
      (Explain the agreements and disagreements concerning the factors that may have produced the problem.)
II. These plans have been proposed to solve the problem
   A. Plan No. 1 has been proposed
      (Explain the nature of the plan, its strengths as claimed by its adherents, and its weaknesses as claimed by its detractors.)

B. Plan No. 2 has been proposed
(Explain the nature of the plan and any significant ways in which it differs from the first plan mentioned; describe its advantages as claimed by its supporters and its weaknesses as claimed by its opponents.)
C., D., and so on

Sample Abridged Outline

Specific Speech Purpose: To have my listeners understand that various plans exist for solving the pressing problem of improving financial support of the nation's public school system
Body:

I. One of the most compelling public issues is the financial condition of the nation's public school system
   A. Adequate financial support of the public school system is critically important to the well-being of our country
   B. Although considerable disagreement exists concerning the universality and severity of the need, it is generally agreed that the public school system must secure better financial support
   C. The reasons for the present inadequate financial support for public education are numerous and varied
II. Various plans are being advanced to provide better financial support for the public school system
   A. One possibility is increased local support
   B. Another possibility is increased state support
   C. Another possibility is increased federal support
   D. A fourth possibility is increased support from a combination of governmental levels.

Organizing the Body of the Speech to Entertain

Although any of the major patterns conceivably might be used to organize the Body of the entertaining speech, probably the Time and Topical patterns are most frequently employed.

Time Pattern. When presenting a personal experience, a factual or fictional narrative, a diverting treatment of a process, or a buoyant handling of a historical continuity, you may arrange the main ideas in a chronological order.

Sample Abridged Outline

Specific Speech Purpose: To have my listeners be diverted by a narration of my adventures during my first and last boar hunt

Body:

I. Stalking the boar
II. Struggling with the boar
III. Escaping from the boar
IV. Retreating to the safety of civilization

Topical Pattern. If the entertaining material in the Analysis List does not contain a time sequence, it may lend itself to grouping under conventional categories or under certain characteristics, purposes, effects, duties, assets, liabilities, or parts of the basic topic.

Sample Abridged Outline

Specific Speech Purpose: To have my audience be amused by my description of several professorial stereotypes

Body:

I. The "pacer" type of professor
II. The "bifocal" type of professor
III. The "man-about-town" type of professor
IV. The "introvert" type of professor
V. The "big-wheel" type of professor

Organizing the Body of the Speech to Persuade

Any persuasive speech can be structured by a Topical, Criteria-Matching, or Problem-Solution formula. Under somewhat unusual circumstances the Implicative Pattern might be employed. (Because the Time and Space are used very infrequently to structure the persuasive speech, they are not discussed in this section.)

Topical Pattern. If you wish to persuade your listeners to accept a new program or course of action, or to rationalize such an existing belief, the first-degree headings of the Body could represent "reasons for acceptance." If you wish your listeners to reject a proposal, or to reinforce their prior decision for rejection, the major heads could be "reasons for rejection." If you wish your listeners to believe, or to intensify their existing belief, that some proposition or opinion is—or is not—true, reliable, effective, or desirable, the primary headings could be "reasons for belief."

In arranging the contentions, or reasons, your intent is to help listeners perceive an analogous relationship between their self-systems and what you are saying. Place first and last those headings that your particular audience probably would consider most persuasive and most interesting, with the less persuasive ones in the middle. Attempt to phrase each primary argument in such a manner that it impinges upon some basic want or desire of the hearers. Then, if you are able to establish this contention, you will be capitalizing upon the listeners' "inner springs of response" and will be encouraging closure with your position.

Sample Abridged Outlines

(1) *Specific Speech Purpose:* To have my audience be motivated to develop skill in oral communication

Body:

- I. By developing your skill in oral communication you will serve your personal interests
  - A. You will achieve greater self-realization
  - B. You will improve your social relationships
  - C. You will increase your professional and economic opportunities
- II. By developing your skill in oral communication you will serve more effectively your community and nation
  - A. Effective speech is necessary for the successful promotion of civic efforts
  - B. Effective speech is the basic means of protecting freedom of speech and, thereby, all of our national freedoms

(2) *Specific Speech Purpose:* To have my audience believe that censorship is undesirable

Body:

- I. Censorship is self-defeating
- II. Censorship is aesthetically indefensible
- III. Censorship is antidemocratic

(3) *Specific Speech Purpose:* To have my audience believe that the political convention system should be reformed

Body:

- I. The convention delegates should be selected by more democratic means
- II. The convention should be made more representative
- III. The convention should be smaller
- IV. The convention should meet every year

Criteria-Matching Pattern. Unlike the Topical Pattern, which can be applied to any kind of persuasive proposition, the Criteria-Matching sequence is limited to propositions of "fact." Note that in this usage the word "fact" is enclosed by quotation marks. Such a "fact" is alleged by the speaker to be true, but, prior to the speech, it had not been incontestably demonstrated. Furthermore, such a "fact" is an allegation that is subject to probable proof by rhetorical means; it is not an undebatable truth subject to absolute verification by means of science. To prove or disprove a proposition of "fact," the speaker must rely upon the available evidence and logical-emotional reasoning. If the "fact" in question can be put in a test tube for analysis, laid upon a scale for weighing, or inserted in a maze for experimentation, it is not a debatable proposition and does not lend itself to proof or disproof by the methods of rhetoric.

Here are some sample propositions that allege that a particular thesis or opinion is—or is not—a "fact," that is, is true, valid, accurate, useful, workable, meritorious, and so on: Jack Nicklaus is the best golfer in history; the UN is no longer an effective instrument for international understanding; American freedoms are endangered by the extreme right; "pop" quizzes are unfair; the legal profession is overcrowded; John le Carré's *Smiley's People* is delightful reading. Notice that these propositions do not advocate the adoption of a new policy or course of action; they merely allege that a controversial assertion is true, that is, is a "fact."

Two basic steps are involved in the organization of a proposition of "fact" by the Criteria-Matching system. First, the speaker must determine the standards, or criteria, that the proposition would necessarily have to meet before it could be considered a "fact." Second, he must demonstrate that his proposition matches these standards. If the standards accurately measure probability, and if the proposition meets all of the standards, the proposition is a "fact"; if the proposition does not meet the criteria, it is not a "fact." To demonstrate this procedure, let us assume that you have applied at a large construction firm for the position of structural engineer to be stationed in South America. The personnel director pulls from his files a manila folder containing the carefully determined requirements the successful candidate must possess. Here are some of the questions the director might ask: "Are you a graduate of a recognized engineering school?" "Was your grade average "B" or better?" "Can you speak Spanish?" "Have you had a minimum of five years' experience as a structural engineer?" "Can you provide suitable references?" If you could answer "yes" to each of these questions, you would be an acceptable candidate. You would have demonstrated your proposition of "fact": "I am qualified for the position of structural engineer with this firm."

Suggestive Format for Criteria-Matching Pattern

Body:

I. Criterion No. 1
   A. Defend this criterion as being a suitable standard of measurement
   B. Show how the proposition meets this criterion
II. Criterion No. 2
   A. Defend this criterion as being a suitable standard of measurement
   B. Show how the proposition meets this criterion
III. Criterion No. 3
   A. Defend this criterion as being a suitable standard of measurement
   B. Show how the proposition meets this criterion

Sample Abridged Outline

Specific Speech Purpose: To have my audience believe that the BMW 320i has the highest performance of any car in its price range

Body:

I. Criterion No. 1: acceleration
   A. This criterion is a suitable standard of measurement
   B. According to tests, the BMW 320i has the best acceleration of any car in its price range

II. Criterion No. 2: braking
   A. This criterion is a suitable standard of measurement
   B. According to tests, the BMW 320i has the best brakes of any car in its price range

III. Criterion No. 3: handling
   A. This criterion is a suitable standard of measurement
   B. According to tests, the BMW 320i has the best handling of any car in its price range

IV. Criterion No. 4: tire reserve
   A. This criterion is a suitable standard of measurement
   B. According to tests, the BMW 320i has tire reserve that is equal to any car in its price range

V. Criterion No. 5: fuel economy
   A. This criterion is a suitable standard of measurement
   B. According to tests, the BMW 320i has the best fuel economy of any car in its price range

As you may have observed, the basic difference between the Criteria-Matching Pattern and the Topical Pattern, as the latter applies to propositions of "fact," is that the Topical arrangement would not contain substantial analyses of the criteria being employed. Thus, to convert the previous outline to a Topical Pattern, all of the "A" headings would be omitted and all of the "B" headings would be raised to first-degree status. As first-degree headings they would constitute "reasons why" the listeners should accept that the BMW 320i has the highest performance of any car in its price range.

Problem-Solution Pattern. Any speech that urges an audience to accept a new policy or course of action is employing problem solution. Such speeches attempt to prove that the existing situation—*status quo*—could be improved through the adoption of a particular plan or program. If the speaker can reasonably assume that the listeners realize the necessity for remedial action, he might omit a separate discussion of the problem or might cover it quickly in the Introduction; in such a case, he would probably organize the Body around a few compelling "reasons for adoption"—thus employing the Topical Pattern (see p. 137). On the other hand, if the listeners do not recognize, or do not accept, the existence of a problem, the first major persuasive task of the speaker is to establish the need for improvement; only then can he successfully propose corrective measures. In using this Problem-Solution Pattern, the following sequence may be employed.

Suggestive Format, Problem-Solution Pattern

Body:

I. Problem Step (Need Argument)

A. Importance of the problem

(This heading is included here to indicate the total thought sequence. As we have seen, however, it is an excellent means of stimulating initial audience interest and, therefore, could be placed in the Introduction as part of the Favorable Attention Step. Before listeners will give close attention to the analysis of a problem, they must identify with it sufficiently well to recognize that it possesses significant meaning for them as well as the community. Problems of genuine importance, especially those involving abstract principles or freedoms, or those concerning exigencies that seem remote in time or space, may not be so recognized by the audience—unless the significance is compellingly set forth by the speaker. Naturally, in addition to directing attention here to the importance of the problem, the speaker must throughout the speech keep the audience keenly aware of the implications of the problem and its solution.)

B. Nature of the problem

(Demonstrate clearly and persuasively the existence of a need that should be satisfied, a situation that should be improved, a genuine and serious problem that should be solved. Before accepting a new policy, an audience must believe that the existing situation is unsatisfactory. If no need for change exists, why should a new policy or program be instituted? In order for a health commissioner to persuade the city council to prohibit bathing at the municipal beaches, he would have to prove that the water was polluted and unsafe for swimming.

One method of handling this heading is to divide the problem into its major aspects or phases. Later, when you come to heading II, B, "The plan will solve the problem," you will show how your plan will improve each of these aspects.)

C. Cause(s) of the problem

(If the causative factors are obvious, if they seem unimportant to the determination of a solution, or if you have covered them in your discussion of the nature of the problem, you may not wish to include this heading. For instance, in a speech urging that the county commissioners should apply for urban renewal funds to relieve the downtown slums, you should demonstrate persuasively the need for improvement, but it perhaps may not be necessary for you to document a detailed analysis of why over the years certain areas gradually declined into slums.

At times, however, the validity of your solution will depend upon how accurately you have analyzed the cause of the problem. If speaking to a school board about a delinquent child, you must be accurate in your diagnosis of the causes that motivate the boy's antisocial behavior. In this case, an incorrect analysis may result in an unsatisfactory solution. Perhaps you believe that the child's unorthodox conduct is produced by an unfavorable home environment. Therefore, you urge that the boy be taken from his parents and placed in the city's home for unwanted and wayward children. Your plan will not solve this problem, however, if the real cause lies in a severe hearing loss. Because the child cannot understand directions and class instruction, he believes he is dull and inferior to other children—hence he becomes a disciplinary problem.)

II. Solution Step (Plan Argument)
   A. Explanation of the plan
   (Explain clearly and in adequate detail the policy or course of action that you are advocating. Understanding precedes conviction. Thinking auditors will reject a "pig in a poke" proposition; they will want to know precisely the nature of the plan they are being asked to endorse. Unless the proposal is clear, all of your efforts at persuasion may fall upon deaf ears.

   The amount of explanation depends upon the complexity of the plan and the understanding of the listeners. If you are urging the Civil Service Board to fire a policeman, your "Explanation of the plan" would probably consist of a simple declaration: "Gentlemen, in view of the proven charges against this man, the only course of action is to fire him immediately." If you are advocating the establishment of a permanent United Nations police force, however, you would have to explain carefully the nature of the force: the number and types of troops; how the members would be selected; how the force would be financed; what controls would govern the actions of the force; and so on.)
   B. The plan will solve the problem
   (Prove that the adoption of your proposals would solve the difficulties you alleged in the Problem Step under heading I, B, "Nature of the problem." Frequently a student speaker is surprised and somewhat offended when fellow classmates refuse to accept his undocumented assertion that his plan will improve the *status quo.* Unless you possess tremendous prestige, critical listeners will demand that you demonstrate the workability of your plan; they will not be jarred from customary patterns of thinking and behaving by unsupported claims.)
   C. The plan can be put into effective operation
   (In many cases the acceptability of an argument hinges upon the speaker's proof that his proposals can be carried out. A plan that *theoretically* would solve an existing problem but that for one reason or another cannot be put into *practical operation* is not a solution at all. Student speakers have been known to assert that the best way to stop cheating in universities is for everyone to be honest. Naturally, if all students were completely honest, no cheating would exist. But how can this ideal of universal honesty be converted into practice? If suggesting that a $7 million garage be constructed in the downtown area to help solve the parking problem, you must prove not only that your plan would reduce appreciably the existing parking difficulties but also that it is feasible, that is, that adequate financing can be secured, a proper site is available, that an exception to the zoning ordinances can be obtained, and so on.)
   D. The plan is the best solution available
   (When the audience is aware of several possible solutions to the problem, you may wish to demonstrate that yours is the most satisfactory one. The technique of accomplishing this purpose is called the *method of residues.*

When a chemist pours a fluid into a test tube and filters off the liquid, the solid material remaining is the residuum or residue. Likewise, when a speaker takes up competing plans one at a time and shows specifically why each is less satisfactory than his, he eliminates them as "answers"; the only remaining answer—the residue—is his plan. *Caution:* A wise speaker attempts to keep the attention of the persuadee centered on the goods and services rendered by his plan. Therefore, if your listeners are not apt to think of counter proposals, if they are emotionally conditioned in favor of another policy, or if time limitations or other circumstances preclude your demonstrating that your plan is clearly superior, you probably should not employ the method of residues.)

E. The plan will not create additional severe problems
(As in the case of heading D, use *caution* in applying this contention. If you claim that your program will not create serious new problems, you may provoke negative thinking on the part of the persuadees. You will have placed yourself on the defensive and may cause your listeners to suspect that you are attempting to camouflage a weak case.

Sometimes, however, this argument must be openly advanced and persuasively defended. Conceivably, listeners might recognize that the implementation of a particular plan might solve an unsatisfactory condition, that it could be put into effective operation, and that it is the best of the proposed solutions—but for compellingly good reasons they might still reject the proposal. In solving an existing problem, the remedy might create new difficulties that are as bad or worse than the original ones—the treatment might be worse than the ailment. If, to alleviate a severe cold, an injection of penicillin is administered to a patient who is allergic to the drug, the patient may die. If advocating the adoption of federal aid to education, you probably would need to prove that such a program would not result in thought control of the schools. Such a consequence would be far more disastrous than the present problem of inadequate financial support of the schools.)

Because of its complexity, the Problem-Solution Pattern is illustrated by a sample outline that is more fully developed than the other sample outlines used in this chapter.

Sample Outline

Specific Speech Purpose: To have my audience believe that the United States should adopt a program of compulsory health insurance for all citizens
Body:

I. The existing system of private medical care is unsatisfactory
   A. The securing of the most effective system of medical care is of paramount importance
      1. To the nation
      2. To the individual citizen

B. The present system of private medical care has failed to meet the nation's needs
  1. The general health of the nation is unsatisfactory
  2. People of the middle and lower income groups cannot afford adequate medical care
  3. Certain areas of the country have a disproportionately small share of the available medical facilities
  4. Medical research is not funded adequately

C. The inadequacy of our present system is primarily caused by its means of financial support
  1. The fee-for-service system makes the cost of medical care prohibitively high for many people
  2. The fee-for-service system does not permit adequate emphasis upon preventative medicine
  3. The fee-for-service system does not provide adequate means for the expansion of medical facilities and a suitable increase in the number of doctors and nurses
  4. The fee-for-service system causes doctors to establish their offices in sites that seem to promise lucrative practice
  5. The fee-for-service system does not provide adequate financial support for research

II. A system of compulsory health insurance for all citizens should be adopted

A. A program of compulsory health insurance is both simple and practical in nature and could be effectively administered
  1. All persons would be insured
  2. All medical expenses would be covered
  3. The cost of the program would be met by means of an increase in the federal income tax
  4. The program would be administered by the Department of Health, Education, and Welfare
  5. Except for the removal of the fee-for-service means of payment, all aspects of the present system of medical care would be preserved

B. Compulsory health insurance for all citizens could answer the nation's needs
  1. It could improve the general health of the nation
  2. It could provide adequate medical attention for all persons regardless of income
  3. It could provide a fair geographical distribution of medical facilities
  4. It could provide funds for medical research

C. A program of compulsory health insurance for all citizens could be put into effective operation
  1. As I have demonstrated, the plan could be efficiently and effectively financed
  2. I have also proved that the program could be successfully administered
  3. The public wants such a program established
  4. Sufficient medical personnel and facilities could be provided to make the plan work

D. Compulsory health insurance for all citizens is the only means of answering the nation's health needs

1. Extended voluntary health insurance programs would not meet the need
2. Health insurance programs sponsored by local or state governments would not meet the need
3. Expanded federal health insurance for the aged would not meet the need
4. Of all the possible programs only the plan for compulsory health insurance for all citizens would possess the financial support and comprehensive scope necessary to meet the nation's needs

E. The adoption of a program of compulsory health insurance would not create serious problems
1. It would not adversely affect the doctor-patient relationship
2. It would not overburden the available medical facilities
3. It would not regiment the medical profession
4. It would not reduce the attractiveness of medicine as a profession
5. It would not further the cause of socialism

The previously stated caution, that formats for the different patterns of organization are intended to be suggestive rather than prescriptive, is especially applicable to the Problem-Solution sequence. The Problem-Solution Pattern described will fit almost any speech urging the adoption of a new policy; it is a broad highway, well marked and well mapped. Nevertheless, you should not slavishly follow the pattern. Feel free to adjust it to meet the particular needs of your audience, the time limitations, or the character of the available evidence. One possible abbreviation of this outline is to organize the Body of the speech around the "B" headings of main heads "I" and "II." Thus, the speaker would establish the existence of a particular phase of the general problem and explain how his plan will answer this phase; he then would demonstrate the existence of a second phase and how his plan will remedy this phase, and so on.

Implicative Pattern. Occasionally a speaker may feel that, because of the nature of the materials or the probable attitudes of the listeners, a direct presentation of his views in a standard Topical, Criteria-Matching, or Problem-Solution sequence would encounter impossible resistance: perhaps the listeners have heard so many appeals on his theme that they have insulated themselves with a protective envelope of disinterest; perhaps they have strong emotional predispositions in favor of a competing viewpoint; or, perhaps they have rigid objections to the speaker's proposals.

In such cases the speaker may wish to approach his subject obliquely by means of the Implicative Pattern. In the Implicative Pattern, before the speaker explicitly presents direct arguments in support of his views, he offers information that guides the listeners indirectly toward closure with his position. A student nurse used the Implicative Pattern to motivate classmates to afford clear passage to ambulances. Her prespeech analysis of the listeners revealed that many of them refused to cooperate with the siren, considering such cooperation to be an abridgment of their personal freedoms. In her speech the student nurse gave several extended examples in which lives had either been lost or endangered because traffic had been slow to give way to the ambulance. Only after citing these cases did the speaker turn to her direct plea to cooperate immediately with the siren. She outlined her speech in the manner indicated below.

Specific Speech Purpose: To have my listeners be motivated as drivers to give way to ambulances on emergency missions
Body:
I. Example No. 1—failure of traffic to yield passage to an ambulance
II. Example No. 2—failure of traffic to yield passage to an ambulance
III. Example No. 3—failure of traffic to yield passage to an ambulance
IV. Example No. 4—failure of traffic to yield passage to an ambulance
V. As a driver you should cooperate immediately and fully to provide passage for an ambulance

---

Summary

After determining the Specific Speech Purpose, and during or following the process of gathering the raw material for the speech, you should prepare the basic framework of the Body. In order to plan the thought structure of the Body, you must understand the principles of organization:

(1) Since the primary function of the outline is to show thought relationships, you should learn to employ a standard system of symbols and indentations.

(2) You should learn how to select the first-degree headings, the major ideas you wish to communicate. In securing the main heads of the Body, the first step is to prepare an Analysis List—a physical or mental listing of the different points you might want to present in the talk. The second step is to evolve from the Analysis List a tentative group of two to five major ideas under which can be arranged pertinent supporting points. The third step is to apply to these tentative first-degree heads the following criteria: Do the headings cover the subject matter inherent in the Specific Speech Purpose? Is each heading a direct division of the Specific Speech Purpose? Is each a single, independent thought unit? Does each possess substantially the same degree of importance as the others? Is each phrased in parallel grammatical structure with the others? Do strong ties of logical and psychological association unite the headings and provide the

listeners with a progression of thought that will enable them to move toward your position?

(3) After finalizing the selection of the first-degree points, you should turn to the choice of headings of second-degree. Subject each of these potential headings to the same tests of suitability that you applied to the first-degree points.

In your attempt to organize the Body into a sequence that will be strategically influential in helping the listeners to perceive analogical relationships between their self-systems and what you are saying, thereby extending themselves toward closure with your position, your Specific Speech Purpose, you must keep in mind the demands imposed not only by your Specific Speech Purpose but also by the listeners' knowledge of, and attitudes toward, the subject and toward you as the speaker, by the speech occasion, and by the nature and availability of developmental materials.

In structuring the Body of the informative speech, let the first-degree heads represent (1) periods of time or the chronological steps of a process (Time Pattern), (2) areas in a geographical sequence (Space Pattern), (3) natural, traditional, or convenient categories (Topical Pattern) that may utilize either an "order of understandability" or an "order of importance or interest," (4) a causal sequence (Cause-and-Effect Pattern), (5) or a problem-solving sequence (Problem-Solution Pattern) that explains the method by which a problem was solved or the plans that have been proposed to solve an existing problem.

In organizing the Body of the purely entertaining speech, you probably would dispose the main heads according to either a Time or Topical Pattern.

In planning the Body of the persuasive speech, you could employ the Topical Pattern for almost any type of speech purpose, the Criteria-Matching Pattern for propositions of "fact," and the Problem-Solution Pattern for speeches recommending a new policy or course of action. Infrequently, you may decide that your persuasive material could best be presented in an Implicative Pattern.

Exercises and Assignments

1. Attempt to take lecture notes in your various classes in outline form. Be especially alert to catch guideposts given by the professor, such as, "The second cause is . . . ," "Now let's look at certain economic implications . . . ," or "Perhaps of most importance . . ."
2. As a means of reviewing for tests in your various classes, reorganize your

lecture notes in outline form. Do you find that this procedure helps make clear formerly obscure thought relationships and facilitates memorization?

3. Outline a speech from *Vital Speeches* or from some other collection of speeches.

4. Rearrange the following main and subheads in proper outline form.
Specific Speech Purpose: To have my audience be informed about the Fulbright Program under Public Law 584

I. Objectives of the program
  A. Offers broadening experiences for American scholars and specialists
II. Description of the awards
  A. Maintenance allowance
  B. Levels of awards
  C. Duration of awards
III. Eligibility requirements
IV. Book and incidental allowances
V. Application procedure
  A. Must be a citizen
  B. Must be in good health
  C. Liability of grantee to tax
  D. Must have a Ph.D. for a research grant and at least three years teaching experience for a teaching award
VI. Selection of grantees
  A. How to obtain application forms
  B. When to apply
  C. Principal criteria for selection
  D. Stages in the selection process
VII. Plan promotes international understanding

5. Structure the following items into a Problem-Solution Pattern that supports this *Specific Speech Purpose:* To have my audience understand that the conquest of Iwo Jima was a costly victory over a major obstacle to the successful culmination of the War in the Pacific.

The conquest of Iwo Jima was the key to the air war against Japan
Final mopping up extended into April
(Solution Step:) The conquest of Iwo Jima by American forces represented a costly victory
(Nature of Problem:) Iwo Jima was a strongly defended island bastion
(Nature of Program:) The battle plans were carefully drawn
The actual invasion required a month of heavy fighting
(Problem Step:) The occupation of Iwo Jima by the Japanese represented a major obstacle to the successful culmination of the War in the Pacific
The Japanese lost an island outpost, Lieutenant General Tadamichi Kuribayashi, and an entire garrison
The physical characteristics of the island also made a successful assault more difficult
The preinvasion bombardment failed to destroy the island's defenses
The victory proved to be the bloodiest engagement yet encountered by the marines
The Japanese commander Lieutenant General Kuribayashi had about 23,000 men under his authority

(Estimation of Results:) In perspective, we would have to assess the Iwo Jima campaign as a successful and necessary military venture, but one tragically costly in human life and suffering
The conquest of Iwo Jima would open the way for the assault on Okinawa, 362 miles southwest of the main Japanese island of Kyushu
D day was originally set on January 20, 1945, but unforeseen events caused a postponement until February 3 and then to February 19
(How Program Solved the Problem:) The conquest of Iwo Jima required an extended and bitterly fought campaign
The victory helped make inevitable our triumph over Japan
(Importance of Problem:) Because of its strategic location 750 miles south of Tokyo, the conquest of Iwo Jima was vital to the war effort
General Kuribayashi had skillfully planned his island defenses to withstand bombardment and direct assault
The plans called for close coordination of air, sea, and land forces
In October 1944, the Joint Chiefs of Staff directed Admiral Chester Nimitz to take Iwo Jima

6. Place the following heads in their appropriate coordinate and subordinate relationships.

defensive strength
fielding
double-play combination
offensive power
pitching
home-run power
skilled base running
reserve strength
managerial strength
coaches
catching
manager
utility outfielders
utility infielders

CHAPTER 7

Developing the Body of the Speech: Understanding Kinds of Content

The subject of Chapter 6 was the selection and disposition of the main ideas of the Body—the basic thought structure, consisting of headings of first and second degree. If you have chosen these headings well, you have evolved a structure that is strategically influential in encouraging maximum movement on the part of the listeners. Nevertheless, by themselves, primary and secondary headings present only a sparse framework or pattern of thought; they are mere statements or assertions without the supportive materials necessary to make them clear, vivid, and impressive.

In this chapter and Chapter 8 our concern is how to develop primary and secondary points so they are maximally effective in answering or satisfying your rhetorical problems, that is, in responding to the demands imposed by the understanding, interests, values, attitudes, and behaviors of the audience, the particular nature of the occasion, the ethical and logical demands of the subject, and the speaker image you project. Your task is to engage the listeners in a continuing interaction as you work sequentially through the outline of the Body. You accomplish this interaction by means of supporting materials. Such materials should enable your listeners to experience areas of identification with your ideas-feelings and sequentially to enlarge these areas of identification. It is in the process of enlarging the areas of identification that the listeners extend themselves toward closure with your position, or Specific Speech Purpose.

You should view your supportive materials as representing rhetorical choices or decisions. They constitute options that you have selected from among those available to you as being the best answers or satisfactions to the rhetorical needs with which you are confronted. If you have chosen the supporting materials well, you may move your listeners during your development of the main points of the Body as far as possible, under the circumstances of the situation, toward closure with your position.

In this chapter we are concerned with understanding the different kinds of content, called Forms of Support. Just as the builder has certain materials that he uses to construct a house, so, as a public speaker, you have definite materials that can be utilized to develop the primary and secondary headings. Instead of plaster, lumber, and mortar, you may use illustrations, statistics, comparison, contrast, testimony, explanation, and visual aids.

The typical manner of using Forms of Support is to state the heading under consideration, present the supporting materials, and then show how these materials have helped develop the point. Each item of support should fit smoothly into the developing sequence of thought. In terms of outlining, each item should develop, amplify, or clarify its immediately superior heading. In terms of effect, each item should be skillfully adjusted to the total speaking situation.

To encourage listeners to move toward closure with your position, your supporting materials must provide them with the means within their hierarchy of values, interests, and beliefs to identify or, at least, to relate as closely as possible with your proposals. Then your supporting materials must supply the listeners with the means of reinforcement that will enable them to continue to extend themselves, to move toward closure. In selecting and applying each item of support, ask yourself questions such as these: Under the existing circumstances, will it encourage the listeners to engage actively in a continuing interaction with me on this subject? Will it capture and "hold" their attention? Will it help them to associate my point with their wants, interests, and needs? Will they understand and accept it? Will they adjudge it consistent with their system of moral and ethical values? Will they regard it as compatible with my speaker image?

Let us now examine the various forms of supportive materials. For each type we consider some of its strengths and weaknesses, certain overlappings, and various suggestions for its effective use. In Chapter 8, "Developing the Body: Understanding Methods of Development," we shall take up certain methods or procedures that apply to all Forms of Support, enabling the speaker to use the kinds of content with maximum effectiveness in developing his ideas.

Illustration (Example)

From the earliest days of man's history, the storyteller has commanded rapt attention. An illustrative narrative vividly presented has high interest value. Everyone enjoys hearing a story. Because of the persuasiveness and interest-provoking qualities of the narrative, Christ resorted almost exclusively to it as his teaching methodology. Aristotle taught that "examples function like witnesses—and there is always a tendency to believe a witness." Lincoln stated that the average person is "more easily influenced and informed by illustrations than in any other way." Henry Ward Beecher characterized the example as "a window in an argument." James A. Winans, one of the patriarchs of modern speech teaching, called the illustration "the very life of the speech." Norman Vincent Peale stated, "The true example is the finest method I know of to make an idea clear, interesting, and persuasive." Perhaps of all the forms of support the example is the most adaptable and the most effective.

What is an illustration? It is the narration of a happening or an incident that amplifies, makes persuasive, or brings into clearer focus the point under consideration. The chief power of the illustration is that it tells a story vividly, thereby making possible a combined appeal to both the intellect and the emotions. The three types of illustration are the detailed factual, the undeveloped factual, and the hypothetical.

The Detailed Factual Illustration

Nature and Purpose of the Detailed Factual Illustration. This type of example is an extended narration of a true occurrence or event. It tells the story of how something happened. The use of dialogue and of detail—concerning the motives, appearance, and behavior of the persons involved, the locality, weather, smells, sounds, actions, and the like—enable the speaker to paint a graphic word picture that carries the audience along as the story unfolds. The detailed factual illustration offers persuasive evidence. In a sermonic address to a Disciples of Christ laymen's convention, former President Jimmy Carter supported his contention that "individual exemplification of the life of Jesus provides a stable social core for America" by describing several personal religious experiences. To prove that the state boxing commission should be more vigilant in its efforts to retire fighters who risk permanent injury, you might relate the true story of a particular fighter: because the commission permitted this boxer to continue fighting even after he had absorbed terrific and repeated batterings, the boxer became "punch drunk." If told convincingly and supplemented by additional evidence, your example should exert an impelling effect.

The detailed true illustration also promotes interest and clarity. To illustrate the neighborliness of the man who just moved in next door, you might tell how he came over to help you cut the grass one morning and even brought some clippers to trim the hedge. Relating the story should vividly clarify your statement that the man is a good neighbor.

In the following excerpt from a sermon by Dr. Norman Vincent Peale, notice how the speaker develops a true narrative in such a manner as to encourage maximum inspirational effect.[1]

Statement of Main Head

If you want true and permanent peace of mind, you have to get close to God. Get Him into your life, let His spirit drive deeply into your personality.

Detailed Factual Illustration

A friend of mine who operates *The American Surgical Trade Association Journal* sent me a story . . . of a hard-pressed surgeon in one of the hospitals of our city. He had grown irritated from over work, and came to perform an operation in an irascible mood. All was in readiness in the operating room when they wheeled in a beautiful girl who had been badly injured in an accident. She did not know she was considered a hopeless case. The nurse who was to give the anaesthetic said, kindness in her voice, "Relax and breathe deeply."

The girl looked up at the nurse and asked, " Would you mind very much if I repeated something my mother taught me when I was a child? I would like to say the twenty-third Psalm."

The nurse looked at the doctor and he nodded. The girl started: "The Lord is my shepherd: I shall not want."

The surgeon listened as he washed his hands. The attendants were very quiet. They had heard this Psalm in churches and cathedrals, but here it seemed to have a deeper meaning." . . . though I walk through the valley of the shadow of death, I will fear no evil: for Thou art with me . . ."

The nurse started to give the anaesthetic, but the doctor said, "Hold it. Let her finish." Then he said to the patient, "Go on, honey, say it to the end. Say it for me, too."

As she finished the doctor looked down on her. He was at peace, relaxed. His skillful hands were ready now, and peace was in his heart. The operation was a success.

Application to Main Head

Queer, isn't it, how peaceful all of us have become. What have we done? Nothing but call attention to some of the most familiar words we know. And these are just a few of the words out of the Book which drive deeply to the essence of human nature with its therapy.

Do you want peace? Get near to God—that is the answer. . . . All basic and lasting peace is from God.

Suggestions for the Effective Use of the Detailed Factual Illustration. (1) The illustration must be relevant. Resist the temptation

[1]This excerpt comes from the sermon "Peace for the Troubled Heart," delivered at the Marble Collegiate Church, New York City. Used by special permission of Dr. Peale.

to use an example merely because it is a "good story." Because of the interest-getting qualities of the illustration, listeners will remember first the example and then the point it amplifies. A strained relationship between the illustration and its major head will inevitably produce confusion and misunderstanding.

(2) Make clear to the audience the relationship of the example to the heading it supports. Recall that in the preceding excerpt the speaker showed explicitly the application of the illustration to the point.

(3) Use sufficient detail to be clear and vivid, but avoid blunting or obscuring the point with unnecessary particulars.

(4) Develop the example in a plausible manner. In order to stimulate formation of the desired picture in the minds of the listeners, details should be presented in the proper order. A discussion of a border dispute between India and Pakistan probably should include in the narration an explanation of the topography. Otherwise the auditors may be uncertain as to the nature of the terrain. Once they have mentally placed the scene in a river valley or in rice-paddy country, confusion will result if you say, "Oh, I forgot to mention that these men were fighting in mountainous country with cliffs sometimes as sheer as elevator shafts."

(5) While remaining consistent with the facts, tell the story in such a fashion that it will facilitate listener identification. Do not strain truth or credulity in the process; but, within the limitations of factual reporting, tailor the story to the particular speaking situation. Do not ignore the needs, values, and interests of those who listen.

(6) Use a sufficient number and variety of illustrations. A general audience will usually include various economic, social, and intellectual levels and a correspondingly wide range of interests, attitudes, and experiences. One example may be insufficient to support an important point, since it may not be equally interesting or meaningful to all of the listeners. Therefore, when necessary, use several illustrations drawn from the major fields of interest represented in the audience. The utilization of several examples to support a particular head adds logical and psychological strength by offering a more comprehensive coverage and by giving the impression of presenting a formidable mass of evidence.

(7) Occasionally it may be necessary to defend your examples as being fair representatives of the available evidence, rather than exceptions.

(8) Use the Factors of Interest (discussed in the next chapter) to develop the example. If deficient in its appeal to involuntary attention, much of its power will be lost.

(9) The details used to develop the example should be accurate. For instance, if you use an illustration from the shop because some of the listeners are foremen, you must demonstrate an exact grasp of information. Otherwise, not only your example, but your entire speech may be discredited.

The Undeveloped Factual Illustration

Nature and Purpose of the Undeveloped Factual Illustration. This type of example is undetailed, condensed, and true-to-fact. Consisting of only essential elements, it is much shorter than the typical full-length illustration. Of course, a maximum word length cannot be assigned to the brief example. The basic point to remember is that some detailed factual illustrations might be as long as ten or fifteen minutes, whereas some undeveloped ones might be less than ten seconds.

The short illustration has several important values. Since the abbreviated example requires less time than the detailed one, a greater number of condensed illustrations can be presented within a given period. Thus the speaker is enabled to present a more adequate coverage and to appeal to additional fields of interest

Robert T. Oliver, author and educator, in his lecture "Writers Are People" shows that it is possible to compress much supporting evidence into a short space of time by means of the abbreviated example.[2]

Statement of Main Head

I should like to add just a few words about how writers go about their business. . . . While other people occasionally think about writing, they do it. . . . Those who can write apparently do; and those who don't apparently can't. Inspiration, at least, surely has little or nothing to do with it.

Short Illustrations

For many years I have made a cursory search of literary history, finding all the examples I could of inspirational writing. There are few instances. Julia Ward Howe wrote "The Battle Hymn of the Republic" in a burst of inspiration. Francis Scott Key was moved to write the "Star-Spangled Banner" during the night he spent on a British battleship while it shelled Fort Henry in Baltimore Harbor. Lord Byron, when he was sixteen years old, published a volume of poetry which was savagely attacked in the *Edinburgh Review*. When Byron read the review, he shut himself up all night long in his study with a bottle of wine and a ream of paper. In the morning he emerged with his white-hot satiric poem on "British Bards and Scotch Reviewers"—a poem still worth reading.

Restatement of Main Head

But these are exceptions, and there are mighty few of them to be found. Real writers work hard at their job, just as systematically and with as little regard for inspiration as do carpenters or chemists.

Short, Illustrations

Sinclair Lewis is a fairly typical specimen of the writer at work. He rented an office and spent five hours a day in it—writing, not waiting for the Muse to strike. He made it a practice to enter his office, put a sheet of paper in the typewriter, and start writing. Of course he had to throw a good many sheets away—but he forced his mind into concentrated activity, and he got his writing done.

Jack London wrote 2,000 words a day, day after day, week after week, month after month. I have an enormous admiration for his

[2]Used by special permission of Dr. Oliver.

Restatement of Main Head

tenacity and productivity. Two thousand words may not seem like a lot; I myself, on occasion, have written as many as six or seven thousand at one long sitting. But the real secret is continuity and regularity. The real secret is to regard writing as a job to be done, and to settle down to doing it, without ever stopping to inquire whether the mood, or the conditions, or the time is right.

Short Illustrations

Examples of this sort could be multiplied endlessly—for this is truly the way in which writers do their job. Anthony Trollope was a postal inspector in England who decided to write novels. He accomplished it by going into his study every evening after dinner and writing for two hours. If he finished a chapter halfway through his stint, he simply began another. Once he completed a novel when his work period was only half ended. Instead of stopping to celebrate, he pulled out another sheet of paper, wrote the title of his next novel at its top, and kept on with his work. . . .

In Elmira I have visited the study of Mark Twain, where he completed *Huckleberry Finn*. It was hard work and he didn't enjoy it; but as in all his writing, he simply stayed with it, day after day, regardless of how he felt. This, too, is the way Melville wrote Moby Dick—and no doubt it is the way Shakespeare wrote his plays. To cite my own experience at this point is truly a descent from the sublime to the ridiculous. But I can only testify that sometimes I enjoy writing and sometimes it is like going to the dentist—but I do it anyway, regardless of feelings, and I must say I don't seem to notice that the quality is affected for better or for worse by the state of mind. Inspiration, in short, doesn't seem to have anything to do with it.

Restatement of Main Head

The use of the terse example for making a swift survey is shown in the following passage from one of President Kennedy's "State of the Union" messages, as reported in the *Philadelphia Inquirer*.

Statement of Main Head

I can report to you that the state of this old but youthful Union, in the 175th year of its life, is good.

Short Illustrations

In the world beyond our borders, steady progress has been made in building a world of order. The people of West Berlin remain both free and secure. A settlement, though still precarious, has been reached in Laos. The spearpoint of aggression has been blunted in Vietnam. The end of agony may be in sight in the Congo. The doctrine of troika is dead. And, while danger continues, a deadly threat has been removed from Cuba.

At home, the recession is behind us. Well over a million more men and women are working today than were working two years ago. The average factory workweek is once again more than 40 hours; our industries are turning out more goods than ever before; and more than half of the manufacturing capacity that lay silent and wasted 100 weeks ago is humming with activity.

Application to Main Head

But we cannot be satisfied to rest here. This is the side of the hill, not the top. The mere absence of war is not peace. The mere absence of recession is not growth. We have made a beginning—but we have only just begun.

The Hypothetical Illustration

Nature and Purpose of the Hypothetical Illustration. When you are unable to secure a relevant factual example or when you wish to apply a story more closely or more vividly to the particular needs of your listeners than a true-to-fact example will permit, you may wish to use an imaginary incident or happening.

The hypothetical illustration is a vivid method of explaining a complicated or technical process. For example, instead of describing how a theater panel board controls lighting effects, place an imaginary technician at the board to pull the appropriate switches, turn the wheels, and punch the buttons. The narration of such a fictitious situation adds human interest to what otherwise might be dull explanation.

The hypothetical illustration is also an excellent method of predicting future events or of making the future seem graphically real. As an example, during a "skull-practice session" prior to a bowl game, a football coach, worried about his team's postseason lethargy, tried to revitalize the squad. A continuation of the team's half hearted preparation, he warned, would lead to dire results. He then proceeded to relate a fictitious play-by-play development of the game, with its fumbles, missed blocks, and faultily executed pass patterns; he pictured the gloom of the badly defeated squad on the long bus and plane ride home and the embarrassed, awkward welcome that awaited them upon return to campus; he even quoted comments by television and newspaper reporters as well as snatches of the conversation of disappointed student supporters

In his address to an audience of more than 200,000 massed in front of the Lincoln Memorial in late summer of 1963, Martin Luther King, Jr., used this striking hypothetical illustration to vitalize and clarify his appeal.[3]

Statement of Main Head

I am not unmindful that some of you have come here out of great trials and tribulations. . . . Go back to Mississippi, go back to Alabama, go back to South Carolina, go back to Georgia, go back to Louisiana, go back to the slums and ghettos of our northern cities, knowing that somehow this situation can and will be changed. Let us not wallow in the valley of despair.

Extended

I say to you today, my friends, even though we face the difficulties of today and tomorrow, I still have a dream. It is a dream deeply rooted in the American dream.

I have a dream that one day this nation will rise up and live out

[3]Copyright 1963 by Martin Luther King, Jr. Reprinted by permission of Joan Daves.

the true meaning of its creed: "We hold these truths to be self-evident; that all men are created equal."

I have a dream that one day on the red hills of Georgia the sons of former slaves and the sons of former slave-holders will be able to sit down together at the table of brotherhood.

I have a dream that one day even the state of Mississippi, a state sweltering with the heat of injustice, sweltering with the heat of oppression, will be transformed into an oasis of freedom and justice.

Hypothetical

I have a dream that my four little children will one day live in a nation where they will not be judged by the color of their skin but by the content of their character.

I have a dream today.

I have a dream that one day, down in Alabama, with its vicious racists, with its Governor having his lips dripping with the words of interposition and nullification, one day right there in Alabama little black boys and little black girls will be able to join hands with little white boys and white girls as sisters and brothers.

I have a dream today.

Illustration

I have a dream that one day every valley shall be exalted, every hill and mountain shall be made low, the rough places will be made plane, and the crooked places will be made straight, and the glory of the Lord shall be revealed, and all flesh shall see it together.

Application of Illustration to Main Head

This is our hope. This is the faith with which I return to the South. . . . With this faith we will be able to hew out of the mountain of despair a stone of hope . . . knowing that we will be free one day.

Suggestions for the Effective Use of the Hypothetical Illustration. In addition to the suggestions mentioned previously for the detailed factual illustration, there are several additional points you should consider when using the fictitious example.

(1) Never present a hypothetical example as being true-to-fact. Such intellectual dishonesty violates your moral obligation to the listeners and to truth, and, if detected, will prejudice your audience against you and your speech.

(2) Ordinarily, avoid using an invented example if a true one is available.

(3) The hypothetical illustration should be consistent with reality. It should appear reasonable, probable, and capable of happening. Wild flights of the imagination usually add little to the logical development of thought.

(4) Recognize the limited effectiveness of the hypothetical example as a means of logical proof. Since the audience realizes that the hypothetical did not actually happen, other forms of support, such as the factual illustration, quotation, or statistics, usually will be more persuasive as logical validation. The relative power of the hypothetical and factual illustration was once vividly demonstrated by a mother who was having difficulty keeping her two young sons from putting things in their ears and

noses. Her recitation of hypothetical examples of possible harmful effects failed to impress the youngsters. But, after one of the boys was sent to the hospital with an infected ear, the mother had a compelling true example to discourage such behavior.

Statistics

Nature and Purpose of Statistics. Statistics are figures that help the speaker develop a point. When skillfully presented, statistical data is both informative and persuasive. Unfortunately, however, it is one of the most misused forms of support. Too frequently speakers are so subject-centered in their orientation that they forget the limitations of their listeners. Instead of supplying a freshet of simplified, interpreted, and dramatized data, they often pour into the ears of the listeners a flood of confusingly complex, raw, and deadly dull numbers.

A claim by a speaker that it costs less for a family today to send a child to college than it did a generation ago would demand documentary proof that could be provided only by statistics. In support of his claims, the speaker might point out that according to the Carnegie Foundation for the Advancement of Teaching "the net cost of higher education per student—for subsistence and tuition—has actually gone down in constant dollars by about 9 per cent" since 1929-30. The base period 1929–30, he should explain, was selected "because it was the last academic year of 'normal' time before the full impact of the Depression." In further substantiation of his point, the speaker could cite Foundation findings that although tuition costs have "risen consistently since 1929–30, this rise has been only one third as fast as the rise in real per capital income. In addition, while in 1929–30 state, local, and federal governments contributed only a few per cent of the cost per student of higher education, combined government funding now accounts for more than 70 per cent. Subsistence costs of students are now paid in part by such programs as veterans' and Social Security benefits and Basic Opportunity grants, while in 1929–30 such support was nonexistent."

The assertion that "the heart is a strong, tough, and durable organ" is a sterile abstraction. You could give specificity and vividness to the concept by saying something like this:

> "How much do you know about nature's most perfect pump? I'm speaking about the terrific power plan that is your heart. If your car were as efficient as your heart, you could drive 1,000,000 miles without going to a garage for a motor overhaul. In a single minute, the heart beats about 72 times and produces enough energy to lift a 78-pound dumbell a foot off the floor. In an

average lifetime, the heart beats nearly 3,000,000 times and generates enough energy to lift the *U.S.S. Missouri* out of the water. As you probably know, the blood supplies the body with vital nutrition, carries away wastes, regulates the water balance, equalizes the body temperature, distributes various glandular secretions, and aids in the defense against disease. To accomplish these functions the heart must push a continuous flow of blood through a complex network of tubes. If the heart falters for even a moment, unconsciousness ensures. If it stops for more than a few minutes, you die. How much blood do you think your heart must pump each minute even when you are resting? Two pints? Maybe three? The answer is five quarts. During my five-minute speech your heart has pumped over six gallons of blood. If you are normally active today, your heart will pump about 5,000 gallons. If you live an average life span, your heart will pump a total of nearly 130,000,000 gallons. How long do you believe it takes for the blood to make a complete circuit from heart-to-arteries-to-capillaries-to-veins and back to the heart? Fifteen minutes? An hour? The answer is a little over a minute. May I suggest that the next time you are in a reflective mood you might give thanks for the strong, sturdy heart which labors so durably in your behalf."

Suggestions for the Effective Use of Statistics. The following suggestions should help make your statistics more interesting, meaningful, and persuasive.

(1) Not only should you make certain that the statistic closely supports the heading it is intended to develop but you should also be sure that this relationship and its implications are clearly recognized by the listeners.

(2) Do not use too many statistics. A speech crammed with figures usually produces confusion and apathy.

(3) Avoid being overprecise. The rounding off of figures makes them easier to understand and to remember. For instance, it would be sufficiently accurate to say "eight and a half billion" rather than $8,474,867,-293.51—and there would be only two numbers instead of a confusing total of twelve. Simplifying statistics to approximate accuracy is even more important when presenting several sets of figures. Of course, under certain circumstances exactness is essential. The purpose for which the statistics are being used should determine whether approximate or exact accuracy is desired.

(4) To make statistics meaningful, bring them within the sohere of the experiences and interests of the listeners. Mere numbers have little value unless interpreted according to the needs and understanding of the auditors. For example, the terms "millions" and "billions" are used glibly by government planners, military experts, and the lay public. Even if we

realize that a billion dollars is a thousand times greater than a million dollars, the term still lacks tangibility. Recognizing that such abstract figures are beyond the comprehension of most of us, Alexander Summer, president of the National Association of Real Estate Boards, explained the difference between millions and billions: "A million dollars in crisp new $1,000 bills would make a pile eight inches high. But if we tried to pile up a billion dollars we'd find that it stretched up in the sky 110 feet higher than the Washington Monument." A statement that an anniversary edition of the *Miami Herald* required 1,182,000 pounds of newsprint and 23,600 pounds of ink was made more vivid by the explanation that the newsprint would fill twenty railway boxcars and the ink would fill more than ten thousand quart milk bottles—or nearly every ballpoint pen south of the Mason-Dixon line.

(5) A thinking audience will be more likely to accept statistics if you can attribute them to some recognized source, as the Department of Agriculture, the American Automobile Association, *The Statesman's Yearbook,* or UNESCO.

(6) With tongue in cheek, Carlyle wrote, "you may prove anything by figures." Since everyone knows that self-interest often motivates the slanting of statistical evidence, you may at times have to defend your statistics by demonstrating that the compiling agency—even one generally accepted as reliable—is free of ulterior motives.

(7) Occasionally even a reputable, well-meaning source may disseminate phony, not knowable, hard-to-trace, or distorted statistics. Therefore, you may need to demonstrate to your listeners that your figures meet tests such as the following: Are the data accepted by experts and corroborated by other findings? Are the samples fairly selected and sufficiently numerous? Do they cover the area adequately? Have the data been accurately reported and classified? Have they been correctly interpreted with proper inferences drawn? Even the most carefully prepared figures from the most reputable sources bear careful scrutiny. Writing in *Fortune,* Daniel Seligman branded as "phony" any meaningless or hard-to-trace statistic, even though attributable to a reputable source. Some of his examples: the statement from the FBI that the annual "crime bill" of the United States is $22 billion; the National Safety Council's appraisal that the "economic loss" resulting from traffic accidents totals $6.2 billion annually; the *Nation's* pegging of the rat population of New York City at 9 million; television psychologist Joyce Brothers' declaration that "the American girl kisses an average of 79 men before getting married." And, according to a news item in the *Miami Herald,* even the United States Weather Bureau may at times be suspect:

> Weather Bureau officials revealed Tuesday they have been keeping Miami's 18-day run of 90-and-over temperatures out of northern newspapers by sending them cooler Miami Beach readings. . . . Because of the change, the highest "Miami" reading to appear in

> northern papers during July was only 89 degrees. . . . The change means that "Miami" temperatures—in northern papers—will be lower in the summer and higher in the winter. Gordon E. Dunn, chief of the Miami bureau, said the switch was made partly because of Dade's [Dade County—Miami's county] dependence on tourism. . . .

(8) Do not use outdated statistics. The value of most statistics, and some in particular, declines rapidly with the passage of time. For instance, a "best seller" sales report may be accurate at the time of release, but two weeks later may be badly out of line with current sales.

(9) Avoid an indiscriminate or misleading use of the term *average.* An umbrella label, the word *average* represents three different measures: in a series of figures, *mean* is the quotient, found by dividing the sum of the items by the number of items; *mode* is the figure that occurs most often; *median* is the figure that falls midway between the two extremities, so that half of the items are on one side of it and half on the other. Thus, if part-time salesman A earns $10,000 a year, B earns $10,000, C earns $12,000, D earns $12,400, E earns $15,000, F earns $26,000, and G earns $48,000, the mean salary is $19,055, the mode is $10,000, and the median is $12,400. Select the kind of average that best represents the core meaning of the statistics and, perhaps, explain to the listeners the appropriateness of your usage.

(10) At times statistics may be made more acceptable by referring specifically to the source where they may be found, for example, the *New York Times,* December 19, 1982; the September 23, 1982, issue of *Newsweek;* or last night's edition of the local paper.

Comparison (Analogy)

The analogy is a form of reasoning in which resemblances are noted between objects, ideas, or institutions and inferences are drawn on the basis of the similarities. The two types of comparisons are the literal and the figurative.

The Literal Comparison

Nature and Purpose of the Literal Comparison. The literal comparison compares ideas or objects of the same class, such as rivers to rivers, cities to cities, automobile to automobile, and disease to disease.

One function of the literal comparison is to serve as logical proof. The basis of analogical reasoning is this: if two things possess essentially comparable characteristics, a proposition that is true of one may be true

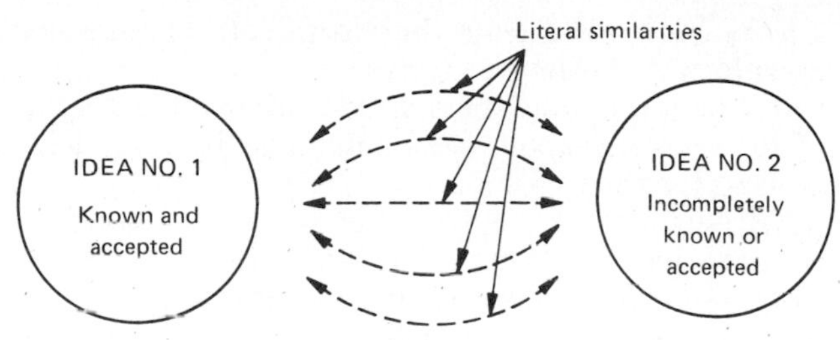

Fig. 7. Literal Comparison

of the other. Sometimes listeners may be motivated to endorse a formerly unacceptable inference concerning an idea if they are shown the resemblances between that idea and a second idea of which they approve. In addressing the National War College, Charles H. Smith, Jr., chairman of the board, Chamber of Commerce of the United States, based his entire argument upon the logical proof and psychological implications inherent in an extended comparison, excerpts of which are presented.[4] By means of analogy, Mr. Smith tried to establish as an inexorable law that the fighting effectiveness of a country's military force depends upon the strength of that country's socioeconomic system. In accordance with this principle, the Romans won their conflict with the Greeks and Napoleon lost to the British. Because the covering law remains constant, the strength of the U.S. armed forces of today depends upon the strength of the country's socioeconomic system. As an extension of this thought, Mr. Smith wanted to establish that present and previous socialistic practices had weakened the American socioeconomic system—and therefore the military effectiveness—by financing major social programs through deficit spending.

> I'm sure you all remember King Pyrrhus from Military History I. But I'd like to review a little of that history to make a point. The time was roughly 280 BC, the scene Tarentum, a Greek colony on the heel of the Italian boot.
>
> The people of Tarentum had dealt cavalierly with some quaint barbarians from the North and—not being very warlike themselves—they began to worry about the possible consequences.
>
> In the name of Hellenistic unity and brotherhood, they appealed for help to Pyrrhus of Epirus.
>
> Pyrrhus, in the name of Hellenistic unity and brotherhood, had conquered half of Macedon. He was one of the best generals of his time. And he was itching for something else to conquer, but he realized that he'd gone about as far as he could safely go in his immediate neighborhood. So he welcomed the invitation from Tarentum.
>
> In the spring of 280 he arrived on the Italian peninsula with an army of 25,000.

[4] *Vital Speeches*, October 15, 1974, pp. 20–21.

The barbarians from the North called themselves Romans. Pyrrhus fought them three times.

He won the first battle, in 280, after a hard fight—largely by use of his secret weapon, elephants. The Romans lost a total of 9,000 men to Pyrrhus's 4,000.

At Asculum, in 278, they met again. And again, Pyrrhus won. The Romans lost 6,000 men, Pyrrhus lost 3,500. But among the 3,500 were most of his generals and his best troops.

It was at Asculum that he made the remark by which his name enters our language: "One more such victory and I am undone."

And he was right.

They met a third and final time at Beneventum, in 275. The Romans won that battle decisively. Pyrrhus returned home with only 8,500 of the 25,000 men he had when he started.

He died three years later, when an old woman on a rooftop in Argos threw a chamber pot at him. Which proves, I guess, that not all old generals just fade away.

In terms of tactical ability, Pyrrhus and his Roman opponents were closely matched. What Pyrrhus could not match was the total Roman system; the combination of high morale, administration, organization and economics that enabled the Romans to keep coming back for more.

Pyrrhus and his army were wholly exposed. They could not recover from a single major defeat. The Roman armies, like the tail of a lizard, were expendable extensions of a system able to regrow what it had lost.

King Pyrrhus's Roman campaign may not be the first example in history of the essential link between military strength and socioeconomic strength, but it is probably the most famous.

After the fall of Rome, as you know, the Western world experienced a long era of feudal economics and personal generalship.

I believe many historians cite the defeat of Napoleon Bonaparte to mark the end of this period; the end of the time when the ruler of a country could personally direct the details of major battles. Ever since, war has become an increasingly complex matter of transportation, communication, coordination, supply and technology.

It's interesting to note, in passing, that economics was one of Napoleon's major weaknesses as a ruler.

In his biography of Napoleon, Vincent Cronin comments on the technological and economic backwardness of the French Empire, in contrast to Great Britain.

Napoleon, he says, "considered economic sacrifices a small price to pay for equality and the rights of man. He who thought in terms of honor believed that others must think in those terms also. It was not true. The ordinary people of the Empire thought of their comforts and of attractive novelties in the shops."

Napoleon had other faults, of course. I understand the British considered him a little weak on naval strategy.

In any case, the point is that we have now reached a stage in his-

> tory where the military forces of a nation can be worse than its socioeconomic system, but they cannot be better.
>
> It is our technological capacity that limits our ability to forestall a nuclear war as well as our ability to win one, if "win" is an applicable term. It is our economic strength that determines the amount of national resources that can be devoted to lesser wars at an acceptable cost to civilian morale. And of course, it is our economic strength that determines our technological capacity.
>
> So the resources, morale and technology in support of a modern military effort are determined by a nation's economic base.
>
> At any given time, we have a finite amount of resources available to devote to the satisfaction of our needs and desires. We may shift resources from one sector of the economy, or one industry, or one government program to another. But the total of claims on our resources cannot exceed the total of those resources.
>
> I realize that that statement sounds so simple and so obvious you may well wonder why I make it.
>
> I make it because, simple and obvious though it is, we have been running the country lately in a fashion that suggests either ignorance of this fundamental truth or a willful decision to ignore it.

A second purpose of the literal comparison is to make ideas clearer by comparing a known or understood idea with one that is unknown or misunderstood. At the ceremony commemorating the 175th anniversary of the signing of the Declaration of Independence, Harry S. Truman, then President, used the following analogy to make more explicit the difficulties in setting up the United Nations Organization[5]—thereby promoting both understanding and conviction.

> We believe in the United Nations. We believe it is based on the right ideas, as our own country is. We believe it can grow to be strong and accomplish its high purposes.
>
> But the United Nations faces stern, determined opposition. This is an old story. The Declaration of Independence was also met by determined opposition. A spokesman for the British King called the Declaration "absurd," "visionary," and "subversive." The ideas of freedom and equality and self-government were fiercely opposed in every country by the vested interests and the reactionaries.
>
> Today, the idea of an international organization to keep the peace is being attacked and undermined and fought by reactionary forces everywhere—and particularly by the forces of Soviet communism.
>
> The United Nations will not succeed without a struggle, just as the Declaration of Independence did not succeed without a struggle. But the American people are not afraid. We have taken our stand beside other free men, because we have known for 175 years that free men must stand together. We have joined in the defense of free-

[5] *Vital Speeches*, July 15, 1951, p. 578.

dom without hesitation and without fear, because we have known for 175 years that freedom must be defended. . . .

There is another way in which our situation today is much like that of the Americans of 1776. Now, once more, we are engaged in launching a new idea—one that has been talked about for centuries, but never successfully put into effect. In those earlier days we were launching a new kind of national government. This time we are creating a new kind of international organization. We have joined in setting up the United Nations to prevent war and to safeguard peace and freedom.

Suggestions for the Effective Use of the Literal Comparison. (1) The analogy should be well adapted logically and psychologically to the total speaking situation.

(2) The essential elements of the two things involved should be comparable. One of the chief weaknesses of the analogy as a means of logical proof is that the characteristics of any two ideas, objects, institutions, or relationships must necessarily vary considerably. Therefore, it is essential that the two things under comparison be alike in significant details and that the points of similarity be as numerous as possible.

(3) Since differences inevitably will exist between the halves of an analogy, do not attempt to conceal genuine dissimilarities. Admit them, but show that they do not affect the validity of the analogy you are making. Of course, if unlikenesses do emasculate your particular comparison, avoid using the comparison.

(4) Do not direct attention to unimportant differences; the audience may attach undue significance to them.

(5) The basis for comparison should be understood and accepted by the listeners. To point out similarities between two unfamiliar things merely serves to connect unknowns. Similarly, conviction is not furthered by linking two ideas neither of which is acceptable to the audience.

(6) The facts upon which the analogy is based must be accurate. As in all forms of support, the data used in developing the comparison must be reliable, objective, and verifiable.

The Figurative Comparison

Nature and Purpose of the Figurative Comparison. The figurative analogy stresses unique relationships between objects or ideas of different classes, as a man to a mountain, a government to a ship, a countenance to a thundercloud, or charity to rain. Its chief value lies in its capacity for striking, graphic imagery. An idea frequently assumes greater clarity, significance, and acceptability if singular resemblances can be pointed out between that idea and a second idea that appears to be completely differ-

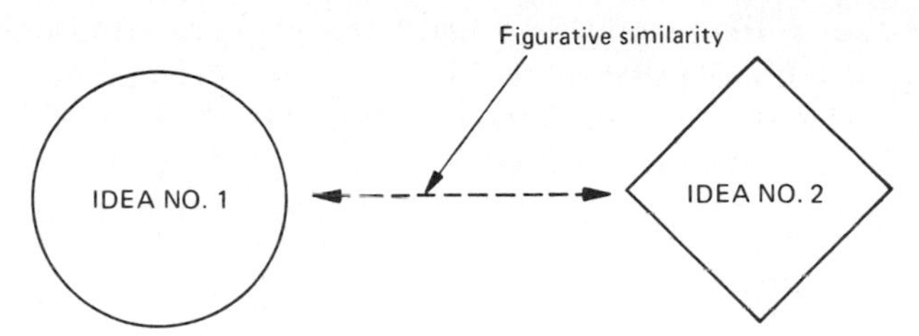

Fig. 8. Figurative Comparison

ent. Usually figurative comparisons are brief and take the form of similes and metaphors.

Richard Gilman attempted to develop an image of Reynolds Price's *The Surface of Earth* by means of this figurative comparison: "'The Surface of Earth' comes to us like a great lumbering archaic beast, taking its place among our literary fauna with the stiff queer presence of the representative of a species thought to be extinct. A mastodon sprung to life from beneath an ice-field, it smells at first of time stopped, evolution arrested." In his funeral oration four generations ago at his brother's grave, Robert Ingersoll expressed a strong emotional appeal with this comparison: "Life is a narrow vale between the cold and barren peaks of two eternities. We strive in vain to look beyond the heights. We cry aloud, and the only answer is the echo of our wailing cry. From the voiceless lips of the unreplying dead there comes no word; but in the night of death hope sees a star, and listening love can hear the rustle of a wing." When evangelist Billy Graham was asked in Australia whether he thought his revivals would produce a lasting effect, he responded with this implied analogy: "The effects of a bath don't last long, but you need it, and it's good for you."

To describe Senator Vandenberg's oratory, Dean Acheson employed this figurative comparison:

> Vandenberg would often be carried away by the hyperbole of his own rotund phrases. My father used to illustrate this very human characteristic by the example of a horse we owned years ago crossing the bridge over the Connecticut River at Middletown. She was gentle and well disposed. But as the buggy began to rumble across the bridge's planking, she would begin to prick up her ears and begin to move faster. More rumble brought more speed, until by the time the Portland shore was reached she was in full gallop and quite a lather. In the same way Vandenberg worked himself up to "a first showdown as to where President Roosevelt's treaty-making power leaves off and that of the Senate begins."

Suggestions for the Effective Use of the Figurative Comparison. (1) Recognize the limitations of the figurative comparison when used as logical validation. Because the things being compared are of different classes, the bonds of similarity usually will be less numerous and more easily refuted than in the case of a suitable literal analogy. The famed psychiatrist Dr. William Menninger once attempted to defend his thesis that more emphasis should be put on cure of mental illness and less on exact diagnosis by stating: "One does not have to know the cause of a fire to put it out." The weakness of this figurative analogy as substantiation was revealed when one critic asked: "In the case of an oil fire wouldn't it be necessary to know that the blaze was caused by burning oil?" The questioner's point was obvious: chemicals, not cascading streams of water, should be used to put out an oil fire. Dr. Menninger's analogy was vivid, but easily refuted.

(2) The figurative analogy should be striking, relevant, appropriate, and credible. Avoid analogies that offer only strained, incongruous relationships.

(3) Usually the figurative comparison should be brief. Unless unusually impressive, it probably should not consume more than a minute.

Testimony

Nature and Purpose of Testimony. Testimony usually takes the form of a direct quotation or a paraphrase and may be drawn from a great variety of sources: a remark by a bus driver, a telecast of a news commentator, a formal state paper by the President, a headline from the evening paper, an advertisement in the classified section, an excerpt from the *Congressional Record*, a dialogue between the attorneys for the defense and the prosecution, statements from a famous historical figure, a verse from the Bible, and so forth.

One advantage of testimony as a form of support is that it is *easily secured.* A quotation may be selected from the billions of words expressed orally or recorded in print.

Frequently, testimony is *persuasive.* An audience that is unwilling to accept an idea or program upon the speaker's personal recommendation may be rendered more receptive if shown that prominent experts or the general public endorse the plan. As Wilfred Trotter states in his *Instincts of the Herd in Peace and War,* we are more sensitive to the opinions of our fellowmen than to any other single influence. Practically all of our actions and thoughts are influenced, if not controlled, by our social consciousness.

Testimony can also be *striking* and *attention-commanding.* A student vitalized the difficulties of cancer research by this quotation:

> Professor Oberling said before the Cancer Institute of Paris, "Today we are sadder and wiser . . . we have the uneasy sensation of knowing both too much and too little at the same time. Too much because we offer a whole series of solutions. . . . The real cause is where all the causes meet. This point, we may be sure, is in the cell. And it is here that we know too little." He goes on to say that the doctors are like one who is asked to explain the workings of an automobile from its external appearance. "We can analyze it, tell what it is made of, what its fuel is, but we may not open the hood."

A direct quotation or a paraphrase may also serve to *clarify* an idea. Examples: to explain the arduous efforts needed for a young singer to qualify for the Metropolitan opera, cite Beverly Sills on the subject; to interpret the seriousness of syndicated crime in the United States, quote the head of the FBI; to illustrate the difficulties of controlling the crowd at the National Open golf tournament, use statements by some of the players or attendants.

There are two major weaknesses of testimony when used as logical proof. Instead of actually proving per se that a certain belief is valid, a specific action is desirable, or that a particular event has happened, such evidence may indicate merely that the person or persons making the statement possess certain opinions. Historians are constantly discovering that traditionally accepted interpretations concerning events of the past need modification; the testimony of previous historians—and their sources—has been inaccurate. Furthermore, in an address before the American Historical Association, famed historian Arthur M. Schlesinger, Jr., admitted that his experiences as a maker of history within the Kennedy administration had caused him to lose faith in the historian's use of testimony—diaries, official documents, and news clippings. Such standard evidence, he said, "is often incomplete, misleading, and erroneous." Occasionally a convict who has served perhaps twenty years is released because belatedly unearthed evidence has demonstrated that he has been wrongly imprisoned. Witnesses had testified against him; a jury had stated that he was guilty; a judge had pronounced sentence; society had accepted the judicial decision. However, such human judgment did not alter the true facts of the case. As a reliable index of the future, the quoted judgment of man is often a weak reed indeed. Perhaps you remember that the British prime minister in 1939 predicted there would be no war, a commentator in 1941 predicted German armies would overrun Russia within six months, the pollsters in 1948 wrote off Harry S. Truman's chances for the presidency, top United States defense and intelligence officials in 1961 apparently endorsed the feasibility of the Bay of Pigs invasion, and almost no political analyst in 1980 predicted a landslide victory for presidential candidate Ronald Reagan.

Another weakness of testimony is that thinking listeners realize that a modicum of research can unearth statements to fit almost any side of any question. Occasional revolutions were advocated as a beneficial tonic by Thomas Jefferson. Child labor was endorsed by Alexander Hamilton. America's participation in the Mexican War was denounced as immoral by Abraham Lincoln. The Old Testament preaches the stern philosophy of an eye for an eye, whereas the New Testament teaches forgiveness and gentleness. Economists differ on the remedies for creeping inflation. Even eye witness testimony to an accident is frequently contradictory.

As you have no doubt already observed, testimony overlaps other forms of support. A direct quotation or a paraphrase may contain statistics, comparison, illustration, explanation, deductive or inductive reasoning, or quotations. The identifying feature that separates testimony from most other forms of support is that the speaker attributes the statements he is making to some source other than himself.

Suggestions for the Effective Use of Testimony. (1) Testimony should be relevant and appropriate to the total speaking situation.

(2) If you have implied that you are presenting an exact quotation, report verbatim. Do not amend the statement in any way, including any characteristics of delivery—like a raised eyebrow and shrug—that might distort the meaning intended by the source.

(3) Avoid lifting a passage out of context in such a way that the meaning will be altered. For instance, the original meaning would be violated if the phrase "If the quarterback is in top form" were omitted from the statement: "If the quarterback is in top form, State will beat Purdue on Saturday."

(4) Indicate to the audience when you are paraphrasing. Your word choice and manner of presentation should faithfully reflect the intended meaning of the original quotation.

(5) Avoid using the words "quote" and "end of quotation" unless it is exceedingly important that the listeners know exactly which words belong to your source. Ordinarily, let a change of pitch, rate, or emphasis indicate the beginning and ending of a quotation.

(6) Refrain from introducing a quotation by a trite phrase such as: "I have a quotation here," or, "I will now read you a quote." Instead say something like this: " Last week in a speech in Chicago, Senator Edward Kennedy stated . . ." or, "On his twenty-first birthday, Theodore Roosevelt wrote these words in his diary. . . ."

(7) Keep quotations short. As a rule, two or three different references are more effective than one long quotation.

(8) The source of the quotation should be intellectually and emotionally acceptable to the audience. Listeners are more receptive to ideas advanced by individuals they know, admire, and trust. If the person (or organization) who has made the quoted statement is unfamiliar, explain why his observations are worthy of acceptance. Mention his title, or his

background of academic, scientific, political, or life experiences that qualify him as an authority in the field. Remember, of course, that expertise in one area does not qualify a person as an authority in nonrelated fields. Further, under unusual circumstances you may wish to demonstrate that the source is reasonably objective and that he has had opportunity personally to examine the facts, preferably at firsthand. As Plautus suggests, "one eye witness is worth ten hearsays." Critical listeners will reject testimony that appears to be motivated by prejudice or self-interest, will insist that the statement be based upon firsthand information, and will place reliance in only those sources possessing reputations for consistent and accurate judgments.

(9) The recency of the quotation may be of considerable importance. One's thinking must undergo alterations in order to adjust to changes in environment. Avoid using an out-of-date quotation to represent the present thinking of an individual, particularly if there is reason to believe that he may have changed his mind.

(10) Sometimes the manner in which the statement was made affects its validity. Was the person emotionally disturbed? Did he make the remark carelessly in an off-guard moment? Did he expect to be quoted? Was the statement carefully prepared and representative of his thinking on the subject? Was it accurately recorded by a responsible agency?

(11) If speaking on a controversial point, you may need to document the testimony. In such a case, specify where you read the statement. If the statement was made orally, explain whether you heard it personally. If you secured it secondhand, where did your informant get his information? How reliable is the intermediary? the original source?

Explanation

Nature and Purpose of Explanation. Unfortunately, explanation cannot be defined more specifically than to say that it is exposition or description for the purpose of making an idea clear, vivid, or persuasive. Broadly speaking, the entire speech to inform may be considered explanation because its sole purpose is to explain—to foster understanding and convey knowledge. In the more circumscribed meaning as a Form of Support, explanation refers to the explication necessary to make intelligible and/or believable a particular superior heading. In the following excerpt, observe how the communicator used explication to make his point clear.

> And just as the good days are exhilarating, so are the bad days [of summer] somewhat frightening—especially when lightning is involved.

That situation has brought words of advice on how to stay alive during electrical storms. Some of the tips from the experts include: Stay indoors, get away from high places. On the farm, don't use farm equipment or metal tools and stop all tractor work. Never go beneath a tree. If you're playing golf, get rid of your clubs, cleated shoes, and umbrellas. If you're in a car, stay there. Don't handle flammable liquids in the open. Don't plug in electrical appliances. Stay off the telephone. Don't swim or go into the water in a small boat. If you're carrying an umbrella, get rid of it. If caught in the open, flatten out on the ground—at least twice as far from the tallest object as the object is high (that's at least 80 feet from a 40-foot tree).

Sometimes, lightning warns you before striking and the National Weather Service suggests, "If you feel an electrical charge, if your hair stands on end or your skin tingles, lightning may be about to strike you. Drop to the ground immediately."

Each individual can keep reasonably safe by following these tips for safety during electrical storms which are almost certain to come with some regularity before summer ends.

To explain the aim of liberal education, Gordon N. Ray (secretary general of the John Simon Guggenheim Memorial Foundation) employed the following exposition:[6]

The aim of liberal education, then, is not primarily the amassing of a large amount of factual information. Rather it is the enlargement of mental capacity that can come through the process of acquiring, ordering, and reflecting upon such information. With this widening of intellectual horizons comes the ability to see things in proportion as they really are, that is to say, the attainment of a degree of wisdom. Learning gives the man who masters it a wider context than immediate experience can possibly provide, though of course such learning has to be proved and validated by experience before it can mean very much. The lessons that result from this process are neither new nor surprising; but they have to be relearned by every generation, and modern life is so complex and misleading that they have become harder than ever to master.

An important method of promoting understanding is the use of definitions. To help the listeners perceive the meaning of a term, you may employ one or more of the following procedures: (1) explain what the term does not mean, as did Dr. Ray in the immediately preceding excerpt; (2) compare or contrast the unfamiliar idea with something that is understood; (3) use one or more factual or hypothetical illustrations to convert the abstract term into picturable reality; (4) describe the nature, function,

[6]Mr. Ray's speech "Is Liberal Education Still Needed" was printed and distributed by Syracuse University.

or historical background of the referent; (5) trace the etymology of the term; (6) provide synonyms; (7) use the *genus et differentia* sequence of placing the word or idea into its logical category, genus, or class and then distinguishing it from other members of that class. As an example of how the *genus et differentia* method works, we might define a free substitution system "T" quarterback in this manner.

General Class	*Differentiating Characteristics*
Under the free substitution system, a "T" quarterback is a football player	(1) who plays exclusively on offense (2) in the backfield (3) of a team employing the "T" formation. (4) He serves as the field general of the team, (5) calling signals from (6) his position directly behind the center. (7) He handles the ball on all except kicking plays, (8) either passing, (9) handing the ball to some other back, (10) or running with it.

Even this definition, which is more detailed than most dictionary explanations, would need further amplification and clarification for an audience unfamiliar with football. In the following excerpt, William Safire used definitions to clarify his point that the conservative movement is split into traditionalists and libertarians.[7]

> Conservatism has two roots: traditionalism and libertarianism. When the right is in opposition, those differences are muted; now, as the right assumes power, the conservative differences will be dramatized.
>
> The traditionalists want government to uphold society's values—to bolster the family unit, to censor the pornographic, to discourage divorce, to encourage prayer, to curb abortion, to lend government sanction to the culture's proprieties. They place a high priority on personal security against crime and on national security against aggression.
>
> The libertarian conservatives are quite different: they may believe fiercely in some or all the above "family values," but they are even more fierce in their belief that government is wrong to legislate morality. Moral matters are for individuals to decide, provided they do not brutalize others. The libertarian (with more consistency than

[7] *New York Times*, November 17, 1980.

the liberal) wants government out of his personal life, and is willing to take the risks and responsibilities of such self-reliance.

That enormous split in conservatism is not a difference in degree ("moderate" versus "extremist") but a difference in kind on the subject of government intervention in citizens' lives.

Suggestions for the Effective Use of Explanation. (1) Explanation should be an integral part of the speech and should be adjusted to the intellectual and emotional needs of the audience.

(2) Although you should avoid oversimplification, your explanations should be instantly intelligible. Avoid involved, abstract discussions. Use easily understood, nonambiguous, nontechnical words. As a student once said, "Spare yourself no pains to save the listener pains."

(3) Keep explanations brief. Long-winded exposition is lethal to audience interest. Be concise. If considerable development is necessary, relieve the tedium of exposition by using appropriate illustrations, analogies, and testimony.

(4) Although an excellent starting-point for the clarification of an idea, exposition usually needs reinforcement through the use of other Forms of Support.

Visual Aids

Nature and Purpose of Visual Aids. Up to this point we have been concerned solely with verbal development. We should recognize, however, that when properly integrated into the speech, visual materials also can serve as examples, comparison, testimony, statistics, explanation, restatement, or repetition.

Experimental, as well as practical, experience demonstrates that more of our learning is acquired by means of the eye rather than the ear and that we learn more quickly, remember better, and are more deeply impressed when both of these senses are utilized. Therefore, you should become skilled in the imaginative use of visual aids such as graphs, charts, maps, diagrams, pictures, photographs, blackboard drawings, scaled or full-size models, actual objects or specimens, films, and slides.

Combining appeals to the eye and to the ear may promote *clarity*. Descriptive words alone are sometimes inadequate to make a point clear. Any parent who has attempted to explain to children the physical appearance of jungle animals is vividly aware that one visit to a zoo would be more instructive than many thousands of words of explanation. An archeologist speaking on the ancient civilization of the Incas and Aztecs could make his discussion more meaningful by incorporating into his lecture

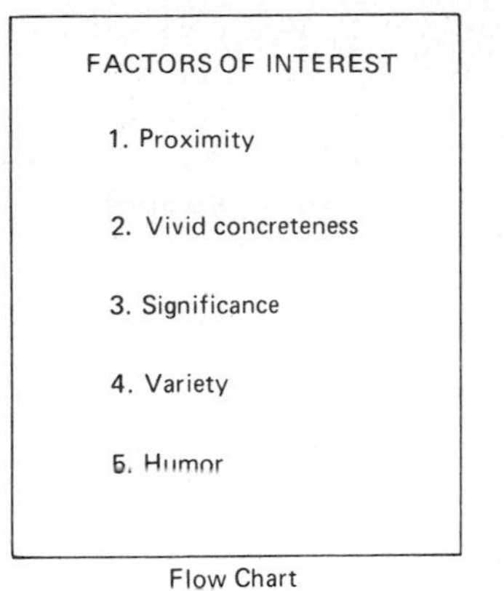

Flow Chart

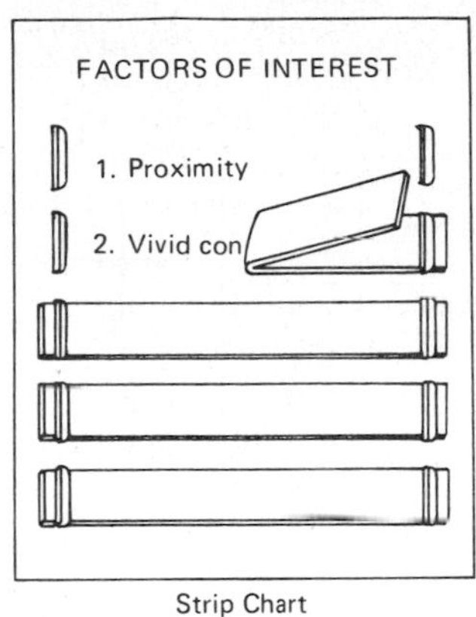

Strip Chart

Fig. 9

large photographs, slides, or motion pictures. A horticulturist could include demonstrations in his lecture on the proper methods of grafting.

Combining appeals to the eye and to the ear may add *interest* to the speech. If attractively prepared and presented, visual aids help to relieve the monotony of the speaker's oral delivery. Who wouldn't be interested in viewing a demonstration of a police dog disarming a man, a film showing the eruption of a volcano, or a working, accurately scaled model of a new type of helicopter?

Combining appeals to the eye and to the ear may serve as superior *logical proof*. According to the old saw, "seeing is believing." A detergent concern once advertised that the suds from a single box of its soap could fill the bed of a tandem truck. When challenged to prove its claim, the company called in photographers and successfully conducted the test. The resulting picture-spread in a national magazine probably persuaded many housewives that the detergent would provide an ample supply of suds for any household chore. A spot-remover salesman might prove the efficacy of his product by deliberately spilling some ink on his tie and then removing the stain through the application of the reagent. In a personal injury suit in California, attorney Melvin Belli used visual evidence successfully to prove his essential point—and secured a $225,000 judgment. The claimant, a fireman, had been injured, when, in passing through a red light, the fire engine had struck a truck. The defense had based its case upon the claim that inasmuch as the truck driver had not heard the siren he had not been given sufficient warning and, therefore, that the emergency vehicle did not have the right-of-way. To demonstrate that the siren was adequately loud, Belli arranged for an aerial photograph of the intersection, had it blown up to huge proportions, and introduced it in the courtroom. As he called up individually twenty-nine persons who lived in the neighborhood, each pointed to his home in the picture and testified

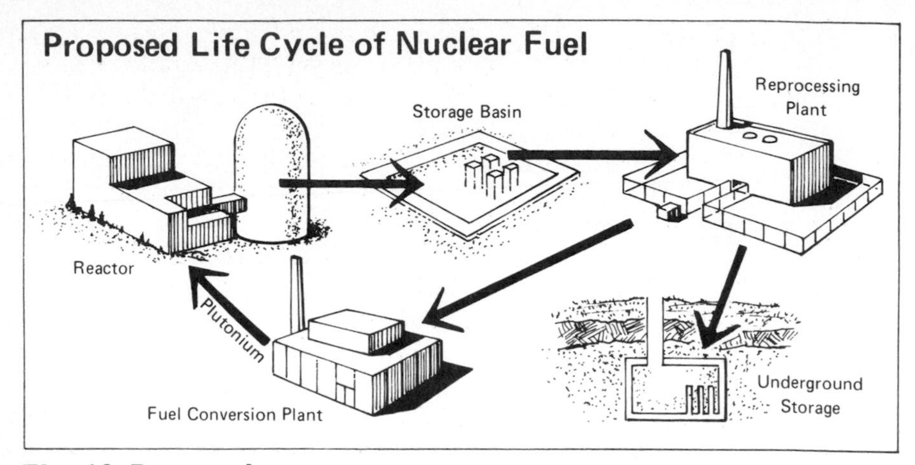

Fig. 10. Pictograph

that he had heard the siren. This impelling visual-aural presentation convinced the jury.

Suggestions for the Effective Use of Visual Aids. (1) Visual material should be adjusted logically and psychologically to the total speaking situation.

(2) The visual aid should supplement, not supplant, the spoken message. Its presentation should not consume a disproportionate amount of time nor center greater emphasis than warranted upon the heading being supported. It should serve directly to amplify, clarify, or prove the point under consideration and should be an integral, nonobtrusive part of the speech.

(3) Visual material should be adjusted to the interests, experiences, and mental capacities of the listeners. Many displays that are suitable for publication in a book or journal are too complicated for public speaking. Furthermore, visual material that is appropriate for a specialized audience may be too technical or involved for a more general audience.

(4) Visual aids should be suited to your abilities for presentation. For example, if you are unacquainted with the operation of a motion-picture projection machine, you probably should either select some other medium or secure the assistance of a skilled operator to run the projector for you. If you are inclined to be nervous in front of an audience, you probably should not attempt a demonstration involving small, accurate, easily observed hand movements. In describing her collection of exotic cups and saucers, a speaker attempted to hold each set as she discussed some of its interesting characteristics. Unfortunately, the slight tremor of her hands—which would have been unnoticed in the presentation of most other aids—caused the cups to dance upon the saucers, setting up a disconcerting and distracting chatter.

(5) Visual material should constitute the most effective use of the time available. Do not use an aid if its presentation will take more time than the demonstration is worth. Weigh the time needed to exhibit the material against its value to the speech.

(6) Select the type of aid that is best suited to your needs, taking into account the expense, effort, and time necessary for its preparation. *Blackboards*, or more accurately *chalkboards*—inasmuch as such boards are produced in a variety of colors—provide one of the quickest, easiest, and most readily available methods of employing visual material. Chalkboard illustrations can be effectuated either before or during the speech. At the proper point in the speech the illustration can be erased or supplemented by the addition of new details. Considerable practice is necessary, however, before you can present chalkboard material with maximum clarity and interest appeal. To promote neatness and dispatch in making diagrams during the speech, you may wish to prepare templates out of card-

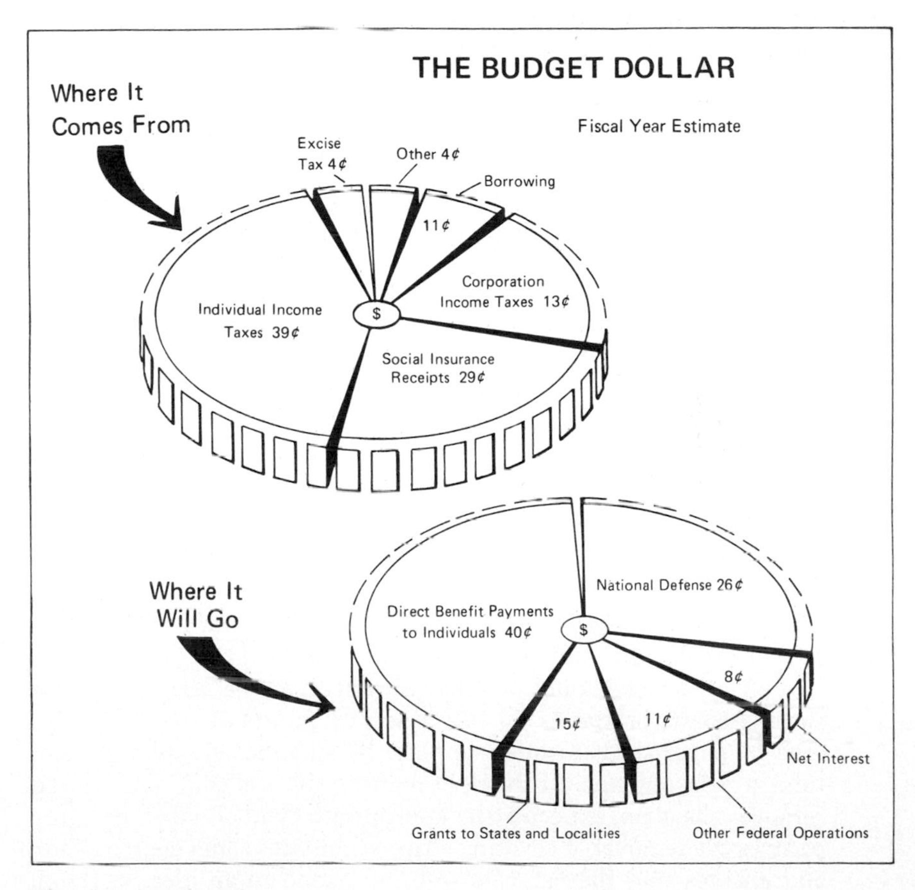

Fig. 11. Pie Graph

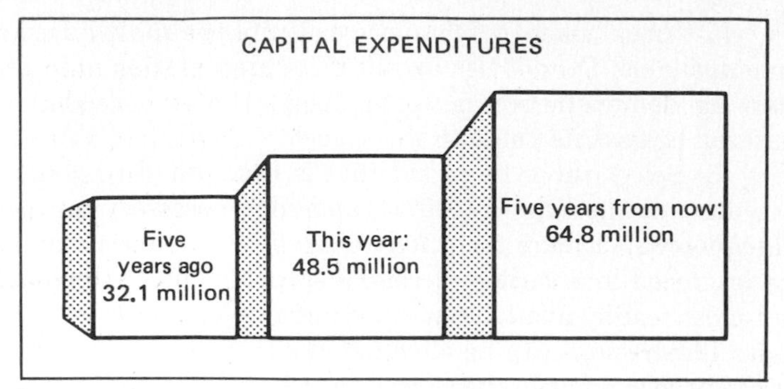

Fig 12. Bar Graph

board or wood that can be placed on the board to serve as guide patterns. A disadvantage of the chalkboard is that, partly because we have been exposed so frequently to chalkboard presentations, this method probably has less intrinsic attention-getting qualities than other types of visual material. Another disadvantage is that chalkboard illustrations often do not possess the sharp delineation and perspective provided in other kinds of aids and may not be as easily seen by large audiences.

Flow charts, often called *organizational charts*, are especially useful to show the basic structure of, or relationships within, a particular organization and to indicate the steps or stages in a process. Such charts serve admirably to present an overview. On the other hand, they may easily become cluttered because of the inclusion of too many details, and sometimes the all-at-once presentation of a complete thought fails to provide an understandable focus upon the constituent parts.

Tree charts are useful for picturizing the history or development of an institution, family, company, or agency.

Table charts are serviceable for presenting important factual data in a concise manner, while making understandable their common relationships. Such tabular lists do not have strong attention-compelling qualities, however, and the temptation is strong for the speaker to include too many figures.

The advantages and disadvantages of *pie graphs*, *bar graphs*, *profile graphs*, *line graphs*, *pictorial* and *semipictorial graphs*, *maps*, and so on probably are sufficiently apparent and need not detain us here.

A brief look should be taken, however, at the *strip* method of presenting charts or graphs. In this procedure, parts of the display are covered by paper strips fastened in place by an adhesive, such as cellophane tape or masking tape. At the right point in the oral continuity the speaker removes the strip, exposing the appropriate symbol, label, or figure. The progressive removal of covering strips stimulates some degree of suspense and ensures that the listeners will not attend to an idea on the display until the speaker comes to it in his speech.

Felt, flannel, and *magnetic boards* are excellent means of visually reinforcing oral announcements, unfolding a step-by-step process, or diagraming the component parts or divisions of some object or thing. If a backing board of Masonite, plywood, or Celotex is covered with felt or flannel, or if the board has a metal surface, cutout materials can be made to adhere to the board by gluing felt, flannel, or small magnets to the back of the objects. When the cutouts are pressed gently against the board, they will adhere until removed. Such boards can be displayed by means of table or "stand-up" easels, which can be purchased relatively inexpensively or borrowed from the audiovisual service department or art department of your school, from the public library, from the YMCA, or from other service organizations.

Opaque projectors, which may be extremely helpful to the speaker, can convert any kind of copy—photographs, magazine illustrations, business letters, and the like—into brilliant screen images. This form of projection, however, has several disadvantages: since opaque projection is secured entirely by reflection, the machine can be used only in well-darkened rooms; the machine is rather large and is awkward to transport; to

Fig. 13. Bar Graph

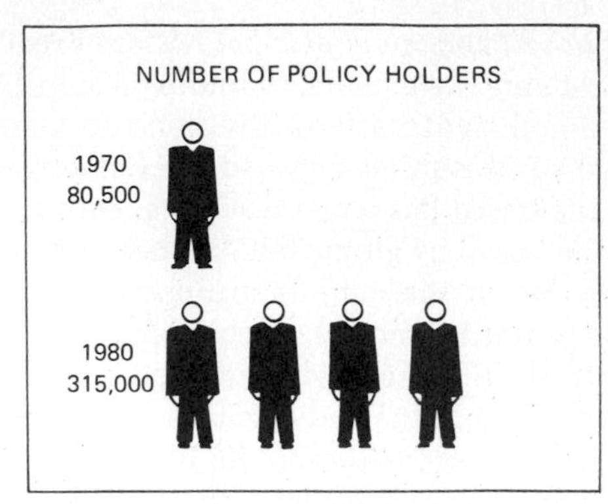

Fig. 14. Figure Graph

operate the projector you must either stand at the machine, thereby placing yourself behind at least part of the audience, or secure the service of an operator who must be well briefed on the sequence and timing of the pictures.

Slide projectors are less expensive than opaque projectors, but can accommodate only slides. As you probably know, you are not dependent upon your own slides; many of the larger universities and libraries have extensive slide collections, and an exceedingly wide range of slides is available commercially. Modern slide projectors have remote control switches that enable the speaker to change slides without leaving his position at the front of the room.

Overhead projectors have several advantages: the projector can be used in a normally lighted room; the speaker operates the machine while standing in front of the room, facing the audience—the projector throws the picture on the screen behind the speaker; whatever the speaker sketches or writes on the machine's writing platform appears simultaneously on the screen; durable, prepared material, called transparencies, can be exceptionally effective. By securing the help of an experienced audiovisual technician, you can employ color and mount overlays on the original transparency. You can thus correlate the visual development with your oral continuity by flipping progressively the overlays, each one adding pertinent new details to the image already on the screen.

Inasmuch as *filmstrips* and *motion pictures*, especially those employing sound, are not widely used during the speech as Forms of Support, a detailed examination of their usage is beyond the scope of this chapter. Perhaps it will suffice to say that in using such visual material, select only films that are adjusted to the total speaking situation, preview the film before using it, arrange proper viewing conditions, integrate the film into the speech so that it occupies the desired degree of prominence and so that its significance and application to your speaking purpose is apparent.

Once you have selected the type of visual aid you will use, consider these further suggestions:

(7) All visual material should be large enough to be seen easily by everyone in the audience; this means every label, every statistic, and, in a picture, every foreground object.

(8) Aids should be sufficiently clear to be understood almost immediately. Avoid cluttering a graph, drawing, diagram, slide, or map with too many ideas: unnecessary details diffuse the focus and distract attention from essential points; if too numerous, necessary details may produce confusion and some important points may be overlooked. Instead of crowding too many significant ideas into a single exhibit, use several displays. And, of course, clarity is promoted by neatness, perspective, balance, use of color, appropriate design, and so on.

(9) Labels for diagrams should be held to the fewest possible number and should be terse, sufficiently large and distinct.

(10) Do not place on the rear surface of the display extensive speaker notes for use during the presentation. In the process of reading such notes, you may tip the aid and thereby reduce its "viewability."

(11) Carefully plan and rehearse the use of the visual aid in advance. By knowing exactly what you are going to do and how to accomplish it, you will avoid wasting precious time during the speech. Your display should be executed with dispatch. If you are to use projected materials, check beforehand on the outlets, length of the cord, the lighting and the position of the projector and screen. The opaque copy, slides, transparencies, or films should be prearranged in the proper order and in the correct position on the conveyor. If using chalkboard diagrams in your speech, practice sketching them so that you can draw them rapidly and accurately while maintaining oral continuity and good eye contact with

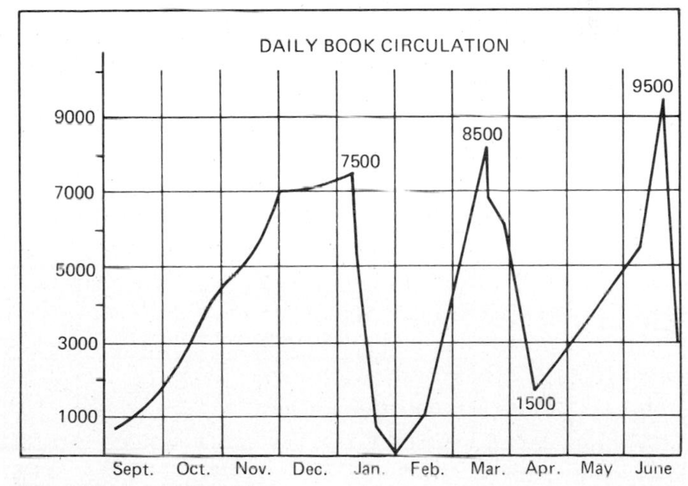

Fig. 15. Line Graph

the listeners. If using an exhibit, ascertain that all mechanical parts are in working order, that all charts, pictures, and so on are arranged in the proper sequence, and that you have ready-at-hand any needed equipment such as pointer, eraser, wall hooks or chart holders, table, cloth on which to wipe hands, clamps, asbestos pads, matches, wrench, string, chalk, or pot holders. If you are using assistants, thoroughly brief them on their jobs and, if possible, go through one or more practice rounds with them.

(12) Unless the chart or picture is on strong, stiff paper, you probably should mount it on a suitable panel; use adequate borders for the mat and possibly use a colored mat to focus attention on the display.

(13) Place the aid in a suitable position for easy viewing. Test its "seeability" by sitting in different locations in the room.

(14) If the aid is multidimensional, plan to turn it several times during the presentation so that its different aspects can be appreciated.

(15) Before the speech, remove from the front of the room any objects that may distract attention from your visual presentation.

(16) In your demonstration do not stand between the visual aid and the audience.

(17) If possible, avoid turning your back upon the listeners. When directing attention to some detail in the display, face the audience, stand either to the left or right of the aid, and point with the hand nearer the display.

(18) Direct your gaze and your discussion to the audience rather than to the visual aid. Inexperienced speakers tend to concentrate on their display; if you lose eye contact with the listeners, you cannot receive feedback from them. Even when completing a drawing, setting up or dismantling a display, or writing on the chalkboard, maintain almost constant visual union with the auditors.

(19) Avoid long, awkward interruptions in oral continuity while you prepare a demonstration or finish a diagram.

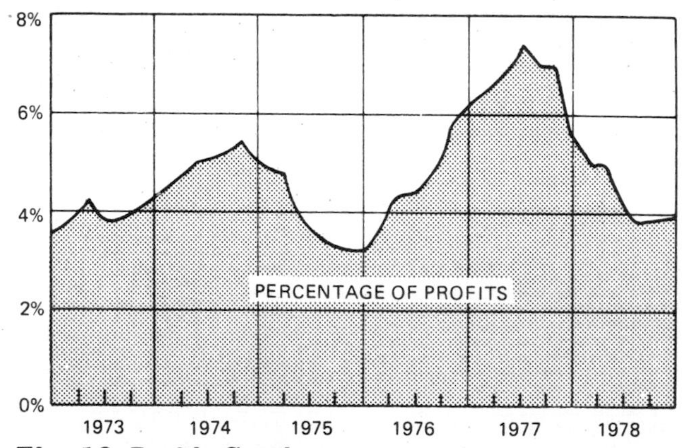

Fig. 16. Profile Graph

(20) In your spoken message, make sure that the listeners appreciate the significance of the visual material and understand its application to the point you are making.

(21) Do not present the visual material until the proper moment in your speech has arrived. If the aid is visible beforehand, some of the listeners' attention will be diverted from the speech; by the time you get to it, because of overexposure the aid may have lost much of its stimulating qualities. When you have completed the demonstration, put the aid out of sight: turn the charts to the wall, place a covering over the specimen, or put the model back into its case.

(22) Up to this point we have been discussing the presentation of visual aids from the speaker's platform. A second method is to distribute visual aid materials, sometimes called "handouts," among the listeners. In using the latter mode, the speaker risks losing valuable time and attention. If the matter is distributed before the speech, the auditors probably will look at it before the speaker is prepared to discuss it, thus distracting attention from the talk and destroying the suspense value of the visual aid. If the material is passed out during the speech, time is consumed and some disturbance is inevitable. If the listeners receive the visual information after the talk, they frequently will throw it away with only a casual inspection. Although speech experts are divided on this point, possibly the best procedure is to have assistants distribute the "handouts" during a pause in the speech. After everyone has a copy or sample, explain the application of the visual aid to the speech; then persuade the audience to lay aside the aid and to concentrate on the remainder of the speech. It is no simple matter, however, to regain their undivided attention. One real estate salesman recognized this difficulty in a speech to prospective homeowners by saying: "And now, ladies and gentlemen, let me suggest that the ladies put their model of the Ruark home in their pocketbooks. And you men, why don't you put yours in your coat pocket? By doing this, you can be sure to take them home for your youngsters to play with. Then, there's a second reason I want you to put them away. To be perfectly candid, I can't compete with these miniature Ruark homes. If you left them out on your laps, I probably couldn't get your attention again this evening."

Summary

To emphasize the close relationship between this chapter ("Developing the Body of the Speech: Understanding Kinds of Content") and Chapter 8; ("Developing the Body: Understanding Methods of Development"), both chapters will be summarized at the end of Chapter 8.

CHAPTER 8

Developing the Body: Understanding Methods of Development

As you will recall, in Chapter 7 we introduced the general function and application of supporting materials. We also identified each kind of speech content (that is, each type of Form of Support), analyzed its nature and purpose, and supplied guidance for its use. We turn now to certain *methods* or *procedures* that apply to *all* kinds of speech content and that enable the speaker to use and interrelate supporting materials in giving substantive, attractive meaning to the basic ideas of the speech.

Didactic Versus Implicative Method

We have already found that the customary method of using supporting materials is to state the main idea, present the Form or Forms of Support, and then show how the materials helped to develop the idea. This direct procedure is sometimes called *didactic*. By their basic nature, all outlines are didactic; when the speaker in his oral presentation follows the sequence of thought represented in the outline, he is thereby applying the didactic method. Thus far, the various sample models we have used to exemplify the different kinds of content have followed the didactic method. This is the order that you probably should follow exclusively in your early speeches.

As you become more experienced in public speaking you may wish occasionally to employ the indirect method of using supporting materials, sometimes called *implicative.* This method is especially useful when you anticipate that—because of negative preconditioning of beliefs, values, or attitudes—the listeners may resist a didactic presentation of the basic idea and its supporting data. In such cases you may improve your chances of securing a favorable hearing by using the oblique approach. That is, you would omit the initial statement of the point; present the supporting materials in such a manner that the listeners are guided to the "correct" understanding or judgment; then, usually, state the point you have tried to establish and show how the supporting material has demonstrated the point.

When Arthur O. Lewis, Acting Dean, College of Liberal Arts at Pennsylvania State University, wished to emphasize to students the importance of liberal education he used this oblique approach.[1]

> More years ago than I like to remember, in the summer before I entered college, an elderly aunt gave me a prized volume of Bacon's *Essays* which she had used some fifty years earlier when she was in college. I no longer remember what she said at the time, but I suspect her intention was to provide me with a touchstone by which I might measure some of the matters I would learn about in college. Although four centuries have passed since these little essays were first published, I continue to find them useful observations on life, and I have had them near me (at this time they are always in my briefcase) for most of my life. I do not always agree with Bacon's ideas on truth, death, adversity, love, nobility, riches, travel, superstition, gardens, fortune and the like, but they are pleasant reading and always thought-provoking.
>
> Although most later editions begin with the essay "Of Truth," the first edition began with the essay "Of Studies." After all these years this little essay still has something to say about education, and, indeed, offers support for the kind of education we believe we are engaged in in the College of the Liberal Arts. "Studies," it begins, "serve for delight, for ornament, and for ability." A twentieth-century Bacon might say that education helps the individual find personal enjoyment, creates social adaptability, and leads to accomplishment in life's occupations. If we followed this recipe for the good life literally, we might very well suggest that students continue studies within the College for the rest of their lives. But Bacon was too worldly to allow for such error. To concentrate too much on studies, he continued, is mere laziness; to use studies only to smooth the way socially is affectation; and to judge only by the rules of scholarship would be disastrous, for only through combining scholarship with experience can one reach true wisdom.

[1]Used by special permission of Dean Lewis.

What studies are useful in Bacon's view? For various reasons he proposes the study of history, of literature, of mathematics, of science, of philosophy, of logic and of rhetoric. Above all, he calls for reading, but "not to contradict and confuse, nor to believe and take for granted, nor to find talk and discourse, but to weigh and consider." However, reading alone will not do, for "reading maketh the full man; conference a ready man; and writing an exact man. . . ." We say it more succinctly: learn to think critically, discuss thoroughly, write exactly.

So what has this got to do with the College of the Liberal Arts in 1980? I suggest that an examination of the baccalaureate graduate requirements would demonstrate that we have not departed very far from the wisdom of a much earlier day. For me, a quite personal demonstration of the value of a liberal education is that in looking for something I might say in this first issue of the academic year, I went back to one of those great works which my own liberal education had introduced me to so many years ago. Surely that must be some small measure of the success of Bacon's concept of education and ours.

Reiteration

A second method or procedure you should keep in mind in using supporting materials is *reiteration.* To enable listeners to understand the meaning of a new idea or appreciate its significance, you need to do more than merely offer a bare statement of the thought. If this were not so, a speech—or advertisement, directive, admonition, and the like—could be reduced to a few terse assertions that, when presented to an audience, would be interpreted correctly and stored "permanently" in the memory. Because listeners possess severe limitations of attention, knowledge-wisdom, retention, and objectivity, some amplification and reiteration of the speaker's ideas are necessary. In a broad sense, you are employing amplification and reiteration whenever you use any kind of speech content, that is, any Form of Support, to develop an idea. In a more restricted sense, reiteration consists of either restatement or repetition.

You are using restatement when you say the same thing over again in different language, and repetition when you repeat in identical phrasing. Through the use of slogans or provocative phrases, repetition may exercise a powerful emotional appeal. In his tribute to the late President Kennedy, delivered before the draped bier at the Capitol rotunda, Senator Mike Mansfield used this poignant phrase five times: "And so, she [Mrs. Kennedy] took a ring from her finger and placed it in his hands." In his speech to the Washington peace marchers, cited earlier in Chapter 7, Martin Luther King, Jr., repeated again and again the phrase: "I have a dream." Unless skillfully used, however, repetition can easily become monotonous. Restatement is less likely to prove tiresome and has the advantage of adding fresh insights and new dimensions to the original idea. In his speech explaining how authors go about their task of writing, Robert T. Oliver frequently restated his thesis (see pp. 155-156). Notice also in various other models we used to illustrate the different kinds of content that the speakers frequently used restatement to make their ideas clearer and more impressive.

In using reiteration, you should adjust restatement and repetition to the needs of the audience and the subject. What is appropriate in one situation might be monotonous and redundant in another. Reiteration promotes clarity and emphasis, and may exert an emotional appeal; but, in the sense that it constitutes the repeating of an idea, it does not advance the thought—it does not move beyond the boundaries of the original idea. Important names, dates, and figures should be repeated at least once. An unusual name might be spelled out for easier comprehension. Important ideas probably should be repeated at least twice. Recognize that the rhetorical question (one that does not require an answer, as does the direct question—look ahead to page 338) may serve as an effective method of restating an idea. In his speech at the annual commemorative observance of the birth of Thomas Jefferson, Bower Aly contrasted Jefferson's principles of democracy with the current practice of democracy by repeatedly asking, "Are we worthy to praise Thomas Jefferson?" Recognize, too, that all of the Forms of Support, including visual aids, may serve as means of reiteration. For example, in this passage a student used a paraphrase and a brief quotation to repeat an idea:

> Peace to the common man depends upon *universal* freedom. Lincoln said that America could not exist half free and half slave. I say to you, neither can the world! On the *New York Times's* editorial page, of recent date, we read this question and answer, addressed to Americans from the troubled blacks of South Africa: "Do you suppose you can keep that idea [that all men are equal] locked up in a single country? . . . We say that free men can no longer be free *alone* . . . they must be free *together.*"

Cumulation

A third method or procedure you should consider in using supporting materials is *cumulation.* One of the most useful means of building an idea into a strategically influential structure, cumulation consists of presenting a tightly ordered series of allied items in support of a point. The speaker's intent in using such a construction is to produce the impact of magnification. The cumulative effect developed by the presentation of a succession of items may be considerably stronger than would be justified by the psychological or logical merits of the data, considered as isolated pieces of evidence. In our earlier discussion of the illustration, we showed how the fitting together of a number of examples or specific instances might give the impression of amassing an overwhelming amount of evidence. Of course, any of the Forms of Support might be used in a tightly structured sequence to evoke a cumulative effect.

Inference

A fourth method or procedure you should bear in mind in using supporting materials is *inference.* You cannot use any supporting item without making some inference—direct or implied—concerning it. You can neither escape employing one or more of the different kinds of content in developing an idea nor avoid making certain implicit claims about this content. When you use supportive materials, you are presenting separate bits of evidence that you allege possess close affinitive relationships to each other and a supportive relationship to the main idea. You are adding to the facts in several significant ways: you have selected and drawn from their hiding places the individual pieces of data and you have clustered and shaped them into a pattern of thought-feeling. The conceptual glue that holds this pattern together consists of the inferences you inevitably make concerning the interrelationship of the pieces and the relationship between the pieces and the idea they are supposed to develop. So, for each item of support there is no way you can avoid making verbal or implied inferences about it, inferences that you wish the listeners to accept. The value of the data you present lies largely in their inferential value to the point you are making. *So important are the different kinds of inference* (inductive, causal, alternation, condition, and category) *that we devote special attention to them in Chapter 9.*

Intensification

A fifth method or procedure you should exploit in using supporting materials is *intensification;* that is, you should attempt to maximize their appeal to the spontaneous attention of the listeners by applying certain

Factors of Interest, or Factors of Intensification. Before considering these Factors, let us look quickly at some aspects of attention.

The Nature of Attention

As William James has said, to a newborn infant the world is a "blooming, buzzing confusion." Gradually, his environment becomes more meaningful because he learns to focus attention upon specific elements in his surroundings. He is soon able to interpret and to respond to a nursing bottle, grandma's cooing and gurgling sounds, and brother's friendly tickling. This process of concentration, or selection from a multiplicity of stimuli, becomes more important as his neuromuscular system matures. The environment, in conjunction with memories of past experiences and physical states of being, presents such a host of stimuli that the human organism lacks the ability to respond to the totality of the situation. Since we cannot respond to everything about us or within us, we must consciously or unconsciously choose that to which we shall attend. An extreme example of the principle of the selection of stimuli is the "absentminded" professor who fails to recognize students or colleagues on the campus. Although he may be unaware of crossing streets, opening doors, or hearing salutations from friends, he is not absentminded. On the contrary, his mind may be working furiously to solve, let us say, a knotty problem in statistical mechanics, or to determine why a rhesus monkey suddenly became frustrated in a manipulation motivation experiment. Through years of careful discipline he has learned how to barricade his mind against interfering stimuli.

The necessity for the selection—and, of course, rejection—of stimuli does not cease when an individual becomes part of an audience. In an imaginary, but fairly typical, audience, the striking brunette in the third row may repeatedly glance at her new diamond ring. Her basic interests of romance and wedding plans may conflict with her attempts to listen to the speech. The little man sitting behind her may be emotionally disturbed because of a dispute with his wife. Perhaps there is an air of hostility between him and his plump wife in the next seat. They may find their emotional problems more absorbing than the speech. The important-looking gentleman on their right may be engrossed in planning promotional schemes for his advertising firm. The burly, ruddy-faced individual near the aisle may be worried over his team's performance in Saturday's game. Whom should he start at end? Will the tackle's knee mend sufficiently for him to play? Is the team psychologically ready? What did the president of the booster's club mean this afternoon when he said, "Let's hope you win this one, John"? The woman in the back row may have difficulty in keeping her two children quiet. Probably she now feels that the speech is not worth her struggles to maintain family decorum. In short: *The speaker is in direct and constant competition with memories, needs, emotions, problems, physical states of being, and other stimuli, which attempt to crowd into the conscious minds of the listeners.*

If you are like most persons, you sometimes read a page or even an entire chapter in a textbook or trade manual before you realize that you have assimilated almost nothing. There has been little, if any, acquiring of information, because you were not attending. Other stimuli have captured your attention; the stimuli furnished by the printed symbols in the book have been too weak to cross the threshold of response. In a like manner, unless listeners give attention to a speech, they cannot receive information, be entertained, or be persuaded. To be an effective speaker you must "sell" your listeners on attending to the stimuli supplied by yourself and your speech. Perhaps your most important single problem is to capture favorable attention and, inasmuch as attention tends to wane, to keep renewing it. Only by claiming the favorable interest of the listeners can you engage them in a continuing "dialogue" that will enable them to move progressively toward closure with your position.

Sometimes auditors may feel compelled to listen because of their respect for the speaker, or their need to glean sufficient information to pass an examination, and so on. Relatively few persons, however, have the ability to force themselves to concentrate throughout a thoroughly boring speech, even a short one of ten minutes. Of course, as the length of the speech increases, the difficulties in maintaining interest multiply. Instead of relying upon voluntary or willed interest, attempt to make your message so interesting that the listeners will be carried along spontaneously, without conscious effort on their part. Fortunately, certain techniques, sometimes called Factors of Interest, or Factors of Intensification, may be used to encourage spontaneous attention. Before incorporating any supporting material—including visual development—into a speech, evaluate its interest appeal in terms of elements such as proximity, vivid concreteness, significance, variety, and humor.

Factors of Interest (Factors of Intensification)

Proximity. One of the complaints of the peace-keeping troops returning from Korea in recent years has been that the American public is little interested in their sporadic confrontations with the Communists. The reason for this disinterest is obvious: the average American does not perceive a direct connection between his immediate existence and the Korean demilitarized zone, or DMZ. A generation ago the complaints of our troops in Korea was much more caustic: Americans seemed relatively unconcerned with a "police action" halfway around the globe. Despite the thousands of battle deaths, Kaesong, Panmunjom, Shunsen, Inje, Heartbreak

Ridge, and the Iron Triangle seemed far away to most people. Although the supply of whole blood fell more than two hundred thousand pints below the armed services' standards for safety, appeals for blood donors brought only a sluggish response. Unlike the Vietnam struggle—and especially unlike World War II when every home was directly affected—there was during the Korean War no violent disruption of industry, economy, entertainment, or home life, except for an unfortunate minority. For those with loved ones in the fighting, the Korean War had poignant personal meaning. For them, news from the shell-pocked front might involve the life, death, maiming, or capture of a son, husband, or sweetheart. But, for most Americans, the conflict was too remote from their daily lives to cause them to realize that it was their war. So, too, the DMZ of today is so far away, Americans have difficulty in remembering that it is their peace. As the years have passed, the Korean War—and even the more recent Vietnam struggle—have disappeared from our thoughts. To the typical college freshman of today, the Korean Seoul, Pyongyang, and Inchon, as well as the Vietnamese Saigon, Haiphong, and Pleiku, are only names, awkward to pronounce and difficult to spell. Further removed from the present are Dumbarton Oaks, Bizerte, Lidice, Eniwetok, and Kula Gulf—names of places where events occurred that stirred our entire nation and most of the world. Much more remote, nearly obscured by the associated fragments of events that scholars call history, are the names Argonne, Saint-Mihiel, and Ypres-Lys—names that were once thought to be "destined to live forever."

As we learned in Chapter 3, the speaker must estimate the potential receptivity of his listeners, and he must adapt his materials to their anticipated responsiveness so that he promotes and reinforces identification. The core concept in this analysis is the self-system of the listener. As we have defined it, the self-system is the complex of functionally interrelated anchors—or patterns—that give continuity and being to an individual. These patterns determine how we view the world and respond to it, that is, how we perceive, judge, decide, remember, imagine, and react. With certain exceptions, our lives revolve around our own interests, needs, and values. Compelling qualities of attention are less frequently evinced in that which is distant in time, space, interest, or feeling. As the following diagram illustrates, other things being equal, the closer the speech materials come to the "bull's-eye"—the person's self-system—the greater will be their appeal to his involuntary attention.

By bringing your supporting material as close as possible to the wants, experiences, cultural patterns, and desires of your listeners, you help them to establish and reinforce identification with your speech. Such identification is essential to promote the maximum movement of the listeners toward closure with your position. Through proximity, you are harnessing for your speaking purposes the vast energy potential that exists in the memories and pre-existing beliefs, ideas, values, and feelings of

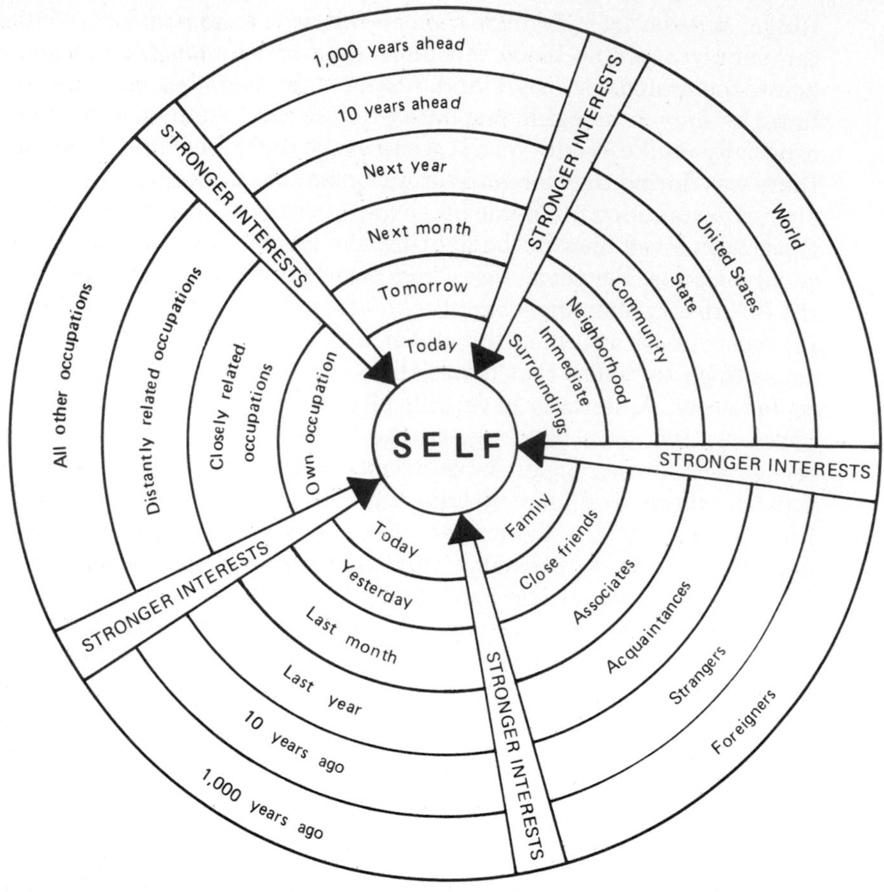

Fig. 17. When Other Factors Are Equal, We Usually Are More Interested in That Which Concerns Us Directly.

your hearers. You are using the "built-in" tendencies of response as a sort of generator, which, when supplied the proper fuel—proximity—may produce powerful new energy in the form of cerebral or glandular reactions.

Do not be content to discuss how the President's tax reform measures will affect people in general; tell how it will affect your listeners. If you are speaking in Philadelphia, your audience will be more concerned about the local transit strike causing them personal inconvenience than about a similar strike in Pocatello, Idaho. Because it is closer to their personal concerns, a typical middle-aged audience will be more interested in a reference to the problem of excessive weight than will a youthful group. A meeting of union men will probably have little curiosity in a description of the canapés, the imported china, the fashionable dresses, or other details concerning Mrs. William A. Barfield's afternoon tea. The same men, however, may have a keen interest in a statement concerning the annual carpenter-bricklayers' barbecue. Usually a class in public speaking will be more concerned about President Ronald Reagan's methods of speech preparation than about those employed by Pericles. As one adult student said, "Pericles may have been a great Grecian orator twenty-five hundred years ago; but so what? He's only a name to me."

As other examples of the use of proximity: mention someone in the audience by name; call attention to some object in the room or on the platform; refer to something previously said by the chairman or some other speaker on the program; or present a hypothetical illustration involving the members of the audience.

Also, note Martin Luther King's use of proximity in his speech at the Lincoln Memorial (see Chapter 7).

Vividness. As is well known, the words used by a public speaker are vocal symbols capable of stirring up meanings in the minds of the listeners. Through common acceptance, such symbols have come to stand for certain objects, ideas, actions, or relationships. Communication is possible because both the audience and the speaker have attached similar meanings to the words. Such semantic principles are accepted unquestioningly by nearly everyone. Many inexperienced speakers, however, fail to transfer theory into practice. Judging from the jejune, trite, ambiguous language that they sometimes use, they conceive of language as a kind of wrapping paper that can be used to package an idea as if it were a pound of butter. Language does not give or transfer meanings; it can only stir up meanings. To stimulate desired meanings in the minds of the auditors, the speaker not only must think in terms of specific reality but also must develop his supporting materials so that, instead of being dully abstract, they are vividly impressive.

In Chapter 15 we shall explore how the speaker selects language that is specific, concrete, and vivid. Here let us examine *imagery* as an important aspect of vividness.

Concrete thinking on the part of the audience can be promoted by the use of imagery. Imagery, expressed through the language of the speaker, sets off in the hearer's neuromuscular system a complex pattern of neural events based upon memory of previous stimulation. Thus, the listeners may vicariously experience sensory impressions somewhat similar to those they would feel in the actual presence of things being discussed.

Consider how limited would be the meaning conveyed if a speaker should say "The two men had a conversation." The word symbol *conversation* has little imagery value. Vividness could be achieved, however, by giving snatches of dialogue and by describing the physical appearance of the men, the way they shook hands, and the intensity with which they spoke and gestured during their conversation. If you were telling an audience about your visit to the New Orleans waterfront, you could employ almost all of the various types of imagery. *Visual* imagery could be invoked by describing the physical characteristics of the ships tied up at the docks. *Auditory* imagery could be stimulated by telling of the boat whistles, the creaking noise of the loading cranes, the cries of the gulls, and the shouts of the longshoremen. *Olfactory* imagery could be utilized by mentioning the smells of the dank holds of the ships, of the stagnant water, and of the pineapples and bananas being unloaded. *Motor* or *kinesthetic* imagery could be employed by describing the straining efforts of the men in the holds moving the cargo into a position under the hatches. *Tactile* imagery could be used by recounting how, in the semi-darkness, you felt your way along the rough surface of a bulkhead. Even *gustatory* imagery could be brought into play by mentioning the bitter taste of the strong coffee you were served aboard one of the ships. By such use of imagery, you would encourage listeners vicariously to "see," "hear," "smell," "taste," and "feel," that is, to experience sensory perceptions roughly similar to those they would have in an actual visit to the waterfront. Notice the imagery used in the various illustrative excerpts in this chapter—for example, the excerpt on page 201 concerning the first friction match and the excerpt on page 159 concerning nature's most perfect pump.

Significance. Some years ago, the most destructive hurricane of the century pounded the North Atlantic. The ferocity of the storm, its significance to the lives and economic welfare of seamen and landsmen, made it front-page news. Many people noted with interest that the westward passage of the luxury liner *Queen Mary* was delayed several days, and that among the detained passengers was Prime Minister Winston Churchill who, with his retinue of thirty-five ministers and advisers, was on his way to a conference with the President. One of the most thrilling sagas of man's struggle against the sea grew out of this storm. The seven-thousand-ton freighter *Flying Enterprise,* seven days out on its Hamburg-New York crossing, was disabled by fifty-foot waves. Although her hull and deck were cracked and she was reeling helplessly, her captain, Kurt Carlsen, refused to join the crew and passengers in abandoning ship. About a week later, the British tug *Turmoil* arrived and secured a tow line to the stricken vessel. Countless persons followed eagerly the reports of Captain Carlsen's valiant efforts to bring his ship and his million-dollar cargo of automobiles, pig iron, and coffee beans into Falmouth harbor. Finally, when less than forty-five miles from port, the steel tow line snapped, Carlsen was taken aboard the *Turmoil,* and the *Enterprise* surrendered to the crashing seas. At Falmouth a crowd of 10,000, including 350 newsmen, greeted the skipper; he received numerous offers to make personal appearances and endorse various products; upon his return to New York, half a million people cheered his ticker tape parade up Broadway.

What made this storm, along with its corollary adventures, so absorbing to people on both sides of the Atlantic? In answer, it *possessed general significance* and *it appealed to certain vital motivations of the observers.*

Develop supporting materials so that they possess general significance. The storm in reference here was tremendous in duration and intensity, causing property damage of several hundred million dollars. A small gale, being much less significant, would have received little, if any, attention from the public. Since the *Queen Mary* was one of the most majestic ships afloat, people were interested in her difficulties, but had little curiosity about the hundreds of smaller craft that were similarly inconvenienced. Winston Churchill was considered by many to be the "Man of the Century." Whatever happened to him was of interest to much of the world. Furthermore, Mr. Churchill's visit to Washington was no casual matter. Among the major problems scheduled for discussion with the President was the resolving of important differences concerning the defense posture of the "free world."

If the storm captured attention because of its general significance, we can reason from this that other events—as well as speech materials—may stimulate interest if they possess general significance. As a speaker you may promote attention by discussing vital subjects and by selecting illustrative materials that concern significant matters. For instance, in the following series, note that ordinarily the items in the left column would possess much higher interest appeal than those in the right.

a scientific breakthrough	a routine experiment
the crucial play in the recent world series	an unexceptional play during a sandlot game
a major social movement	a localized, ephemeral social action
a tragic train wreck	a minor collision
a dangerous murderer sought by an FBI dragnet	a sneak thief wanted by the local sheriff for petty larceny
a statement by the President	an opinion by a local citizen
an epoch-making decision	a cracker-barrel judgment

Naturally, this does not mean that audiences will invariably be more interested in materials that concern the generally significant rather than the less important. General significance is only one of several Factors of Interest or Factors of Intensification. A minor topic especially rich in some other quality, such as proximity, might be more stimulating than a nationally important consideration.

Develop supporting materials so that they appeal to significant wants. Supporting materials have stronger appeal to spontaneous attention if they evoke significant needs, cultural patterns, habits of thought and feeling, and desires of the listeners. Because of the principle of proximity, the individual members of the audience will respond more readily if the speaker appeals to their own impelling concerns. Through derived interest, however, listeners are also attentive to the operation of basic wants in the lives of others.

Much disagreement exists concerning the identity and the nature of basic human wants, even whether one ought to analyze a person's behavior in terms of its principal drives. Nevertheless, it may be helpful to the beginning speaker to consider that various options are available to link supporting material to the built-in potentialities for response that exist within the listener, that is, the predispositional readinesses that seem—at least in Western cultures—to be almost universally true of human nature.

The best-known authority on significant wants has been Abraham Maslow, who arranged his conception of human beings into a pyramid "built out of the layers of human needs." At any time, the most pressing wants are those that "dominate an individual's behavior, despite their position in the hierarchy as a whole." Although Maslow has modified his pyramid slightly over the years, its essential character can be described in this way. The base comprises physiological or survival needs—the avoidance of hunger, thirst, pain; the second level, safety and security needs; the third level, belongingness and love needs; the fourth level, esteem or ego needs; and the fifth level—the top of the pyramid, self-actualization needs—"the need to grow as a person—to satisfy one's potential to the fullest."

Although Maslow's pyramid may be useful to you in developing supporting materials, you may find even more helpful the following discussion of human wants. This analysis—while compatible with Maslow's conceptions—is especially adapted for the public speaker.

Nearly everyone welcomes change, excitement, and adventure—in safety and moderation, of course—as relief from the monotony of daily routine. Some doctors have suggested that most of our aches, tiredness, frustrations, and minor ills are caused by boredom. To escape from humdrum, we take vacation trips, visit night spots, go hunting, attend football games and, also, respond empathically to materials involving the dramatic, the exciting, and the unusual. The story of Captain Carlsen stimulated attention because he was fighting to save his life, his ship, and his cargo. We are almost always interested in significant struggles of man against the elements, man against himself, man against man, team against team, and army against army. Here was adventure one could experience vicariously from the safety of an armchair. Here was action, suspense, and bravery. A sharp contrast to the impelling qualities of the Carlsen story is afforded by the experience of the author. About the time Captain Carlsen was being picked out of the water by the *Turmoil,* the author was adrift in a skiff off the Florida coast. Night had settled and sharp swells pitched the light boat violently. Being a landlubber, he was somewhat alarmed at his predicament. He was in no genuine danger—the violent storm that was battering the North Atlantic was many hundreds of miles away; lights on the shore were easily visible; the outboard motor was soon coaxed to life; and, furthermore, minor mishaps of this sort are common occurrences to fishermen. When, upon returning home, he attempted to recount his "adventure" to his wife, she interrupted gently and said, "Tell me later, dear; it's time for the newscast, and I want to hear about Captain Carlsen and the *Flying Enterprise.*" Although exciting to the author, his experience was so commonplace it would fail to interest others.

Because listeners are interested in change, excitement, and adventure, you may encourage their attention by developing your supporting materials to appeal to this significant want.

Another of our fundamental interests is to be secure and comfortable. This basic want helps keep us relatively content to live within our normal, safe sphere. It regulates our response to the impulse to seek change, excitement, and adventure. Self-preservation and maintenance of physical and psychological well-being represent universal wants; everyone tends to respond to this essential requirement.

In developing supporting materials, recognize that, although listeners are primarily concerned with their own physical well-being, through self-identification they may also become interested in the struggles or needs of others to save their lives and to maintain their health and well-being—as in the case of Captain Carlsen.

Also, in using supporting materials keep in mind that, in these times of inflation, high taxes, and economic slowdown, listeners are acutely conscious of the need for economic security. They wish to protect themselves and their families from economic hardships resulting from unemployment, sickness, injury, and old age. They want to increase the value of their property, get a good job, maintain job security, raise their salary, save on fuel bills, pay less for groceries, and so on.

Inasmuch as the tensions of our times are also reflected in our interest in, and need for, psychological comfort, consider how your supporting materials may be developed to impinge upon the listeners' feelings of mental security. For instance, when suggesting a new belief or program, you might demonstrate that your program is not totally strange but is based upon the known, the familiar, and the traditional. Also, you could promote psychological comfort by showing listeners how your program will help them maintain and increase their prestige and influence.

The desire for satisfactory status is one of the most impelling wants. Much of our goal seeking is conditioned by our desire for *social* approval. We want to fit in, to be accepted, liked, and admired by the groups to which we belong, or to which we would like to belong. For most of us, our manner of thinking, dress, and behavior is based largely upon our social consciousness. Most of us are eager to acquire power and authority over others, partly because these accomplishments in turn lead to higher personal and group esteem.

Self-status, a correlative of group status, is central to much of our goal-directed behavior. Some psychologists say that to some extent each of us lives in a cracked-mirror world; that is, we wish so strongly to have high status in our own eyes that we see ourselves differently from the way others see us. We tend to rationalize our failures; we may overlook our deficiencies and focus on our assets; we often close our eyes to the selfish aspects of our seeking and convince ourselves that our behavior is prompted by altruistic motivations. In the attempt to adjust satisfactorily one's image, as seen by one's own self, some persons employ escape mechanisms, such as projecting one's own faults to others ("Everybody would cheat if he could get away with it."); seeing in one's self virtues that are not there ("If the newspaper says Henry is civic minded, then I am civic minded too. I'm as good as he is."); decrying those attributes that cannot be attributed to one's self ("Who cares if Margaret can talk learnedly on any subject? She bores me, the show-off."); distorting liabilities of character or personality into assets, as prejudice into rational convictions, or hypercritical fault-finding into disinterested inquiry. ("I'm not being nosy, and I hate gossip; I'm just interested in the poor dear.")

Therefore, in using supporting materials try to relate what you are saying to the listeners' significant want for satisfactory *self* and *group* status. They will be encouraged to establish analogical relationships between their self-systems and your speech if you point out how their status may be maintained or enhanced, or how the status of others is, or has been, affected.

Almost everyone possesses a deep-rooted interest in companionship, loyalty, affection, reverence, and sex. In using supporting materials, you can generate interest by utilizing this significant want. Americans are, by and large, a gregarious people. We are a nation of joiners. Much of our social and business life is conducted on a basis of friendship. We have feelings of loyalty and affection, ranging from weak to intense, toward those who hold similar social, political, religious, or economic beliefs. Conversely we may experience antipathy or dislike toward those whose beliefs, values, attitudes, or behaviors differ from our own. References to either our friends or enemies may attract attention, as may allusions to the sentimental attachments of the listeners, such as their university, place of employment, hometown's baseball team, or favorite rock star.

All of us are aware of the transitory quality of life. Most of us possess deep feelings concerning the Creator and the unknown reaches that at both ends of our mortal existence stretch into incomprehensible eternity. Respect, awe, and love of God are, according to some psychologists and historians, basic elements not only of the American heritage but also of our personal nature as well-integrated personalities. Therefore, supporting materials that touch upon their sense of reverence will interest many listeners.

Interest in sex is evidenced by even the octogenarian. Many women are said to choose perfumes, clothes, and cosmetics that will enhance their attractiveness to men. Sales promotion experts realize that the sex appeal of a shapely model in, let us say, a shave soap commercial on television will attract masculine attention. The male viewer, of course, can hardly avoid noticing that the person reciting the advertiser's claims is a seductive female who not only exudes sexuality but also implicitly predicts sexual conquests for the lucky users of the soap. Similarly, listeners attending a speech may be interested in appropriate allusions to sex in the speaker's supporting materials.

All of us wish to live our lives with as much personal freedom as possible. In using supporting materials, remember that, like everyone else, listeners want freedom from unreasonable external restrictions for themselves and are interested in the efforts of others to achieve such freedom. The Thirteen Colonies fought the Revolutionary War, in part, at least, to free themselves from what the Colonists thought were excessive restraints on trade and commerce imposed by England. A similar spirit of independence is now agitating many of the countries of the Third World. It is true, of course, that social behavioral patterns undergo constant incremental change as societal values alter and that values change under the pressure of nonconformity. Nevertheless, in the main, we obey the customs of society and expect others to do so. We resent control, however, when it impinges too sharply upon our freedom of action. How can you as a speaker utilize this significant want in developing supporting materials? Perhaps these examples will suffice in explanation. If you are developing a point concerning family relations, your listeners may identify with a youth who rebels against dictatorial parents. If you are discussing advantages of living in the country, your listeners—especially if they are city apartment dwellers—may be interested in your portrayal of the greater freedom from external restraints afforded by rural living. If you are addressing libertarian conservatives about proposed government regulations, your listeners may respond attentively to materials showing that such regulations are unwarranted invasions of one's personal freedom.

Before leaving the topic of significance, it should be made clear that our catalog of impelling interests is intended to be suggestive, rather than prescriptive, and that our coverage, like any brief treatment of such complex matters, tends toward oversimplification. One should not consider attention as a kind of electronic connection operating automatically, as when a plug (speaker-selected stimulus) is attached to a live current (audience needs), producing immediate, controllable energy. As dynamic life forces in communicative situations, the significant human needs do not function in isolated stimulus-response patterns; the listener must be considered in terms of his total being and his environment. Man's responses to his needs are conditioned by habit, memories, his moral-ethical concepts, and social pressures. Nearly always more than one want influences a person in a particular communicative situation, and he may be torn between wants of relatively equal intensity. The strength of a particular want may vary somewhat among persons of different age groups, social status, economic levels, and so on. Also, the intensity of a particular want varies within the individual, partly according to its current degree of gratification-deprivation.

A knowledge of the significant human wants helps us to understand that, although it may frequently seem irrational, human behavior is typically goal directed. To enlist man's better nature to work in the best interests of himself and of society is the function of responsible speaking.

Variety. Any constant source of stimulation such as the ticking of a clock or the steady drone of a speaker's voice quickly loses its capacity to provoke a response. If we attempt to concentrate on the key of a typewriter, we soon find our attention wandering. Yet we can lose ourselves in an NBA championship game or an Oscar-winning movie partly because such entertainment possesses variation of pace and kind of activity. Variety or change may be only the "spice" of life but it is a necessity for the speaker. If your speech content is monotonously the same, you will put your auditors to sleep. Therefore, you should consciously build variety or change into your development.

Here are some specific suggestions for the application of the principles of variety in developing the main heads of the speech.

(1) Do not overuse any single Form of Support, say, statistics. The sameness of the type of material may produce boredom. Therefore, appeal to the listeners' need for change by weaving into the talk an appealing selection of the different Forms of Support.

(2) When using a particular Form of Support in a series for cumulative effect—as was discussed on page 187—apply the principle of variety in your choice of amplifying materials used. For instance, the excerpt from Professor Oliver's speech on "Writers Are People," page 155, contained several consecutive factual illustrations, yet each example brought out an idea sufficiently different from the others that it renewed interest.

(3) If you appeal exclusively to a single type of imagery, say visual, your audience may tend to find your discussion tiresome. Instead, stimulate various sensations appropriate to what you are saying. You will not

only improve the attention-catching and attention-renewing quality of your materials but also their capacity to evoke understanding.

(4) Direct your materials toward a variety—not just one or two—of the significant wants. Except under unusual circumstances, listeners are potentially receptive to all of the wants discussed just previously. By appealing to a variety of wants, you will appeal to your listeners' need for change—and you will be more persuasive, too.

(5) After you have mastered the didactic method of constructing the ideas of the speech, you might for the sake of change, occasionally employ the method of implication (see pages 185-186).

(6) At times, vary the typical declarative form of discourse by using interjections or by asking rhetorical or direct questions (see Chapter 15).

(7) Break the standard language flow by occasionally inserting snatches of conversational dialogue. Such dialogue may offer change, novelty, a sense of movement, and perhaps, even some suspense. In your brief sketch you might assume the different roles, even—while being careful not to overdo—altering your voice and manner to indicate the different characters.

(8) Inasmuch as most speech materials have little suspense value, when possible, stimulate curiosity. For instance, when telling a story or joke save the punch line for a climax at the end.

(9) On the one hand, although we are interested in new experiences, new ideas, new products, and new sights, an audience sometimes becomes jaded by a speaker's dwelling for too long on the "new." On the other hand, although we are also interested in familiar sights, long-established beliefs, accustomed ways, and customary products, audiences may become bored by continual reference to the "familiar." In such a situation, you could appeal to the listeners' desire for variety by pointing up what is familiar in the new, or new-in-the-familiar.

In the following example, notice not only the speaker's effective use of imagery, snatches of conversation, and suspense, but especially also his new-in-the-familiar method of development.[2]

> Jean Saugrain and his two companions sat in the doorway of the hut, watching their redskin captors whip themselves into an insane frenzy. The beat of drums, pounding out a ceremonial death dance, reached a maddening tempo.
>
> One of the three white men, his nerves nearing the breaking point, leaped to his feet. "You should have let us make a fight for it, Saugrain," he said angrily.
>
> "It was useless, Monsieur," the little Frenchman replied, and his companions knew that was true. Saugrain was wise in the ways of

[2]From the radio-television program "This Is the Story," copyrighted by Morton Publishing Company, Inc. Used by special permission.

the frontier—even of this vast, unknown hostile land into which no white man had ever set foot before. Indian country had been his life, since he had given up a successful career as a Paris chemist and come to America during the Revolution.

Outside the hut, the drums were suddenly silenced, and a stillness ensued that was even worse than the savage beat. A warrior, looking fierce in his warpaint, dropped a bundle of dry brush in front of the door of the white men's prison.

"What does that mean?" Saugrain was asked.

"It is not food, Messieurs," replied the Frenchman. "It is part of the death ceremony. I fear—" Saugrain broke off and a sly smile crept onto his lips. "But, wait! There is perhaps one chance."

The little ex-chemist stepped outside the hut and knelt beside the Indian, who was trying to ignite the brush with sparks from pieces of flint. Then, as his companions watched, Saugrain took a sliver of wood from his pocket, drew it across a stone and set it afire!

In a moment, the entire Indian village was gathered about Saugrain. Awestricken, they watched him repeat his magic. In the end, the elders of the tribe, certain he was the embodiment of some great spirit, gave Saugrain and his friends their freedom, for death was unthinkable after witnessing such a miracle.

To Saugrain's friends, it was a miracle, too. They had never before seen a friction match for the simple reason that *Jean Saugrain was its inventor.*

Stranger still, however, is the fact that the appearance of—*The First Friction Match* not only saved the lives of three men, but gave America much of its *great western empire,* for the two men who owed their lives to Jean Saugrain and his matches were—*Lewis* and *Clark*—leaders of the exploration party that established America's claim to the vast . . . *Pacific Northwest Territory!*

(10) The occasional use of relevant, appropriate humor can provide a variation in mood, content, and tempo. Listeners grow weary of following serious arguments or instruction and welcome brief humorous diversions that break tensions and relieve formality.

Humor. Fresh, sparkling, appropriate humor can be of great value in getting and keeping the attention of an audience. As we have just seen, humor is an excellent means of providing a change of pace, relieving tensions, and promoting congeniality. Listeners rarely maintain an attitude of indifference or dislike toward a speaker who can stimulate them to smile or laugh. Humor can also provide an enjoyable means of making ideas clear, vivid, and persuasive. Chauncey M. Depew, once one of the nation's greatest after-dinner speakers, considered that much of his effectiveness lay in his ability to use humor as a means of implanting ideas in the minds of the listeners. In attending to his pointed wit, Depew's audiences involuntarily opened their minds, at least slightly, to persuasion.

In using humor, you should ordinarily keep in mind certain cautions.

Do not poke embarrassing fun at any person or minority groups present in the audience. Avoid insinuating comments, such as stating that you saw Joe Smithers at the Golden Shores Club last week with a blonde. The audience may roar at Smither's discomfiture; but, even if it is obvious that you are only kidding, perhaps a problem exists that you don't know about, and he or Mrs. Smithers may resent your low-grade humor. A speaker once acutely embarrassed a dignified circuit judge by relating how the last time the judge visited the community he had become inebriated and caught a plane to Denver instead of his intended flight to New York. Unless you are certain that your auditors will appreciate humor of this type, you should use only innocuous material.

Instead of ridiculing individuals or minorities present in the audience, perhaps poke a little fun at yourself. Although easily overdone, a witty, mildly belittling anecdote about yourself may be good for a laugh and further serves to prove that you are a "regular fellow" and no "stuffed shirt." During his presidential campaigns, Norman Thomas stimulated involuntary attention by occasional references to his repeated failures to secure the presidency. Even non-Socialists could not help liking a man who was so candid. On the other hand, such deprecating humor can sometimes have negative results. According to pollsters, some persons felt less inclined to vote for Adlai Stevenson after hearing him make self-disparaging quips.

Avoid off-color humor. Such humor may have a place in nightclubs or at stag dinners, but be very careful about using it at ordinary public speaking occasions. One does not need to be smutty in order to be funny.

Be brief. Make every word count. If necessary, write out the humorous material as you think you might give it in the speech. Rework the phrasing until you have eliminated verbiage, leaving a concise, swift-moving development. The object of this written exercise is not necessarily to produce a passage for you to repeat verbatim in your speech, but rather to clarify the essential elements in your own mind.

Be enjoyable. Humor should provide a pleasant, amusing diversion—a form of adult play in which you and the listeners share a "sense of well-being." Humor is not amusing if it provokes disturbing emotions of fear, disgust, anger, sorrow, and so on.

Consider humor as a spice or tonic, not a staple. If the general theme of your speech is serious, be careful that the overuse of humor does not make it difficult or impossible to regain the serious attention of the audience or impair your credibility. Solving serious problems does not fit the role of clown.

Use only relevant humor. Humor should arise out of the speaking situation and should relate directly to the subject, audience, or occasion. Furthermore, the application of humor to the matter under discussion should be apparent to the listeners. The involuntary attention thus evoked will help the auditors move toward closure with the speaker's informative or persuasive position. Conversely, irrelevant humor may distract attention from the speaker's point and may make his speech purpose more difficult to achieve.

Avoid stale material. To be appealing, ordinarily humor should be fresh, new to the listeners. Therefore, be cautious when borrowing material from widely read magazines, standard joke books, or recent telecasts of a popular comedian. If your audience knows what you are going to say, your humor usually loses much of its punch. When using the humor of others, you might try to make it as much your own as possible: change the names of the characters; alter the background of the story; use new twists and angles; make special adaptations to fit your audience and the speaking situation.

Learn to use other types of humor besides stories, puns, and anecdotes. Sparkling, original humor can be found in a witty turn of phrase, mimicry, a clever bit of repartee with the chairman, hyperbole or understatement, a pointed reference to some aspect of the occasion or speech situation, a touch of irony, ridiculous comparison or contrast, an unexpected twist to a familiar quotation or poem, and so on.

Summary

In Chapters 7 and 8 we have been concerned with principles of development. The primary and secondary heads of the Body represent only a skeletal framework. They must be developed by means of supporting materials. To fulfill each heading you want to structure it in such a way that it—along with the other headings in the speech—becomes a strategically influential encouragement to the listener to engage with you in a continuing cyclical interaction. It is in this dialogue that the listener extends himself toward closure with your position. If the headings have been well chosen to answer the demands imposed by the total speaking situation (that is, the ethical, logical, and psychological requirements of the topic; the understanding, interests, and attitudes of the audience; the particular requirements of the occasion; and the speaker image you project) and if the headings are substantiated by supportive context, which is also well chosen to meet the rhetorical needs inherent in the situation, then the unfolding message may serve to move the listeners as far as possible, under the prevailing circumstances, toward acceptance of the speaker's message. In fleshing out the headings you may choose from among these kinds of content, that is, Forms of Support: extended and short factual illustrations, hypothetical illustrations, statistics, literal and figurative comparisons, testimony, explanation, and visual aids.

In addition to containing suggestions for the specific use of the individual types of supporting material, Chapters 7 and 8 contain a discussion of five basic methods of developing the Forms of Support that warrant your special concern: didactic versus implicative methods; reiteration; cumulation; inference (which receives particular attention in Chapter 9); and intensification. The treatment of intensification included an analysis of Factors of Interest or Factors of Intensification: proximity; vivid concreteness; significance, variety, and humor.

Exercises and Assignments

1. From the written text of a speech by some prominent person, pick out each Form of Support used and evaluate the speaker's use of Methods of Development. Ask yourself questions such as these: Would the greater use of implication improve the interest values of the presentation? Did the speaker make adequate appeals to significant wants? Did the speech possess suitable qualities of vivid concreteness?
2. Prepare a three-minute speech constructed around two or three factual illustrations.
3. Analyze a news report by some prominent television commentator to discover and evaluate the Forms of Support and the Methods of Development used.
4. Write a description of some event or happening. Use as many of the various types of imagery as possible.
5. Prepare a five-minute speech employing as many of the significant wants as possible.
6. Can any one of the Factors of Interest be selected as the most important? If so, which? Why? If not, why not?
7. Which of the Forms of Support are best suited for logical proof? Which are the least suited? Why?
8. Make a careful study of one of the Forms of Support. Deliver in class a brief report on its strengths and weaknesses as logical proof and on its capacity to clarify and to interest.
9. Give a five-minute talk in class on the importance and the nature of a particular Method of Development. Also, be sure to tell how a speaker could make practical use of this Method.
10. Explain to the class why a particular significant want discussed in this chapter deserves to be considered as an important motivating force in our lives. Tell how it can be used in speechmaking. As in Exercises 8 and 9, use plenty of examples to illustrate your ideas.

11. In your reading and listening-observing at school, home, and at your job, be alert to the use and misuse of supporting materials. For a period of one week, keep a written record of noteworthy examples. Sample item from the Associated Press: "Individuals who take their tax returns to the Internal Revenue Service for help can expect accurate assistance less than half the time, a House hearing was told yesterday. For those who itemize deductions, the IRS accuracy falls to 25 per cent, and the record for private professional assistance—including attorneys and certified public accountants—is about the same. . . . The data . . . were presented by Ralph Nader's Tax Reform Research Group. IRS Commissioner Donald C. Alexander praised the Nader analysis and said Congress must bear the primary responsibility for the situation because 'the law is too complex.'"

CHAPTER 9

Developing the Body: Applying Principles to Speeches of Basic Types

This chapter is designed as a continuation of Chapter 7: "Developing the Body of the Speech: Understanding Kinds of Content" and Chapter 8: "Developing the Body: Understanding Methods of Development." It serves two purposes: (1) to apply essential concepts covered earlier to developing the Body of speeches of basic types and (2) to introduce significant new concepts especially in regard to developing the Body of persuasive speeches.

Developing the Body of the Informative Speech

In informative speaking you seek to provide worthwhile information clearly and interestingly, to widen mental horizons, and to bring the unknown or misunderstood into the realm of correct interpretation. You do this for a very practical reason. You wish to enable your listeners to extend themselves, to change themselves, to make the greatest possible movement, under the situational circumstances, from their initial position of knowledge-understanding toward your position, as represented by your Specific Speech Purpose. To accomplish this, you must adjust what you say and how you say it to the demands imposed by the total situation: the speech occasion, the readiness of the listeners to be influenced, the requirements of your topic, and yourself as the speaker. You know all of these purposes and requirements from your reading of previous chapters. Now let us look briefly at some applications that may be especially helpful in preparing informative speeches.

The Supporting Material Should Encourage the Listeners to Engage with You in a Continuing Dialogue

Although this admonition is true for all communication, some inexperienced speakers have difficulty in appreciating that informational speaking should entice the auditors into a continuing cyclical interrelationship with the speaker. It is a truism that only during this mutual exchange can extension, or movement, of the listeners take place. Nevertheless, some speakers concentrate to such an extent on the subject matter that they forget their pragmatic purpose in speaking: to effect closure between their position and their listeners'. Too many beginning speakers consider that emotional feelings and human needs are associated only with persuasive speaking. Everything that has genuine meaning in our lives is colored with emotional overtones. All image-evoking words and phrases possess connotative, emotional values as well as denotative, intellectual meanings. We eat, sleep, love, hate, marry, beget offspring, bury our deceased loved ones, and strive to excel upon a logical-physiological-emotional basis. Therefore, accept that the attitudes, desires, and prejudgments of your listeners condition their receptivity to informational materials.

You should consider the ability of the listener to understand and remember the informational matter. What is the extent of the listeners' experience and knowledge concerning the subject and the point immediately under development? What is their probable level of comprehension? Their ability to assimilate new ideas? Their grasp of the terminology implicit in such a discussion? As a freshman engineering student once epitomized this point, "What is the audience's 'learnability' quotient on this subject?"

Also, attempt to determine the reasons why the listeners do not already know and understand the material. Is the reason merely the lack of opportunity or exposure? Insufficient interest or curiosity? The protection of some personal interest by not knowing or understanding (as, disinterest in modern art may cloak a sense of inadequacy in dealing with abstractions)? If you can ascertain such causes, try to respond to them in the way you develop the supportive materials.

The key to developing the Body of the informative speech—as in the case of any other speech—is to adjust materials to the self-systems of the listeners. When possible, you should develop each heading in such a way that the listeners will identify with what you have to say and will want to follow and to understand. Only in this way will the auditors be induced to enter creatively and actively into a continuing dialogue with you.

The Supporting Materials Should Demonstrate that you Possess Proper Attitudes as a Speaker

Often in giving informational speeches, students tend to dissociate themselves from the speaking situation. They seem to think that their function is merely to fill the allotted time with factual material, somewhat similar to the task of a bag boy at a supermarket checkout counter who fills sacks with customer-purchased cans, boxes, bottles, packages, bars, tubes, cartons, jars, and so forth. Interestingly enough, these same students sometimes complain that some of their instructors seem insufficiently interested in their students or in their teaching. To be an effective informative speaker, you should be dynamically enthusiastic about your subject and about communicating your material to the listeners. If you are truly excited, your attitudes will be reflected in the material you select and the manner in which you present it. Recognize that you are in a position to be of real service to your listeners. Instead of concentrating on your own reactions, think actively and deeply about the demands of the total speaking situation. Only by becoming sensitively attuned to your proper role as the speaker, to the demands of the audience and occasion, to the requirements of your topic, and to the process of communication can you expect to develop effectively the Body of the informative speech.

Maintain an attitude of objectivity toward the informational materials. Naturally, since you are enthusiastic about your subject and wish to interest and inform your listeners concerning it, you cannot be completely detached. Within this limitation, however, an informative speaker is expected to be impartial, honest, and accurate. If you present an assertion as being factual, you should have made all reasonable efforts to ascertain that it is indeed a fact. Furthermore, you should avoid confusing fact with opinion. A fact is a known, verifiable "truth;" an opinion is an interpretation, judgment, or belief resting on grounds insufficient to produce "certainty." Thus, the statement that O. J. Simpson received a $2,500,000 contract for playing three years with the Buffalo Bills is, or is not, a fact; the assertion that he is the best running back in the history of professional football is an opinion. Avoid permitting your biases to cause you to make subjective value judgments, to emphasize disproportionately certain aspects of the subject, or to be inconsistent in the application of standards to the various items under consideration. Since your listeners assume that you are a disinterested observer and reporter, you must be faithful to that image. If you wish to take a position on an unsettled issue, alert the listeners concerning the controversial nature of the item and explain that you are advancing a personal conclusion. Otherwise, you may seem to be attempting to indoctrinate your listeners while posing as an informative speaker.

The Supporting Materials Should Facilitate Interest-Understanding-Retention

Viewed from one angle, this heading implies a sequence: interest precedes understanding, and understanding precedes retention. From a different perspective, however, the goals—to promote interest, understanding, and retention—may be considered a single target: the speaker should evaluate each item of development in terms of its qualities to promote each of the three goals—to interest, to facilitate understanding, and to encourage retention. Here are some specific suggestions to implement the "Methods of Development" discussed in Chapters 7 and 8.

Without being obtrusive, link the developmental materials to the wants, experiences, and interests of your listeners. Keep before the listeners the general significance of the subject, and do not let them forget that the topic has important consequence to them. Try to link the materials to the listeners' interest in change, adventure, and excitement: point up relevant conflicts and struggles; depict action and movement; focus on the newness of the topic or the changes it will produce in their pattern of living. Show how the topic has affected or will affect the listeners' economic, physical, or psychological security. Underlying your development may be the theme that a knowledge of your subject can promote higher group status or self-realization. If you can legitimately do so, tap the listeners' interest in companionship, loyalty, reverence, affection, and sex. Maybe you should relate the supporting materials to the personal freedom of the listeners or of other persons.

Present informative supporting materials in such a vividly concrete and specific manner that the audience will be able to construct mental pictures of what you are saying. Avoid vague and generalized phrasing. Instead of "statistics indicate," say, "The Institute of Public Opinion yesterday released the results of a poll in which 3,500 Chicago housewives were interviewed . . ." Consciously attempt to evoke appropriate imagery: visual, auditory, olfactory, kinesthetic, tactile, and gustatory. Sensitize yourself to the effective use of specific and graphic detail by the regular reading of informational magazines, such as *Time, Newsweek, Sports Illustrated,* and *National Geographic.*

When possible, explain the unknown or misunderstood by linking it to something already familiar to the listeners. As we saw on page 161, a "billion dollars" or the number of pounds of newsprint and ink required to produce an anniversary edition of the *Miami Herald* are incomprehensible abstractions, requiring conversion to familiar realities. Similarly, to mention the number of board feet in a giant Sequoia would be meaningless to the average person; convert the unknown into the familiar by explaining how many seven-room houses this amount of lumber would construct. To describe the sensitivity of the BMEWS (Ballistic Missile Early Warning System) radars in Greenland, Alaska, and England, point out that if one were erected in Chicago it could detect and report the arc of a tennis ball tossed in the air in New Orleans.

As a result of your evaluation of the listeners' level of comprehension, you should be able to anticipate which terms and concepts require definition, description, or classification. Also, you should be able to estimate the amount and kind of explication and narration that is necessary to make each point clear and understandable, without belaboring it. Do not depend exclusively upon explanation, however. In supporting the major headings of the Body, make liberal use of vivid illustrations, figurative and literal comparisons, quotations, and statistics; provide the necessary amount of restatement and repetition; when feasible, supplement oral materials with visual aids or demonstrations.

Add verve and brightness to the informational materials by the occasional use of humor, figures of speech, bits of dialogue, unusual contrasts, references to your connections with the subject or to certain experiences shared by you and the audience, personification, rhetorical and direct questions, suspense, and so on.

Provide ample guidance for the listeners by means of transitions, summaries, and interpretations. Although the procedure should depend upon the total situation, probably you should summarize briefly each main head before taking up the next, making clear the logical relationships that couple the headings together. A sergeant instructing ROTC students at rifle practice might link together the main divisions of his discussion in this way: "Now that we are acquainted with the techniques of firing from the standing and kneeling positions, let us move on to the prone method of firing." In explaining "How Food Becomes Fuel," one authority used this terse transition: "After digestion and absorption the body's next major task is to distribute the nutrients to the cells. . . ."

Sometimes you may wish to employ obvious signposts, like "First . . ."; "The second major function . . ."; "The last point to remember. . . ."

In addition to tying together the main divisions of the Body, you should make clear the application which each supporting item bears to the point under discussion and to the speech purpose. Your listeners should always be posted on how to integrate your materials with their existing knowledge, so as to produce a meaningful learning experience. Furthermore, you should help them to evaluate the relative importance of the individual supporting items. Do not require them to digest and assimilate great quantities of raw data. If a particular concept is of paramount significance, alert the listeners so that they will appreciate its importance.

In discussing the continuing crisis of South Africa, a speaker might focus attention by saying, "This background is essential to anyone who wishes to think clearly and fairly about what is going on in South Africa." In addressing the current relationship of the United States with China, a speaker might say, "To see in proper perspective the present association of the two countries, it is necessary to understand first the lasting imprint left on Chinese thinking by Chairman Mao Tse-tung."

Give the auditors any assistance necessary to enable them to follow easily the development of your thought. Perhaps say something like: "The French President's reply to the British request raises several questions . . ."; "The controlling fact in this conflicting testimony is . . ."; "Perhaps you can already see that two different patterns of response are beginning to emerge"; or, "All this chemical dissection has one purpose: to break down the chyme from the stomach into molecules that can disappear, by absorption, into the veins and lymph ducts." Sometimes, a directive may be in order: "Remember this name"; "Listen to this"; "I want you to hold on to this point"; "Don't forget this key formula"; "Write this down"; "Plan to use this procedure again in a few minutes when we come to . . ."; "Think about this approach."

Developing the Body of the Entertaining Speech

As you will recall, in the entertaining speech your major, if not sole, intent is to provide your listeners with a refreshing diversion from routine problems and obligations. Although most effective speeches probably contain elements of entertainment, only the speech to entertain has as its primary purpose the amusement of the audience.

It is an oversimplification to say, however, that in developing the Body of the entertaining speech you should select materials primarily for their entertainment value rather than for their usefulness to inform or persuade. The term *entertain* means to hold attention agreeably. The subject matter and speaking occasions for entertaining speeches vary so widely that generalizations tend to be misleading. In selecting speech materials to fit the total speaking situation, you must consider all of the typical aspects of the occasion and the audience. In addition, you must adjust the materials to the degree of serious intent of the speech itself. A minority of entertaining speeches are completely free from any serious purpose—as in the case of the speaker at a fun-night gathering who wishes to provoke his audience to raucous laughter. From this extreme position, the degree of serious intent in entertaining speeches represents a continuum stretching toward the opposite extreme at which the serious aspects may be virtually as important as the entertaining ones. Some public lectures are primarily entertaining in order to attract an audience, particularly if an admission is charged and the lecture is not sponsored by a civic group. Such speeches, however, often contain much information about the billed topic of, say, "Marine Life Found in the Great Barrier Reef of Australia," "The Sights and Sounds of the Kasbah," or "Little-Known Facts about Well-Known People." Also, entertaining speeches may contain varying degrees of persuasion: a travelogue on "Interesting Customs of Family Life in India" may also seek to stimulate reflective thinking concerning the culture of other peoples; a dramatic narrative on "Skin-Diving for Treasure in the Florida Keys" might also contain a "soft sell" argument for Florida as a vacationland; a speech on a fantasy topic such as "COMPUTERS and Man in 1995" might have the secondary function of sensitizing the listeners to the problems attending man's adjustment to machines. The more important the secondary serious purpose, the stronger should be the resemblance of the supporting material to that which is appropriate for speeches to inform or persuade.

Inasmuch as pleasure and relaxation are mainly states of bodily feeling and mental attitudes, and inasmuch as the audience is not expected primarily to retain factual information or to accept or reject courses of action, the structure of the Body may be casual and relaxed. This does not mean that entertaining speeches do not require careful preparation. It does mean that the primary purpose of the supporting materials is unique: to provide a swift, sure, interesting development of thought; not basically to implant new understanding or belief, but to divert pleasantly the listeners. Although the sequence of ideas should flow smoothly and easily, there may be little need for internal summaries or a careful amassing of data. Statistics, reiteration, definitions, and appeals to general significance and to most primary wants may have somewhat less application to entertaining than serious speeches. On the other hand, you may find that in entertaining speeches you can make effective use of examples, analogies, episodes, variety, comedy, exaggeration, incongruity, irreverence, and appeals to the listeners' interest in pleasant change, adventure, and excitement.

As general rules, supporting materials should emphasize the buoyant rather than the heavy, the graphic and lively rather than the complicated and exact, the sanguine rather than the pessimistic. Use those materials that emphasize freshness and brightness. Use suspense, but do not let it become somber or painful. Use imagery, but avoid laborious descriptions. Use fast-paced exposition and narration, but avoid dull analysis.

In your selection and presentation of supporting materials, you should reveal yourself as a friendly, animated speaker who is completely in harmony with the relaxed, congenial mood of the audience and the speech occasion.

Developing the Body of the Persuasive Speech

Before we consider the developing of the Body of speeches to convince, stimulate (reinforce or impress), and actuate, we should review basic principles. The function of the persuasive speaker is to influence others to believe, feel, or act in a desired manner, that is, to move the listeners as far as possible under the existing circumstances toward closure with the speaker's position, his Specific Speech Purpose. In carrying out his persuasive function, of course, the advocate must remain consistent with high ethical standards and with the logical requirements of his subject. (We have frequently touched upon ethical standards and "logical requirements" in previous chapters and shall look at them from a different perspective on page 224.)

Although the development of all speeches should be audience centered, this point is possibly of the greatest significance in the persuasive speech. Charles Perelman, dean of the Faculty of Humanities, Free University, Brussels, Belgium, once said that "persuasion is essentially adapting yourself to your listeners. You must meet them where they are. To do this you have to know where they stand, what they believe, what they think is important, what they consider relevant or not relevant. Persuasion is to lead the audience, but you have to come to them where they are." In Chapter 2 it was suggested that a speaker does not persuade a listener; he merely enables the listener to persuade himself. All the advocate can do is to supply the means, the resources, to the listener that may enable him—if he so desires as a free agent—to change himself. The present way one thinks, feels, and behaves is essentially the product of one's past. Modifying one's present belief-value-knowledge system involves a stretching or extending of that system. One accepts new beliefs, or reinforces old ones, only through analogy, integrating the new with the established patterns of belief-feeling. And, it is the existing hierarchical structures of beliefs and values that determine the acceptability of the suggested modification. Thus, the self-system—the complex of functionally interrelated anchors that we discussed on pp. 27–28—must change; but, and this is crucial to the process of understanding persuasion, it is *through* the self-system that the change is effected. The self-system basically controls how, and the extent to which, the individual will respond to particular persuasive entreaties.

Extending this line of thought, we can assert that a listener persuades himself only to the extent that he identifies with the speaker's message. To enable your listeners to identify with your materials, two basic steps are necessary. First, by careful study of your potential listeners you may discover their differences and their common denominators of desires, experiences, cultural patterns, interests, beliefs, knowledge, and attitudes, especially as they relate to the subject and to you as the speaker. As part of your analysis of the demands of the total situation, prior to selecting your Specific Speech Purpose, you attempted to determine the status of your listeners' knowledge of and attitudes toward you and your subject. You also tried to discover the causes for your listeners' attitudes, beliefs, and behaviors. And you sought to establish a hierarchy of values, interests, and desires that you and your Specific Speech Purpose share with the listeners and that will provide realistic commonalities for building your message into a strategically influential appeal. Only after you have estimated your rhetorical needs in establishing and reinforcing identification will you be ready for the second step: consider the options available to you concerning the types of supporting materials and the methods of development and, keeping in mind the rhetorical needs you confront, select those options that will best facilitate listener-speech identification. In this way, the listeners will be encouraged to persuade themselves that logic and their best interests compel them to accept your proposals.

The remainder of this chapter is concerned with the specialized requirements for developing the Body of the persuasive speech.

The Speech to Convince

As you will remember, on controversial issues the basic opinion of the audience determines whether the speaker's purpose is to convince or to stimulate (impress or reinforce). To convince a listener is to convert his mind-set *from* opposition, neutrality, or indecision *to* affirmation or agreement. Listeners who are hostile to the speaker's proposals and who personally feel deeply involved in the matter are vastly more difficult to persuade than those auditors who are neutral or uninformed. If persuasion consists of movement—or change in the self-system—which is voluntary, if it is the self-system of the persuadee that determines the acceptability of a suggested new belief-feeling, and if the persuadee rejects the change in his self-system recommended by the speaker, then the speaker may have very little, if any, chance of effecting closure. It will be exceedingly difficult or impossible for the speaker to establish, and expand, beachheads of relevant identification with the listeners. For the definitely or extremely hostile listener, the greatest movement toward closure that a speaker normally can reasonably expect to achieve is to alleviate hostility; for such listeners, supportive materials ordinarily should be directed toward reconciliation, lessening of animosity, and furthering of understanding. In a single speech the possibility of converting the highly involved, strongly opposed listener (on a matter of genuine consequence, of course) is unlikely—even if you are able to present some superordinate goal that transcends the differences between you and the listener. If the suggested change falls within the "latitude of rejection" of the highly motivated and hostile listener, it will be rejected. Therefore, in the following discussion we are primarily concerned with those listeners whom you have a much greater chance of moving toward closure: those who range from the uncommitted to the moderately opposed.

Identification and the Speech to Convince. To move uncommitted and moderately opposed listeners as far as possible toward closure with your position, you should select and develop your supporting materials in such a manner that they will encourage your listeners to *identify with you as the speaker.* To facilitate such listener identification, you yourself must be likeable and believable. Your hearers must consider you to be a morally responsible person of goodwill who is sincerely interested in being of service to them. If you genuinely desire to promote the best interests of the auditors and are sensitive to their emotional and intellectual needs, your warmth and sincerity should permeate all that you say. To lead the neutral or critical auditor, you must demonstrate confidence in your cause, in the intrinsic merit of your listeners, and in your competency as a person and as a speaker. Naturally, the listeners will expect you to be knowledgeable, dynamic, positive, and definite. They will also demand that you follow the golden rule: you must be fair-minded toward your listeners' beliefs and attitudes if you expect them to be fair-minded toward your proposals. Avoid seeming to indict or to lecture your listeners. Be especially courteous toward other speakers on the program who may differ with you. As Rufus Choate pointed out, "neither intolerance nor sarcasm is argument"; when directed toward the listeners' beliefs and attitudes, such discourtesy will alienate those whom you wish to convert. If you can do so unobtrusively, possibly build up your prestige by mentioning special study or experiences that enable you to speak with authority; be willing to admit minor weaknesses in your argument; recognize the strong points in the opposing contentions; admit that others agree with your listeners; constantly try to establish common ground by emphasizing relationships or experiences that you share with the listeners, by stressing agreement upon basic goals or principles, and by accepting as much as possible of their views; perhaps acknowledge your appreciation of the idealistic or humanitarian motivations of your listeners; possibly indicate that you would like to agree but cannot because of your assessment of the facts; do not claim for your evidence more than is warranted; in some cases, minimize the use of value judgments—let your evidence do the talking for you.

Your supportive materials should also be developed in such a way that they will encourage the listeners to *identify with the substance of your message.* Adjust what you say to the logical-psychological needs of the audience. In speaking to an audience that is both uninformed and unprejudiced concerning the subject, you may be able to secure acceptance of your views by merely supplying necessary information. If the listeners are undecided because of conflicting beliefs-attitudes or are opposed because of logico-emotional convictions, your supporting materials must make a coordinated appeal to their reasoning and feelings. "In building an argument from a state of doubt over a chasm of inaction to a state of belief the speaker works like an engineer," so one writer believes. "The proposal for which" the speaker "would gain acceptance is like the roadway of the bridge. The roadway is supported by strong piers of evidence, firmly sunk into the rock of human attitudes. Just as the engineer should see that the piers of his bridge are well designed to support the weight upon them, so should the builder of an argument see that his reasoning is valid to support the proposal." To effect "permanent" persuasion, you must do more than to divert listeners from their objections. Short-term persuasion may be secured by means of graphic human interest stories, appeals to sympathy, personal magnetism, and so forth. Such persuasion soon wears off, and the persuadee returns to his original position of doubt or disbelief. In his estimation of the rhetoric of a labor spellbinder, Stanley Levey compared the agitator to Billy Graham: "He stirs up his audience and they decide there and then to go straight. But the next morning, when the word and the presence are gone, they fall back happily into all their old bad habits. . . . He makes it all sound so simple. But after he has said it, what have you got? How long will they . . . remember it? What does it mean?" To make conviction stick, you should remove objections by logical means. Naturally, your listeners will resist your efforts at persuasion. If they are predisposed against your proposals, they may seek eagerly to pick holes in your case. If they detect, or think they detect, weaknesses in your logic, they may find this sufficient reason to reject your entire argument.

Inference and the Speech to Convince. The following suggestive guides may enable you to help your listeners draw appropriate inferences from your materials.

Inductive reasoning. Underlying much of our discussion in Chapter 7 of supporting materials was *induction,* or reasoning from specific evidence to general conclusions. The treatment of the illustration, comparison, testimony, and statistics contained considerable guidance in testing the validity of data as inductive evidence. Hostile listeners especially will be critical of the inductive process by which one uses individual items of proof to establish the truth of a contention. Therefore, you should select only that evidence that will bear critical scrutiny and that obviously supports closely its superior heading. Buttress each major contention with enough evidence to satisfy the audience that the base of your inductive argument is sufficiently comprehensive. Perhaps demonstrate that your evidence is representative of a preponderance of available data and is not isolated or extraordinary. If a preliminary examination of the audience has indicated various specialized areas of interest, draw some of your corroboration from those areas. Help your listeners to understand the meaning of each item of support and to appreciate its function in the inductive development. Since all elements of proof will not be equally significant, direct special attention to your most telling points. In fitting the pieces of evidence into the inductive pattern, be careful to avoid ambiguity or distortion. Critical listeners will be only too eager to find, or to think they have found, awkward links in your logical associations.

Causal reasoning. We made an earlier acquaintance with *causal* reasoning in Chapter 5 in connection with the Cause-and-Effect and Problem-Solution patterns for organizing the main heads of the Body. Here we are concerned with the effective use of causality ("this produces that" type of reasoning) to develop the major contentions. The basis of causal reasoning is that for every happening there is a cause. Such reasoning is an addition to the relevant "facts." It involves an inference or judgment, alleging a causal relationship among the "facts." The cause-to-effect sequence argues from an accepted fact to an alleged result. It always involves a chronological pattern such as (1) from the more distant past to the more recent past—Jimmy Carter's stand on abortion cost him the vote of numerous Catholics in the 1980 election; (2) from the past to the present—the bad fall the jockey took yesterday will make him overly cautious today; (3) from the present to the future—the refusal of Congress to pass a major tax bill will cause a recession. The effect-to-cause pattern moves from an accepted fact or result backward in time to the alleged cause(s). This order may proceed (1) from the present to the past—your failure has been caused by inadequate preparation; (2) from the more recent past to the more distant past—the Bay of Pigs fiasco was caused by faulty intelligence evaluations in the CIA. In using causation do not assume that critical listeners will accept your undocumented assertions; prove the existence of a causal relationship. Do not oversimplify or assign false causes. And, do not argue that, merely because one event occurs before another, the first happening produces the second.

Analogical reasoning. Also in Chapter 5 we encountered *analogical reasoning* in relation to the use of literal and figurative comparisons. When you draw inferences based on resemblances or differences that exist between two things—or among more than two—you should attempt to make the relationship both logically and psychologically acceptable to the listeners. The suggestions given on pp. 162–168 should help you to facilitate listener identification with the basic half of the analogy and to promote the willingness of the listener to make the inferential leap to the second half of the analogy, thereby moving somewhat closer toward closure with your basic position. Your task, of course, is to make credible the inference that, because two things are similar in one or more significant ways, a particular proposition that is true of one of them may also be true of the other, a conclusion which, if accepted, will cause appropriate change in the way the listeners view your basic contentions. The hostile audience will be especially unwilling to accept this change and will attempt to reject the basic half of the analogy, the linkage between the two halves, and the resulting conclusion. Therefore, you should anticipate such resistance and plan your development accordingly.

Disjunctive reasoning. A fourth type of reasoning is alternation ("It is either this or that"). Sometimes you may legitimately tell your listeners that they must choose between a small number (usually two) of ideas, policies, or courses of action. In doing so, beware of the "exaggerated gamut." A critical audience will reject your "magnifying the gulf" between your side and the opposition, as in offering the choice between prosperity and depression, good and evil, truth and lie, love and hate. Would many Republicans or independent voters accept the assertion that "the Republican party is the party of the wealthy and privileged and the Democratic party is the party of the people"? Would many Democrats accept the smear that "the Democratic party is the party of war and socialism, whereas the Republican party is the party of peace and individual freedom"? If offering alternate courses of action, include all relevant possibilities. Analytical listeners will probably recognize any artificial limitation of choices. To say that a university must either go "big time" or discontinue football is to overlook potential courses of action. A college could de-emphasize football by joining with like-minded schools in a "play for fun" conference; it could abolish intercollegiate football and inaugurate an intensive intramural program, and so on.

Conditional reasoning. A fifth type of reasoning is *condition* ("If this happens, then that will follow"). In the conditional argument, you assert that *if* particular circumstances occur or *if* certain requirements are met, *then* specified results inevitably will follow. Examples: "If the Upper Colorado Basin project is adopted, the dinosaur remains in Echo Park will be destroyed"; "Bet on the challenger: if he lasts through the sixth round, he will outpoint the champion." When presenting a conditional argument, you may need to demonstrate that the hypothetical conditions are likely to occur, and that, once they do come about, the alleged results will ensue. This means that in some cases you may need to prove both the "if" (antecedent) clause and the "then" (consequent) clause of each conditional argument. For instance, in attempting to persuade a faculty member not to accept a better paying position elsewhere, a dean might use this argument: "If the state legislature grants the university the requested increase in appropriations, the administration will improve significantly the faculty salary structure." In this situation the disgruntled professor would expect proof that the legislature would pass the desired appropriation measure and, further, that the university administration would use the funds to raise salaries.

Categorical reasoning. A sixth type of reasoning is *category.* This mode of thought proceeds from a general or universal premise to a particular conclusion: what is true of an entire category or class should also be true of any member of that category. The categorical process follows this line of reasoning: general premise—"All members of Phi Beta Kappa are extremely intelligent"; intermediary step—Tim Wilson is a member of Phi Beta Kappa"; particular conclusion—"Therefore, Tim Wilson is extremely intelligent." In speechmaking, the categorical pattern (commonly called a *syllogism*) is rarely stated in its complete form. Typically, one or more of the steps are so obvious that they are omitted. You might merely assert, "Tim Wilson is a Phi Beta Kappa, a real brain." Despite the omission of one or more steps, the listener can expand the remaining part(s) into the full pattern for a better analysis of the logical relationships.

When speaking to neutral or hostile auditors, be especially rigorous in using these criteria to test the validity of categorical reasoning:

(1) *Is the general premise "sufficiently universal"?* Nearly everyone would agree that members of Phi Beta Kappa are very intelligent. Usually, however, the general premise needs some qualifications. Public speaking deals with probabilities rather than certainties; true universality is exceptional rather than common. Instead of "all effective speakers prepare their speeches," it would be more accurate to say that "practically all effective speakers prepare their speeches if they have the opportunity." Some speakers such as Patrick Henry and Clarence Darrow apparently made little formal speech preparation. Then, too, almost every speaker is forced occasionally to speak impromptu.

(2) *Is the general premise true?* Avoid reasoning from a questionable or untrue general assumption. A partisan once charged, "Of course Smithers is an arch conservative. His brother was once president of the NAM." By expanding these statements into the full pattern, we have: "Any man whose brother has ever been president of the NAM is an arch conservative. Smithers' brother formerly was president of the NAM. Therefore, Smithers is an arch conservative." Because the general premise of this speaker is subject to question, the particular conclusion may be inaccurate. Perhaps Smithers is a reactionary, but no proof has been offered.

(3) *Is the specific case a member of the general category?* Unless it is, no reliable conclusion can be drawn. For instance, every criminal trial hinges upon this criterion. According to law, all those guilty of committing crimes must be punished. The task of the prosecutor is to prove that the

defendant committed a crime, that is, the specific case (the defendant) is a member of the general category (all those guilty of committing crimes).

Emotions and the Speech to Convince. If human minds worked with the cool efficiency of computers, we could end here our overview of the Body of the Speech to convince. The motivations, habits, and biases of critical listeners may cause them to reject a well-reasoned argument. "People speak in the name of truth," Charles Perelman states, "but truth has to be accepted as such. Otherwise, they [the persuadees] say you consider this a truth, but for us it's all a mistake." A good many years ago, William James pointed out that it is insufficient to plant an idea in the mind of another; to effect persuasion, you must enable the persuadee to identify with the idea, that is, the idea must be made emotionally attractive. Hence, when possible to do so, each appeal you make to reason should also constitute an appeal to a want or to a habit of thinking-feeling. As you develop your logical argument, consider how to make the "truth" appear to your listeners to be the "truth." As much as possible, start from premises that are warmly endorsed by the hearers and, employing their line of thinking, reason toward the desired conclusion. Help your listeners to think more rationally by relieving any emotional need to disagree. Encourage them to want what you are proposing. You can make your ideas more attractive to the listeners by using one or more of these methods: Demonstrate unobtrusively that your proposals do not conflict with their interests and attitudes. If such a conflict undeniably exists, possibly admit it; but minimize it by showing that there is no conflict on important goals or that your program is rooted in other needs or attitudes possessed by the auditors. When possible, emphasize the positive by showing that, instead of being in conflict, your proposals actually reinforce the listeners' existing attitudes. In this way, you would be harnessing your hearers' will-to-believe in the support of your ideas. Sometimes, you can reduce friction between your ideas and those of the listeners by using *implication*. Instead of stating the point and then offering proof, you may present the supporting materials in such a way that the auditors are gently guided through their own reasoning toward the "correct" judgment. In this method, only after giving all of the evidence would you state the point you were trying to establish.

Additional Suggestions for the Speech to Convince. Consider these further guides for speaking to neutral and moderately opposed auditors.

(1) Your persuasive goal should be to "win over" the listeners, rather than to overwhelm them. Do not construct a case; build a bridge to understanding and agreement. If your aim is to pile up an impressive total of debater's points, you may "prove" the argument—but lose the audience. Ignore nonessential differences. Use the methods previously discussed to

bring closer together your basic position and that of the audience. Do not shoulder a greater burden of proof than is necessary to achieve your persuasive goal, and use reasoning and evidence as means of narrowing—not widening—the gulf between you and your listeners. Heed the advice of La Rochefoucauld: "True eloquence consists in saying all that is necessary, and nothing but what is necessary."

(2) Keep before your listeners the major lines of your case. By summarizing (in some cases, each major contention should be summarized before moving on) and by coupling the main heads with smooth transitional phrases, you can give the speech added momentum. The addition of each new argument should help to propel your speech toward the persuasive goal. If your speech marches, if it seems to sweep swiftly and surely toward its objective, the listeners are more likely to be caught and carried toward belief.

(3) When possible, use visual materials to strengthen your contentions. Seeing is believing. The most dramatically persuasive use of visual aids that this writer has observed occurred during the Cuban crisis of 1963. In a ninety-five-minute television briefing Secretary of Defense Robert S. McNamara attempted to convince the American people that the Russian missiles had been withdrawn from the island. Previous verbal assurances had failed to relieve public apprehension. Therefore, as his chief means of proof McNamara used scores of greatly enlarged reconnaissance photographs taken at both low and high altitudes. For many persons, this visual evidence was compelling proof that the missiles were gone and the missile sites had been destroyed.

(4) To use the Forms of Support most effectively, keep in mind their uses and limitations. For instance, the literal comparison is usually better logical confirmation than the figurative analogy, although the latter possesses splendid attention-getting qualities and at times is unexcelled in giving clear insight or perspective. Factual illustrations are more convincing verification than are hypothetical examples, but fictitious examples may permit a closer application to the individual members of the audience. Statistics are difficult to remember and typically dull, but can be compelling evidence if interpreted in terms of the audience's experience and interest. The use of testimony has intrinsic deficiencies as logical proof in part because a little research can uncover numerous attestations on either side of most controversial issues. If both the quotation and its source are acceptable to the audience, however, testimonial endorsement is highly effective. Robert T. Oliver and Rupert Cortright go so far as to say, "Since authority is the oldest means of persuasion known to man, it is not surprising that it is also the most universally effective." Repetition, according to some authorities is especially useful in speeches to convince: That which at first seems unpalatable may gradually, upon repeated exposure, seem less strange and undesirable. The influence of repetition is much greater, of course, when applied during a sustained campaign

than in a single speech; but if the listeners are neutral or opposed primarily because of unfamiliarity with your ideas, repetition, along with restatement and explanation, may be quite effective.

The Speech to Stimulate (Reinforce or Impress)

Much of what you have just read concerning the development of speeches to convince applies to speeches to stimulate (reinforce or impress), *providing* you keep in focus two controlling factors: the function of this type of speech and the audience to which it is directed. On controversial issues, the speech to stimulate is directed at audiences who are already in substantial agreement with the speaker. On noncontroversial topics—that is, on topics involving beliefs-values-attitudes-behaviors which are universally accepted by society (see pages 85–86)—when the intent is to arouse interest or feelings, the stimulating speech may be pointed to apathetic listeners, as well as to interested ones. Like any other type of speech, the stimulating one must be audience-centered. As you have just been reminded, the audience of the stimulating speech agrees with the speaker. Because the audience is essentially in harmony—emotionally as well as intellectually—with the speaker, identification is much easier to establish and maintain than with the neutral or hostile audience. An attempt to convince such an audience would be pointless. Inasmuch as it already is convinced, it needs to be impressed or stimulated to a stronger agreement. It needs to have its beliefs-values-attitudes-behaviors reinforced.

In developing the Body of the stimulating speech, your problems in *projecting the appropriate speaker image* are somewhat less acute than in the convincing speech. Inasmuch as you do not represent an alien belief, no ideational-emotional gulf separates you from the audience. The listeners should be less critical of you, less skeptical of your motives, and far less inclined to reject out-of-hand your proposals. In point of fact, the positive attitudes that the listeners hold toward your subject may be extended to you, as a defender of this point of view. The more intense their feeling toward the subject and the closer your association with the subject, ordinarily the more affirmative will be their reactions to you as the speaker.

Likewise, your efforts to *appeal to the logical-psychological needs of* the favorably disposed audience should be much easier to realize than when addressing the neutral or, especially, the hostile audience. In planning the logical-psychological development of the Body, recognize that the stimulating speech does not have to remove or circumvent the basic objections of the listeners; it does not seek to convert uncertain or hostile auditors; instead, its function is to reinforce existing beliefs-values-attitudes-behaviors—to expand the already established major areas of identification between speaker and listener.

Polarity and the Speech to Stimulate (Reinforce or Impress). A key concept in understanding the stimulating speech is *polarity.* As used here, polarity refers to the positive orientation of the thought-feeling responses of the listeners toward a specific polar point: the speaker's persuasive intent. The degree of polarity is high when the ideational-emotional responses of the auditors flow smoothly and noncritically toward the persuasive goal. The degree of polarity is low when listeners retain heterogeneous attitudes and beliefs toward the topic, when they think and feel as individuals rather than members of an in-group, when they resist suggestion and subject the speaker's evidence and reasoning to critical or hypercritical scrutiny. In convincing speeches, polarity is low, partly because the listeners' will-to-believe may run counter to your proposals. In stimulating speeches the polarity potential of the listeners may be much higher, partly because their will-to-believe supports your idea. Your speech development should correlate reasonably well with the intensity of the listeners' predispositions. When a person adopts an idea or a program, he tends to develop a complex of attitudes concerning it. If it assumes immediate and considerable significance to him personally, his logico-emotional attachment to the belief grows in intensity and becomes entangled with values and attitudes concerning related beliefs. As a general rule, the stronger and more pervasive his personal and subjective values and attitudes concerning a particular belief, the less critical the person is likely to be of the evidence and reasoning that reaffirm his beliefs. In the speech to convince you may have the difficult, and sometimes impossible, task of contending with hostile logico-emotional factors; in the speech to stimulate, the chief roadblocks you encounter may be apathy, sluggish awareness, or dull sensitivities.

Logic-Ethics and the Speech to Stimulate (Reinforce or Impress). The foregoing should not be interpreted to mean that either logic or ethics is unimportant in stimulating speeches. You should arrive at your convictions only after an exhaustive examination of the facts and a painstaking application of reasoning and ethics to the facts. You should never compromise your beliefs to please an audience. Such a practice is indefensible on both moral and pragmatic grounds. Over the long pull, the pandering speaker is recognized as such and his ethical proof is drastically reduced. Furthermore, although their beliefs and actions may be rooted in emotions, men do reason logically, or think they do. Therefore, an extremely emotional appeal, or one that is obviously pitched at the emotions, will answer the logical-psychological needs of only irrational auditors and may offend others. At the opposite extreme, an exclusively logical approach will leave the listeners "cold." A median position, then, is in order: *your development of the Body of the stimulating speech should be as logical as the nature of your listeners permits.*

Unethical Artifices and Strategems and the Speech to Stimulate (Reinforce or Impress). The statement of purpose for the stimulating speech (to reinforce values and attitudes, to impress or stimulate listeners to stronger agreement) implicitly endorses a combined appeal to thinking and feeling. Your problem is to assign appropriate roles to both logic and emotions. The astute, if uncomplimentary, student of human nature Machiavelli once stated, "Men in general judge more from appearances than from reality. All men have eyes but few have the gift of penetration." Machiavelli would accept this extension of his statement: when their self-interests or cherished beliefs are involved, men tend to be less objective. Realizing this truism, some unscrupulous speakers seek to manipulate the favorably oriented audience by means of unethical artifices and stratagems, such as the following.

(1) *Irrelevant evidence.* A sound argument must be directed to the point, to the merits of the case. A speaker may appear to be constructing a sound argument, however, if he uses illustrations, comparisons, statistics, or testimony that seem to support the point, though they are irrelevant.

(2) *Half-truths and lies.* Not infrequently speakers deliberately or unconsciously distort evidence to the extent that it no longer resembles objective truth. Also, they may assert as factual that evidence which is undocumented, merely conjecture, or opinion.

(3) NON SEQUITUR *conclusion.* A speaker may affirm a conclusion on the basis of reasoning or supporting materials that do not prove the point, although they may seem to do so. For instance, if arguing against tax reforms a speaker might refute one of the arguments for it; if he then claims to have destroyed the whole case for tax reforms, he is affirming a non sequitur conclusion.

(4) *Irrelevant conclusions.* If a point is difficult to prove, the speaker may deliberately ignore the real issue—and prove something else. If speaking to a religiously oriented audience on the constitutionality of Bible reading in the schools, a speaker might sidestep the issue of constitutionality and prove instead that religion is vitally important or that because Bible reading in the schools is prohibited by Supreme Court decision the cause of religion is injured.

(5) *Obfuscation.* To meet minimal requirements for logical development, language must be clear, precise, and consistent. A means of avoiding the rational examination of certain issues or evidence is deliberately to obscure the matter in a smoglike blanket of language. In what purports to be a straightforward accounting, the speaker may destroy meaning by inserting in key positions terms that are intentionally vague, ambiguous, shifting in meaning, contradictory, abstract, or unfamiliar to the listeners. His explanations may be so involved, technical, or crowded with citations that the listeners lose sight of the point. Because the

speaker appears to be sincerely trying to foster understanding and because the hearers agree with his basic views, this deception may go undetected.

(6) *Unscrupulous speakers use many other clearly unethical methods, such as deliberate faulty generalizations, faulty particularizations (deductions), and faulty causation.* No attempt here has been made to catalog all such methods and no claim is made that such practices are peculiar to stimulating speeches. The unscrupulous speaker will use dishonest methods whenever he believes he can "get away with it." His chances for escaping detection are better, however, when speaking to relatively *noncritical* listeners in the stimulating speech than to *hypercritical* auditors in the convincing speech.

The Ethically "Gray Area" and the Speech to Stimulate (Reinforce or Impress). Now that we have eliminated dishonest practices we enter a "gray area" in which the rhetorical methods are ethical or unethical depending upon their usage in the particular situation. If your listeners are unwilling to "hold still" for a dispassionate examination of all relevant aspects of the topic, you may wish to employ rationalization. Having already made up their minds, the listeners may want merely to hear reasons and evidence that support their beliefs. This justification is reasoning *after the fact.* The "right" answers have already been determined, and the listeners may need assurance that their beliefs are "correct," "worthy," "humanitarian," "in tune with the past and in step with the future," and so on. To meet such listeners "where they are," you should recognize that they are inclined to view the facts through their biases. Rationalization (self-justification) is an inescapable fact of life. On some issues your listeners may be unwilling or unable to reason systematically. The logical-psychological needs of these listeners may require generous appeals to the emotions. Even in such cases, however, the ethical speaker should never take license with the truth.

Among the more common appeals to rationalization are the following somewhat overlapping methods.

(1) *Assuming the point.* If a speaker is convinced that logic and ethics support his basic contentions, and *if the audience agrees,* he customarily assumes, rather than proves, the validity of his points. From this base of agreement, his developing material may stress the significance or application of his argument.

(2) *Appealing to popular feeling or prejudice.* Whenever a Republican addresses a Lincoln celebration or a Democrat speaks to a Jefferson-Jackson dinner, he appeals—whether he wishes to or not—to the emotional prejudgments of the listeners. If they did not share in the values, attitudes, beliefs, policies, and, perhaps, in the need for the party to win the next election, they probably would not have paid the $100 banquet charge.

(3) *Appealing to sympathy or pity.* Human sensitivities sometimes transcend logic. They give meaning, richness, and dimensions to life. They help to make us humane, different from the unfeeling machine. To motivate an audience to experience sympathy or pity for another person may be ethical or unethical. If the speaker wishes the listeners to help a flood victim with contributions of money or clothes, an appeal to sympathy and pity may be legitimate. If the speaker wishes to cause the audience to acquit a defendant of a crime that he has committed, an appeal to sympathy and pity may not be legitimate.

(4) *Shifting the burden of proof.* Logically, he who affirms or denies a point of view must assume the necessary burden of proof or disproof. In speaking to noncritical listeners, a speaker may challenge the opposition to disprove his arguments "if they can." This attempt to shift the burden of proof becomes a fallacy only if he assumes that the inability of his opponent to disprove his case thereby establishes its truth. One cannot logically discharge a burden of proof by declaring that others must either refute it or accept its validity. For example, a professor who wanted his university to shift from a term to a semester calendar committed a fallacy when he demanded that the administration prove that the term system was superior to the semester. If the administration did not respond to his demands, he claimed, this failure would prove the semester system was better.

(5) *Transferring emotional approval.* An exceedingly common method of stimulating favorable attitudes toward an idea or thing is to couple it with some emotional source of respect, authority, reverence, or affection: it should be accepted because highly respected individuals or organizations endorse it ("Mr. Reagan thought enough of the Easter Seal campaign to make a national television appeal in its behalf"); it is traditional ("Fee-for-service medical practice is part of our American heritage; it has always been a part of the American way of life"); it is new ("X-O ought to be good; it's the newest miracle drug"); it is folksy ("The senator likes to barbecue chickens in his backyard for family get-togethers"); it is scientific ("The XYZ corporation is the leading name in electronics research; so, this tube has to be the best"); it is associated with proven beliefs, programs, and so on ("This boy should be given a football scholarship; his three older brothers all played good ball for State U").

(6) *Arguing to the man.* A speaker may attempt to color the listeners' reactions to an individual in order to influence their reactions to his views. By referring to a person's associations, personality, appearance, war record, family, love for children or animals, reputation, community service, and so on, the speaker constructs the kind of image that may "rub off" on his ideas, that is, will make the ideas either more or less attractive. Sometimes, of course, the credibility of a person's ideas depends upon his credibility as a person. When an Atlanta insurance agent claimed to have overheard a telephone conversation in which University of Georgia Ath-

letic Director Wally Butts passed on to University of Alabama coach Bear Bryant information concerning Georgia football plays, conclusive factual proof was not ascertainable; at least until the legal judgment was made in the resulting civil suit, public belief or disbelief in the charges depended upon the image of credibility projected by the three men.

(7) *Oversimplifying.* Even at best, public speaking tends to compress and simplify issues. At the rate of 150 words a minute, a speaker utters only 1,500 words in ten minutes—hardly enough for an exhaustive examination of even an uncomplicated topic. In addition to the time factor, the listeners' limitations of power of attention, knowledge, and objectivity encourage compression and simplification. Especially in speaking to favorably oriented listeners, the speaker is tempted to ignore qualifications, extenuating circumstances, differentiating characteristics, and so on. He is inclined to speak of absolute values, simple cause—direct result, obvious need—infallible solution, and so on.

(8) *Using stereotypes, ridicule, and sarcasm.* Speakers often use stereotypes, ridicule, and sarcasm to rally the support of favorably oriented listeners. By disparaging "outsiders," the speaker may draw the in-group members (speaker and listeners) closer together. By employing stereotypes, the speaker may evoke attitudes—ideas that the listeners bring "ready-made" to the speaking situation. When appropriate to the situation, such use of labels, loaded words, and slogans helps to unify the audience and to make complex matters seem understandable and solvable.

(9) *Applying the "bandwagon" technique.* The "bandwagon" is sometimes used to hurry into stronger agreement those listeners who are in basic agreement with the speaker but hesitate to commit themselves more deeply to his proposals. The speaker may capitalize upon the "herd instinct" by claiming that the listeners (or, all "right-minded" people) universally and wholeheartedly support his proposals. The plea may be implied, or open: "Go with the crowd! Those who hesitate will be isolated and lonely. Don't be left out! Get on the bandwagon before it passes you by!"

The foregoing and other methods of rationalization are used in convincing speeches, in addition to stimulating ones. They are especially successful however, when directed to the relatively noncritical audience of the stimulating speech. When rationalization is used to *supplement* logic, it may be ethical; when used to *supplant* logic or to serve ignoble ends, it is dishonest and should be avoided.

Additional Suggestions for the Speech to Stimulate (Reinforce or Impress). In addition to logic, stratagems, and rationalizations, various other means often are used to stimulate an audience to stronger agreement. Any means that will cause listeners to think, feel or behave as a positive unit will promote polarity. Unification of the listeners is promoted if the meeting is held in a location rich in relevant emotional attachments, such as a religious edifice, union hall, or fraternity house; if symbols such as the flag, the cross, trophies, pictures of respected leaders are prominently displayed; if listeners are crowded together in a room just large enough to accommodate them. Some speakers consider that emotions may sweep more easily over an audience if the members are in close physical proximity to each other and if the audience fills the available seats with persons sitting in the aisles and standing along the walls. Unification is fostered by getting the listeners to engage in symbolic actions, such as reciting the Boy Scout oath, singing fraternal songs, pledging allegiance to the flag, saying the Lord's Prayer, reading from a prayer book, or standing or sitting in unison as part of a ritual. Unification is encouraged by stimulating the listeners to overt response, as laughing, smiling, clapping their hands in applause, cheering, booing, holding up hands in response to a question, and so on.

To impress favorably oriented listeners, you may stress beliefs, emotions, and experiences that you share with them and that are relevant to the point; emphasize that the members of the audience endorse your ideas; as unobtrusively as necessary, underscore your argument both with proof that your proposals will benefit them and society and with positive reasons why they are "right" to believe the way they do. You may encourage listeners to reinforce their beliefs by proving the logical merit of your proposals and by demonstrating appropriately that the proposals promote their interests: their physical, psychological, or economic security; their personal freedom; their desire for recognition and influence; their pride in the community; their love of country; their loyalty for customs and traditions; their affection for family and friends; their reverence for God or religion; their interest in sex; their desire to experience excitement, adventure, and change.

Definitely and extremely favorable auditors are potentially highly polarized. They may be hungry for strong positive assertions, sweeping generalizations, impelling slogans, and dynamic calls for action. For such listeners, especially, phrase your supporting materials in such vividly concrete language that they easily formulate the mental-emotional images. Recognize that, as Donald W. MacKinnon (director, Institute of Personality Assessment and Research at the University of California) put it, "the unconscious operates more by symbols than logic." Keep the pace moving swiftly and smoothly toward the persuasive goal. Do not frustrate like-minded listeners by forcing them to follow your speech through a labyrinth of overly involved explanation or overly technical documentation. As in any speech, use variety in the selection of the Forms of Support and Factors of Attention. Humor can be very useful as a means of unifying and energizing the favorably oriented audience, particularly if the humor makes your proposals seem more attractive and the alternatives less so. In the stimulating speech, your use of humor perhaps may be somewhat less reserved and more incisive than in convincing speeches, and may include irony, burlesque, caricature, quips, parody, incongruous comparisons and contrasts, hyperbole, understatement, and unusual twists of familiar statements or poems.

The Speech to Actuate

As you will recall, the actuating speech differs from convincing and stimulating (impressing or reinforcing) ones in that it attempts to produce direct observable action on the part of the listeners. Its intent goes beyond mere intellectual or emotional affirmation; it seeks to motivate a specific response in the near future. Although the actuating speech can be directed to any audience, whether favorably oriented, neutral, or hostile to the speaker's POINT (review Figures No. 4—page 86, No. 5—page 87 and No. 6—page 88), only listeners who are in vigorous agreement with a policy are likely to carry out a requested action. Strong affirmation usually precedes action. This means that by the time you have finished presenting the supporting materials of the Body—or at least, by the time you have completed your Summary Step in the Conclusion—the listeners must have moved *from* their original position *to* one of such strong agreement that they are ready to act. Naturally if the listeners bring to the meeting "built-in" patterns of intellectual-emotional opposition, it is usually unrealistic to expect that a single speech will convert them into active supporters. To meet your listeners "where they are," follow the advice given earlier in this chapter for speeches to convince and to stimulate (reinforce or impress). In developing the Body, keep in mind, of course, that your purpose represents the ultimate challenge to a speaker: to get others to do as he wishes.

Summary

This chapter was designed as a continuation of Chapters 7 and 8. In developing the Body of the informative speech, you should plan the supporting materials to encourage the listeners to engage with you in a continuing dialogue, to demonstrate that you possess proper attitudes as the speaker, and to facilitate interest-understanding-retention. In the entertaining speech, your major, if not sole, concern in using supporting materials is to provide your listeners with a refreshing diversion from routine problems and obligations. In the speech to convince, you should plan the supporting materials to enable the listeners to move *from* opposition, neutrality, or indecision *toward* agreement. In the speech to stimulate, you should design the supporting materials to impress or stimulate the favorably oriented listeners, to enable them to reinforce their existing state of agreement. In the speech to actuate, you should select and develop the supporting materials in such a way that listeners are motivated to do something you wish.

Exercises and Assignments

1. Prepare a five-minute speech for class presentation in which you discuss some of the major differences between the development of the Body of the speech to inform and that of the speech to entertain.
2. In a five-minute talk explain some of the differences in the types of supporting materials and Methods of Development that you might employ in preparing speeches to inform, entertain, and persuade.
3. Give a five-minute talk in which you explain some of the similarities and differences in the style of delivery for speeches to inform, entertain, and persuade.
4. Discuss for the class the use of significant wants in the speech to entertain; the speech to inform; the speech to persuade.
5. In a short report, contrast the role of "implication" in the speech to inform with its usage in the speech to persuade.
6. Make a brief talk explaining your answer to the question: "Is the 'yes' technique as used in persuasive speeches unethical?"

CHAPTER 10

Developing the Introduction of the Speech

As in the business interview, the successful outcome of the public speech depends in part upon initial impressions. No effective salesman would walk into the office of a stranger, sit down at the desk, and begin to transact business. Instead, he would introduce himself and state the purpose of his call before attempting to make a sale. Similarly, under ordinary circumstances the public speaker should not launch into the middle of a speech; some sort of Introduction is needed. Because the initial impression that the speaker makes upon his listeners is so important, some speakers believe that the Introduction is the most important section of the speech. Many years ago Quintilian pointed out that "there is no point in the whole speech where confusion of memory or loss of fluency has a worse effect, for a faulty Introduction is like a face seamed with scars; and he who runs his ship ashore while leaving port is certainly the least efficient of pilots."

Understanding the Principles of Development

The appropriate length of the Introduction varies considerably, depending upon the circumstances involved; however, a serviceable estimation of the length of the typical Introduction is about 10 per cent of the entire speech. The substance of the Introduction likewise depends upon the total situation; in general, the Introduction serves as a bridge between the initial reaction of the listeners and the speaker's major ideas, as presented in the Body—or, as Cicero suggested, it serves to *answer the rhetorical needs* usually present at the beginning of a speech: "to render hearers well disposed toward the speaker, attentive to his speech, and open to influence."

The Introduction prepares the hearers *psychologically*—by stimulating favorable interest in the speaker and his message—and *logically*—by orienting them to the basic thrust or purpose of the speech and the nature of the Body. As a serviceable formula for your first speeches you may consider that the favorable attention materials comprise the first heading of the Introduction and the clarifying materials the second, as shown.

Specific Speech Purpose:
Introduction:
I. Favorable Attention Step
II. Clarification Step
Body:

In your later speeches, you may wish to discard the formula or to adjust it to the particular speaking situation: under some conditions you might prefer to begin the speech with a Clarification Step; upon other occasions your attempts to stimulate a receptive attitude on the part of the listeners may also serve to orient them to the subject, thus obviating the need for a separate Clarification Step, and so on.

Keeping in mind that the formula is designed to be a flexible tool, consider the following suggestions for preparing the Favorable Attention Step and the Clarification Step.

Stimulating Favorable Attention

Through past experience with dull speakers, the American public has been conditioned to expect the worst. Therefore, even though curiosity or respect for you as the speaker may cause an audience to listen fairly attentively for the first minute or so, you must establish yourself at the outset as an interesting, friendly, animated speaker with a worthwhile message. Unless you successfully "sell" both yourself and your speech, the initial attention of the audience may soon be dampened and can be rekindled only with difficulty.

Let us look now at some of the various options at your disposal for fostering favorable attention in the Introduction.

Refer to the Significance of the Subject. One of the most reliable methods of securing immediate attention is to "identify" your topic with the desires and needs of the listeners. Do more than point out the importance of the topic to people in general; go a step further and make clear the application to the members of the audience. As unobtrusively—yet as impellingly—as possible, demonstrate that your message will save them money, save them time, make them more popular, increase their earnings, reduce their automobile insurance rates, improve their appearance or their health, protect them from bodily injury, and so on.

Thomas P. Pike began his speech ("Alcoholism in the Executive Suite") to the Town Hall of California by stressing the significance of alcoholism to society and to his listeners.[1]

> I am deeply grateful for this invitation to speak to you today about alcoholism. This dread disease is our nation's # 1 health problem and our # 3 killer, ranking only after heart disease and cancer as a cause of death. It needs to be talked about more and understood better in forums such as this.
>
> Whether you realize it or not, it is virtually certain that you have a problem with alcoholism in your organization, because 5 percent to 10 percent of all employed persons in this country are alcoholics. Of the ten million alcoholics in this country, over half of them are on government or corporate payrolls and are currently robbing their employers blind. The total national economic impact of the disease of alcoholism in our society is a staggering $43 billion per year.
>
> Alcoholism is an insidious disease, poorly understood, unjustly stigmatized, and it is an illness around which our society has created a dense fog of fallacy, myth, and false moral condemnation. Its victims are subjected to a hideous conspiracy of concealment and it's a hidden disease, which, like the iceberg, shows only the tip. It is treated too often by being ignored and. . .denied.
>
> The public ignorance on alcoholism is massive and it is a national disgrace. President Nixon once stated that "Our greatest foe in combatting alcoholism is ignorance."
>
> To bring some of the light of truth into this vast arena of human darkness and suffering, and to bring the message of hope and help which is available to the suffering alcoholic and his employer, is the prime purpose of a personal crusade in which my wife and I have been privileged to engage for over thirty years. . . .
>
> Now, before I tell you something about occupational alcoholism, which, believe me, exists all the way from the production line to the executive suite, let me tell you a little about my own long and losing battle with John Barleycorn, and then share with you some overviews on alcoholism generally, and its effects on our work force in particular.

[1] *Vital Speeches,* January 1, 1980, p. 166.

Use Humor. Although frequently misused, humor can be an excellent method of stimulating favorable attention. Inasmuch as the opening remarks probably constitute the most conspicuous part of a speech, be especially careful to follow the suggestions in Chapter 7 for the use of humor. It is perhaps sufficient here to state that any witty pleasantry, banter with the chairman, playful jibes at someone in the audience, novel twist to a common saying, good-humored irreverence, clever exaggeration or understatement, humorous story, and so on, must be genial, fresh, relevant, appropriate—and brief. Here are some sample situations in which humor was used to secure interest:

(1) A human-relations expert began to talk on courtship in this manner: "Courtship has been semiseriously defined as that short interlude between lipstick and mopstick."

(2) John A. Howard, when president of Rockford College, used this method to start his speech at the Opening Convocation, Rockford College, Rockford, Illinois:

> Two caterpillars were crawling across a lawn one day when a handsome butterfly flew overhead. One caterpillar was heard to remark to the other, "Some folks may think that's the way to live, but you couldn't get me up in one of those flimsy things for a million dollars."
>
> This morning I want to share with you some thoughts about liberal arts education which appears to be carrying on very much like the grumpy caterpillar just quoted. The potential is there, but the creature, seemingly ignorant of its potential, is somewhat obtuse in its thinking and earthbound in its performance.

(3) At a meeting of a local bar association a judge introduced his speech ("The Social Responsibilities of the Legal Profession") like this:

> According to a story told by the late Judge Hollister, the gate between heaven and hell broke down one day. When Saint Peter discovered the condition of the gate he called to the devil: "Hey, Satan, it's your turn to fix it this time."
>
> "My apologies, sir," replied the boss of the land beyond the Styx. "My men are much too busy to worry about a broken gate."
>
> "Well, then," growled Saint Peter, "I'll sue you for breaking our agreement."
>
> "Yeah?" retorted the devil. "Where will you get a lawyer?"

Tell an Illustrative Story. An example of the use of personal experience as a Favorable Attention Step is afforded by a mother who urged the members of a local PTA to make their homes "child safe." Several years previously this woman had left on a bedside table an open bottle of aspirin from which her three-year-old daughter had swallowed a near lethal dose.

By telling of this near tragic experience and by showing that many youngsters are involved in home accidents, the woman encouraged the members to listen to her suggestions for improving the safety of the home.

Factual illustrations other than personal experiences may also be used effectively to capture initial attention.

(1) In attempting to place into interesting perspective the decision to integrate the power-generating systems serving France and England, Hallowell Bowser employed several examples.[2]

> Every student of history knows that the most stirring and momentous events have a way of taking place without benefit of torchlight parades, or road signs pointing to the scene of the excitement. The Wright brothers' first flights at Kitty Hawk, the departure of Columbus's tiny fleet from Palos, and the trial runs of Daimler's automobile are among the historic events that were greeted by profound silence in contemporary journals.
>
> This human propensity for ignoring great events so bemused Brueghel that he painted a notable canvas in whose foreground a peasant stolidly plows his field, while in the background Icarus ends his legendary flight by plunging into the Aegean, unnoticed by the workaday world. It would be a pity indeed if one of the potentially crucial events of this decade, the forthcoming cross-Channel power exchange between France and England, went similarly unremarked.

(2) A speaker soliciting funds for the Red Cross might introduce his subject by relating a specific instance in which that organization had provided dramatic assistance to distressed people.

(3) If seeking to impress the need for safety upon workmen newly assigned to the construction of an underground missile installation, a foreman might secure *initial* attention by telling how a former worker had lost his life because momentary carelessness had caused his crane to topple over the lip of the one-hundred-foot shaft.

Although the narration of an actual happening is usually much more effective, the relating of an imaginary occurrence can also be used to secure attention.

(1) In the Favorable Attention Step of a speech on the construction of storm shelters, the speaker could describe how a tornado might differently affect two hypothetical families, one of which had built a shelter and the other had not.

(2) The following excerpt from a student speech demonstrates a different type of fictitious story:

> Sometime during childhood we all read or were told the enthralling fantasies of the "Arabian Nights." In the story of Aladdin and his lamp, you will remember that Aladdin had lost the magic lamp,

[2] *Saturday Review,* July 3, 1961, p. 26.

> the rubbing of which produced a genie bound to carry out all of its owner's wishes. Feeling certain that the lamp had been found by someone in the village, Aladdin conceived an ingenious idea. Disguising himself as a peddler and carrying a basket loaded with bright new lamps, he proceeded from one street to another in the village, crying, "New lamps for old! New lamps for old!" Soon there appeared an old man who sought to trade the battered lamp Aladdin was seeking for a bright, shiny new one.
>
> Perhaps we of America, like the aged man in the fable, have traded an old lamp for a shiny new one!

Use a Stimulating Quotation. A frequently employed method of creating involuntary attention in the Introduction is to use a striking, brief, relevant quotation. Naturally, you are not limited to quotations taken from written works, but may select oral testimony as well.

(1) Before the election of 1980 a speaker began an address to a conservative audience with this quotation:

> Herman Kahn believes that a "major change is taking place in the country after a decade of dominance by eastern liberal transcendentalists who did their best to wreck the country by embracing a set of values that did little to solve the country's problems." According to Kahn, "square values and square politics are in the ascendency." I accept Kahn's conclusions and make them the text for my speech.

(2) A minister wishing to stimulate his hearers to re-examine their own actions and thinking in the light of Christian doctrines began his sermon like this: "Walpole once said, 'In my youth I thought of writing a satire on mankind, but now in my age I think I should write an apology for them.'"

(3) A journalist addressing a woman's club on the role of literature in modern civilization introduced his topic in this manner:

> Books are not dull, inanimate, unimportant sheets of paper attached to cardboard bindings. Without the written recordings of man's thoughts and emotions civilization would be impossible. Clarence Day has expressed well the importance of books in these words: "The world of books is the most remarkable creation of man. Nothing else that he builds ever lasts. Monuments fall. Nations perish. Civilizations grow old and die out—and after an era of darkness—new races build others, but—in the world of books are volumes that have seen this happen again and again—and yet live on—still young—still as fresh as the day they were written—still telling men's hearts of the hearts of men—centuries dead!"

Ask the Audience a Striking Question. An easy way to test the "striking" quality of a question is to turn it into a declarative statement. Unless the resulting sentence is stimulating, the question itself will not be so. When turned into a declaration, the query "Do you watch television?" becomes "You do watch television." Obviously such a sentence has little attention value. Avoid asking dull, flat, pointless questions or insulting ones, such as the following: Do you engage in corrupt business practices? Are you unconsciously cruel to your children? Do you cheat in filing income tax returns?

Here are some examples of how the stimulating question has been used to secure initial favorable attention.

(1) A civic leader addressing a group of adults on juvenile delinquency used this as his Favorable Attention Step:

> What would you do if your son came to you this evening and said, "Dad, I've just killed a man"? What would be your emotions when he poured out his story that he had been drinking and, as he was speeding home, his car struck a pedestrian? Your son a hit-skip driver? A juvenile delinquent? Of course not, you say. But this very situation confronted a friend of mine this spring. He didn't think it could happen either—but it did!

(2) A football coach speaking to a rabid high school crowd at a bonfire rally started off his "pep talk" by asking the question "Are you with the team?" (He knew, of course, that the students were frenetically partisan and that the asking of this question would give them a chance to let off steam. Under ordinary circumstances such a question would lack stimulating qualities.) After the noise had partially subsided, the coach asked, "Do you think we're going to win?" This offered the students another opportunity to participate.

(3) A student discussing his experiences at a summer resort in North Carolina began his talk in this manner: "Have you ever found a six-foot-long diamondback rattlesnake in your closet? Well, I did last summer. . . ."

Make a Pithy, Provocative Statement. The provocative statement is used in much the same manner as the striking question. An ordinary, dull phrase—or a series of them—will not gain attention. To catch interest, a sentence must be different; it must be intriguing. It should not, however, seem strained, or contrived, or an awkward striving for the sensational.

(1) In the opening of his lecture to the Bread Loaf Writers' Conference, Robert Frost used several pithy statements:

> You don't have to know how to spell to write poetry. You can be rather loose in your syntax as far as I am concerned. You don't have to know how to punctuate at all. Poe has nothing but dashes in his poems because he left punctuation to his printers. . . .

(2) In an address before the Radio and Television News Directors' Assocation, Edward R. Murrow began with these challenging comments:

> This just might do nobody any good. At the end of this discourse a few people may accuse this reporter of fouling his own comfortable nest; and your organization may be accused of having given hospitality to heretical and even dangerous thoughts.

(3) Public speakers could profitably study the trenchant, interesting methods used by *Time* magazine to introduce its articles. An article about Francois Mauriac and other "confused" Europeans opened with this striking statement:

> The difference between a confused intellectual and an ostrich is that the ostrich cannot manufacture its own sand.

Refer to the Audience, Occasion, or Purpose of the Meeting. By identifying yourself or your proposals with certain associations, pleasant experiences, ideals, beliefs, desires, interests, or attitudes of the listeners, you may foster a favorable reception of your message. To illustrate:

(1) In his address to the San Francisco Press Club, Stansfield Turner, Director of the Central Intelligence Agency, attempted to promote favorable interest by pointing out similarities between himself and his listeners—before recognizing potential areas of conflict.[3]

> It is always a treat to have a chance to exchange ideas with the press. I believe that our two professions, journalism and intelligence, have a great deal in common. We have in common the task of finding the facts about what is going on in the world; you primarily, for the American public; we, primarily for the American government.
>
> Beyond that, we both recognize the great importance to each of us of protecting our sources of information. I admire those newsmen who have been willing to go to jail rather than to disclose their sources. I assure you that we too will go to considerable lengths to protect ours.
>
> The appreciation of the value of an exclusive is another common professional characteristic. For you, it can provide an important edge over your competitors. For us, it can give the President of the United States an important edge of advantage when competing or negotiating with others.
>
> There is also another interest we have in common. We both must possess some fundamental protections under the law if we are to continue to be effective for our country. For you, the most fundamental protection is the freedom of speech which is guaranteed by

[3] *Vital Speeches*, October 1, 1980, pp. 753–54.

the First Amendment of the Constitution. For us, it is the guarantee of a reasonable degree of secrecy, without which we simply cannot function. And, it is here that our interests sometimes appear to collide. It may seem to you that we are ready and eager to dispense with the privileges of the First Amendment in the pursuit of secrecy. Nothing could be further from the truth.

(2) A civic leader talking to a Little League club might tell the youngsters of seeing Dave Kingman hit three home runs in New York the day before, mention that fifteen years earlier he had been a member of this same club, or refer to his long friendship with the club's director.

(3) In his Favorable Attention Step, a commencement speaker might describe his own feelings and emotions at his graduation two decades previously, or state that immediately after the program he was flying to Madison, Wisconsin, to attend his son's graduation.

If you are a visitor speaking at a regularly scheduled meeting of an organization or if you are addressing a special meeting called for a specific purpose, you probably should refer in the Introduction to the audience, occasion, or purpose of the gathering. In the opening of his address to the All-European Conference in Helsinki, Leonid Brezhnev made these references to the speaking situation.[4]

All of us who take part in the final stage of the Conference on Security and Cooperation in Europe feel the unusual character of this event and its political scope. It can be said with confidence that the same feeling is shared by millions upon millions of people in all the countries participating in the conference, and not in those countries alone. Together with us, they are in the process of comprehending what is presently taking place in the capital of Finland.

What has made the top political and state leaders present in this hall adopt such an attitude to the conference?

The answer seems to be that the results of the conference are linked with expectations and hopes never before engendered by any other collective action during the period following the well-known allied decisions of the postwar time.

The people who belong to the generation which experienced the horrors of World War II most closely perceive the historical significance of the conference. Its objectives are also close to the hearts and minds of the generation of Europeans which has grown, and is now living, in conditions of peace and which quite justly believes that it cannot be otherwise.

The soil of Europe was drenched with blood in the years of the two world wars. Top political and state leaders of 33 European states, and of the USA and Canada have assembled in Helsinki in

[4] *Vital Speeches,* September 1, 1975, p. 674.

> order to contribute, by joint efforts, to making Europe a continent which would experience no more military calamities. . . .
>
> This is why the hour has struck for the inevitable collective conclusions to be drawn from the experience of history. And we are drawing these conclusions here. . . .

Compliment the Audience. One of the most effective—as well as most dangerous—methods of identification is to compliment your hearers. All of us appreciate commendation. If a person is intelligent enough to admire us, we tend to believe that he has used similar good judgment in arriving at other ideas, and may listen to him somewhat less critically. Recognize, however, that an audience is quick to sense and resent too obvious or extravagant praise. Therefore, compliment an audience only if you are sincere, if the situation seems appropriate, and if the compliment can be phrased so that it not only *is* genuine but also *seems* genuine.

As in social conversation, opportunities—and necessities—sometimes arise in public speaking situations for the speaker to pay his listeners genuine compliments. Let us look at sample situations.

(1) If you are the guest of a corporation, labor union, university, or social organization, and have been treated courteously and generously, good manners may require you to refer to this hospitality in the Introduction. On Herbert Hoover's seventy-fourth birthday some fifteen thousand Iowans gathered in an all-day celebration in his honor. After a picnic dinner and a parade of bands and drum corps, Mr. Hoover rose to speak:

> I am deeply grateful for your reception and the honor which you do me today. I deeply appreciate the many thousands of kindly acts and kindly wishes which have marked the day. They come both from those of you who are present and from many parts of my country—which adds to my gratitude. . . .

(2) If you are an outsider speaking in a city or state famed for its scenery, sports, fashion centers, climate, educational institutions, industry, or the like, you may signify your recognition of the prominence for which the community is noted. In speaking to the Economic Club of Detroit, E. Douglas Kenna, president of the National Association of Manufacturers, attempted to secure favorable attention with this compliment.

> I am honored to be in Detroit because of what this city stands for—not just for this country but throughout the world. Detroit is the hub of the competitive system. It's the cradle of the mass production dynamism which helped create the miracle of America. . . .

(3) If either the listeners or the organization you are addressing has had a distinguished past, you may be justified in referring to this record.

William J. McGill, then president of Columbia University, used this compliment to begin his speech to the National Conference on the Causes of Popular Dissatisfaction with the Administration of Justice:

> It is an honor and a privilege to address this distinguished audience commemorating the 70th anniversary of Roscoe Pound's classic paper on the causes of popular dissatisfaction with the administration of justice, but I am also a bit intimidated by the honor.
>
> A national conference of jurists and eminent scholars of the law chosen especially for their competence in considering the philosophical underpinnings of American justice offers no easy forum to an untarnished legal virgin. . . .

(4) If either the listeners or the sponsoring organization has recently achieved an honor—especially if that honor has a direct connection with the meeting—you may need to recognize this distinction in the introduction of your remarks. Arthur G. Hansen, president of Purdue University, opened his address at the Purdue University Commencement with this recognition of the achievement of his hearers:

> One of the pleasurable aspects of being President of this University is the privilege of being the first to officially congratulate you on reaching this important milestone in your life. The diploma you will receive shortly symbolizes the many efforts you have put forth and the commitment you have made to reach this goal. You need not be told that it has come at a price. We feel certain, however, that as you move into your earned positions in the world, you will feel the price paid was well worth it. Your degree distinguishes you. Wherever you go you can say with a genuine sense of pride, "I am a graduate of Purdue University."

(5) If the listeners have had to wait through several hours of ceremony, oratory, or presentation of awards, or if they have had to combat inclement weather to attend the meeting, you can voice your appreciation. Many years ago in Freeport, Illinois, Stephen A. Douglas began a rejoinder to Abraham Lincoln with this deft compliment:

> The silence with which you have listened to Mr. Lincoln during this hour is creditable to this vast audience, composed of men of various political parties. Nothing is more honorable to any large mass of people assembled for the purpose of fair discussion than that kind and respectful attention that is yielded not only to your political friends, but to those who are opposed to you in politics.

(6) If you have been generously applauded upon being introduced, you might thank the listeners for the warmth of their welcome. For example, a university president, recently victorious in his struggles to secure a

higher appropriation from the state legislature, was given a cheering ovation from the faculty at the annual end-of-the-school-year meeting. In response, the president said:

> Thank you. . . . Thank you. . . . Thank you for your most kind welcome. . . . I rather suspect, however, that a few of those cheers were for the good news recently announced at the state capitol. (Laughter and applause)

Preparing the Audience for the Body of the Speech

To orient the audience to the Body, you may follow the Favorable Attention Step with a Clarification Step. As the term indicates, the Clarification Step should "clarify," that is, make apparent the nature and purpose of the talk and give necessary preliminary explanations and definitions. In planning the Clarification Step, you could use one or more of the following three methods.

State the POINT of the Speech. Frequently the inexperienced speaker fails to make clear the basic thrust of the speech or the nature of the response he is seeking. From such a speech the members of an audience may form vague, or even sharply conflicting, conceptions of the POINT of a speech. Every effective speech, business letter, board meeting, serious conversation—every communicative situation—not only has a POINT or purpose, but all persons involved know what that POINT is.

Although it is not always necessary or desirable to use this method—as we shall see a little later—the listeners will have no reason to mistake the purpose of your speech if you tell them expressly what your POINT is. If you cannot phrase your intent in a concise, definite statement, it is vague to you and will, therefore, be even less distinct to your listeners. To orient the listeners to the POINT of your message, merely paraphrase the Specific Speech Purpose. Naturally you should avoid using a fragmentary sentence, such as "Football safety," or the label "Specific Speech Purpose" in some such manner as: "My Specific Speech Purpose is to inform you concerning football safety." Instead, you could say something like this: "In the next few minutes, I would like to explain how several recent equipment changes are making football a safer sport." To illustrate further:

(1) Senator Edward M. Kennedy began his celebrated speech, August 12, 1980, to the Democratic National Convention with this statement of the POINT:

> My fellow Democrats and my fellow Americans: I have come here tonight not to argue for a candidacy, but to affirm a cause.

> I am asking you to renew the commitment of the Democratic Party to economic justice. I am asking you to renew our commitment to a fair and lasting prosperity that can put America back to work.

(2) In a report to the American people following his return from a meeting with Soviet Premier Nikita Khrushchev, President John F. Kennedy used as his opening sentence this statement:

> I returned this morning from a week-long trip to Europe and I want to report to you on that trip in full.

(3) As an indication that rhetorical principles transcend national boundaries, when Mr. Khrushchev returned to his country following the previously mentioned conference with Mr. Kennedy, he introduced his message with this statement:

> Today I should like to express some thoughts, some considerations of mine about the meeting and talks with Mr. Kennedy in Vienna.

(4) In the Introduction of his speech ("American Foreign Policy in the Midst of the World Revolution") to the annual convention of the Pennsylvania Nurses Association, Robert T. Oliver combined his Favorable Attention Step and Clarification Step: first, he pointed out the directions his speech was *not* going to take; then he indicated the area his message would cover and why he had selected this purpose.[5]

Text

Reference to Audience and Occasion

Two different ways occurred to me of adapting my remarks for this evening particularly to this audience. One way was to discuss the sick world—and no one can doubt it is highly feverish—in terms of diagnosis and treatment. This was tempting, because as nurses you know that laymen commonly are concerned with symptoms rather than with causes of diseases, which often gives a ludicrously false notion of what is wrong and what needs to be done about it. I think it would not be difficult to demonstrate that laymen also make the same error in thinking about international relations.

The second method of adaptation that also seemed appealing for a time was to select those particular aspects of the world situation that might be of special interest to your profession—the growth of population, the prevalence of hunger, the lengthening of the life span through public health measures, the problems of the rapidly developing underdeveloped nations. This method also had some appeal,

[5]Used by special permission of Dr. Oliver.

for what we all are primarily concerned about is the welfare of individuals, regardless of national boundary lines and ideologies.

Statement of POINT

What I have decided to do, however, is to talk to you simply and straightforwardly about how we ordinary American citizens can set about analyzing the world situation in an effort to make sense of it—to see where we are going, and why, and what our future is likely to be. This is the kind of problem that concerns all of us, not as nurses or as professors, but as men and women with our own lives to live and with the future of our children to think about.

Significance of topic

Outline

Introduction

Combination Favorable Attention Step and Clarification Step

I. Two different ways occurred to me of adapting my remarks for this evening particularly to this audience
   A. To discuss the sick world in terms of diagnosis and treatment
   B. To select particular aspects of the world situation that might be of special interest to your profession
II. I decided to talk about a problem of universal significance: how we ordinary citizens can set about analyzing the world situation in an effort to make sense of it

Explain How You Plan to Develop the Body. To facilitate your listeners' understanding of the materials that will be presented in the Body, you may provide them in the Introduction with a preview of what is coming. This is analogous to reading the Preface or the Table of Contents before reading the book itself. You should recognize, however, that although this method serves splendidly to provide proper focus, it does not possess strong attention-compelling qualities.

Here are some examples.

(1) A student who wanted to convince his audience that off-track betting should be legalized stated his POINT and listed his main arguments like this:

> I believe that we should legalize off-track betting in our state for several reasons. First, we have to realize that our inability to enforce existing anti-gambling ordinances is making a mockery out of law enforcement. Second, the state is losing at least fifty million dollars in revenue a year since there is no tax on illegal gambling. Third, attempts to enforce anti-gambling ordinances cost the state thousands of dollars a year. Fourth, off-track betting is no more immoral than legalized track betting or bingo games. Fifth, the gangster element which now directs off-track betting, could be effectively curbed if such betting were legalized and controlled.
>
> Now let me take up the first of these contentions. . . .

(2) Look ahead to pp. 248–249 to see how Harry S. Truman began a speech by combining an explanation of how he planned to develop the Body with other introductory materials, including a statement of the POINT.

(3) In his speech to the executives of Litton Industries, John A. Howard, director of the Rockford College Institute, followed a Favorable Attention Step with an explanation of the way he intended to develop his message.[6]

Text

Humorous Story

A story is told of a knight who returned to his castle at twilight. He was a mess. His armor was dented, his helmet skewgee, his face was bloody, his horse was limping, the rider was listing to one side in the saddle. The Lord of the castle saw him coming and went out to meet him, asking, "What hath befallen you, Sir Knight?" Straightening himself up as best he could, he replied, "Oh, Sire, I have been laboring in your service, robbing and raping and pillaging your enemies to the west." "You've been WHAT?" cried the startled nobleman, "but I haven't any enemies to the west!" "Oh!" said the knight. And then, after a pause, "Well, I think you do now."

Application of Story to the POINT

There is a moral to this story. Enthusiasm is not enough. You have to have a sense of direction. Private enterprise, like the bedraggled knight, is not at its best these days. This morning I want to pose to you the possibility that the troubles which beset the business community may arise because it does not have a very clear idea of who its opponents are and as a result, is focusing much of its defensive energies upon the wrong targets. The sense of direction is amiss. . . .

Explanation how Speaker Planned to Develop the Body

I want to focus our attention on just three large areas of problems and suggest what I believe to be the source of those problems, so that remedial action can be aimed at the causes rather than at the symptoms, as is now the case. The three areas are:

1. *Problems of overzealous regulatory interference* in matters of occupational safety and health, the environment, affirmative action, etc.

2. *Financial problems* including inflation, rising taxes, high interest rates and the scarcity of capital.

3. *Problems having to do with irresponsible conduct* involving theft, vandalism, arson, bribery, embezzlement, rough tactics by unions, the failure to give a good day's work for a good day's pay, and so on. . . .

All right, we have our agenda laid out for us.

[6] *Vital Speeches,* May 15, 1980, p. 450.

Outline

Introduction

I. Favorable Attention Step
   A. A story is told of a knight. . .
   B. There is a moral to this story
II. Clarification Step
   A. The business community does not have a clear idea of who its opponents are
   B. I want to focus our attention on three large areas of problems

Provide Necessary Background Explanations. Frequently, you will find that the definition of key terms will be helpful, if not essential, in orienting the audience to the topic.

(1) In a preceding illustration concerning off-track betting, the speaker probably should have included in his Clarification Step a definition of this type of gambling. Uninformed persons in the audience might believe that off-track betting included dice, roulette, bolita, and the numbers games. Such misinformation might prejudice them against the speaker's proposal.

(2) A speaker arguing that basic nonagricultural industries should be nationalized must answer several questions about the topic before he can proceed with his address: What is meant by "nonagricultural industries"? Which industries are included? Which are excluded? What is meant by "nationalized"?

Sometimes your audience will need general background information on the subject before it is competent to follow you easily. For example, a young man who addressed an organization concerning his participation in a recent national weight-lifting contest realized that his listeners possessed little knowledge of weight lifting.Therefore, he prepared the audience for the Body of his speech by supplying background explanation. He began with a concise history of the sport, told of the relatively widespread interest in weight lifting throughout the world, and then explained the nature and scoring of the two Olympic lifts used in AAU competition: the snatch, and the clean and jerk. As a result of this Clarification Step, the audience was adequately oriented toward the subject.

In order to understand the present significance or meaning of your topic, the audience may require some explanation of previous events pertinent to the subject.

(1) A world traveler speaking about modern China might wish to trace briefly the history of China in order that his listeners might understand better the present patterns of thought and behavior.

(2) A naval officer discussing the new Trident missile as a strategic

weapon might preface his remarks with a brief narration of the developmental history of the missile.

(3) President Harry S. Truman, announcing that a state of emergency would be proclaimed on the following day, December 16, 1950, explained briefly in the Introduction the events that had necessitated such a proclamation.[7]

Text

Statement of the POINT

I am talking to you tonight about what our country is up against, and what we are going to do about it.

Reference to Significance of Topic

Our homes, our nation, all the things we believe in are in great danger. This danger has been created by the rulers of the Soviet Union.

For five years we have been working for peace and justice among nations. We have helped to bring the free nations of the world together in a great movement to establish a lasting peace.

Historical Background Information

Against this movement for peace, the rulers of the Soviet Union have been waging a relentless attack. They have tried to undermine or overwhelm the free nations, one by one. They have used threats and treachery and violence.

In June the forces of Communist imperialism broke out into open warfare in Korea. The United Nations moved to put down this act of aggression, and, by October, had all but succeeded.

Then in November, the Communists threw their Chinese armies into the battle against the free nations.

By this act, they have shown that they are now willing to push the world to the brink of a general war to get what they want. This is the real meaning of the events that have been taking place in Korea.

Reference to Significance of Topic

That is why we are in such grave danger. The future of civilization depends on what we do—on what we do now, and in the months ahead.

We have the strength and we have the courage to overcome the danger that threatens our country. We must act calmly, wisely and resolutely.

Statement of the Main Ideas of the Discussion

Here are the things we will do:

First, we will continue to uphold . . . the principles of the United Nations. . . .

Second, we will continue to work with the other free nations to strengthen our combined defenses.

Third, we will build up our own army, navy and air force and make more weapons for ourselves and our allies.

Fourth, we will expand our economy and keep it on an even keel.

Now, I want to talk to you about each one of these things.

[7] *Vital Speeches,* January 1, 1951, p. 162.

Outline

Introduction

I. Clarification Step: I am talking to you tonight about what our country is up against, and what we are going to do about it
II. Favorable Attention Step: Our home, our nation, all the things we believe in are in great danger
III. Clarification Step: This danger has been created by the rulers of the Soviet Union
   A. For five years we have been working for peace and justice among nations
   B. Against this movement for peace, the rulers of the Soviet Union have been waging a relentless attack
IV. Favorable Attention Step: The future of civilization depends upon what we do
V. Clarification Step: Here are the things we will do:
   A. First, we will continue to uphold . . . the principles of the United Nations
   B. Second, we will continue to work with the other free nations to strengthen our combined defenses
   C. Third, we will build up our army, navy, and air force and make more weapons for ourselves and our allies
   D. Fourth, we will expand our economy and keep it on an even keel

Avoiding Common Faults of the Introduction

Although in preparing the Introduction a speaker may err in a wide variety of ways, the following are probably the faults most commonly made.

Being Apologetic. If you imply that you are going to do poorly, the audience will be conditioned to expect an ineffective speech and will tend to believe (even though unjustifiably) that it *is* unsatisfactory.

Being Long-Winded. Get to the point. Do not bore your listeners with a wordy, rambling Introduction. Time yourself in your rehearsal periods; and, unless there is a genuine need for a longer Introduction, keep your preliminary remarks within 10 per cent of the total speech length.

Being Antagonistic. Do not use unnecessary controversial material. Do not be dogmatic with groups who might disagree with you. Do not make offensive, slighting remarks. Do not make false assumptions about your audience. Do not be patronizing. Do not use unsavory humor.

Being Irrelevant. Not only must all material have a direct application to the subject, the audience, or the speech occasion but the application must also be clear to the audience.

Applying Principles to Speeches of Basic Types

Now that we have examined the principles for developing the Introduction we are ready to see how these principles may be applied to planning Introductions of speeches of basic types.

Planning the Introduction of the Speech to Inform

Because the speech to inform is designed to promote understanding, assimilation, and retention, the Introduction should usually contain both a carefully planned Favorable Attention Step and a Clarification Step. In view of the previous discussion of basic principles, perhaps it is enough here to direct your attention to certain special considerations concerning the application of principles to informational speaking.

A common mistake committed by inexperienced speakers is to assume that the auditors will be interested in the subject because they "ought to be" or because the speaker himself is interested. Such individuals may subconsciously assume the attitude expressed by James Smith's Glendoveer: "'Tis mine to speak, and yours to hear." Although you legitimately may identify your own interests with the topic or refer unobtrusively to your qualifications to speak on the subject, you probably should not tell an audience that these considerations determined the selection of your subject. Such a procedure is speaker-centered: it serves to identify your own self with the subject; but, beyond establishing your credentials, does not link the listeners with the speaker-message. As you discovered earlier in the text, persons learn best and remember best when they identify the proffered information with their own interests and needs. Of the eight methods we have discussed for securing favorable attention in the Introduction, perhaps the best means of promoting the identification of listeners with informational materials is to stress the significance and interest of the subject. Point out explicitly—though not baldly—how the subject may directly affect the lives of the listeners. If you cannot find a direct application to their interests, choose a different topic.

The Clarification Step is of exceptional importance to informative speaking: by preparing the audience for the Body, you facilitate learning and retention. Until you acquire experience, it is probably best to state in a simple brief sentence the essential idea or concept that you wish the hearers to learn about or to understand. After stating the POINT, perhaps explain concisely how you will approach the topic in the Body: when you wish to direct attention to important steps, stages, or procedures covered in the Body, you can summarize them or list them formally in a one-two-three-order. If the auditors may not understand the meaning of all terms basic to the subject, provide the necessary definitions. If the listeners' grasp of the subject background is inadequate for them to see the topic in its proper perspective or to follow your analysis easily, offer preliminary explanations. Also, remember that the final sentences of the Introduction should provide a smooth transition in thought and mood from the preliminary section of the speech to the Body.

As you will remember from Chapter 3, listeners respond most readily to speakers who project an appropriate image, that is, who seem to possess character, knowledge, goodwill, and desirable qualities of personality. Therefore, in the Introduction you must not only *possess* appropriate attitudes toward yourself, the purpose to inform, the informational materials, and the audience but also must *demonstrate* your possession of such attributes by suitable language, content, and delivery. Of course, such demonstration must be natural and uncontrived. For instance, if seeking favorable attention by citing your qualifications or experience, do not permit such references to become obtrusive or ostentatious.

In short, the Introduction of the informative speech should do everything possible to facilitate the proper intellectual and psychological reception of the information to be presented in the Body.

Planning the Introduction of the Speech to Entertain

In presenting a speech that seeks only to divert the listeners, you may not find it necessary to group the material into an Introduction, Body, and Conclusion. Since the audience is not being asked to acquire new understanding or to accept or reject courses of action, the only function the Introduction would serve is to prepare the audience to be entertained. For instance, in Mark Twain's famous entertaining speech on "The Oldest Inhabitant—the Weather of New England," the introductory comments are virtually indistinguishable from the remainder of the speech. As the following excerpt indicates, the speech starts with a general indictment of the weather (Introduction) and then moves to a bill of particulars (Body), the variety of the weather being the first complaint:

> Gentleman:—I reverently believe that the Maker who made us all makes everything in New England—but the weather. *(Laughter.)* I don't know who makes that, but I think it must be raw apprentices in the Weather Clerk's factory, who experiment and learn how in New England for board and clothes, and then are promoted to make weather for countries that require a good article and will take their custom elsewhere if they don't get it. *(Laughter.)*
>
> There is a sumptuous variety about the New England weather that compels the stranger's admiration—and regret. . . .

As you know, however, most entertaining speeches have a secondary purpose of providing information or promoting persuasion. The more important this secondary function becomes, likewise the more important becomes the Introduction. Nevertheless, even in entertaining speeches that possess serious import, the introductory materials should be brief, buoyant, and sprightly. If present, the Clarification Step should not seem too obvious, too heavy, or overorganized. Since the primary purpose of the speech is to divert the listeners pleasantly, the opening must not become mired in technical definitions, explanations and so forth.

As far as the speaker image is concerned, you must be thoroughly tuned to the demands of the particular speaking situation, that is, to the purpose of providing entertainment, to your diverting speech materials, to the exigencies of the occasion, and to the audience's initial degree of willingness to be entertained. By reflecting geniality, optimism, and verve, your manner and mood will encourage the listeners to relax, forget problems and obligations, and to delight in being diverted.

Planning the Introduction of the Speech to Persuade

You will remember that in persuasive speeches your purpose is to influence the listeners to change their opinions, deepen their existing convictions, or adopt new courses of action. Because persuasion involves the logical and psychological prejudgments of the listeners, they may be conditioned positively or negatively toward you and/or your proposition. Auditors are not always partisans, of course. Frequently, they may be basically neutral or undecided concerning your proposal or yourself as the speaker.

The Favorable Audience. In addressing a *favorably disposed* audience, you will encounter no irrational opposition. On the contrary, your listeners' will-to-believe has conditioned them toward an acceptance of your proposals. Nevertheless, when seeking to reinforce long-established beliefs that are taken for granted, such as patriotism or reverence, you may experience initial difficulty in arousing interest. Under such circumstances, an extended Favorable Attention Step may be necessary. Conversely, of course, the Favorable Attention Step may sometimes be abbreviated when addressing a highly polarized audience. Also, in some stimulating speeches, the nature of the subject or the audience may indicate that orienting materials may be minimized or, occasionally, omitted.

Until you gain experience, however, you should include in the Introduction both a Favorable Attention Step and a Clarification Step. By their combined means, the Introduction should awaken interest in the pre-existing bonds of common feelings, beliefs, and experiences. Furthermore, it should help prepare the listener for a personal reaffirmation and intensification of appropriate attitudes. In his address to the Conference of European Communist and Workers' Parties in East Berlin, Leonid Brezhnev used this Introduction, which was well suited to a favorably disposed audience.[8]

> Dear Comrades, the delegation of the Communist Party of the Soviet Union warmly greets the participants in this conference of communist and workers' parties of Europe. We convey to you the feelings of brotherly friendship and militant solidarity from the fifteen and a half million Soviet communists. We also cordially thank our comrades from the Socialist Unity Party of Germany and personally Comrade Honecker for their attention, for the excellent organization of our conference.
>
> Present in this hall are the leading figures of twenty-nine communist parties of Europe. Gathered here are people who devoted their life to the struggle for the rights of working people; for a new, just social order; for a really lasting peace among peoples. Our parties work under different conditions and tackle various tasks, shaping their tactics and strategy according to the concrete situation in their respective countries. But all of us are participants in a single struggle, all of us are moving in the same direction and all of us are united by a common, noble ultimate goal. This is why for us European communists it is useful, in the interests of our common cause, to exchange views and discuss such important and topical themes as peace, cooperation, security and social progress in Europe.

The Primarily Neutral Audience. In attempting to persuade a *primarily neutral audience,* you probably can anticipate a relatively objective initial hearing. If the auditors are undecided because they lack information, your Introduction should be tailored to help them identify their interests and needs with the topic and to stimulate them to want to hear the informative-persuasive materials you will present in the Body. If the listeners are neutral because they have not yet made up their minds, your Introduction probably should emphasize basic points of agreement that exist between you and the listeners. If you make this initial identification persuasively clear, the listeners may find it easier to adjust their speaker-message identification to accommodate the proposals that you will present later.

As long as you stress points of accordance, the audience has no logical course other than to agree with you, and you are encouraging positive, affirmative thinking. Offer the listeners as much opportunity as possible to think "YES," and as little as possible to think "NO," Any of the methods discussed earlier in this chapter may be utilized in the Favorable Attention Step to encourage an atmosphere of goodwill and sympathetic, attentive listening.

[8] *Vital Speeches,* August 1, 1976, p. 610.

As a novice, you probably should invariably plan to use a Clarification Step in speaking to a neutral audience. Remember, of course, that this segment of the speech also must be adjusted as effectively as possible to the needs of the particular audience. Understanding and conviction may be advanced by employing one or more of the following standard elements: a diplomatic statement of the POINT; a brief explanation of the arguments you plan to advance; the definition of any potentially confusing terms; an explanation of the background or recent history of the topic.

The Hostile Audience. When you address an audience *hostile* to your program, the opening minutes of the speech may determine whether the group will afford you a reasonably objective hearing. Ordinarily, at the outset you should seek to establish common ground with your auditors. The psychological set of the "hostile" listeners conditions them against your case and very possibly against you as the speaker. They have identified their interests and needs with policies or beliefs that are counter to yours. Until you establish some rapport—some commonality of belief, or purpose, or attitude—they will effectively resist your persuasion. In the Introduction, follow the advice contained in a hit song that was popular a generation or so ago: "accentuate the positive" and "eliminate the negative." By stressing basic points of agreement, you may narrow the logical and psychological gamut between you and your listeners, and, thereby, encourage a more objective hearing of the arguments you will present in the Body. Frequently a speaker and an audience who seem to be poles apart actually desire the same end results; they clash only in the paths or means to be employed in realizing the objectives. Fortunately, no public-speaking situations exist in which no elements of common ground are present between speaker and audience; should such an impasse ever exist, speechmaking would be useless—the time would be at hand when all persons would have need to hide "themselves in the dens and in the rocks of the mountains."

Of course, in order for you to encourage listeners to be fair-minded toward you and your ideas, you must be fair-minded toward them and their beliefs. Although you should be thoroughly convinced of the rightness of your cause, you should not forget that the people to whom you are speaking also believe, or think they believe, their convictions are right and just. All of us are fond of our ideas and opinions. We resent any bald attempt by a speaker to change our minds. If we had not successfully rationalized our position, we would probably have already altered our views. When approached tactlessly, we close our minds to new, unwelcome proposals. On the other hand, if approached courteously by a speaker who evidences respect for our beliefs and who identifies his policies with what we think are our best interests, we feel somewhat less on the defensive—hence, may tend to listen more objectively.

Before you can reach common ground with those who disagree with your recommendations, you must meet several requirements:

First, understand that others view the matter differently from the way you do, that their beliefs are sincere, and that they have convinced themselves that reason and justice are on their side. Beware! It is easy to tell yourself: "Yes, I know they think differently. That's why I'm going to change them." Such a speaker does not really accept the fact that his listeners *believe* differently and *feel* that they are justified in thinking as they do.

Second, attempt to find the basic reasons for the listeners' objection to your proposals. Since the listeners are products of their environment, you should be able to determine the causes for their beliefs. In the process, you may discover a surprising amount of logic on their side that you had not thought of before.

Third, ascertain what the listeners believe the elements of common ground to be. If you held their beliefs, how would you wish to be approached on this problem? Of course, you cannot stress common relationships, beliefs, interests, and feelings in the Introduction and then abandon this courteous, conciliatory approach during the remainder of the speech.

Let us look at two instances in which speakers were compelled to seek common ground with hostile audiences.

(1) A college fraternity was being split into two rival groups over the expulsion of a member. At the meeting called to vote upon the question, a leader of the wing favoring expulsion rose to speak. He began by expressing a deep love for the fraternity and stated that he was sorry for the hostility among the members and was ashamed of his own acerbity. He read several letters from prominent alumni urging amicable settlement of the problem. He admitted that both sides desired what was best for the fraternity and that the only real controversy involved the means of attaining this goal. He explained that, since the issue was so important to the well-being of the fraternity, he wished to present his arguments as dispassionately as possible and, furthermore, that he anticipated hearing a spokesman from the other side; by this sharing of ideas, he hoped that differences might be speedily reconciled. His mild, conciliatory approach did much to millify the opposition. Indeed, the opposition had to agree with everything he had said. By means of a friendly agreeable manner of introducing his case, the speaker had encouraged the other side to listen more objectively.

(2) In addressing the people of Zambia on the U.S. policy toward Southern Africa, during the early period of the American attempt to resolve the political problems of Rhodesia, former Secretary of State Henry Kissinger confronted an audience that was critical of the United States and highly suspicious of its motives. To reduce this opposition,

Kissinger approached his topic from the standpoint of his listeners. In an extended Introduction, he minimized differences, evinced respect and appreciation for his listeners, stressed an optimistic future, and emphasized common bonds of beliefs, aspirations, and traditions that exist between the people of Africa and those of the United States.[9]

> President Ford has sent me here with a message of commitment and cooperation. I have come to Africa because in so many ways, the challenges of Africa are the challenges of the modern era. Morally and politically, the drama of national independence in Africa over the last generation has transformed international affairs. More than any other region of the world, Africa symbolizes that the previous era of world affairs—the colonial era—is a thing of the past. The great tasks you face—in nation-building, in deepening the peace and integrity of this continent, in economic development, in gaining an equitable role in world councils, in achieving racial justice—these reflect the challenges of building a humane and progressive world order.
>
> I have come to Africa with an open mind and an open heart to demonstrate my country's desire to work with you on these great tasks. My journey is intended to give fresh impetus to our cooperation and to usher in a new era in America policy.
>
> The United States was one of the prime movers of the process of decolonization. The American people welcomed the new nations into the world community and for two decades have given aid and encouragement to economic and social progress in Africa. And America's responsibilities as a global power give us strong interest today in the independence, peace and well-being of this vast continent comprising a fifth of the world's land surface. For without peace, racial justice and growing prosperity in Africa, we cannot speak of a just international order. . . .
>
> Our differing perspectives converge in a common purpose to build a secure and just future for Africa. In active collaboration there is much we can do; in contention or apart we will miss great opportunities. . . . It is time to find our common ground and act boldly for common ends.
>
> Africa is a continent of hope—a modern frontier. The United States from the beginning has been a country of the frontier, built by men and women of hope. The American people know from their history the meaning of the struggle for independence, or racial equality, for economic progress, for human dignity.
>
> I am not here to give American prescriptions for Africa's problems. Your program must be African. The basic decisions and goals must be African. But we are prepared to help.
>
> Nor am I here to set African against African, either among your governments or among factions of liberation movements. African

[9] *Vital Speeches,* May 15, 1976, pp. 455–56.

problems cannot be solved and your destiny cannot be fulfilled except by a united Africa. America supports African unity.

Here in Africa the range of mankind's challenges and potential can be seen in all its complexity and enormous promise. The massive power and grandeur of nature is before us in all its aspects as the harsh master and as a bountiful servant of mankind. Here we can feel the rich and living cultures which have changed and invigorated art, music and thought around the world. And here, on this continent, we are tested, all of us, to see whether . . . humanity will be the victim or the architect of its destiny. . . .

One is struck by the similarity of philosophy in the American Declaration of Independence and in the Lusaka manifesto. Two hundred years ago, Thomas Jefferson wrote: "We hold these truths to be self-evident, that all men are created equal, that they are endowed by their Creator with certain unalienable rights, that among these are life, liberty and the pursuit of happiness. That to secure these rights, governments are instituted among men, deriving their just powers from the consent of the governed."

And seven years ago, the leaders of east and central Africa declared here in Lusaka that: "By this manifesto we wish to make clear, beyond all shadow of doubt, our acceptance of the belief that all men are equal, and have equal rights to human dignity and respect, regardless of color, race, religion or sex. We believe that all men have the right and duty to participate, as equal members of society, in their own government."

There can be no doubt that the United States remains committed to the principles of its own declaration of independence. It follows that we also adhere to the convictions of the Lusaka manifesto. . . .

On this occasion I would like to set forth more fully American policy on some of the immediate issues we face—in Rhodesia, Namibia and South Africa—and then to sketch our vision of southern Africa's hopeful future.

As mentioned before, the initial reaction of the audience to the image projected by the speaker is perhaps more important in persuasive speeches than in informative or entertaining ones. In informative and entertaining speeches, the speaker attempts to provide a service for the listeners. He may ask nothing of them except to avail themselves of the proffered information or entertainment. Conversely, in persuasive speeches the speaker seeks a specific commitment from his hearers. His purpose is not merely to provide a service, it is to gain from the listeners some active involvement: to change their minds, or reaffirm allegiance, or engage in some overt activity. Because such commitments may involve pocketbooks and sensitive attitudes and beliefs, the listeners are likely to be critically analytical of the speaker—particularly if he represents the "other side."

The following suggestions, especially true for persuasive speeches, may, of course, be applied to all types of speeches. If you have reason to believe that the listeners may be opposed to you personally, recognize that such antipathy may color their reactions toward your proposals, and attempt to develop the Introduction in such a way that opposition may be lessened. For instance, if your auditors regard you as a "stuffed shirt," reveal yourself in your opening remarks as being an unassuming person, free from ostentation. Although easily overdone, possibly telling a brief joke at your own expense will relieve antagonism. If your listeners believe you to be egotistical, possibly you should avoid references to yourself in the Introduction; concentrate attention on your proposals, and demonstrate by style, content, and delivery that you are modest and unpretentious. If your auditors feel that you are intolerant or radical, indicate in your first sentences (and throughout the speech, of course) that you are amiable, temperate, and conciliatory.

Summary

The Introduction serves to answer the rhetorical needs that are usually present at the beginning of a speech. In order to provide a bridge between the initial reaction of the listeners and your major ideas, you may prepare the listeners both *psychologically*—by stimulating their favorable interest in you as the speaker and in your message—and *logically*—by orienting them to the nature and purpose of the Body. In the Favorable Attention Step, you may stimulate favorable interest by employing one or more of the options at your disposal, such as the following: (1) referring to the significance of the subject; (2) using humor; (3) telling an illustrative story; (4) using a stimulating quotation; (5) asking the audience a striking question; (6) making a pithy, provocative statement; (7) referring to the audience, occasion, or purpose of the meeting; (8) complimenting the audience. In the Clarification Step, you may orient the audience to the Body by using one or more of the options available to you, such as these: (1) stating the POINT of the speech; (2) explaining how you plan to develop the Body; (3) providing necessary background explanation. In planning the Introduction, be especially careful to avoid common faults, such as being apologetic, long-winded, antagonistic, or irrelevant.

Inasmuch as speeches to inform, to entertain, and to persuade have different purposes, each of these basic types of speeches requires a somewhat different kind of bridge between the initial reaction of the listeners and the speaker's major ideas, as presented in the Body.

Exercises and Assignments

1. Analyze the methods used by various news commentators to begin radio broadcasts or telecasts. Notice that a program frequently begins with the reporter's listing the main items of news; then, following a commercial, he discusses each of the items in detail. In such cases would the original listing serve as a Favorable Attention Step as well as a Clarification Step? Why, or why not?

2. Read the Introductions of several speeches to discover in each case the speaker's methods of capturing attention and of preparing the listeners for the Body. In what ways do you think the Introductions could be made more effective?

3. Attend a sermon by a minister or rabbi who is recognized as being an outstanding speaker. What does he do to get your attention at the outset? If a text is read, observe how it serves as a partial Clarification Step. Can you think of any way in which his Introduction could be improved?

4. For one of the persuasive speeches you have presented, or will present later, prepare *three* different Introductions. Each of the Introductions should be designed to meet the requirements of one of the audiences represented in the following list: an audience that is (1) favorably disposed toward you and your subject; (2) affirmatively disposed toward you but negatively disposed toward your subject; (3) negatively disposed toward you but affirmatively disposed toward your subject; (4) hostile toward both you and your subject; (5) favorable toward you and neutral or uninformed toward your subject; (6) negative toward you and neutral or uninformed toward your subject; (7) neutral or uninformed toward you and your subject; (8) neutral or uninformed toward you and negative toward your subject; (9) neutral or uninformed toward you and favorable toward your subject.

5. Begin your next speech with the relating of a short personal incident that has a close relationship to your speech subject. (Possibly you will experience less nervousness when beginning a speech in this way.)

6. In future speeches in class attempt to use more than one method of achieving favorable attention in the Introduction. By carefully planning what you are going to say, you need not exceed the 10 per cent average length of Introductions.

7. In a short talk to the class explain the "Yes Technique" in the Introduction as used by the persuasive speaker.

8. Why should you avoid beginning a speech by stating the title in a fragmentary sentence?

9. In your judgment, would the speech to convince or the speech to stimulate require the more carefully planned Clarification Step? Why?

CHAPTER 11

Developing the Conclusion of the Speech

Even the simplest forms of social communication require some sort of "conclusion," or ending. When closing a conversation with an acquaintance, do you cease talking abruptly, turn your back, and walk off? Don't you almost instinctively employ some concluding phrases, such as "Well, I've got to catch my bus, Harry. Come by the house when you have time."? When concluding a telephone call, don't you indicate your intention to hang up by saying something like this: "It was good to talk with you, Bob. I'll see that you get the papers by tomorrow morning. Good-bye."?

A suitable closing is even more important in a public speech than in a social conversation. The way you end a speech always influences the listeners' reactions to what you have said in the Body and sometimes is a determining factor in your efforts to inform or persuade. The power of the Conclusion was shown following the first Alger Hiss trial when a juror explained that she had been uncertain as to Hiss' guilt until the summation of the State's case by the prosecutor.

Understanding the Principles of Development

The nature and length of the Conclusion depend upon all the demands involved: the Specific Speech Purpose; the length of the talk; the character of the material covered in the Body; the probable status of the listeners' understanding, knowledge, and receptivity; the speaker's prestige and personality; and the influence of the speaking occasion.

How long should a Conclusion be? Perhaps the most effective answer is the reply made by Abraham Lincoln when asked how long a man's leg should be: "Long enough to reach to the ground." Although the length of the typical Conclusion may be about 5 per cent—or somewhat more—of the total speech length, considerable variation exists in particular cases. If the subject matter of the Body is complicated, thereby necessitating a detailed review, or if an extended appeal to the feelings seems advisable, the Conclusion may be longer than customary. Under no circumstances, however, should the Conclusion be any longer than is necessary. As Quintilian warned, "If we devote too much time to the final recapitulation, the Conclusion will cease to be an enumeration and will constitute something very like a second speech." If the theme is relatively simple and the material has been clearly and logically presented, the Conclusion may be abbreviated. For example, Andrew Kaul III concluded a high-school graduation address (entitled "The Great Delusion," a warning against accepting the programs of "Liberalism") with this concise summary:

> In closing, I appeal to you young men and women, for your own sakes, to *keep* America the land of opportunity.
>
> Don't be taken in by the "Great Delusion."
>
> Your future is in your own hands; hang on to it.

Aristotle used only four words—which translate into four sentences in English—to conclude his treatise *The Rhetoric:* "I have done. You have heard me. You have the facts. I ask for your judgment."

In your effort to be brief, however, do not go to the extreme of being disconcertingly abrupt. Follow this rule of thumb: the Conclusion should be long enough *to crystallize the thought of the speech, to promote the proper mood, and if suitable, to stimulate specified action on the part of the listeners.* (The last of these functions, applicable only to the Conclusion of actuating speeches, is treated in detail under the speech to actuate, later in this chapter.)

To promote the proper mood in the Conclusion, you should attempt to enable your listeners to identify more strongly with the subject and your Specific Speech Purpose. To accomplish this you may vitalize the implications of the speech by emphasizing the significance, application, or pervasiveness of the topic; stress relevant goals, aspirations, or feelings that you share with the listeners; predict future success for relevant programs sponsored by the audience; or seek to intensify the attitudinal agreement of the listeners. Your speech must not grind to a dull, uninteresting stop. An impotent, mumbled close may nullify a previously established favorable speaker-audience relationship. Your Conclusion should "pack a punch." That is, it should end the speech on a high note of favorable interest; it should leave the listeners with the lasting recognition that you have presented effectively a message of significance; it should accentuate in the listeners the psychological mood that will be most helpful to the securing of the Specific Speech Purpose.

To help crystallize the thought of the speech in the Conclusion, you may tie up any loose threads of thought; make clearer or reinforce the materials previously discussed; reemphasize the basic thrust; or recapitulate the essential points.

Clarify the Thought and Promote the Proper Mood of the Speech

Although the methods for promoting the appropriate mood and clarifying the thought of the speech do not lend themselves readily to categorizing, perhaps the following discussion of basic options will prove helpful to you.

State the POINT of the Speech. As mentioned in Chapter 10, the stating of the POINT (that is, the basic thrust or intent of the speech, which, of course, is a paraphrase of the Specific Speech Purpose) during the Introduction brings the speech into "exact" focus, so that the listeners will anticipate the direction and boundaries of the speech. Not infrequently in the Body of a speech the central theme becomes partially submerged under the accumulation of examples, quotations, statistics, references to authority, and so on. In such cases, it may be advisable to focus final attention upon the essential point or message. To restate the POINT concisely in the Conclusion improves clarity but does little to promote the proper mood. In the following excerpt from a student's speech advocating increased federal aid to education, the restatement of the POINT helps to clarify and reinforce the basic contention but offers scant interest appeal.

> In the ten minutes allotted to me I have endeavored to show you convincing, powerful reasons why the federal government should shoulder a greater part of the burden of supporting the public school systems of our nation. America must adopt a more extensive, more effective program of federal aid to education.

Customarily the speaker should follow a restatement of the POINT with some amplification. In his address to the Awards Convocation at Duke University, Gordon N. Ray (then secretary general of the John Simon Guggenheim Memorial Foundation) stated his speech purpose and then attempted to foster lasting acceptance by personalizing his message.[1]

[1]Printed and distributed by Syracuse University.

My theme in this address has been to urge the continued relevance of liberal training in today's world, to assert that the wisdom which can come from such training remains the most precious acquirement that education has to offer. Students often fail to realize the extent to which their future lies in their own hands. Goethe . . . said that what a man in youth wishes to be, he will become after a fashion in later life. So it behooves you to consider your ambitions carefully in the light of such wisdom as you may be able to bring to bear on them, because they will probably be realized, though not exactly in the way you expect. Mental indolence, seeking favors, and taking the easy out will in time become habits. "The burnt Fool's bandaged finger goes wabbling back to the Fire." The result in mature life will be an easy job, but a job as insignificant and badly rewarded as unresponsible jobs usually are. On the other hand, constant intellectual cultivation and a delight in overcoming difficulties will lead on from opportunity to opportunity, keeping always before you that wide range of choices for the future which is the real definition of success. So ends my lay sermon, and it is appropriate that I should turn for my final words to a verse in Proverbs. . . . "Wisdom is the principal thing: therefore get wisdom; and with thy getting get understanding."

List the Main Ideas of the Speech. A clear, concise method of summarizing in the Conclusion is to list the main ideas of the speech in a formal "one, two, three" order. There is no better way of enabling the audience to remember specific points than to list them in the Introduction, analyze them in the Body, and relist them in the Conclusion. Usually, however, such a formal stating of main points in the Conclusion does little to promote the appropriate mood and, furthermore, may seem a bit bald—too much like an academic lecture, too stilted and monotonous. A safe generalization is to use this method only when it is essential that the audience retain specific points, arguments, phases of a program, or directions and, when using this method, to do more than merely list points—include some explanation, a restatement of the POINT, or an indirect review.

In the following examples the speakers have clarified the thought of their speeches by a formal listing of main ideas. (1) To conclude his speech before the General Assembly of the United Nations, Andrei A. Gromyko used this formal review.[2]

It is the opinion of the Soviet Union that some of the top-priority tasks today are as follows:

1. To proceed in practice to a Cyprus settlement, stop the violence against that country and its people, secure respect for the sovereignty, independence and territorial integrity of that State. . . .

2. To resume urgently the work of the Geneva Peace Conference

[2] *Vital Speeches,* November 1, 1974, p. 39

on the Middle East to solve the questions of establishing a just and durable peace in this area.

3. To complete the Conference on Security and Cooperation in Europe at an early date by adopting, at the highest level, decisions assuring a peaceful future for Europe.

4. To reach specific agreements at the Soviet-American strategic arms limitation talks, the multilateral negotiations on the reduction of armed forces and armaments in Central Europe and in the Committee on Disarmament.

5. To take measures to implement the decisions of the Sixth special session of the General Assembly of the United Nations on strengthening the economic independence of developing States.

No one would venture to claim that the solution of all these problems, and of others, to which we have drawn the attention of this Assembly, is an easy task. But their solution is necessary and feasible. It is worthwhile for all States really interested in developing peaceful and reasonable forms of international intercourse to work for this end. The Soviet Union will not be lacking in efforts aimed at facilitating the establishment of durable and lasting peace on earth.

(2) In concluding his talk to the National Association of Accountants on "The Disclosure of Information: A Challenge to Corporations in the 80s," Donald P. Rogers attempted to personalize his message, listed the main points of the Body, and restated the basic thrust of the speech.[3]

Many of you will be responsible for making disclosure decisions, many of you will participate in making disclosure decisions, and many of you will be called upon to advise your clients on disclosure decisions. I hope that you will consider the points I've discussed tonight.

1. The effects of disclosure are not as terrible as we fear,
2. Public attitudes strongly support disclosure, and
3. Public policy will promote more disclosure in the future.

After you have considered these points, I think you will decide that the best disclosure strategy is one of deliberate, voluntary disclosure and aggressive, honest communication.

Review Informally. Perhaps the most widely used and most flexible method of concluding a speech is to review the major ideas presented in the Body and/or the implications of the basic theme. In most cases an informal review is preferable to a formal listing of points: it affords a much better means of promoting the proper mood; it seems less academic, teaching without appearing so obviously to teach.

(1) In his defense of "Standard English" to the Fellows, American

[3] *Vital Speeches,* May 1, 1980, p. 433.

Council on Education, Benjamin H. Alexander (president, Chicago State University) concluded with this informal review.[4]

> I use this occasion as a forum to present my views because you are in the forefront of non-traditional education. It is important that you as believers in non-traditional education speak out when the non-traditional approach to education is being bastardized. The non-traditional student, as well as the traditional student, cannot succeed unless he has been trained from the beginning in Standard English. Standard English—not Black English or Brown English or White English—is the only foundation for effective reading, speaking, writing and learning.
>
> As an educator and a black man who as a child was very poor himself, I plan to speak out on every occasion against this blatant plantation mentality. The poor blacks of this nation are not inferior; they do not need the crutch of Black English. Most of them are able and willing to meet standards. They don't want to turn back the calendar to plantation days.
>
> I urge you to join me in battling this paternalism in education. Join with me in saying—Standard English—the hell with anything else! As educators we must set as our objectives the raising of standards, not their lowering. In my view, to do otherwise is to admit that we are not educators—we are *hustlers*.

(2) Speaking to the Democratic National Convention, 1980, Senator Edward M. Kennedy used this extended informal review to crystalize the thought of the speech and to promote the proper mood.[5]

> In closing, let me say a few words to all those I have met and all those who have supported me at this convention and across the country.
>
> There were hard hours on our journey. Often we sailed against the wind, but always we kept our rudder true. There were so many of you who stayed the course and shared our hope. You gave your help; but even more, you gave your hearts. Because of you, this has been a happy campaign. You welcomed Joan and me and our family into your homes and neighborhoods, your churches, your campuses, and your union halls. When I think back on all the miles and all the months and all the memories, I think of you. I recall the poet's words, and I say: "What golden friends I had."
>
> Among you, my golden friends across this land, I have listened and learned.
>
> I have listened to Kenny Dubois, a glassblower in Charleston, West Virginia, who has ten children to support, but has lost his job after 35 years, just three years short of qualifying for his pension.

[4] *Vital Speeches,* May 1, 1980, pp. 439–40.
[5] *Vital Speeches,* September 15, 1980, p. 716.

I have listened to the Trachta family, who farm in Iowa and who wonder whether they can pass the good life and the good earth on to their children.

I have listened to a grandmother in East Oakland, who no longer has a phone to call her grandchildren, because she gave it up to pay the rent on her small apartment.

I have listened to young workers out of work, to students without the tuition for college, and to families without the chance to own a home. I have seen the closed factories and the stalled assembly lines of Anderson, Indiana, and South Gate, California. I have seen too many—far too many—idle men and women desperate to work. I have seen too many—far too many—working families desperate to protect the value of their wages from the ravages of inflation.

Yet I have also sensed a yearning for new hope among the people in every state where I have been. I felt it in their handshakes; I saw it in their faces. I shall never forget the mothers who carried children to our rallies. I shall always remember the elderly who have lived in an America of high purpose and who believe it can all happen again.

Tonight, in their name, I have come here to speak for them. For their sake, I ask you to stand with them. On their behalf, I ask you to restate and reaffirm the timeless truth of our party.

I congratulate President Carter on his victory here. I am confident that the Democratic Party will reunite on the basis of Democratic principles—and that together we will march toward a Democratic victory in 1980.

And someday, long after this convention, long after the signs come down, and the crowds stop cheering, and the bands stop playing, may it be said of our campaign that we kept the faith. May it be said of our party in 1980 that we found our faith again.

May it be said of us, both in dark passages and in bright days, in the words of Tennyson that my brothers quoted and loved—and that have special meaning for me now:

I am a part of all that I have met . . .
Tho much is taken, much abides . . .
That which we are, we are—
One equal temper of heroic hearts . . . strong in will
To strive, to seek, to find, and not to yield.

For me, a few hours ago, this campaign came to an end. For all those whose cares have been our concern, the work goes on, the cause endures, the hope still lives, and the dream shall never die.

(3) Abraham Lincoln typically closed his speeches by means of an informal review. The Conclusion of his First Inaugural Address tells us vividly that the basic purpose of the speech was to help preserve the Union and to cast odium upon the Southerners if they seceded:

My countrymen, one and all, think calmly and well upon this whole subject. Nothing valuable can be lost by taking time. If there be an object to hurry any of you in hot haste to a step which you would never take deliberately, that object will be frustrated by taking time; but no good object can be frustrated by it. Such of you as are now dissatisfied, still have the old Constitution unimpaired, and, on the sensitive point, the laws of your own framing under it; while the new administration will have no immediate power, if it would, to change either. If it were admitted that you who are dissatisfied hold the right side in the dispute, there still is no single good reason for precipitate action. Intelligence, patriotism, Christianity, and a firm reliance on Him who has never yet forsaken this favored land, are still competent to adjust in the best way all our present difficulty.

In your hand, my dissatisfied fellow-countrymen, and not in mine, is the momentous issue of civil war. The government will not assail you. You can have no conflict without being yourselves the aggressors. You have no oath registered in heaven to destroy the government, while I shall have the most solemn one to "preserve, protect, and defend it."

I am loath to close. We are not enemies, but friends. We must not be enemies. Though passion may have strained, it must not break our bonds of affection. The mystic chords of memory, stretching from every battle-field and patriot grave to every living heart and hearthstone all over this broad land, will yet swell the chorus of the Union when again touched, as surely they will be, by the better angels of our nature.

Review Indirectly by Means of Quotation, Comparison, or Example. An excellent method of promoting the proper mood or of crystallizing the thought is to incorporate into the Conclusion a quotation, a comparison, or an example that epitomizes the purpose or tone of the speech. Such an indirect summary usually serves as a supplementary review. Except under most unusual circumstances, it should not be used as the sole method of reiteration, but should be conjoined with a statement of the POINT, a formal enumeration, or an informal review.

Quotation. Of the three means of summarizing indirectly suggested here, the quotation is the easiest to apply and is by far the most frequently used.

(1) A student closed a philosphical address on happiness with this brief informal review, followed by a quotation:

Happiness, one of God's best gifts, is bestowed upon us freely. There is plenty for all. It does not announce itself with blaring trumpets, for it is a quiet element that is found in the simple things of life. It is true, as Ruskin wrote: "All the real and wholesome enjoyments possible to man have been just as possible since first he was made of the earth—to watch the corn grow, and the blossoms set; to draw hard breath over a plowshare or spade; to read, to think, to love, to pray—these are the things that make men happy."

(2) At the Opening Convocation, Rockford College, then president of that institution, John A. Howard, used a statement of the POINT and a quotation to conclude his claim that "the liberal arts are urgently needed":[6]

> It is time for a ringing declaration that the traditional liberal arts have not passed the time of their usefulness, but instead were never more urgently needed.
>
> I will conclude with a quotation which states that declaration for us. It is a passage from Gordon Chalmers' book, *The Republic and the Person:*
>
> Bruno Walter had been pursued from place to place in Germany and Austria by the pogroms of central Europe. His son-in-law, crazed by the horrors, killed his wife, Walter's daughter, and then committed suicide. Walter said in the winter of 1940–41 to his friends, referring to the Beethoven opera, *Fidelio,* he was about to conduct: "This music says 'Yes' to all who ask if courage and sacrifice and endurance and fortitude can win against a cruel tyranny. . . . Somehow this music tells us that happiness is deeper than unhappiness. Many of you know the tragedy of my life, yet I can say that. There is joy to be had even through grief. In the depths of my heart I know it, and I know that ignorance of this may lead ultimately to defeat and suicide."

Comparison. To find or evolve a comparison that epitomizes the purpose of the speech and that promotes the proper mood is often difficult. Sometimes the speaker can discover in the writing and speaking of others a suitable comparison; more frequently, however, he must evolve the comparison, drawing it from the essence of the speech.

In his address to The National War College, Charles H. Smith, Jr., then chairman of the board, Chamber of Commerce of the United States, concluded with this statement of the POINT, informal review, and comparison:[7]

> Despite [the] demonstrated superiority of the free market system, there are many distinguished leaders from both government and business who warn that future generations of Americans—perhaps even the next generation—will witness the elimination of free enterprise in America—the elimination of capitalism, and the substitution of state ownership of the means of production and a centrally planned economy. . . .

[6] *Vital Speeches,* November 1, 1974, p. 60.
[7] *Vital Speeches,* October 15, 1974, p. 25.

> If our free market economic system outperforms every variation of government owned and government planned economies, we must ask ourselves why it is that so many knowledgeable people are freely predicting the early demise of the free market system in America. Those of us who realize that all of our freedoms—freedom of the press, freedom to work at a job of our own choosing, freedom to bargain collectively—yes, even political and religious freedom are based on the freedom of the market place and the private enterprise system; those of us who realize this must quickly find the reasons for the threat to our free market economy and rally to its defense. If Grayson, and Goldwater, McCracken and Burns are correct, we don't have much time left in which to reverse the direction in which our economy is drifting.
>
> And when I use the word "drifting," let me suggest the analogy of a Sunday sailor drifting lazily down the Upper Niagara River. It's a warm sunny afternoon, and the current is not yet so rapid that the amateur skipper is alarmed about the rapids ahead that lead to complete destruction at the Falls. There is still time and opportunity to change course and work our way back upstream; or at the very least, work our way over to the shoreline where we can tie our craft to a sturdy tree to prevent being caught in a current that will sweep us over the Falls. The thunder of impending doom is still only a faint rumble in the far distance.
>
> But the longer we procrastinate in changing course, the more dangerous becomes our position. It is high time that we begin to identify and seek to avoid currents that can carry us downstream at an ever accelerating pace until we reach a channel from which there is no possibility to return.

Example. As in the case of the comparison, you may experience some difficulty in selecting a factual or hypothetical example that will concisely and graphically crystallize the thought and promote the proper mood.

To make more vivid the basic message of his speech, a student used this factual example:

> In summation, let me ask you once again not to drive an automobile if you have been drinking. Don't be another Frank Hollis. Frank was my roommate last year in the dormitory. He liked to drink his way from bar to bar, and then, about two in the morning, would drive home singing and having a great time. One morning Frank didn't come in. When I left the room to go over to Louie's café to get breakfast, I thought he had spent the night with some buddy. Frank didn't come to his 8:30 class. I didn't know it at the time, but at the hour Frank should have been taking notes in history, the state police were pulling his body out of his partially submerged car in the river. He had turned a corner too fast and his car had skidded out of control into the river. The pathetic thing was that only the front seat was covered with water. But poor Frank drowned in three feet

of water because he was too drunk to know enough to crawl into the back seat. My sincere advice to you is not to drive if you've been drinking. Don't take the chance of becoming another Frank Hollis.

Avoiding Common Faults of the Conclusion.

In preparing the Conclusion, be especially careful to avoid these faults, which are among those most commonly made by inexperienced speakers.

Being Apologetic. As in the Introduction, to offer excuses in the Conclusion may be a reflection of inadequate self-confidence. If you have conscientiously planned your speech and have delivered it to the best of your ability, you are entitled to the appreciation of the audience.

Being Abrupt or Long-winded. To present a smooth "rounding off" of the thought and mood of the speech, avoid halting abruptly, as though being called to the telephone, or continuing on and on, overlooking various opportunities to close.

Introducing Important New Points of View. As you will recall, the place for the initial introduction of major ideas is the Introduction or Body—not the Conclusion.

Being Irrelevant. The use of such matter blurs or distorts the final focus of the speech.

Drastically Altering the Mood. Inasmuch as the final impression may be even more important than the initial one, avoid permitting an unsuitable deviation from the mood established throughout the speech.

Applying Principles to Speeches of Basic Types

We turn now to the application of these principles to the planning of Conclusions for speeches of basic types.

Planning the Conclusion of the Speech to Inform

Throughout the Introduction and Body of the informative speech you have attempted to promote understanding, assimilation, and retention. The Conclusion represents your final opportunity to foster favorable attitudes toward you and your informational topic, bring the substantive elements of the speech into final panoramic view, and re-emphasize the critical points in order to fix them enduringly in the minds of the listeners.

To encourage a lasting positive reaction to the subject, you might restress the significance of the topic, its application to the lives of the listeners, its immediacy, its universality, its popularity, its unusualness, its antiquity, its modernity, its patriotic, humane, or reverential values, and so on. Such re-emphasis should be relevant, sincere, and in good taste, and should help the listeners carry away from the speech a sense of identity or involvement in the subject.

If the speech is short or unusually clear, perhaps a restatement of the POINT is sufficient to provide final focus and effect retention. Much more frequently, however, inasmuch as retention of the new knowledge is ordinarily even more important for the speech to inform than for other basic types, the Conclusion should provide a somewhat more extensive review.

If your listeners must remember specific rules, procedures, or principles discussed in the Body, you should repeat them in the Conclusion. Probably the formal listing of points appears more frequently in informative speeches than in entertaining or persuasive ones. Even in informative speeches, however, you should carefully estimate whether this means of promoting clarity and retention will in your particular speech compensate for its dull and academic flavor. More commonly, you will wish to review the salient points or concepts of the Body, linking and telescoping them in such a manner that the speech purpose is crystallized and the ideational content of the speech is brought into final focus.

Naturally, you also may promote favorable attitudes and clarity by using one or more appropriate, brief quotations, comparisons, or illustrations.

Sometimes in the Conclusion you may employ a modified "action step," suggesting that your listeners continue their new-found interest in the subject and, perhaps, concisely providing "how," "what," "when," and "where" guidance for the securing of additional information. As an example of a representative Conclusion for a speech to inform, in concluding a lecture to an academic audience on the topic "The Emergence of the Concept of Southern Oratory," Waldo W. Braden used this informal review.[8]

Text

In summary, the image of floridity and the belief that Southern oratory is different from the speaking of other sections dates back before the Civil War. The school readers reinforced and popularized the concept with brief eloquent passages from ceremonial speeches.

[8]Used by special permission of Dr. Braden.

They probably helped to perpetuate the myth by encouraging the students to imitate flowery models and mellifluous delivery.

It is evident that most early Southern literary historians and anthropologists contributed significantly to the image of Southern oratory as well as to the formal study of the subject. . . .

The Southern historians, doing little more than parrot the literary historians, continued to perpetuate an image with little study or analysis. They were influenced by frontier camp meetings, stump speaking, political harangues, and ceremonial speaking—often eulogies of Southern heroes, such as Patrick Henry, John Randolph of Roanoke, Robert Y. Hayne, William Yancey, and Seargent S. Prentiss.

It seems [to me] that a study of Southern oratory based upon apologists and heroes, portions of ceremonial speeches, secondary reports of casual observers, and sensational occasions such as frontier camp meetings and stump speaking is bound to be myth-encrusted.

Outline

Conclusion:

I. The image of floridity and the belief that Southern oratory is different from other sections dates back before the Civil War
  A. School readers reinforced and popularized the concept
  B. Early Southern literary historians and anthropologists contributed to the image
  C. Southern historians continued to perpetuate the image
II. A study of Southern oratory based upon apologists and heroes, ceremonial speeches, secondary reports of casual observers, and sensational occasions is bound to be myth-encrusted

In regard to speaker image, it is probably sufficient to consider that in the Conclusion what you say and how you say it should be consistent with the image you have established and maintained throughout the Introduction and Body: the image of an intelligent, well-meaning, personable speaker who is especially knowledgeable on the topic, eager to communicate new understanding to the listeners, and sensitive to the listeners' needs and interests—particularly as they relate to the new knowledge.

Planning the Conclusion of the Speech to Entertain

Inasmuch as the "pure" speech to entertain does not seek to provide listeners with new understanding or to persuade them to accept or reject courses of action, the Conclusion serves merely the function of promoting the proper mood, that is, to bring the speech to a graceful, smooth close leaving the audience with the positive impression of having been pleasantly diverted. Typically, a few well-turned phrases are sufficient. If a longer Conclusion seems advisable, the materials should be sparkling, buoyant—and brief.

In Mark Twain's entertaining speech "The Oldest Inhabitant—the Weather of New England" (see excerpt from the Introduction to this speech on p. 251), the closing sentence centers final attention on the basic thought and mood of the speech:

> Month after month I lay up hate and grudge against the New England weather; but when the ice-storm comes at last, I say: "There. I forgive you now; the books are square between us; you don't owe me a cent; go and sin some more; your little faults and foibles count for nothing; you are the most enchanting weather in the world."

If your entertaining speech has a secondary function of informing or persuading, you should adjust the nature of the Conclusion accordingly: the more important the function of informing or persuading, the more your Conclusion should resemble the typical Conclusion of the informative or persuasive speech.

In bringing your speech to a close, you should, of course, continue to be relaxed, genial, and positive. Your speaker image should encourage the listeners to retain their pleasant feelings of optimism and buoyancy.

Planning the Conclusion of the Speech to Persuade

In your efforts to persuade the audience to think, feel, or do as you wish, the Conclusion must be an important consideration. Although the basic task of persuasion should have been accomplished in the Body, the Conclusion may be decisive—if it stimulates, or fails to stimulate, in the listeners a lasting impression of being personally involved, and of having heard a compelling address to their judgment-sentiment.

Speech to Convince. The speech to convince aims at the future, that is, it attempts to alter the convictions-attitudes-behaviors of the auditors "permanently," to establish the new concepts so firmly that the listeners will not revert to previously held positions or heed the "siren" calls of later persuaders.

The initially uncommited audience. In order to establish the basis for belief in those speeches that are directed to the *initially uncommitted audience,* the Introduction and Body should have presented a closely knit, factual rationale, cast in as nonargumentative a form as possible and tailored as effectively as possible to the logical and attitudinal predispositions of the listeners. The Conclusion is not the place to introduce significant new arguments or documentation—the place to do that is in the Body. The Conclusion provides the opportunity to bring together the basic contentions and evidence so that the listeners can gain an *in toto* grasp of the case; it affords the means of directing to the listeners a final appeal to accept the reasonableness and desirability of the new policy. Although the typical Conclusion probably should be primarily factual and logical, you should not overlook the need to encourage a lasting identification of the listeners with the basic thrust of your speech—the residual message. Consider the possible use of relevant and tactful allusions to the self-interest of the listeners or of appeals to the ideals, aspirations, or values endorsed by the listeners. In most cases you could appropriately use a restatement of the POINT and an informal review, which could include one or more quotations, comparisons, or illustrations. Less frequently, the Conclusion might contain a formal listing of major arguments.

The initially hostile audience. In concluding a speech addressed to an audience that was *initially hostile* to your proposal, you probably should re-emphasize the basic elements of agreement or identification and diplomatically review the arguments you have presented.

For example, in speaking to the people of Zambia concerning the U.S. policy toward Rhodesia, Henry Kissinger confronted an audience that was sharply critical of the policies and motives of the United States. On pp. 255–257 we saw how Kissinger tried to establish beachheads of identification with his listeners during the extended Introduction of his speech. Now let us see how in the Conclusion Kissinger re-emphasized those beachheads of identification (which, of course, he had attempted to expand in the Body) and reviewed the basic proposals he had advanced in the Body.[9]

> Today I have outlined the principles of American policy on the compelling challenges of southern Africa.
>
> Our proposals are not a program made in America to be passively accepted by Africans. They are an expression of common aspirations and an agenda of cooperation. Underlying it is our fundamental conviction that Africa's destiny must remain in African hands.
>
> No one who wishes this continent well can want to see Africans divided either between nations or between liberation movements. Africans cannot want outsiders seeking to impose solutions, or choosing among countries or movements. The United States, for its part, does not seek any pro-American African block confronting a block supporting any other power. Nor do we wish to support one

[9] *Vital Speeches,* May 15, 1976, p. 459.

faction of a liberation movement against another. But neither should any other country pursue hegemonial aspirations or block policies. An attempt by one will inevitably be countered by the other. The United States therefore supports African unity and integrity categorically as basic principles of our policy. . . . The United States supports Africa's genuine nonalignment and unity. We are ready for collaboration on the basis of mutual respect. We do so guided by our convictions and our values. Your cause is too compatible with our principles for you to need to pursue it by tactics of confrontation with the United States; our self-respect is too strong to let ourselves be pressured either directly or by outside powers.

What Africa needs now from the United States is not exuberant promises or emotional expressions of good will. What it needs is a concrete program which I have sought to offer today. So let us get down to business. Let us direct our eyes toward our great goals—national independence, economic development, racial justice—goals that can be achieved by common action. . . . Let us prove that these goals can be realized by human choice, that justice can command by the force of its rightness instead of by force of arms. . . .

So let it be said that black people and white people working together achieved on this continent—which has suffered so much and seen so much injustice—a new era of peace, well-being and human dignity.

Speech to Stimulate (Impress or Reinforce). On controversial issues, as you remember, the anticipated audience attitude determines whether the persuasive speech should be aimed toward conviction or stimulation (impression or reinforcement). When the audience initially is favorably oriented to the speaker's policy, the Introduction and Body should capitalize upon the initial reaction of the listeners so that they are brought into stronger logical and emotional agreement. When this has been accomplished, the Conclusion serves as a final stimulant, closing the speech on a high point of interest and logical-emotional affirmation.

In comparison to the Conclusion of the convincing speech to the previously uncommitted audience, the Conclusion of the stimulating speech may have somewhat less need to crystallize the thought by a factual and logical review of the speaker's arguments and a somewhat greater need to appeal to emotional and rationalized values.

As a general guide, which you must apply with caution, the emotional component of the Conclusion can be gauged to the emotional affirmation of the audience: the more intense the emotional agreement, the stronger and more sweeping can be the appeal. Naturally, any address to the feelings should be sincere and appropriate.

Very possibly you will find that the method of formal listing is less appropriate for the speech to stimulate than for speeches to convince or inform. Such an obvious, and usually flat, recapitulation may interfere with your attempts to build up to a final peak of attention. Your use of the other standard procedures—restatement of the POINT, informal and indirect review—should be carefully adjusted to the ideational needs of the subject and to the values, attitudes, and behaviors that you and the listeners share in relation to the topic.

Upon acceptance of the Sylvanus Thayer award at the U.S. Military Academy, West Point, General Douglas MacArthur delivered a moving address on "Duty, Honor, and Country." In his Conclusion, General MacArthur furthered his speech purpose of impressing the corpsmen by restating the POINT, reminding the West Pointers of their great responsibilities, tying an evocative personal reference to his theme, and bidding the corpsmen good-bye:[10]

> Your guidepost stands out like a tenfold beacon in the night: Duty, honor, country.
>
> You are the lever which binds together the entire fabric of our national system of defense. From your ranks come the great captains who hold the Nation's destiny in their hands the moment the war tocsin sounds.
>
> The long, gray line has never failed us. Were you to do so, a million ghosts in olive drab, in brown khaki, in blue and gray would rise from their white crosses, thundering those magic words: Duty, honor, country.
>
> This does not mean that you are warmongers. On the contrary, the soldier above all other people prays for peace, for he must suffer and bear the deepest wounds and scars of war. But always in our ears ring the ominous words of Plato, that wisest of all philosophers: "Only the dead have seen the end of war."
>
> The shadows are lengthening for me. The twilight is here. My days of old have vanished—tone and tints. They have gone glimmering through the dreams of things that were. Their memory is one of wondrous beauty, watered by tears and coaxed and caressed by the smiles of yesterday. I listen then but with thirsty ear, for the witching melody of faint bugles blowing reveille, of far drums beating the long roll.
>
> In my dreams I hear again the crash of guns, the rattle of musketry, the strange, mournful mutter of the battlefield. But in the evening of my memory I come back to West Point. Always there echoes and reechoes: Duty, honor, country.
>
> Today marks my final roll call with you. But I want you to know that when I cross the river, my last conscious thoughts will be of the corps. . . .
>
> I bid you farewell.

[10] *Vital Speeches,* June 15, 1962, pp. 520–21.

Speech to Actuate. Only speeches *to actuate* have as the principal purpose the impelling of listeners to perform definite acts in the immediate or fairly soon future. Therefore, the Conclusion of the actuating speech usually should do more than promote the proper mood and clarify the thought; it should also contain a direct appeal for action, sometimes called the Action Appeal.

The substance of the Action Step depends upon the character of the overt response desired, as well as the exigencies of the speech occasion, the audience, the nature of the materials previously presented, and so on. In general, however, the Action Appeal should not only indicate clearly the nature of the desired action, and how-where-when it is to be accomplished, but it should also constitute a postive logico-emotional appeal to perform the action. Ordinarily the Action Appeal of speeches on important social, political, or philosophical themes cannot make as concrete an appeal for overt response as can the Action Appeals of speeches with limited themes, such as contributing to the cancer drive, purchasing a gas refrigerator, or voting for a particular candidate.

The Action Appeal should always make the response as desirable and as easy to accomplish as possible. (Avoid vague, trite requests such as, "Write to your Congressmen." Many people do not know the name of their Congressman. Do you? If someone should ask you to write your city commissioner, state representative, U.S. Representative, or U.S. Senator, would you know the man's full name and his mailing address? Wouldn't you be more likely to write and post the letter if the speaker gave you and the rest of the audience stamped and addressed envelopes?)

The Action Appeal should constitute an effective address to the emotions as well as to the intellect. According to William James, we accept a new belief or policy of action only when the new idea possesses sufficient emotional attractiveness. Audiences usually are not moved to action by intellectual appeals, devoid of emotional fiber. On the other hand, invocation of emotions will prove ineffective unless the listeners have previously been brought into substantial agreement with the speaker. Furthermore, maudlin, affected, overdone, insincere appeals to the emotions are generally ineffective. Listeners will resent, and rightly so, any obvious play on their feelings. Never use an emotional plea because you think it is a good rhetorical "trick." Exercise a discriminating judgment based upon moral considerations and a genuine respect for the intelligence of your audience. Only well-reasoned appeals, which are well integrated into the continuum of the entire speech, will constitute a persuasive Action Appeal.

Occasionally the Action Appeal may constitute the entire Conclusion. More frequently, however, it should be used in conjunction with a formal, indirect, and/or informal review. Examples: (1) In concluding his summation speech in the White-Knapp murder case, Daniel Webster

summarized the case for the prosecution by means of an informal review; then he employed an Action Appeal to impel the jurors to take the necessary step—ballot to send the defendant to the noose:

Text

Informal Review

Gentlemen, I have gone through with the evidence in this case, and have endeavored to state it plainly and fairly before you. I think there are conclusions to be drawn from it, the accuracy of which you cannot doubt. I think you cannot doubt that there was a conspiracy formed for the purpose of committing this murder . . .; that you cannot doubt that the Crowninshields and the Knapps were the parties in this conspiracy; that you cannot doubt that the prisoner at the bar knew that the murder was to be done on the night of the 6th of April; that you cannot doubt that the murderers of Captain White were the suspicious persons seen in and about Brown Street on that night; that you cannot doubt that Richard Crowninshield was the perpetrator of that crime; that you cannot doubt that the prisoner at the bar was in Brown Street on that night. If there, then it must be by agreement, to countenance, to aid the perpetrator, and, if so, then he is guilty as principal.

Action Step

Gentlemen, your whole concern should be to do your duty, and leave the consequences to take care of themselves. You will receive the law from the court. Your verdict, it is true, may endanger the prisoner's life, but then it is to save other lives. If the prisoner's guilt has been shown and proved beyond all reasonable doubt, you will convict him. If such reasonable doubts of guilt still remain, you will acquit him. You are the judges of the whole case. You owe a duty to the public, as well as to the prisoner at the bar. You cannot presume to be wiser than the law. Your duty is a plain, straightforward one. Doubtless we would all judge him in mercy. Towards him, as an individual, the law inculcates no hostility; but towards him, if proved to be a murderer, the law, and the oaths you have taken, and public justice demand that you do your duty. With consciences satisfied with the discharge of duty, no consequences can harm you. There is no evil that we cannot either face or fly from but the consciousness of duty disregarded. A sense of duty pursues us ever. It is omnipresent, like the Deity. If we take to ourselves the wings of the morning, and dwell in the uttermost parts of the sea, duty performed or duty violated is still with us, for our happiness or our misery. If we say the darkness shall cover us, in the darkness, as in the light, our obligations are yet with us. We cannot escape their power, nor fly from their presence. They are with us in this life, will be with us at its close; and in that scene of inconceivable solemnity, which lies yet farther onward, we shall find ourselves surrounded by the consciousness of duty, to pain us whenever it has been violated, and to console us so far as God may have given us grace to perform it.

Outline

Conclusion:

I. I have gone through with the evidence in this case, and have endeavored to state it plainly and fairly before you
  A. I think there are conclusions to be drawn from it, the accuracy of which you cannot doubt
  B. I think that you cannot doubt the following:
    1. There was a conspiracy formed for the purpose of committing this murder
    2. The Crowninshields and the Knapps were the parties in this conspiracy
    3. The prisoner at the bar knew that the murder was to be done on the night of the 6th of April
    4. The murderers of Captain White were the suspicious persons seen in and about Brown Street on that night
    5. Richard Crowninshield was the perpetrator of that crime
    6. The prisoner at the bar was in Brown Street on that night
    7. If there, then it must be by agreement, to countenance, to aid the perpetrator, and, if so, then he is guilty as principal

II. Gentlemen, your whole concern should be to do your duty and leave the consequences to take care of themselves
  A. Your duty is plain
    1. You will receive the law from the court
    2. You must discharge your responsibilities under the law
  B. With consciences satisfied with the discharge of duty, no consequences can harm you
    1. A sense of duty pursues us ever
    2. We cannot escape from the pain of duty violated or the consolation of duty performed

(2) A few hours before a disastrous hurricane struck southern Florida, a student in an adult public-speaking course in Miami brought a box of Sterno stoves to class and attempted to sell them. In the Conclusion of his talk, he summarized informally the arguments presented in the Body and then used an Action Appeal.

> During my talk I have demonstrated to you how simple it is to operate the Sterno Cook Stove. I even fried an egg and brewed a pot of coffee. As I have told you, the ten-thirty advisory from the weather bureau states that a severe hurricane will strike the Miami area sometime this evening. You need a Sterno Cook Stove because electricity possibly will be cut off during the storm to avoid electrocutions from fallen wires. You can't go out to a restaurant during the hurricane. The storm may last through the night and through tomorrow. If the storm doubles back as the one did on the west coast of Florida this summer, it may last even longer. What's more, elec-

trical service in some parts of the city may be off for ten days to two weeks. Buy a Sterno Cook Stove from me for three ninety-nine, and you can have as many cups of coffee as you want during the storm. On this little stove you can heat the baby's formula, cook a pan of beans, or prepare an entire dinner. Three ninety-nine is a small investment. This morning I started out with twenty-five stoves, and I've sold fifteen already. Don't wait until this afternoon or tonight to buy a stove from me; I doubt that I'll have any left. I have only ten stoves here. Let me see the hands of those who want one. If you don't have the money with you, you can pay me the next class period. Now, how many of you want stoves?

(3) Perhaps the most famous Action Appeal in the history of American public speaking constitutes the Conclusion of Lincoln's Second Inaugural Address.

With malice towards none; with charity for all; with firmness in the right, as God gives us to see the right, let us strive on to finish the work we are in; to bind up the nation's wounds; to care for him who shall have borne the battle, and for his widow and orphans; to do all which may achieve and cherish a just and lasting peace among ourselves and with all nations.

In the Conclusion of the persuasive speech, your speaker image must be consistent with that which you have maintained throughout the Introduction and Body, that is, a reasonable, ethical, intelligent person who is seriously concerned about the topic under consideration; who is decisive, energetic, and confident; who understands and respects the attitudes and beliefs of the listeners; who (keeping in mind his ethical responsibilities as well as pragmatic resources) identifies himself and his cause with the needs and better nature of his listeners, and who is not self-seeking but is interested in providing a service for his listeners and the larger public.

Summary

The nature and length of the Conclusion depend upon all of the circumstances involved. In general, the length of the typical Conclusion may be about 5 per cent—or somewhat more—of the total speech length, and the functions of the typical Conclusion are to crystallize the thought of the speech, promote the proper mood, and, in the case of actuating speeches, impel specific action on the part of the listeners. Although the basic task of moving listeners toward closure with the speaker's position should have been accomplished in the Body, the Conclusion may be decisive if it produces, or fails to produce, in the listeners a lasting impression of being personally involved and of having heard a compelling address to their thinking-feeling-behaviors. The Conclusion, then, provides the final psychological-logical impulsion to move the listeners toward closure.

To accomplish the purposes of the Conclusion, one or more of the following procedures may be employed: state the POINT of the speech, that is, the basic thrust or speaker's intent; list the main ideas; review informally or indirectly by means of quotation(s), comparison, or example.

Care should be taken to avoid common faults such as apologizing, being disconcertingly abrupt or long-winded, introducing important new points, including irrelevant material, violating the proper mood, or losing the attention of the listeners.

Because the general speech purpose is one of the most important conditioning aspects of the total speaking situation, speeches to inform, entertain, and persuade require somewhat different types of Conclusion.

Exercises and Assignments

1. In concluding a speech delivered before the Convention on Individual Liberty at Billings, Montana (sponsored by the Montana Chamber of Commerce), Dean Russell used this exhortation:

> Thus, the final decision rests on the attitude of each individual American. If enough of us accept the degrading idea of a Welfare State—a Relief State, a Slave State—the process will soon be completed. But if enough individual Americans desire a return to the personal responsibility that *is* freedom, we can have that too.
>
> Before choosing, however, consider this: When one chooses freedom—that is, personal responsibility—he should understand that his decision will not meet with popular approval. It is almost certain that he will be called vile names when he tries to explain that compulsory government "security"—jobs, medicine, housing, and all the rest—is bad in principle and in its total effect; it saps character and strength by encouraging greed and weakness; it destroys the individual's God-given responsibility for self-help, respect, compassion and charity; in some degree, it automatically turns all who accept it into wards of the government; it will eventually turn a proud and responsible people into cringing dependence upon the whims of an all-powerful state; it is the primrose path to serfdom.
>
> No, the choice is not an easy one. But then the choice of freedom never has been easy. It never will be easy. Since this capacity for personal responsibility—freedom—is God's most precious gift to mankind, it requires the highest form of understanding and courage.

What kinds of listeners would respond positively to Mr.Russell's appeal? Why would they? What kinds of listeners would respond negatively? Why would they? How would you characterize Mr. Russell's use of language and motive appeals?

2. For your next speech in class prepare two different Conclusions. In one follow a statement of the POINT with a formal listing of the main ideas of the Body. In the second state the POINT, and then give an informal review of the material covered in the Body. Record the two Conclusions and determine which one is superior.

3. Attend an evangelistic service. Near the close, did the speaker grow more emotional? If he did, why did he? If he did not, why not?

4. A student once stated that most radio or television commercials consist exclusively of an Action Step. Was his reasoning valid?

5. Study the Conclusions of at least five printed speeches. Which methods of summarizing seem to predominate? In what ways could the Conclusions be improved?

6. Should emotional appeals to action in the Conclusion always be avoided when speaking to the well educated? Why or why not?

7. During the next round of speeches in class, pick out the best and the poorest Conclusions. Be prepared to defend your judgment before the class.

8. Keep a written record of the most common "sins" of the Introduction and of the Conclusion that you hear in speeches on the campus and in the community.

9. Deliver a sales talk in class in which you close with an Action Step. Do your hearers agree that your Conclusion is impelling? Does it answer the questions: what, how, where, and when?

10. Close one of your class speeches with an indirect method of summarizing, that is, by quotation, illustration, or comparison. Make sure that your material is relevant and interesting.

SECTION IV

Delivering the Speech

Essential Purpose of Section IV: to enable the student to deliver his speeches with effectiveness

Platform etiquette and conduct
- Before the speech (pp. 295)
- Beginning the speech (pp. 295)
- During the speech (pp. 296)
- After the speech (pp. 296)

Dress and appearance

Use of a public address system
- If present, a public address system should be used (pp. 297)
- Keep within close range of the microphone (pp. 298)
- Maintain normal volume and projection (pp. 298)

Chapter 13: Rehearsing the Speech

Where to rehearse (pp. 301)

When to rehearse (pp. 302)

How to rehearse
- The preliminary phase in rehearsing is to fix the speech in the mind (pp. 303)
- The second phase in rehearsing is to polish the delivery of the speech (pp. 304)

Chapter 14: Using the Body and Voice in Delivering the Speech

Using the body effectively
- The importance of bodily action (pp. 308)
  - Bodily action helps to clarify meaning
  - Bodily action helps to achieve emphasis
  - Bodily action facilitates adjustment to the speaking situation
  - Bodily action helps to secure and maintain interest and attention
- Developing effective bodily action (pp. 310)
  - Eye contact
  - Facial expression
  - Posture
  - Movement
  - Gestures

Using the voice effectively
- Six attributes of the effective speaking voice (pp. 315)
  - Audibility
  - Pleasantness
  - Variety
  - Animation
  - Fluency
  - Clarity
- Acquiring the attributes of an effective speaking voice (pp. 317)
  - Audibility and pleasantness are primarily the products of proper habits of breathing, phonation, and resonation

Variety, animation, and fluency necessitate a flexible voice
Clarity depends upon the distinctness and "correctness" with which you speak

Chapter 15: Using Language in Delivering the Speech

The nature of language

Words are symbols having meaning only in terms of the associations established between the symbol and the object or concept to which it refers (pp. 335)
A symbol never tells everything about the object or concept to which it refers (pp. 335)
Thought cannot be transmitted, but can only be stirred up in the listener (pp. 336)
Word meanings are constantly changing (pp. 336)

Specific guides for the effective use of language

Language should be chosen for its oral qualities; it is primarily meant to be heard, not read (pp. 337)
Language should be adapted to your own personality, your audience, and the occasion (pp. 338)
Language should possess clarity (pp. 339)
Language should be sufficiently objective (pp. 341)
Language should be vivid and impressive (pp. 342)
Language should include an abundant stock of connective and transitional words and phrases (pp. 345)
Language should be arranged into clear and varied sentences (pp. 346)
Language should be chosen from a constantly increasing speaking vocabulary (pp. 347)

CHAPTER 12

An Introduction to Delivery

The preceding sections have dealt with developing proper perspectives concerning public speaking, understanding the basic demands upon the speech, and preparing the speech. We are now ready to consider the principles of delivering the speech. Chapter 12 concerns an overview of speech delivery; Chapter 13 contains suggestions for rehearsing the speech; Chapter 14 contains advice for using the body and voice; Chapter 15 concerns the use of language in delivering the speech.

How important is delivery in determining the total effectiveness of a speech? Perhaps the best answer to this question was made by Cicero when he wrote, "many poor speakers have often reaped the rewards of eloquence because of effective delivery, and many eloquent men have been considered poor speakers because of an awkward delivery." Occasionally, an audience will be attentive to a speaker with inferior delivery—if he has a significant message. With sound, interesting ideas and a strong desire to share them with others, one may move an audience in spite of deficiencies in delivery. Awkward, unsophisticated students sometimes hold classes spellbound by presenting inherently interesting ideas. A speaker who holds a position of authority may—by virtue of his rank—maintain the attention of his audiences, despite poor delivery. Although such instances indicate that sometimes a speech may be well received without good delivery, we cannot conclude that presentation is, therefore, unimportant. Because of inadequate delivery, many speeches of genuine significance are failures. Accept Aristotle's admonition that "success in delivery is of the utmost importance to the effect of a speech."

As noted in Chapter 1, some students mistakenly believe that to pursue the development of good delivery is fruitless—that some speakers are "naturally good," whereas others are doomed to permanent ineffectiveness. Of course, those individuals with pleasant voices, good articulation, quick minds, fluent tongues, and attitudes of confidence will need less training in delivery than others less generously endowed. Nevertheless, the talented novice can greatly improve his skills in delivery, and with conscientious practice and training the ineffectual beginner can develop effectiveness on the platform.

One of the problems confronting the author of a practical guide to public speaking is that, although training in speech presentation is critically important to the novice, "it is the sort of training that is least amenable to transmission in a written treatise." Saint Augustine had this in mind when he advised that beginning speakers would "more readily learn eloquence by reading and hearing the eloquent" and by practice "than by following the rules of eloquence." Also, like modern teachers, Saint Augustine was disturbed lest training in delivery should cause the student to be overly concerned with rules and techniques during the presentation of his speeches. Saint Augustine counseled that at the time of utterance the speaker should be concerned with reaching his listeners: "I think there is hardly a single eloquent man who can both speak well and think of the rules of eloquence while he is speaking. And we should beware lest what should be said escape us while we are thinking of the artistry of the discourse."

The principles discussed in Section IV, "Delivering the Speech," should be considered as suggestive guides, not as arbitrary rules. Delivery is intimately related not only to the totality of the immediate speaking situation but also to the purpose and personality of the speaker. Within reasonable bounds, the guides to delivery should be interpreted to fit the individual. For example, in the matter of gesture, the naturally demonstrative speaker will gesticulate far more frequently than the less dynamic speaker. Although gestures aid anyone addressing a visible audience, all speakers should not be expected to use exactly the same kind or amount of physical expressiveness.

Basic Principles of Delivery

Effective Delivery Makes Full Use of Both the Visible and Audible Codes

You may have read in your morning paper the text of a speech which you attended in person or watched on television the previous evening; or you may have examined the text of a speech before you heard it delivered. In either case, you possibly were struck by the difference between your reactions to reading the speech and to hearing it. In one instance, the printed text may seem clearer and more persuasive; in another, listening to the speech may seem more rewarding. Delivery is a major factor accounting for the differences.

Delivery consists of that visible and audible activity by which the speaker communicates his ideas and feelings to his listeners. As a beginning speaker, you should be concerned with acquiring skill in the use of both the audible and visible codes. Your voice can do much more than merely produce the sounds that in various combinations become language; it can emphasize significant ideas by changes in pitch, intensity, and rate; it can convey delicate nuances of meaning through the use of inflections; it can enhance emotional appeal by an appropriate use of pause, stress, pitch variability, and modification of timbre. The visible code, consisting of posture, movement, gesture, and facial expression, may also aid in pointing up specific meanings and in strengthening emotional appeals.

Admittedly, some successful speakers may have rasping voices or cloudy articulation, or may commit minor errors of syntax or grammar, and so on; others may tend to be wooden or mechanical, lacking adequate bodily expressiveness. Such speakers are effective *despite*—not because of—their limitations in delivery. If they possessed better skills in delivery, their general speech effectiveness probably would be enhanced. Recognize that the skillful use of both the visible and audible codes can mean the difference between an indirect, lifeless, uninspiring performance and a meaningful, stimulating message.

Effective Delivery Is Adapted to the Total Speaking Situation

Effective delivery is well adjusted to the demands imposed by the speaker himself, the speech, the audience, and the occasion. The modern writer in making this point could scarcely do better than to turn to the testimony of the famed medieval scholar Alcuin: "The whole manner of delivery should be fashioned to accord with the nature of the place where the speech is made, with the materials available to the speaker, with the persons concerned in the case, with the speaker's subject, and with the particular occasion. Some materials, to be sure, should be delivered in the vein of simple narrative, others in the vein of authoritative advice, and still others in the vein of indignation, or of pity, if the voice and the delivery are to befit a particular kind of subject." The following suggestive elaboration of Alcuin's statement may provide the basis for further thinking on your part.

(1) Adaptation to the audience. Academic or intellectually inclined groups may prefer a somewhat more restrained and dignified delivery

than do the ebullient delegates to a political or labor convention. Small audiences expect a somewhat quieter and more informal manner than do large gatherings in dignified spacious surroundings.

(2) Adaptation to the occasion. Although a pep rally may be addressed with great informality, a memorial service will call for dignity and solemnity in presentation. A nominating speech at a political convention will call for more vigorous projection than will a lecture on Victorian poetry to a women's study club.

(3) Adaptation to the subject. If you wish to entertain a nightclub audience with broad humor, you would use an informal manner and, probably, considerable movement, gesticulation, and vocal dynamics. If you wish to convince a review panel of judges to sustain the school board's decision concerning the firing of a teacher, your delivery probably should be earnest, direct, and sincere, without pyrotechnics.

(4) Adaptation to the speaker. Audiences usually expect a youthful speaker to be more energetic and physically expressive than an elderly speaker. One's profession may also influence the manner of presentation expected. Persons may anticipate greater formality and restraint from a physician, judge, or college dean than from a professional football player, a famous comedian, or a gossip columnist.

If you have the proper "feel" for the total speaking situation, you will almost automatically adjust your delivery to the constraints imposed by your purpose and speech materials, the audience, the occasion, and yourself as the speaker.

Effective Delivery Is Sincere

Listeners are far more likely to believe what a speaker says if they are convinced that he believes it. Even a suggestion of insincerity may result in failure. For example, one student ruined what was otherwise a moving speech on the value of prayer by winking slyly as he said, "Even sophisticated intellectuals find solace in prayer." From that point on, his listeners doubted his sincerity. The best way to give the impression of sincerity is to *be sincere*. Do not plead causes in which you do not believe. If you are dishonest with yourself and with others, such chicanery very likely will "show through" your synthetic sincerity. Ralph Waldo Emerson pointed out, "What you are . . . thunders so that I cannot hear what you say." In an interview with the author, Harry S. Truman observed that the speaker "must believe what he is saying. . . . As for sincerity, the public is quick to detect and reject the charlatan and the demagogue. It may be deceived for a brief period, but not for long."

Apparent insincerity is sometimes a serious problem for novice speakers. Although completely in earnest, a speaker may give the impression of hypocrisy or indifference because of poor eye contact, shifting from one foot to another, bored facial expression, hesitant utterance, and so on. Instead of being evidences of dissimulation, such delivery characteristics may be manifestations of insecurity. Nevertheless, they may damage his credibility. The answer to this problem is, of course, to develop a confident, lively, direct style of communication.

Closely related to sincerity is the concept of the *ethical responsibility* of the speaker. In a materialistic civilization in which many believe in achieving personal ends at any cost, effective speaking, like atomic energy, may be used to further evil causes. As discussed in Chapter 1, inasmuch as many unethical persons are eager to use their persuasive powers to make the worse cause appear the better, it is the obligation of the responsible citizen to use his speaking ability in the interest of good causes.

The character of the speaker is an exceedingly important factor in determining his effectiveness. The speaker with a reputation for honesty, reliability, and dependability may succeed where a more polished and experienced performer will fail, if the motives or character of the latter are subject to suspicion. If you are to maintain a reputation for integrity, avoid taking any side of any question for the sake of momentary personal gain. Otherwise, audiences may become convinced that you are without principle, and then you will find it difficult to secure acceptance of those ideas in which you really believe.

Effective Delivery Is Modest and Unassuming

To the unsure, stumbling beginner, modesty is not a problem. With increased confidence acquired by successful experience, a few students develop exalted opinions of themselves. The overly confident beginner, of course, has this distorted viewpoint at the outset. If such conceit is apparent to the listeners, it will surely—and justifiably—irritate them. To be genuinely effective, a speaker should possess a well-integrated, mature personality, essential elements of which are the realistic assessment of one's own personal assets and liabilities and the appreciation of the intrinsic merit of others. Few persons have accomplished enough prior to their middle years to warrant feelings of superiority. Effective speakers, like most successful persons, recognize that modesty is an indispensable asset in interpersonal relations. Therefore, they avoid the ostentatious parading of knowledge, vocabulary, or cleverness.

Effective Delivery Is Confident and Assured

The speaker is a leader in the sense that he wishes to lead his listeners to new positions of understanding, belief, or feeling. To lead others one must be able to lead one's self. A requisite for leadership is confidence in one's own worth as a person and as a speaker. If you apply the suggestions in Chapter 1 to control nervous tension, you should feel the comforting assurance of having done everything possible to prepare yourself intellectually and psychologically for your speech. When you rise to speak, think and act positively and soon you may begin to feel self-assured. Remember that "nothing succeeds like a successful attitude."

Effective Delivery Does Not Attract Attention to Itself

Many years ago, William Jennings Bryan's Chautauqua lectures attracted large humbers of auditors, some of whom came primarily to admire his "magnificent delivery." A generation or so ago, grade school students memorized and declaimed (but scarcely understood) orations originally delivered to the ancient Romans. Today, partly because television and radio emphasize an intimate, very direct style of delivery, exhibitionism on the public platform has become passé. We give speeches primarily because we have something to say that we feel needs to be said; we attend speeches primarily because the speaker has something to say that interests us. Good delivery does not attract attention to itself, but rather to the speaker's ideas.

Effective Delivery Is Enthusiastic and Animated

As Bulwer-Lytton pointed out, "Nothing is so contagious as enthusiasm; it moves stones, it charms brutes. Enthusiasm is the genius of sincerity and truth accomplishes no victories without it." Before you can move others, you must feel moved yourself. If you are alert and animated, your listeners probably will reflect to some extent your enthusiasm. A dull, dour, flaccid speech personality rarely engenders an eager response. Animated delivery results primarily from a *lively desire to communicate.* If you believe in your ideas and are strongly motivated to share them with others, your presentation is likely to be alert, vigorous, and dynamic.

Modes of Delivery

Several modes of presentation are available to the speaker. He may (1) *memorize,* (2) speak *impromptu,* (3) *read* from manuscript, or (4) speak *extemporaneously.* Novices should avoid the first mode, use the second only when opportunity for preparation does not exist, and employ the third only when the situation is formal and exactness of language or careful timing is essential. For most persons, extemporaneous delivery provides the mode of greatest effectiveness in the majority of situations.

Avoid the Memorized Speech

Because the beginning speaker fears that he will be unable to find the right words and remember his ideas, he may be tempted to memorize his entire speech. He reasons that this will relieve him of the necessity to think on his feet during a period of emotional strain.

Admittedly, skilled and experienced performers on the stage, before the television cameras, or on the public-speaking platform may recite long memorized passages with seeming spontaneity. We should also recognize that the novice speaker may employ limited memorization to advantage. For instance, he should learn the sequence of ideas he wishes to present, and possibly, he may commit to memory a joke, short quotations, figures—if not too numerous, a punch line, a few sentences at the beginning or ending of a speech, and so on. Nevertheless, speech teachers strongly urge the typical beginner not to memorize entire speeches. Why? Consider these reasons:

(1) If you begin to speak in public by employing the *memoriter* method, you may make more difficult and less likely, your acquisition of adequate skill in speaking extemporaneously or impromptu. If you memorize to escape the task of converting ideas into language, you may experience acute discomfort later when you attempt, or are forced by circumstances, to think on your feet. Practice is necessary to develop facility in symbolizing ideas on the platform. Memorization not only fails to provide this practice but it also produces habits of thought and expression directly counter to spontaneous utterance. Such habits augment the difficulty of symbolizing under stress.

(2) One who memorizes is in constant danger of forgetting. If you forget a line, your whole machinery of memorization may be disastrously thrown off, and by the time you are able to return to your memorized track the effectiveness of your speech may have been severely damaged.

(3) Memorized speeches usually sound mechanical. The speaker tends to concentrate upon remembering the next word or phrase rather than upon the communication of his ideas. His delivery and speech personality suffer as a result.

(4) Although a student may find time to memorize an occasional short speech, the busy adult is unable to devote enough time to commit full-length speeches to memory. After you have acquired experience, feel free to experiment with the *memoriter* method, if you wish to do so; for your early speeches, however, avoid this mode of delivery.

Make the Best of the Situation If You Are Forced to Speak Impromptu

The impromptu speech is treated in detail in Chapter 16 as a special type of speech. Because it is also one of the modes of delivery available to the public speaker, brief reference to it is made at this point.

To speak impromptu means to speak on the spur of the moment, without specific preparation. When asked unexpectedly "to say a few words," the speaker must do most of his thinking while speaking. This is not as difficult as it may appear, since everyone does so whenever engaging in conversation. In public speaking, however, it is a frightening prospect to many, because the situation is more formal and more tension evoking. Even poised speakers, however, are not at their best when speaking without specific preparation. Frequently such improvisation is rambling, prolix, and obtuse. Speak impromptu only when specific preparation is impossible. In such cases, recognize that you are not completely unequipped: you are aware of the needs of the occasion; you have listened to the previous speakers; you possess general knowledge upon which you can draw; and you can use the moments between the request to speak and your first words to plan your opening remarks. Attempt to control nervous stress, forget yourself, and concentrate on communicating your thoughts.

Read From Manuscript Only When the Situation Is Formal and Exactness of Language or Careful Timing Is Essential

We should recognize that in the off-campus world a great many speeches are read from manuscript. Very probably, the large majority of really important speeches are either read from manuscript or partially read, partially extemporized. Especially when the audience is large, the occasion formal, the exactness or felicity of language important, and precise timing essential, experienced speakers often prefer to read their speeches. Also, many busy people, especially those who have not had proper training and sufficient experience in extemporaneous delivery, find it easier to read from manuscript.

Nevertheless, you are advised not to read your early speeches for several reasons:

(1) The classroom speaking situation does not provide an atmosphere that is ideally suited to manuscript speaking; the audience is too small and the mood of the occasion too informal.

(2) Most of your public speaking in real life situations will be extemporaneous. To acquire skill in extemporaneous delivery, you should use that mode in your training speeches.

(3) Your speaking probably will be less effective if you read than if

you extemporize. Only unusual speakers can read speeches in such a manner that both thought and language seem to spring from the actual speaking situation. In most cases, especially with beginners, the speech turns out to be an essay wired for sound.

For Most Situations, Including Your Speech Class, Use the Extemporaneous Mode of Delivery

In this method of presentation, language is coined, for the most part, at the moment of utterance. The advantages of the extemporaneous mode were set forth eloquently more than two hundred years ago by the Frenchman Fénelon: The extemporaneous speaker "speaks naturally, he does not talk in the manner of the declaimer. Things flow from their source. His utterances are lively and full of movement. Even the warmth which possesses him converts itself into terms and figures that he will not be able to prepare in his study." Although Fénelon admitted that men "can compose some lively speeches" in their studies, he protested that in most cases "actual delivery adds to them a still greater liveliness. Moreover, what you find in the heat of battle is concrete and natural in a quite different way. It has a casual air and lacks the artifice of almost all discourses composed in leisure. We must add that the skillful and experienced speaker adjusts subject matter to the effect that he sees it making upon the listener; for he notices very well what enters into the mind and what does not enter, what attracts attention, what touches the heart, what does not do these things." We should recognize, however, that although Fénelon's indictment of *memoriter* and manuscript speaking does not apply to skilled practitioners, his statement is a provocative endorsement of the extemporaneous mode.

You may extemporize with or without notes. In either case, during the rehearsal period fix your ideas and their sequence firmly in mind.

(1) Delivery without notes: Although the use of notes is perfectly acceptable, some advantages accrue from eliminating their use. Inasmuch as many beginning speakers tend to refer to notes more frequently than necessary, your speaking may be more direct and communicative if you do not take notes to the platform. If you use notes, you should not become so dependent upon their psychological reinforcement that you fear to speak without them. If you will deliver one or more of your early speeches without notes, you will discover that you can speak without the assistance of memory prompters. Delivery without notes makes mandatory, of course, the careful memorization of the outline structure of your speech.

(2) Delivery with notes: Using notes need not constitute a barrier between you and the audience, providing you refer to them only infrequently and unobtrusively. As general suggestions, put note cards on a

lectern, if one is available, or hold them in your hands. Do not place them on a low table, if reading them will necessitate obvious bending or stooping. Use relatively small, inconspicuous cards or sheets of paper but do not attempt to hide the fact that you are using them. If you need more than one card, number each and write on one side only. Keep notes as few in number as possible and phrase each entry concisely. Become so familiar with the sequence of your ideas that only rarely will you need to prompt your memory. In advising young ministers, Cotton Mather suggested, "Let your *notes* be little other than a *quiver,* on which you may cast your eye now and then, to see what *arrow* is to be next fetch'd from thence, and then, with your eye as much as may be on them whom you speak to, let it be shot away, with a *vivacity* becoming *one in earnest.*" Try to anticipate the need to look at your notes so that this can be done while speaking the last few words of a sentence. Thus, you can avoid a disruptive hesitation before beginning the next point.

Platform Etiquette and Conduct

Before the Speech

Although your speech may be first on the program, your obligations are not completely discharged upon concluding your talk; subsequent speakers deserve courteous attention, and the audience will be quick to notice lack of interest or distracting behavior on your part. If your speech occurs near the end of the meeting, the same rule for courteous attention holds. Excessive random action or preoccupation with your notes prior to and during the other speeches will be offensive to the speakers and may be resented by the listeners, who expect you to listen as attentively as they do.

As the time for your speech draws near, attempt to relax and control nervous tension. Breathing deeply and slowly a number of times usually helps.

Beginning the Speech

Upon being introduced by the chairman, rise and walk briskly but calmly to the speaker's stand. Wait until the chairman has finished his introductory remarks, however, before leaving your seat—do not "jump the gun." As a general rule pause a moment at the speaker's stand and acknowledge the chairman, perhaps with the words, "Mr. Chairman"; although the formality is possibly less closely adhered to than formerly, you should ordinarily recognize the audience, as with the greeting, "Ladies and gentlemen." Under unusual circumstances it may be desirable to acknowledge the presence of very important persons; usually, however, it would be a bit ludicrous to begin with a statement such as "Mr. Chairman, Mr. Mayor, Members of the Board of Trustees, Representative Johnson, Alderman Milton, Police Commissioner Blackwell, Principal Bilbo, Coach Johnson, Fire Chief Lawson, the Reverend Mr. Hast, other distinguished guests, and ladies and gentlemen."

Avoid random action at the outset. If it is necessary to button your coat, adjust your tie, or clear your throat, do so at your seat, not upon reaching the speaker's stand. Such activity will distract your listeners at a crucial time when you need to be establishing favorable interest in you as the speaker and in your subject matter.

Even if the chairman does not announce the title of your speech, start with the first sentence of your introduction. Do not begin a speech by announcing the topic in an incomplete sentence, such as, "How the Russians are Endangering World Peace."

During the Speech

Concentrate on your ideas and your audience in an attempt to make your delivery enthusiastic and communicative. Although you should be alert to the feedback you receive from the listeners and should seek to engage them in a continuing interaction, do not worry excessively about how well you are doing, or whether the audience approves of you. If you lose your trend of thought, pause a moment and attempt to go on with an elaboration of the preceding idea. If you find this difficult, glance at your notes and move on to the next major point. Do not be unduly concerned about the omission of some of your supporting material; unless it is of vital significance, the audience probably will be unaware of your lapse. If you make a mistake in pronunciation or diction, or if you hesitate, cough, or drop your notes, do not pause to apologize; this will only emphasize the distraction. Ordinarily only serious mistakes that alter the meaning you wish to convey should be corrected in the course of the speech.

After the Speech

Although prominent speakers sometimes conclude with "Thank you," it is unnecessary to thank a group for listening unless your appearance was at your own request. If you have done well, they should thank *you*. When your final word has been spoken, you might pause a moment, give a slight nod of acknowledgement if you wish, and return to your seat.

Dress and Appearance

It is exceedingly difficult to generalize in regard to dress and appearance. Perhaps there is only one "absolute" rule: your dress and appearance should fit the demands of the situation—the expectations of the audience, the nature of the speaking occasion, the demands of your purpose, and the character of your own life-style. Audiences regard the speaker's grooming as an indication of the kind of person he is. Therefore, the way you look may either help, or hinder, your attempts to move your listeners toward closure with your position. Despite the extreme informality in dress prevailing at most colleges, the student should not assume that docksiders, tennis shoes, jeans, T-shirts, and sweaters are acceptable dress at public-speaking situations off campus. Your dress does influence how others perceive you. Therefore, dress in a manner that will project an appropriate speaker image. In most situations, the speaker should be neat and well groomed. Listeners notice sharp contrasts, clashing colors, and extremes in the cut and style of the speaker's clothing. The man who wears a blue suit should avoid wearing bright green socks or tan shoes, and should save his dazzling Christmas tie for another day. The woman who is to address a meeting of the Parent-Teacher Association should put aside her eye-arresting frock with the deep cleavage for a more appropriate occasion and choose either a more conservative dress or a suit. For a detailed study of the persuasive effect of clothing, the student should consult John T. Molloy's *Dress for Success,* a work based upon fifteen years of empirical research.

Use of a Public Address System

Webster, Clay, Bryan, and others who spoke prior to the electronic age were forced to depend solely upon vocal projection to reach the back rows of audiences. Because most large auditoriums and meeting halls today are equipped with public address systems, such strenuous vocal activity is unnecessary. Amplifying systems require that some adjustments be made, however, if the speaker is to use them effectively.

If Present, a Public Address System Should be Used

If the sponsors of your meeting have installed an amplifying system, experience has probably indicated that it is needed by most speakers in that particular room when a large audience is in attendance. Although you may be fairly certain that your voice will carry without amplification, it will be better for you to use the public address equipment. The audience will expect you to do so, and will appreciate hearing you without effort.

Keep Within Close Range of the Microphone

Microphones are usually secured to the speaker's stand or placed near it. Speak directly into the microphone from your position behind the lectern. To avoid distracting variations in volume, keep a fairly consistent position in relation to the microphone.

Maintain Normal Volume and Projection

Although a large audience and a spacious room ordinarily require increased volume and projection, remember that the amplifier makes this unnecessary. Avoid sharp increases in volume, which will overload the amplifier. Your rate of speaking will need to be a trifle slower with a large audience, even though you are using a public address system. Do not be disturbed because you can hear your voice as it leaves the amplifier; use what you hear as a guide in adjusting your volume and projection.

Summary

Certain principles and practices are basic to the achievement of effective speech delivery. Good delivery (1) makes full use of both the visible and audible codes, (2) is adapted to the total speaking situation, (3) is sincere, (4) is modest and unassuming, (5) is confident and assured, (6) does not attract attention to itself, and (7) is enthusiastic and animated.

Among the various modes of delivery, the extemporaneous is the most effective for most persons in a majority of situations, including your speech class. Reading from a manuscript may be employed when the situation is formal and exactness of language and timing is required, if sufficient care has been exercised in preparation and rehearsal. The impromptu speech should be avoided if opportunity for preparation exists. Memorized speeches by beginners usually are ineffective.

The speaker should be aware of the essentials of platform conduct and etiquette before, during, and after his speech. His dress, appearance, and manner should be correct and appropriate. If a public address system is provided, he should use it skillfully.

Exercises and Assignments

1. During a round of speeches write a short analysis of the delivery of each of your classmates, using as a guide the basic principles in this chapter. Include both assets and liabilities. Put each analysis on a separate sheet of paper and do not sign your name. Hand the papers to your instructor, who will read them, sort them, and return to each student the various analyses of his delivery. How do your classmates' estimates of your delivery compare with your own? Are there points upon which there is substantial agreement? How will these evaluations help you in future work on techniques of delivery?

2. From among the well-known speakers you have heard, select the three who, in your judgment, are most effective in delivery. Be ready to defend your choice in class discussion.

3. Can you name several recognized speakers who are consistently well received by audiences even though their delivery is only average? Report orally to the class your analysis of the reasons for their effectiveness.

4. Prepare a two- or three-minute speech for extemporaneous delivery and record it. Then write out the speech verbatim, and read it into the microphone. Play back both versions and evaluate the two presentations. Which mode of delivery seems more effective? Why? Do your classmates agree?

5. One speaking assignment could be devoted to a "work session," in which each speaker may be stopped at any time by either classmates or instructor to point out deficiencies in delivery and to suggest improvements. Following each interruption, the student should attempt to remedy the deficiencies noted as he resumes speaking. (Caution: inasmuch as some students may find this procedure to be disconcerting, participation should be voluntary.)

6. Write two speech topics on separate pieces of paper. Each topic should ask for an opinion or point of view on some common subject-matter area. Be certain that your topic is general enough to permit any student to speak on it from his general knowledge. Place these topics, along with those of your classmates, face down on a table at the front of the classroom. As each student goes before the group he will pick two slips, and, after selecting one of the two topics and discarding the other, speak on it for two or three minutes. Compare the delivery of each student in this impromptu session with his delivery of prepared speeches.

7. Arrange to use a public address system in one speaking assignment. If your school does not own one, your city library may have such equipment available for rent at a nominal fee. In presenting your speeches, observe the rules noted in this chapter for the effective use of such equipment.

CHAPTER 13

Rehearsing the Speech

The last time you witnessed a collegiate or professional football contest weren't you impressed by the deceptive ball handling, the hard, efficient blocking and tackling, and the smooth, integrated operation of the offensive and defensive units? Do you remember that critical fourth down play-action pattern during the third quarter? How the man in motion drifted out to the left side of the line, as though getting in position to go downfield for a pass? How the quarterback faked a handoff to the fullback, who plunged into the line? How the quarterback then faded farther to the rear, apparently to toss a long aerial downfield, only to turn suddenly and throw a short bullet pass to the tight end? Recall how that player sprinted for the right side of the field, how blockers cleared a path for him, and how beautifully the runner timed his stride to avoid tacklers as he swivelhipped his way to a first down? Watching a well-integrated football team in action, we realize only vaguely the tremendous time and effort that goes into the training and conditioning programs of such a team.

Just as in football and all other sports, practice is essential in dramatics. The first time a cast runs over the lines of a play the rendition is uninspiring. There will be many rehearsals before the curtain can be raised on a finished performance. Innumerable hours of rehearsal also are necessary for successful concert appearances by singers, pianists, dancers, and violinists.

It is perhaps unnecessary to add that almost all effective speakers rehearse their speeches in some form before delivering them. Only an extremely limited few are so talented that they can speak with maximum effectiveness without some rehearsal. Much of what passes for impromptu shafts of oratory has been carefully prepared. The famed eighteenth-century English orator Richard Brinsley Sheridan worked out much of his "impromptu" wit and rebuttals in advance of utterance. Winston Churchill is said to have rehearsed a crushing rejoinder as much as a month in advance.

Conceivably, some readers may protest: "I've been talking since I was two and a half. Why should I rehearse my speech? I get plenty of practice in speaking every day." Practice in conversational speaking, yes; in public speaking, no. Ordinary conversation differs from public speaking in several essential ways. Unlike public address, conversation is a face-to-face situation with all parties contributing; there are no silent rows of auditors. Being largely nonpurposeful and disconnected, conversation does not present the need for logical, meaningful continuity delivered by one speaker for a continuous period of five to twenty minutes or longer. The conversational speaking situation does not provide the same strains and stresses as does public speaking. It does not present quite the same problems of poise, projection, clarity of articulation, accuracy of phrasing, posture, or bodily expression. As you well know, there are many adequate conversationalists who are not effective public speakers.

The average speaker cannot present with maximum effectiveness a speech of five or ten minutes without rehearsal. The first time you give a particular speech you are likely to ramble and to be hesitant, repetitious, and awkward in phrasing. By rehearsing you can reduce the likelihood of disconcerting breaks in your thinking process, improve clarity and accuracy of statement, smooth out delivery, acquire more self-confidence, and put more vigor into your presentation.

Now let us examine the three basic factors in your rehearsal: where to rehearse; when to rehearse; how to rehearse.

Where to Rehearse

Effective speakers make use of a wide variety of places for speech rehearsal. One student practices his talks in the shower. A preacher who drives some thirty miles to his pulpit rehearses en route, striking the steering wheel in his efforts to drive home important points. A business executive rehearses in his parlor before the analytical eyes of his wife. Lincoln, as a young man, delivered speeches to lonely fields of corn and pumpkins. Daniel Webster rehearsed even while fishing. Ex-Senator John Pastore sometimes practiced his speeches in his bedroom while dressing. President Kennedy practiced his opening statements for his live, televised press conferences while riding from the White House to the conference at the New State Building. Probably the best place for you to practice is some private room at home or in the dormitory, where you can work undisturbed. If feasible, arrange at least one practice period in the room where the speech is to be delivered, or in a similar location. Both Ronald Reagan and Jimmy Carter carefully inspected the site prior to engaging in their televised debate during their presidential campaign. If you are accustomed to the physical surroundings of the designated hall, you may possess somewhat better poise at the time of actual presentation. Test the acoustics, find how much volume is necessary to carry to the back row. If you are to speak from a raised platform, climb the stairs to the dais and become accustomed to looking out at the seats. If a lectern is present, stand behind it; walk to the side; become accustomed to its physical presence. Even a golf professional like Jack Nicklaus will play several practice rounds to get the feel of a course before engaging in competition.

When to Rehearse

Ordinarily the rehearsal period should not begin until the outline has been completed and all materials gathered. Although a few individuals may successfully violate this rule, the average beginner should complete his speech at least a day in advance of the delivery date. In general, the longer the speech and the more demanding the situation, the longer this interval should be. If you are to give a twenty-minute address at the annual banquet of the interfraternity council, a thirty-minute eulogy of the recently deceased president of your company, or a fifteen-minute summary of the month's activities of your personnel department, you probably should attempt to complete speech composition at least two days before the time for delivery. In this way, you will provide a time cushion in case you should encounter unexpected delays in completing the speech and, if your speech preparation goes according to schedule, will allow time for your speech to "jell" in your mind. Give yourself sufficient opportunity to smooth out some of the rough spots in delivery. Experience will demonstrate the optimum length of the rehearsal period for your particular needs. Perhaps this point of caution should be offered: in your zeal to leave sufficient time for rehearsal, do not finish the organization and development of your talk so far in advance that the speech loses its warmth and vitality.

For most individuals, the rehearsal period should stop before the beginning of the program at which the speech is to be given. Of course, there are exceptions. For instance, President Franklin D. Roosevelt at times silently rehearsed major radio addresses at the banquet table after completing his dinner and before being introduced. However, for most beginning speakers, last-minute practice may tend to increase tension. When waiting to be introduced by the chairman, do not worry about your talk. Try to relax by concentrating your attention on the chairman, on other speakers, on something in the auditorium or by engaging someone in conversation.

How to Rehearse

The following methodology is offered as a suggestive procedure for the beginning speaker. Experience should enable you to work out a system that will answer your own personal needs most effectively. We consider the rehearsal period under two heads: (A) the preliminary program of fixing the speech in the mind; (B) the final program of polishing the delivery of the speech.

The Preliminary Phase in Rehearsing Is to Fix the Speech in the Mind

A generation or so ago speakers might commit to memory entire speeches, which sometimes were more than an hour in duration. In our jet propulsion age, however, few individuals can afford the time for such extensive memorization. (Indeed, some of our civic and political leaders do not even prepare their own speeches, being content to assign the task to secretaries or other subordinates. Once an official of a major charity drive asked the author to have his speech composition class write talks for others to use during the local campaign.) Even if sufficient time were available, few speakers could deliver effectively a memorized talk. As mentioned earlier, you should memorize only the sequence of the ideas you wish to present and, perhaps, brief quotations, a few statistics, jokes, a few important phrases, and the like. Fix firmly in your mind the outline of the speech, even when planning to use notes during the actual presentation. If you have followed carefully the suggestions contained in the previous chapters on organization, you probably will have little difficulty in learning and retaining the outline of even a long speech. (For instance, if you have used parallel phrasing for coordinate heads, memorization of the outline will be greatly facilitated.) Usually, when a student complains that he cannot remember his speech, he either has not obeyed the canons of good speech organization or has not rehearsed adequately.

Here is a possible program for fixing the speech in the mind.

(1) Read over the entire outline *silently* one or more times, endeavoring to concentrate on each point as you go along. Go straight through. Do not stop or retrace any portion.

(2) Read the outline *orally* at least once. Continue through the entire outline without stopping or repeating any section.

(3) Now attempt to give the speech without any recourse to notes. If you cannot remember specific points, go on as best you can. Do not give up until you have made every effort to complete the entire talk. Do not worry if you stumble and falter. As one student said, "It's better to mess up the speech in private than before an audience."

(4) Reread the entire outline silently, then orally. *Think* while you are doing it.

(5) Try again to give the speech completely from beginning to end without reference to notes.

(6) Review the outline, silently and orally, and deliver the speech extemporaneously, without notes, until you have the sequence well in mind.

Notice that the emphasis in the preliminary phase of rehearsing has been to give you a firm grasp of the *total sequence* of the speech. (Every time you interrupt the continuity during this phase of the rehearsal period you encourage forgetting at that particular point during the actual presentation.)

The Second Phase in Rehearsing Is to Polish the Delivery of the Speech

Practice makes permanent as well as perfect. Unless you follow an intelligent program of polishing your delivery, practice may do more harm than good. Admittedly, rehearsing for a particular speech may not correct major, constant faults; however, application of the following points should greatly improve your speech presentation. Do not attend to these guides slavishly; adapt them to your individual needs. After you have acquired some experience, you will be able to plan your own program for polishing the speech.

(1) If possible, get a sympathetic but analytical friend or relative to attend at least one rehearsal and make suggestions. You will be wise, however, to accept with reservation the advice offered by your observer, unless he is a competently trained critic. If no one is available, place several chairs in a row and address the chairs as though people were sitting in them. For at least part of your practice, try to construct in your mind the audience and the situation with which you will be confronted during the actual speech presentation, and rehearse accordingly. As suggested earlier,

if feasible at least one practice period should be arranged in the room (or close approximation) where you will speak. Try to prepare yourself for the total speaking situation.

(2) Possibly spend part of your practice period rehearsing before a full-length mirror. Notice your facial expressions, movements, posture, and gestures. Although such practice has been used by Adolf Hitler, Goodwin Knight, and Billy Graham, who is said to rehearse each new sermon in front of a mirror, many persons find mirror practice disconcerting. Therefore, if you find yourself becoming self-conscious, immediately discontinue this form of practice.

(3) For some speakers—but not for others who find the practice disturbing—the use of a tape recorder is highly desirable for adequate speech rehearsal. If using a recorder, listen critically and make notations along the margin of the speech outline at the appropriate places where improvements in vocal delivery are needed. Do not erase the recordings each time, but check improvement by playing back the various attempts. Avoid overdoing this type of practice; possibly several recordings will be sufficient.

(4) Spread your rehearsal over various intervals instead of concentrating your practice in one or two sessions. Four fifteen-minute periods will be more valuable than a single period of an hour and a half.

(5) Although the number of times one should practice the speech in the second phase of rehearsal will vary according to the individual, the average student should rehearse a five-minute talk to be given in a public-speaking class at least twice. A greater number of repetitions may be needed if the speech is longer or the situation more demanding. *Never practice to the point that spontaneity is injured.*

(6) Use your rehearsal as a final check on speech organization and content. Probably you should avoid making major changes in your speech at this stage. You can, however, make minor changes, such as adding further supporting evidence, inserting a touch of humor, or trimming the length of the speech.

(7) Work systematically to improve both vocal and bodily delivery. If you have been criticized for possessing insufficient animation in previous speeches, here is the chance to practice giving life and vitality to your presentation. Do not be inhibited while rehearsing. Try to force yourself to be more dynamic. Loosen up your facial muscles. Attempt some gestures. If you have had poor posture in preceding speeches, try to stand erect during your practice. Unless you are unusual, your voice is not the supple instrument it should be. In your practice ask yourself these questions: Is my rate of speaking flexible? Does my voice reflect the intellectual and emotional meaning of what I am saying? Does my voice indicate thought phrases satisfactorily? Do my words come smoothly and easily, or are there awkward interruptions in the flow of language? Is my pitch monotonously level? Does my voice lack emphasis? Does it sound strained

and weak? Does it need more projection? Again a word of caution: if such practice makes you feel self-conscious, even after applying guide No. 8 (immediately following), discontinue this phase of your practice.

(8) Every time you rehearse, endeavor to vary your phraseology, vocal inflections, and gestures. Do not let your speech become "canned."

(9) Practice especially those portions of the speech that give you difficulty. Inasmuch as you have mastered the sequence of the talk in the first phase of rehearsal, it is unnecessary to continue to rehearse the entire talk each time. If transitions from one main point to the next are troublesome, practice until they become easier. If you tend to ramble when presenting the Summary Step, practice this portion until your recapitulation is concise. If your attempt at humor seems flat, concentrate on making it more sprightly, gay, and cheerful.

Summary

As in other kinds of public performance, such as sports, drama, and concert work, practice is essential to the public speaker. Intelligent rehearsal should make your delivery smoother and more forceful. Although there are a wide variety of suitable places for practice, a private room at home will probably be most satisfactory. If feasible, at least one practice period should be held either in the room where the speech is to be given or in a similar location. The rehearsal period probably should not begin until the outline has been finished and all materials gathered, and should be completed before the beginning of the program at which the speech is to be given. The actual rehearsal consists of two basic phases: (1) fixing the speech in the mind, and (2) polishing the delivery.

Exercises and Assignments

1. Interview several persons who speak frequently in public so that you may discover their methods of rehearsal. Report your findings to the class.
2. Listen closely to speeches in class to discover which students may have failed to rehearse sufficiently. Also, note which speakers may have rehearsed too much.
3. Prepare a short speech for class in which you describe how some effective speaker in history rehearsed his speeches. For help, consult your speech instructor or librarian.

4. As soon as you have completed the outline for your next speech, and without any rehearsal, record the entire talk. Speak as effectively as you can. Even though you may stumble to a halt several times, go through the entire speech. Do not erase this recording.

5. A continuation of Exercise 4: Practice conscientiously, applying the advice contained in the section "Preliminary Phase in Rehearsing"; then record the speech once again. Do not erase this recording.

6. A continuation of Exercises 4 and 5: Carefully follow the suggestion for the "Second Phase in Rehearsing" given in this chapter. When you think your delivery has attained maximum effectiveness, record the speech for the third time. Play back and compare the three recordings.

7. Prepare for presentation in class a "canned" speech. Memorize not only the exact words to be used but also facial expressions, gestures, and set patterns of pitch, time, force, and vocal quality. In the judgment of your instructor and the class, how does this presentation compare with your customary extempore delivery?

CHAPTER 14

Using the Body and Voice in Delivering the Speech

In this chapter we consider the physical and vocal aspects of delivery, the way you look and sound to your listeners. In Chapter 15, we discuss the use of language in the speech. Now, however, let us turn to an examination of the visible code.

Using the Body Effectively

The visible code includes all observable behavior on the part of the speaker: eye contact, facial expression, posture, movement, and gesture. Before analyzing separately each of these aspects of visual communication, we should consider their general significance to effective speaking.

The Importance of Bodily Action

The importance of bodily action can be appreciated only if you reject certain misconceptions about its place in speaking.

(1) *Visible action is not a distinct and separate activity to be employed or ignored as the speaker sees fit.* If your audience can see you, it is impossible for you to speak without communicating visible meaning.

Even the inadequate physical expression of the "wooden speaker" provides clues concerning his personality and his attitude toward speaking. Moreover, such a speaker inevitably shifts his weight now and then, moves his eyes and head from time to time, and is forced to move his mouth to form words. Inescapably, the visible code is an integral part of the face-to-face speaking situation.

(2) *The speaker is not concerned with visible action as an end in itself.* A gesture inserted for its own sake in a speech is exhibitionism. Bodily action that calls attention to itself at the expense of the speaker's ideas will hinder the achievement of the Specific Speech Purpose.

(3) *Visible action does not replace the audible code; it supplements it.* In attempting to communicate meaning, inarticulate speakers sometimes try to substitute movement, facial expression, and gesture for words. Carried to extremes, this behavior approaches pantomiming and the sign language of the speechless.

(4) *Effective visible action is not artificial or unnatural.* The statuelike, "poker-faced" speaker who asserts that gesture and movement are artificial and unnatural to him usually unconsciously punctuates his conversation with appropriate gestures and facial expression. After he has become accustomed to speaking in public, he is sometimes surprised to discover that he is using the visible code freely and naturally.

Effective bodily action helps the speaker in adjusting to the speaking situation, securing and maintaining interest and attention, clarifying meaning, and attaining emphasis.

Bodily Action Helps to Clarify Meaning. Inasmuch as the language and the paralanguage, or nonverbal, aspects of the speech are directed exclusively to the ear, they employ only one medium of communication. We learned earlier that when possible the speaker should appeal to visual as well as aural reception. Chapter 7 contained detailed suggestions for supplementing words with visual aids, such as pictures, maps, diagrams, models, actual objects, and charts. Now, you should consider that your body is also a "visual aid." Descriptive bodily action is important in clarifying meaning and achieving emphasis. For instance, the lift of an eyebrow, the curl of a lip, or the shrug of a shoulder may convey the meaning of hundreds of words. Also, concepts of distance, size, shape, direction, and speed are frequently more meaningful and vivid to an audience if illustrated by descriptive action. The optimum *distance* from a microphone, the *size* of a dent in a fender, the shape of a modernistic end table, the *direction* taken by a cue ball in a three-cushion billiard shot, the *speed* of a boxer's left jab are typical of concepts which may be pointed up by descriptive action.

Bodily Action Helps to Achieve Emphasis. As suggested, bodily action is an effective means of securing emphasis. The ideational and emotional intent of the speaker should be appropriately reflected in his physical delivery. The speaker may use a wide variety of physical expressiveness to emphasize his thoughts and feelings. For instance, if he tells a light, humorous story, his entire manner should be in keeping with the levity of his remarks. If he exhorts his listeners to "give a big round of applause for the visiting coaches," his manner should underscore the evocation of his words. If he wishes to emphasize the sequential nature of his points, he may enumerate them on his fingers.

Now that we have considered the importance of the visible code, let us turn to the practical utilization of the code in public speaking.

Bodily Action Facilitates Adjustment to the Speaking Situation. As noted earlier, one of the manifestations of stage fright is muscular tension. Unless you employ constructive outlets, your excess energy may find its release in such distracting random action as coin-jingling, nose-rubbing, and head-scratching. If you attempt to bottle up tensions, they may intensify to the degree that some part(s) of the body may begin to tremble, shake, or "freeze" into statuelike rigidity. Beneficial avenues of release lie in animated, vigorous physical and vocal delivery. One of the best ways to achieve partial relaxation of a muscle is to use it. For example, a cramp in a leg muscle can be relieved by "walking it out." As a speaker you can alleviate tension by channeling surplus energy into suitable activity, such as moving the head to emphasize a point, taking a step or two to indicate a transition, or making a hand or arm gesture to reinforce an idea. In this way you will be utilizing bodily action as a means of adjusting to the speaking situation.

Bodily Action Helps to Secure and Maintain Interest and Attention. As you will remember, an unchanging stimulus soon loses its capacity to evoke a response. If you make almost no physical movement on the platform, the visible aspects of your speech present an "unchanging stimulus." Because of the nature of their neuromuscular systems, the listeners will find that the monotony in your physical delivery will make attending to your speech much more difficult. Do not depend exclusively upon speech content or vocal delivery to secure and maintain audience interest and attention. Effective bodily action can be exceedingly helpful in this respect.

Developing Effective Bodily Action

Although for instructional purposes the various aspects of the visible code are treated separately, all are fused in the process of speaking.

Eye Contact. Positive relationships with your listeners depend upon maintaining direct eye contact with them. Most of us like for a speaker to "look us in the eye" when talking to us in conversation or from the platform. When a speaker looks constantly at his notes, the floor, the ceiling, or out the window, we tend to lose interest in what he is saying and may even be inclined to distrust him. Therefore, except for necessary reference to notes or to visual aids, keep your eyes on your listeners, or you may lose them. Single out some individual in the audience, look directly into his eyes and speak briefly to him, and then shift your attention to another person. For small audiences, such as your speech class, try to look at each person several times during even a short speech. For large audiences you can give the impression of looking at everyone by dividing the room into sections and by focusing on individuals in first one section and then another. Each member of an audience likes to believe that the speaker is aware of his presence and is talking directly to him.

Common sins in the use of eye contact. (1) *The "starer":* Avoid merely looking in the general direction of the audience without focusing your eyes upon the group. Listeners are quick to detect a blank stare or a "faraway" look and will react negatively.

(2) *The "flitterer":* To establish visual contact with a listener, you must "hook on" to his gaze so that you both feel a meeting or touching of personalities. If your glance flits from one person to another, no genuine contact is being made.

(3) *The "avoider":* Refusal to look at your listeners is an avoidance reaction and will be so considered by the people you are attempting to reach.

Facial Expression. When speaking to an audience, your face will probably reflect appropriately your thoughts and emotions—provided that you are spiritedly animated and that under normal conditions your face is fairly expressive. If you fall into the "dead pan" category, however, attempt to brighten and enliven your facial expression. Be careful, though, that you do not overcompensate and indulge in random or exaggerated expressions. Two principles may help you to acquire effective facial expression:

(1) Attempt to free yourself from inhibitions to the extent that facial expressions can manifest themselves naturally.

(2) Do not plan and rehearse specific facial expressions for use in a speech. Facial expressions should be spontaneous reflections of your inner state of thinking and feeling. Except in the case of talented and experienced performers, contrived expressions rarely seem genuine; furthermore, they are unnecessary. If you are thoroughly aware of the meaning of what you are saying and are sensitively tuned to the total speaking sit-

uation, your natural expressiveness should provide adequate reinforcement to your words.

Common sins in the use of facial expression. (1) *The "poker face":* Nervous tension often inhibits one's customary facial expressiveness. Although an inexpressive face may help the poker player, it restricts the effectiveness of the public speaker.

(2) *The "mugger":* The repeated and exaggerated posing of this frustrated actor distracts attention from what he is saying.

(3) *The "facial jiggler":* This nervous speaker releases tension by engaging in excessive amounts of facial expression, much of which may have little relation to his intended meaning.

Posture. Although there is no single correct way to stand while delivering a speech, your body should be erect without the exaggerated stiffness of the soldier-at-attention. Relax sufficiently to be comfortable, but not so much that you appear to slouch. As a general guide, you may look best and be most comfortable if your feet are placed about six to twelve inches apart, with your weight resting on the balls of both feet. Your arms may hang naturally at your sides, unless you are using them for gesticulation. For short periods you may rest one or both hands on the lectern. If the situation is informal, you may put either hand in a pocket, clasp hands behind your back, even lean briefly on the lectern, and so on. As a general rule, you should avoid maintaining any of these hand positions unchanged for an extended period of time. After awhile any set position begins to appear stiff and unnatural.

No attempt has been made here to set up rigid rules governing posture. The basic guide to effective posture, as for any other facet of speechmaking, must be, "Does this help or does it hinder me in achieving my Specific Speech Purpose?" The suitability of one's posture depends upon the totality of the speaking situation: the speaker, the speech, the audience, and the occasion. What is suitable in one set of circumstances conceivably may be undignified, ludicrous, or insulting in another. For instance, in a very casual environment, a speaker could promote a desired mood of informality by putting both hands in his pants pockets, or even by sitting on a table; to assume similar positions in addressing the annual banquet of a college honor society would be injudicious.

Appropriate posture in public speaking will be most easily attained if you practice proper bearing under ordinary circumstances. By making good posture a habit, you will not feel uncomfortable when you assume correct position on the platform.

If you have suitable speech attitudes, you will forget yourself in the process of communicating your message to your audience; any real concern about hand positions, stance, and other aspects of bodily action will disappear. If some aspect of your posture is unsatisfactory, your instructor will note it and you can eliminate it before your next presentation.

Common sins of posture. (1) *The "sloucher":* Audiences get the impression that the "sloucher" is too tired to stand up or that he lacks genuine interest in his ideas and his listeners. Members of the audience may find their attention wandering from his speech to his appearance.

(2) *The "leaner":* This speaker clutches any nearby object—table, lectern, the back of a chair, or the like—that will support his weight and clings to it throughout his speech. Audiences may wonder if he could stand unsupported, and as a result may miss part of what he says.

(3) *The "ramrod":* With stomach in, chest out, shoulders back, and chin in, the "ramrod" gives the impression that at any moment he might click his heels and salute. Audiences wish he would relax, so that they could also.

Movement. Under this heading, we are concerned with gross movements of the entire body, such as walking from one position to another on the platform; activity by parts of the body for the purpose of gesticulation is treated later in this chapter.

Movement helps the speaker to attract and maintain attention and to convey meaning. As you know, a moving object usually has a greater capacity to attract involuntary attention than does a stationary one. Changing positions on the platform—as moving from behind the lectern to the right or left, or walking forward a few steps toward the audience—may help maintain audience interest and can even help awaken drowsy listeners. Such movement should be executed naturally and smoothly, of course; if awkward or apparently contrived, it will attract negative attention. Various meanings can be conveyed by movement: for instance, a pause accompanied by a few steps to either side can help to indicate a transition; a move forward can help you to emphasize an important point.

How much movement should you employ? A categorical answer cannot be given: your age and physical makeup, your subject, your physical surroundings, the mood of the audience, and other factors will influence the kind and amount of movement appropriate to the situation. In general, you should avoid extremes: do not remain in one spot throughout a twenty-minute speech (unless you are using a public address microphone); on the other hand, avoid continuous movement. In making a two-minute announcement, you probably would not need to move about the platform; in a five- to ten-minute speech, you might wish to move several times.

As mentioned earlier, the manner in which you approach and leave the platform is also important, since first and last impressions occur at these times. Moderation is again the key. Move at a normal rate, avoiding both nervous rapidity and exasperating slowness.

Common sins concerning movement. (1) *The "statue":* Like his stone counterpart, the "statue" appears incapable of movement.

(2) *The "pacer":* Like a caged lion, the "pacer" walks determinedly from one side of the platform to the other, and then back. His audience may long for the speech to end so that both he and they can rest.

(3) *The "swayer":* The "swayer" rhythmically moves his body from side to side or forward and backward, in apparent imitation of a sea gull on a buoy. As in the case of the "pacer," the movement of the "swayer" encourages the audience to focus on his behavior rather than on his message.

Gestures. A *gesture* is a purposive movement of some part of the body to convey meaning and secure emphasis. If gesticulation is a natural characteristic of animated conversation, it is perhaps even more an integral part of dynamic public speaking. When you are deeply interested in your subject and enthusiastic about communicating it to your listeners, your body will almost automatically enter into the communicative process. Purposeful motions of your arms, hands, head, or shoulders will add clarification and emphasis to the spoken words. As stated earlier, a *descriptive* gesture will make more meaningful such concepts as distance, size, shape, and direction. These gestures usually involve the use of the hands and arms. For example, the size of "the fish that got away" may be indicated by holding the hands, say, eighteen inches apart. A gesture of *emphasis* is used to strengthen the impact of an idea upon the listener so that it will be more readily accepted and remembered. In addition to the wide variety of hand and arm gestures that may be used to reinforce the speaker's words, emphasis may also be achieved by head and shoulder gestures, the most common of which are shrugging the shoulders and shaking or nodding the head.

Common sins in the use of gestures: (1) *Random action:* Speakers frequently substitute distracting random activity for purposive gesture. Such activity includes fidgeting with notes, pencils, buttons, coat lapels, pockets, bracelets, and beads; it embraces wiggling fingers, twisting hands, jerking one's head, rubbing the nose and chin, pulling an ear, running fingers through the hair, taking one's glasses off and putting them on, and the like. By developing facility in gesticulation, the speaker can divert some of his nervous energy into positive outlets.

(2) *Perpetual motion:* Perpetual motion may be as monotonous as perpetual immobility. The speaker who constantly uses his hands will soon lose the reinforcement of meaning that gestures can provide. Gestures should punctuate ideas rather than serve as an ever-present accompaniment to words.

(3) *The abortive gesture:* This gesture is inadequately or incom-

pletely executed. For instance, in the case of an insecure speaker who wishes to push his hands away from his body to indicate revulsion or rejection, the potentially vigorous movement of the arms may be aborted, resulting in only a distracting jerk of the arms and hands. Sufficient practice to "get the feel" of gesturing should put an end to abortive gestures.

Using the Voice Effectively

The vocal aspects of delivery are singularly important to the effective presentation of a speech. The speaking voice produces those sounds (words) that represent the speaker's thoughts, thus audibly conveying his ideas to his listeners. The voice also carries many other messages. It ordinarily reveals the sex of the speaker, and gives a general idea of his age; it provides some clues to his state of health and reflects his emotional condition; it is so intensely personal that one can identify friends, and often casual associates, by a phrase or two spoken over the telephone.

Successful public speakers recognize that the effective speaking voice permits the communication of delicate nuances of meaning, helps create favorable attitudes toward the speaker, and aids in achieving audience acceptance of his ideas. Inadequate vocal delivery, on the other hand, may result in irritation, loss of attention, misunderstanding, and, in severe cases, total loss of meaning. On the speaker's stand and in everyday conversation the effective use of one's voice is basic to successful communication.

We are concerned with the practical use of the voice in the delivery of the speech. Our objective is to provide a brief overview that is suitable to the needs of the beginning public speaker.

Six Attributes of the Effective Speaking Voice

The desirable speaking voice possesses the attributes of audibility, pleasantness, variety, animation, fluency, and clarity.

Audibility. It is obvious that a speaker cannot communicate vocally with his audience unless he can be heard. Every word should be clearly and effortlessly heard by every member of an audience. Because beginning speakers usually are accustomed only to speaking informally in small groups, they often fail to make the vocal adjustments necessary to enable their voices to carry to the periphery of public-speaking audiences. Conversely, they occasionally "over adjust" by blasting their listeners with excessive loudness. To speak effectively, the speaker should adjust his volume and projection to the acoustical requirements of the speaking situation.

Pleasantness. Inasmuch as pleasantness is a highly subjective concept with a multitude of meanings, it is difficult to define. Although scientifically accurate, the explanation that timbre is solely dependent upon the "frequencies and the relative intensities of the partials present in the sound waves" is confusing to most students and, from the standpoint of public speaking, too limited. Perhaps pleasant vocal quality will be best understood by noting those characteristics of voice that are generally agreed upon as undesirable. Unpleasant voices may be harsh, nasal, breathy, or hoarse; the presence of such vocal qualities may seem even more unpleasant if the voice is pitched too high or too low, or if it lacks variability in rate, pitch, or force. The concept of pleasantness is closely related to the other attributes of voice discussed in this section and to the speaking situation. In general, listeners prefer those attributes of voice—as well as those of articulation and pronunciation—to which they have become accustomed.

Variety. Monotony, or insufficient flexibility, is frequently a characteristic of the untrained voice. This deficiency can be attributed to the novice's preoccupation with himself, the strain of communicating with an audience, and inadequately developed habits of vocal variety. The effective voice is a flexible instrument. By subtle changes in pitch, rate, quality, and force, it may reflect every change in the speaker's attitude, every shade of meaning to be conveyed, and every discernible listener-reaction.

Animation. The animated voice is lively, spirited, vibrant, and flexible. It is the product of healthy communicative attitudes, sincere interest in what one is saying, and a keen desire to communicate one's ideas and feelings to the listeners.

Fluency. Fluency refers to smoothness in the flow of words. Lack of fluency may be caused by nervousness, faulty breathing, inadequate preparation, or poor speech habits. It may be manifested in frequent hesitations and vocalized pauses, during which the speaker hunts for the next word. When words finally come, they may be spoken much too rapidly, in an attempt to "catch up." Stop-and-go delivery of this type tends to distract listeners, for they experience difficulty in following the speaker's ideas. Although relatively smooth utterance is a prerequisite for effectiveness, the actual flow of language should vary with the nature of the material presented, the personality of the speaker, and the circumstances of the occasion.

Clarity. Audible voices sometimes lack sufficient clarity to facilitate intelligiblity. Clarity results primarily from precise articulation of the various sounds which, in combination, produce words. Because of precise and energetic articulation, the actor's stage whisper can be clearly understood by every member of his audience; on the other hand, because of cloudy enunciation, the novice speaker's words may be understood only with difficulty, even though he speaks with adequate loudness.

Acquiring the Attributes of an Effective Speaking Voice

Inasmuch as our concern here, as it has been throughout the book, is with practical applications to speaking, we do not involve ourselves in a technical discussion of voice production. For suitable references on that subject, consult your instructor or the card file index of the library. For our purposes it is enough to recognize that the speaker can work systematically to improve his speaking voice.

Audibility and Pleasantness are Primarily the Products of Proper Habits of Breathing, Phonation, and Resonation. Let us see how control over the physical processes of breathing, phonation, and resonation determine the audibility and pleasantness of one's voice.

Breathing. Sound cannot be produced without some motive power to initiate the vibrations that send out sound waves. The motive power for the voice, as well as for the clarinet, saxophone, trumpet, and the like, is air exhaled from the lungs. Any change in the amount or force of this stream of air will affect voice production. Although most of us are not conscious of the regular, rhythmical breathing used to sustain life, we may encounter some difficulty in breathing for public speaking. Breathing to produce speech requires rapid inhalation and slow, sustained, controlled exhalation. To become an effective public speaker, it is unnecessary for you to study the involved musculature of breathing. The chief need of the public speaker in improving his habits of breathing is not to increase lung capacity. According to voice scientists, the breathing capacity of the lungs is not a significant factor for the speaker in voice quality and force or in control over the voice. Surprisingly enough, one does not seem to use significantly more air in ordinary speaking than in casual breathing, and research indicates that in normal speech it is inconsequential whether a speaker breathes primarily "thoracically," "medially," or "abdominally." If you are actively conscious of the need for sustained breath support and are adequately relaxed, your body will probably react appropriately, thus making possible firm, steady vocalization, adequate force for vigorous public-speaking needs, and the delicate variations in loudness and intensity that are so important in conveying intellectual and emotional meaning.

Phonation and resonation. The process by which all voiced sounds are produced is called *phonation.* There is no practical reason for us to examine the extremely complicated muscular movement by which phonation is accomplished; most of this action is not subject to our direct voluntary control.

We hear the vocal *effects* of such muscular action and, by attempting to regulate the effects, we exert indirect control over the speech mechanism itself. Were it not for the phenomenon of resonance, the phonated sound produced in the larynx would be weak, thin, and lacking in fullness, richness, and color. In the human being, the chief resonators are the throat, the mouth, and the nasal cavities. It is thought that the size, shape, and texture of these cavities are primarily responsible for increasing the carrying power of the voice and for providing distinctive, individual quality. Changes in the size and shape of these structures permit differences in timbre that suggest the mood, personality, and emotions of the speaker. In addition, variations in the size and shape of these cavities help produce the sounds of the language. The quality, or timbre, of a sound (or voice) is the characteristic that enables you to distinguish one sound source from another, even though the sounds may be uttered with identical pitch and loudness. It is the attribute that tells you without looking whether a trombonist or saxophonist is "taking the lead."

Vocal quality basically is determined by the processes of phonation and resonation, and is closely related to the pitch and force of the voice, as well as to the speaker's health, attitude, and general emotional state. Timbre may reveal which speaker is angry and which is happy, which speaker is confident and which is frightened. Such emotional states are responsible for changes in the tension of the throat musculature and in the size and shape of the resonating cavities. These alterations result in corresponding modification of the vocal quality. For instance, nearly everyone has experienced a tightening of the throat when afraid; in extreme cases, the frightened person may be unable to utter a sound.

The unpleasant vocal qualities that occur most frequently in public speaking include breathiness, harshness, hoarseness, and nasality. *Breathiness* occurs when the vocal folds fail to approximate, thus failing to close the space between the folds once each cycle; because of this insufficient closure, some of the breath stream escapes unvocalized. *Harshness* is commonly caused by excessive tension in the throat; the voice sounds as if it contains rasping, grating, scraping noise elements. *Hoarseness,* a combination of harshness and breathiness, may be temporary, caused by a cold or a similar respiratory infection, or by improper use of the voice. *Nasality* is the result of too much nasal resonance and may be caused by organic reasons or by poor speech habits. (Insufficient nasality, or denasal speech, is an articular disorder that is usually caused by nasal obstruction, such as enlarged adenoids or congestion from a head cold, but sometimes by bad speech habits.)

If your instructor suggests that you may have a minor vocal problem caused by improper use of the voice, you should secure from him, or from a specialist in speech correction, a diagnosis of the nature and severity of the difficulty as well as suitable reading references and drill materials. The assistance of a well-trained critic is extremely valuable in all phases of speech development, especially in matters relating to vocal delivery. By becoming conscious of an existing need to improve one's phonation or resonation, by securing suitable reference and exercise material, and by practicing remedial exercises conscientiously, the speaker can improve deficiencies of audibility and pleasantness caused by bad speech habits.

Variety, Animation, and Fluency Necessitate a Flexible Voice. An adequately supported voice, clearly produced and richly resonated, will nevertheless be monotonous unless it possesses *flexibility*. We were concerned in the previous section with the development of a pleasant voice; in this section we examine those characteristics of voice that give it variation, animation, expressiveness, and responsiveness. Flexibility increases interest, reveals the speaker's personality, helps clarify the thought, and conveys emotional values. Among the most important variable attributes of voice are *pitch, force,* and *rate*. Although in speaking the three are so interrelated that the listener receives a total impression, they may be examined and practiced separately.

The effective speaking voice has flexibility of pitch. *Pitch* refers to the location of the sound on a musical scale. Variation of pitch is accomplished by moving up or down the scale, either by a pitch *step between* syllables or words, or by a continuous *slide* from one pitch to another. The following discussion of pitch usage includes general pitch level, pitch variations, and pitch or melody patterns.

General pitch level should be appropriate to the age and sex of the speaker. The adult male voice is expected to be lower in general pitch level than the adult female voice; the voice of a child is ordinarily pitched higher than that of the adult. Any extreme variation from these expectations will startle listeners and may hinder effective communication. General pitch level also reflects the emotional state of the speaker. During anger, excitement, or gaiety, most voices tend to rise in pitch; during grief, reverence, or solemnity, the opposite effect may occur.

The optimum general pitch level for the speaker is usually determined by the size and structure of his speech mechanism. Little can be done about these anatomical characteristics—a natural tenor cannot become a bass, although both the tenor and bass may be able to extend the limits of their upper and lower registers. Habitual general pitch should be the same as one's optimum pitch. Attempt to find that pitch level at which the voice is produced most easily and resonated most effectively. Your optimum level will probably be about one fourth of the way up your total range. By keying your general, or most frequently recurring, level to this placement, you will achieve the greatest carrying power with least effort, probably secure the best timbre, and will be able to both raise and lower the pitch with maximum ease. (A habitual pitch level keyed well below optimum pitch may tend to make the voice harsh, hoarse, or breathy.)

Flexibility in pitch will make your vocal delivery more animated, interesting, and meaningful. With the help of your instructor and recordings of your voice, determine whether your delivery is being handicapped by inflexibility of pitch. The intellectual and emotional content of your message constantly changes; to convey the full intrinsic meaning of what you say—and how you feel about what you say—your voice should respond with suitable, constant pitch changes. In the flexible voice, pitch changes may represent a wide continuum from extremely subtle contours to sharp, striking breaks. By practicing exercises, such as those appearing at the end of this chapter, you should improve the flexibility of pitch and develop a usable range of at least one octave. Your next step is to incorporate into your public speaking the steps and slides of animated conversation, permitting the thought and emotion that are to be communicated to dictate the nature and extent of pitch variation.

In your efforts to improve flexibility of pitch, avoid objectionable melody patterns and the exaggerated inflections of "affected" speech. Some beginning speakers force utterance into set pitch patterns that are repeated monotonously during a talk. In the "sing-song" up-and-down pattern, a few words are uttered with a slowly rising inflection, followed by another group delivered with a gradually falling inflection. In the "question" pattern, the speaker inappropriately ends many sentences with upward inflections, thereby making his statements seen indefinite—almost as if he were asking questions requiring "yes" or "no" answers. In the "rising-fading" pattern, the speaker begins many sentences with a sharply rising inflection and ends them with a slowly receding inflection. How does one avoid using the same inflectional pattern to express a variety of different meanings and emotions? By keeping the natural patterns of vigorous conversation. In public speaking one's vocal delivery may be more formal and somewhat louder, but it should remain as much like conversation as the size of the audience and the formality of the situation permit. If you possess good communicative attitudes, are thoroughly sensitive to the meaning of what you are saying, wish eagerly to communicate your message to the listeners, and have developed good habits of vocal usage, your pitch variations automatically will tend to reflect appropriately your meaning and mood.

The effective speaking voice has flexibility of force (loudness). As previously noted, the speaker should adjust his force to the size of the audience and the acoustical conditions, as well as to the mood of the occasion and the subject matter. Although he should avoid excessive force, he must speak with sufficient loudness to be dynamic, to impress his audience with his desire to speak and his interest in the subject. In addition, he should vary his general force level. Continuous use of any level of force—soft, medium, or loud—will grow monotonous and will eliminate variation of force as an effective method for conveying meaning and achieving emphasis.

As part of your self-help program, practice delivering words, phrases, and sentences with a variety of force. Project some passages with maximum loudness, as though addressing a huge crowd, without the help of a public address system; for some passages use the general force level suitable for speaking to an audience of one or two hundred persons; for some passages use the level of loudness suitable for vigorous conversation. When projecting the voice with great loudness, be careful to maintain clear enunciation and to avoid building up excessive tension in the speech musculature. Increase the strength of the airflow from the lungs, but do not attempt to augment loudness by tensing the throat. If the vocal mechanism becomes overly tense, voice quality and clarity of articulation may be impaired.

Read aloud or improvise passages that require different levels of loudness and kinds of quality. Examples: a leader trying to control an unruly crowd about to degenerate into a mob; a lawyer spiritedly arguing a case before a jury; a minister delivering a funeral sermon; a parent telling a soothing bedtime story to a sleepy child.

Real aloud or extemporize passages in which you vary the emphasis you give to various words, phrases, and/or sentences. By making different words—or succession of words—stand out, you can alter the ideational and emotional values. For instance, stress successively the words in this sentence: "This is the pie I baked."

THIS (Not the others on the table) is the pie I baked.
This IS (It really is!) the pie I baked.
This is THE (I just baked one) pie I baked.
This is the PIE (It may look like a cake, but it's not) I baked.
This is the pie I (Me, Bill Winters!) baked.
This is the pie I BAKED (I didn't buy it; I baked it).

In your practice, underscore words or points by markedly *decreasing* as well as *increasing* force. Whereas sharply increasing force is a well-known device for securing emphasis, many speakers do not recognize that decreasing force may secure a similar effect. The latter device, that of "underplaying," can be exceptionally helpful in regaining lagging attention or in stressing a point.

During the delivery of a speech, of course, you should concentrate on communication, letting the meaning of what you are saying determine your amount and variation of force.

The effective speaking voice has flexibility of rate. The speaker's rate of utterance affects his intelligibility and general effectiveness. The average general rate for public speaking is probably between 120 and 150 words per minute. If your overall rate of speaking is slower than 110 or faster than 170 words per minute, it may need some adjustment. An important consideration for the public speaker is the concept of *apparent* rate. Audiences do not sit with stop watches to check the speaker's rate of utterance; their judgment is subjective and is influenced by factors such as pause, vocalized pause, hesitation, clarity of enunciation, and prolongation of vowel sounds. Although Franklin D. Roosevelt spoke more slowly than average, his *apparent* rate was near the average. Conversely, some effective speakers may attain a rate of 175 words per minute without giving the impression of excessive speed.

General rate should fit the total speaking situation: the material presented, the acoustics, the mood of the occasion, the reactions of the listeners, and the personality and feelings of the speaker. If the noise level is high, the audience large, the mood solemn or sorrowful, or the content difficult or important, the speaker's general rate probably should be somewhat slower than customary. Conversely, if the total situation is light, joyful, or exciting, the speaker's general rate probably should be somewhat faster than usual. Thus, a fiery coach attempting to inspire his players in a pregame dressing room exhortation ordinarily would use a more rapid pace than would a minister delivering the invocation at outdoor commencement ceremonies.

Other than varying the average number of words spoken per minute, the most important factors in rate variability are *pause* and *duration of sound. Pause* should be differentiated from *hesitation.* Hesitation is an unintentional interruption in the flow of speech. Typically it is caused by being nervous, being unable to think of the proper word, or losing one's train of thought. Because it reveals uncertainty and short-circuits communication, it should be avoided. Most beginning speakers are guilty of excessive hesitancy, but have not developed effective use of pause. Pause is a purposeful interruption of utterance that serves to emphasize important ideas by allowing them time to "sink in" and that serves to punctuate what the speaker says—as periods, commas, and the like in an essay set off words into thought groups. The basic thought unit of oral communication is the vocal phrase: a word or, more customarily, a group of words that possess a common core of meaning. Although variation in pitch and force are helpful in indicating the beginning and end of vocal phrases, the primary method is the use of pauses. To appreciate the importance of silence as vocal pronunciation, read orally the following sentence; pause only where slanted lines appear; pause momentarily for a single line, somewhat longer for a double line, and longer still for triple lines.

> Yet, even though we may take pride in this achievement/ we know that our democracy, our enjoyment of freedom/ is not so much a gift from the past as a challenge for the future// not so much a reward for old victories as a goal for new struggles// not so much an inheritance from our forefathers as an obligation to those who will follow/// For democracy is never a final achievement// It is a call to an untiring effort to continual sacrifice and to willingness if necessary/ to die in its defense.

In reading this passage, perhaps you felt the impulse to pause in different places from those indicated by the slanted lines. This would not be surprising. To a considerable extent, vocal phrasing is a matter of personal preference. One of the characteristics of a person's oral style is his method of vocal phrasing. In addition to the factor of personal preference, the length of the phrases and the duration of the separating pauses are conditioned by the same factors influencing general rate. For instance, the phrasing indicated in the inset would be suitable for a small informal audience, seated in a room possessing good acoustics. The same vocal phrasing would be inappropriate, however, for a very large audience—especially if the occasion is impressive or the acoustics poor. Under the circumstances just mentioned, the speaker should shorten the length of the thought units and increase the period of silence between phrases, something like this:

> Yet/ even though we may take pride in this achievement/ we know that our democracy/ our enjoyment of freedom/ is not so much a gift from the past/ as a challenge for the future/// not so much/ a reward for old victories/ as a goal for new struggles/// not so much an inheritance from our forefathers/ as an obligation to those who will follow/// For democracy is never a final achievement/// It is a call/to an untiring effort/ to continual sacrifice/ and to willingness if necessary/ to die in its defense.

Duration of sound refers to the amount of time consumed in producing a sound, particularly the vowel sounds. Duration of sound should vary with the material presented, the mood of the occasion, the size of the audience, the acoustics, and the feelings of the speaker. Prolonging the vowel sound in the word "bad," for example, may aid in securing emphasis: "I wouldn't say he did a *bad* job. Greater duration of sounds is also an essential means of slowing general rate when necessitated by solemn, important, or depressing circumstances; conversely, shorter duration of sounds is an essential way of increasing general rate for light or exciting circumstances.

Variety in rate will aid in holding attention, making effective transitions, and attaining emphasis. How can flexible rate be secured? First, listen to yourself and to recordings of your voice and, perhaps, check with your instructor to determine the nature of your needs; second, use the information presented in this section and the exercises at the end of this chapter as the basis for a self-help program to improve your control over general rate, vocal phrasing, pausing for emphasis, and duration of sound; finally, attempt to incorporate your new skills into your public speaking. Of course, when speaking to an audience forget techniques; let the habits you have acquired in practice provide the flexibility of rate necessary to stir up desired responses in the hearers.

Clarity Depends Upon the Distinctness and "Correctness" with Which You Speak. Delivery of a speech in a clear, pleasant voice with sufficient variety in pitch, force, and rate may still be ineffective if articulation and pronunciation are inadequate. In a broad sense, articulation and pronunciation are the processes that are involved in the production of the sounds of a language.

The concepts of articulation and pronunciation are closely related and occasionally overlap. A sound or combination of sounds habitually produced improperly, resulting in impaired intelligibility and comprehension, may be classified as an articulatory problem. Most articulatory difficulties occur in the formation of the consonants, individually or in combinations. A pronunciation error occurs when the sounds of a word are given values, sequences, or accents that are unacceptable to listeners and consequently are judged incorrect. Articulation, then, is primarily concerned with *intelligibility;* pronunciation is a matter of *acceptability,* which is determined by conventional standards.

Unacceptable pronunciation frequently does not interfere with intelligibility. For instance, although many people find "theeayter" an unacceptable pronunciation of the word "theater," this pronunciation is almost universally comprehended. On the other hand, "Sgoweet" for "Let's go eat" is an example of a common slurring error that may impair comprehension. As another example, the indistinct enunciation of the consonant *f* caused the sinking of the submarine *Stickleback.* A navy board of inquiry determined that when a first-class electrician's mate at the controls directed another electrician's mate to "come off" on his panel, the second man heard "come on," and turned the rheostat the wrong way. The mistake tripped circuit breakers and cut off the *Stickleback's* main power. Out of control, she surfaced directly in front of the destroyer escort *Silverstein.*

Using distinct articulation. Many words in our language depend upon a single sound for identification; if that sound is improperly produced or if another is substituted, the word may be lost to the listener, or he may mistake it for another. If articulation is "cloudy" or errors frequent, listeners may be irritated or repelled and may wonder why the speaker has not made some effort to improve. The result may be a failure in communication.

In your efforts to improve articulation, you are concerned with both consonants and vowels: intelligibility is primarily dependent upon the distinctness of the consonant sounds; nevertheless, because the carrying power of the voice is primarily in the vowels, precise enunciation of the vowel sounds is essential.

Common difficulties in articulation are (1) mumbling or muffling, (2) slurring, and less frequently (3) overprecision.

(1) *Mumbling or muffling.* This occurs when the jaws, lips, soft palate, and tongue are not active enough to allow precise formation of the sounds. Habitual laziness in the use of these articulators causes general indistinctness. Difficult combinations of consonants, especially, require energetic and precise movements of the organs of articulation.

(2) *Slurring.* This articulation error takes place when a series of sounds and words are run together so that syllables are indistinctly formed or omitted altogether. *What are you doing tonight?* may be slurred so that it becomes *Whutchadoontnight?* Slurring is frequently caused by excessive speed. Many combinations of sounds require considerable movement by the articulators; unless sufficient time is allowed, these sounds cannot be precisely produced. Even more frequently, slurring is caused by carelessness and habit. When poor sound formation and excessive speed are combined, intelligibility will be impaired.

(3) *Overprecision.* Although overprecision is much less common than indistinctness, it is sufficiently prevalent to warrant a word of warning. When a speaker is unduly conscious of his enunciation, he may make exaggerated use of his articulators, resulting in an affected manner; he may mistakenly accentuate normally unstressed sounds (as *o* of "p*o*lice" or *e* of "D*e*troit"); or he may tend to pronounce the letters instead of the sounds of the language (as pronouncing the *t* of of*t*en," the *l* of "pa*l*m," or the second *b* of "bom*b*er"). Overprecision calls attention to itself at the expense of ideas.

How may distinctness be improved? Begin by analyzing your speech to discover its weaknesses. Many articulatory problems remain uncorrected because the speaker does not know they exist. Record your voice and check your articulation with the help of your instructor. If your speech suffers from general indistinctness, resulting from lazy articulators or excessive speed, begin your program for improvement by slowing down your general rate and by increasing the speed and precision of the jaw, lip, soft palate, and tongue movements. If you have difficulty in enunciating certain sounds, begin by learning to distinguish aurally between the correct and your production of the particular sounds; next drill to produce correctly and easily the sound in isolation; finally, and most difficult, develop the ability to produce the sound correctly in conjunction with others to form various words. Most speakers can improve the clarity with which they articulate difficult sound combinations like the *d* of *nd* and *ld*, the *t* of *ft*, *st*, and *pt*, and the clusters *sk, sks, skt* (from "sked"), *sp, sps, spt* (from "sped"), and *sts*. Practice these sample words:

> se*nd*, be*nd*, ope*ned*, beyo*nd*, fou*nd*; sai*led*, pu*lled*, go*ld*, wor*ld*, mai*led*; li*ft*, si*ft*, gra*ft*er, dra*ft*, fi*ft*een; *st*ill, co*st*, exi*st*ence, toa*st*, *st*op; we*pt*, sle*pt*, o*pt*ical, gul*ped*, ste*pped*; *sk*im, *sk*ill, *sc*oop, ri*sk*, ba*sk*et; de*sks*, ta*sks*, tu*sks*, a*sks*, ma*sks*; a*sked*, ri*sked*, hu*sked*; *sp*ecified, ho*sp*ital, e*sp*ecial, di*sp*air, *sp*eed; ga*sps*, wi*sps*, ra*sps*, gra*sps*, cla*sps*; li*sped*, gra*sped*, ra*sped*; conte*sts*, insi*sts*, ne*sts*, gue*sts*, li*sts*.

Continued practice on exercises such as the foregoing and those found in standard drillbooks on voice and articulation will help build appropriate habits.

Using acceptable pronunciation. Mistakes in pronunciation may distract or even irritate the audience. Such errors can be avoided if the speaker is sensitive to the standards of pronunciation prevalent in the community, and if he is aware of the common types of pronunciation errors.

Follow the Pronunciation Practices of Respected and Educated People in Your Community or Region: We are all aware that different regions tend to produce different dialects. The speech of a native Bostonian, for instance, differs noticeably from that of a Nebraska schoolteacher or of an Alabama newspaper publisher. Such variations do not constitute pronunciation errors, provided the majority of the "intelligent and cultured" persons in the region involved adhere to them. Extreme dialects and other pronunciations below the standards of a region should be modified, because audiences may not find them acceptable. Modifications of a dialect may also be required when an individual moves to a new region, if intelligibility or acceptability is impaired. Foreign accents may be acceptable unless they are so obvious that they are distracting or reduce intelligibility. Regional and foreign dialects tend to become modified as the individual consistently associates with people in a new environment.

Standard pronunciation represents "a complex, arbitrary system of habits which meet social, cultural demands." These habits are social in their origin and function. As a very general rule, one's pronunciation should not attract negative attention; it should conform reasonably well to the expectations of the listeners. If your habits of pronunciation are not compatible with those accepted by most educated people, you should consider whether your best interests require an improvement in your standards of pronunciation.

In general, educated persons use those pronunciations recorded in a recently published standard dictionary. Therefore, when in doubt about the pronunciation of a word, check the latest edition of a standard dictionary. If the word has more than one acceptable pronunciation, make your choice and stick to it—at least throughout the course of a particular speech. At this point it might be wise to caution the speaker to respect but not to worship the dictionary. Consider it an invaluable tool—but neither omnipotent nor omniscient:

(1) The function of a dictionary is not deliberately to set standards, but to *record* "the usage of the speakers and writers of the language."

(2) Dictionaries do not invariably record all usages acceptable by significant numbers of educated speakers.

(3) All pronunciation variants listed are acceptable, unless otherwise stated. The order of listing does not necessarily mean that one pronunciation is more desirable than another.

(4) Dictionaries differ somewhat among themselves concerning the acceptable pronunciations of various words. As an experiment, spend an hour comparing the pronunciations recorded in *Webster's Third New International Dictionary* with those in several standard desk dictionaries.

(5) Because of problems of printing and lexicography, at the date of publication a dictionary is already somewhat out-of-date with current pronunciation practices.

Avoid Common Pronunciation Errors: Although numerous specific errors are made in the pronunciation of words, such mistakes can be grouped into five categories:

(1) *Omissions.* The omission of necessary sounds occurs most frequently at the end of words, as when one or more sounds are omitted in the combinations *sks, skt, sps, sts, kts, kst, nst,* and *ndz* occurring in word endings: de*sks*, a*sked*, cla*sps*, insi*sts*, affe*cts*, glan*ced*, fri*ends*. In addition, omissions frequently occur in the middle of words, as in *libary* for *library, govment* for *government,* and *probly* for *probably.*

(2) *Additions.* Some typical additions of unnecessary vowel sounds are *athalete* for *athlete* and *elum* for *elm.* Representative additions of unnecessary consonant sounds include *acrost* for *across* and *warsh* for *wash.*

(3) *Inversions.* This error results when two sounds are inverted, as in *aks* for *ask, intregal* for *integral* and *hydernt* for *hydrant.*

(4) Substitutions. Such errors are very common, occur with surprising variety, and often are hard to correct. Among the more common vowel substitutions are *tin* for *ten, aeg* for *egg,* and *extri* for *extra.* Represen-

tative consonant substitutions include *liddle* for *little, bat* for *bath, srub* for *shrub,* and *crasy* for *crazy.*

(5) *Misplaced accents.* Misplaced stress occurs very commonly in words such as larynx, cigar, device, infamous, Italian, exigency, formidable, municipal, and hydrometer.

If you have reason to believe that you commit any of these types of pronunciation errors, consult your instructor or plan a self-help program based upon the detailed advice contained in a recently published voice and articulation drillbook.

Summary

Bodily action facilitates adjustment to the speaking situation, helps the speaker to secure and maintain audience interest and attention, and aids the speaker in clarifying and emphasizing meaning. The values of bodily action will be realized by effective use of (1) eye contact, (2) facial expression, (3) posture, (4) movement, and (5) gestures.

An effective speaking voice possesses the attributes of (1) audibility, (2) pleasantness, (3) variety, (4) animation, (5) fluency, and (6) clarity. Audibility and pleasantness are the products of proper habits of breathing, phonation, and resonation. Variety, animation, and fluency necessitate a voice that is flexible in pitch, force, and rate. Clarity depends upon distinct articulation and acceptable pronunciation.

Exercises and Assignments

Exercises to Improve Physical Expression

1. Deliver a three- or four-minute speech demonstrating (1) good and bad posture, (2) properly and improperly executed movement, (3) the most common sins in the use of facial expression, or (4) effective and ineffective use of gestures.

2. *Project in Individual Pantomime:* Choose for class presentation a subject that is well adapted to pantomime. The following suggestions may give you some ideas: (1) Teach an imaginary person to play golf, to dance the tango, to box, to apply cosmetics, to use several wrestling holds, to drive an automobile. Make your choice of subject as original and unusual as possible. Your instructor and classmates will attempt to identify what you are doing. (2) Tell a story without the use of words. Then ask a classmate to retell the story in words. (3) Impersonate a well-known comedian, actor, or public official.

3. *Project in Group Pantomime:* With two or three of your classmates select a narrative or playlet that you can produce in pantomime, with each student

playing one part. Your selection should call for considerable action on the part of each character. Detective stories, adventure stories, and melodramas lend themselves well to group pantomime. Write your own production, if you wish. Limit the presentation to ten minutes.

4. Choose a subject upon which you have strong feeling—something that arouses your indignation or your anger. Exhort your audience to "do something about it." In giving vent to your feelings, make a real attempt to "let yourself go." Move freely about the platform, let your face reflect your emotions, pound the lectern, shake your fist; approach expressive action with abandon, and do not worry about overdoing it.

5. Watch a well-known speaker on television. Give particular attention to his use of the visible code. As part of your observation, for a few minutes turn off the sound while you continue to study his physical delivery. Did he commit any of the common sins of posture, movement, facial expression, or gesture? In what ways did his use of bodily action contribute to or detract from his effectiveness? Report to the class.

Exercises to Improve Vocal Flexibility and Expressiveness

1. Say "are you sure?" with (1) an upward inflection, (2) a downward inflection, and (3) a double inflection (rise followed by fall, or *vice versa*).

2. Choose a poem or the text of a speech that requires a maximum of flexibility in pitch, force, and rate to express adequately its meaning. Practice reading it aloud, attempting to increase vocal expressiveness.

3. Read aloud the following, attempting to express the meaning and mood of each. Do not worry about "overdoing" your interpretation.

a. Your attention, ladies and gentlemen. The main event of the evening, fifteen rounds, for the heavyweight championship of the world. Introducing, in this corner, weighing 225 pounds, wearing white trunks, the heavyweight champion of the world, Larry Holmes.

b. The sneer is gone from Casey's lips, his teeth are clenched in hate,
He pounds with cruel vengeance his bat upon the plate;
And now the pitcher holds the ball, and now he lets it go.
And now the air is shattered by the force of Casey's blow.

Oh, somewhere in this favored land the sun is shining bright,
The band is playing somewhere, and somewhere hearts are light;
And somewhere men are laughing, and somewhere children shout,
But there is no joy in Mudville—Mighty Casey has struck out.

4. Say, "Good morning. How are you today?" so as to express a variety of feelings, such as *eagerness, gaiety, pathos, romance, haughtiness, hurry, disinterest,* and so on.

5. Read the following selection *without pausing except at the slanted lines.* Do you agree in all cases with the suggested phrasing? If not, what are your reasons for disagreement?

HAMLET: Speak the speech,/ I pray you,/ as I pronounced it to you,/ trippingly on the tongue:/ but if you mouth it,/ as many of your players do,/ I had as lief the town-crier/ spoke my lines./ Nor do not saw the air/ too much with your hand,/ thus;/ but use all/ gently:/ for in the very torrent,/ tempest,/ and, as I may say,/ whirlwind/ of your passion,/ you must acquire/ and beget/ a temperance that may give it/ smoothness./ O, it offends me to the soul/ to hear a robustious/ periwig-pated fellow/ tear a passion to tatters,/ to very rags,/ to split the ears of the groundlings,/ who, for the most part,/ are capable of nothing/ but inexplicable/ dumb-shows/ and noise:/ I would have such a fellow/ whipped/ for o'erdoing/ Termagant;/ it out-herods/ Herod:/ pray you avoid it.

1st PLAYER: I warrant/ your honor.

HAMLET: Be not too tame/ neither,/ but let your own discretion/ be your tutor:/ suit the action/ to the word,/ the word/ to the action;/ with this special observance,/ that you o'erstep not/ the modesty of nature;/ for anything so overdone/ is from/ the purpose of playing,/ whose end,/ both at the first/ and now,/ was/ and is,/ to hold,/ as 'twere,/ the mirror up to nature;/ to show virtue/ her own feature,/ scorn/ her own image,/ and the very age/ and body of the time/ his form/ and pressure./ Now this overdone/ or come tardy off,/ though it make the unskillful laugh,/ cannot but make the judicious/ grieve;/ the censure of the which/ one/ must/ in your allowance/ o'erweigh a whole theater/ of others./ O, there be players/ that I have seen play,/ and heard others praise,/ and that highly,/ not to speak it profanely,/ that neither having the accent/ of Christians/ nor the gait of Christian,/ pagan,/ nor man,/ have so strutted/ and bellowed,/ that I have thought some of nature's journeymen/ had made men,/ and not made them well,/ they imitated humanity/ so abominably./

Exercises to Improve Habits of Distinctness and Correctness

1. During one round of speeches jot down every word misarticulated or mispronounced by each speaker. Indicate the nature of the error. Use a different sheet of paper for each speaker. Give each his list at the conclusion of his performance.

2. Carry with you a note pad for a period of one or two weeks. Listen carefully to your friends, family, and business associates for slurring, mumbling, sound omissions, additions, substitutions, and inversions. Note each error on your pad. Arrange the list of words under the headings above and bring to class. In cooperation with your classmates, make a master list of the most commonly mispronounced words. Practice the list and read it aloud to your classmates, who will check for errors.

3. Read orally the following list of frequently mispronounced words. Add to this list words that you believe to be often mispronounced. Check each word in a standard desk dictionary and then in the *Webster's New International Dictionary of the English Language Unabridged.* Do you find the *unabridged* dic-

tionary to be more liberal in accepting pronunciation variants than the desk dictionary? If so, which dictionary is "right"? Why?

battery
because
certainly
athlete
combatant
drought
exemplary
experiment
exquisite
flaccid
forehead
formidable
frailty
generally
gesture
heinous
hundred
impotent
infamous
integral
interesting
intricacies
irrelevant
laboratory
larynx
leisure
library
literature
maintenance
miniature
miserable
naturally
nominative
onerous
orgy
particularly
perspiration
picture
prelate
pronunciation
recognize
sophomore
statistics
superfluous
tremendous
trough
umbrella
vehemence

4. Bring to class a "tongue-twister." Place it on the speaker's table face down. Each student should choose one, glance through it, and then read it aloud. Do it slowly the first time, gradually increasing speed in subsequent readings. Here are some examples that require nimble use of the articulators:

a. Six slim, sleek saplings.
b. Stop at the shop at the top of Schram Street.
c. In January and February there are few athletic exhibitions.
d. Some shun sunshine; some shun shade.
e. He whittled a white whistle from the willow wand which he cut.
f. Shoes and socks shock my shy sister Susan.
g. Fill the sieve with thistles; then sift the thistles through the sieve.
h. The freshly fried flesh of flying fish is fine eating.
i. Much whirling water makes the mill-wheel work well.
j. She sells seashells; does he sell seashells too?
k. Esau Wood sawed wood. Esau Wood would saw wood. All the wood Esau Wood saw Esau Wood would saw. In other words, all the wood Esau saw to saw Esau sought to saw. Oh, the wood Wood would saw! And oh, the wood-saw with which Wood would saw wood. But one day Wood's wood-saw would saw no wood, and thus the wood Wood sawed was not the wood Wood would saw if Wood's wood-saw would saw wood. Now, Wood would saw if Wood's wood-saw would saw wood. Wood would saw wood with a wood-saw that would saw wood, so Esau sought a saw that would saw wood. One day Esau saw a saw saw wood as no other wood-saw Wood saw would saw wood. In fact, of all the wood-saws Wood ever saw saw wood Wood never saw a wood-saw that would saw wood as the wood-saw Wood saw saw wood. And I never saw a wood-saw that would saw as the wood-saw Wood saw would saw until I saw Esau saw wood with the wood-saw Wood saw saw wood. Now Wood saws wood with the wood-saw Wood saw saw wood.

CHAPTER 15

Using Language in Delivering the Speech

Some speakers give only slight consideration to the words they use. Subscribing to the "say what you have to say quickly and be done with it" school, they exhibit little interest in developing an effective oral style, preferring to leave that to the Websters, the Churchills, and the Eric Sevareids. It is true, of course, that superfluous ornamentation and "style for the sake of style" belong to speakers of the past. The tempo of modern society encourages simplicity and brevity. On the other hand, if the speaker limits his concern with language to grammar and fluency, he misunderstands the nature and functions of language in speech.

Language is the heart of communication. Spoken words symbolize the speaker's thoughts, much as printed words represent the writer's thinking. Reinforced by his physical delivery and by his vocal delivery, the speaker's words may stir up desired meanings and feelings in the listeners. Inappropriate language may impair or cause a complete breakdown in the process of communication: ideas may be misunderstood; arguments may seem ineffectual; and emotional appeals may fail. Effective language skills are not the product of an undirected, effortless process "about as automatic as breathing." They cannot be acquired merely by absorbing osmotically the everyday speech around one. Much of this language is clumsy, prolix, and ambiguous. You are urged to accept Wilson Follett's prescription: "To speak or write well means hard work, the taking of sometimes painful thought, the constant rejection of labor- and thought-saving alternatives, and the practice of canons that are mastered only by arduous self-cultivation and discipline."

In a brief textbook on public speaking space permits only a brief orientation to the nature of language and to specific guides for improving oral style. Perhaps this chapter will prove helpful to you in initiating a self-help program to improve your use of language.

The Nature of Language

An effective oral style is based upon an understanding of the nature of language. Perhaps the basic principle of language is that *words are only symbols.* Although this observation seems obvious, few persons fully appreciate that they live in a symbolic world that conditions the way they view themselves and their environment. If we think about it for a moment, it is clear that we do not react directly, and exclusively, with the physical world. Virtually all of our perceptions-judgments-feelings-behaviors involving the empirical world—the physical world out there—are mediated by symbolic values. For each of us the symbolizing process began so early and has been so pervasive and so continuous that we fail to realize how completely our thinking, believing, valuing, and behaving are responses to, and impingements upon, the encapsulating symbolic world.

Students of communication only recently have come to a full recognition that symbolic behavior is intrinsic to all human action and thought, perhaps to all knowing itself. Because of his large brain and intricate neuromuscular system, man is virtually compelled to become a symbol maker and a symbol user. Symbolic behavior is central to man acting as man. It is perhaps the supreme identifying characteristic of humanness. If, as Douglas Ehninger puts it, "man is by nature a creature who automatically translates his experience into symbolic equivalents, and if, in addition to whatever function symbols have in reporting the world, they also express attitudes or feelings about the phenomena referred to, man—whether he wills it or not—constantly is inducing and being induced, is constantly persuading himself when he is silent and persuading others when he speaks. In short, man not only is surrounded by rhetoric; he also is bound by and to it."

Every encounter between humans is a rhetorical encounter in that it necessarily involves the sending and receiving of signals. Almost everything we see, hear, or touch has communicative values. Any observable action that we take is potentially communicative, inasmuch as it has symbolic values that can be interpreted by others. We cannot *not* communicate to others whenever we are in their presence. Even silence on our part has communicative values. Our entire waking time is constrained by the endless producing, receiving, and interpreting of symbols. Intrapersonal communication even pervades our sleep. To secure normal, restorative rest, we must dream, and symbolic behavior is the stuff of dreams. Given the nature of our neuromuscular system, continuous symbolic behavior is inevitable.

In earlier chapters we discussed the transmission of nonverbal symbols by the speaker and their reception and interpretation by the listener, as well as the reverse—the transmission of such symbols by the listener and their impact upon the speaker. We have noted the importance and pervasiveness of body language (facial expression, eye contact, posture, movement, and gesture), paralanguage or vocal delivery (audibility, pleasantness, variety, animation, fluency, and clarity of the voice), and object language (those "objects" with which the person surrounds himself and which represent deliberate choices, as one's grooming, dress, and other evidences of life-style). In this chapter we are concerned with the speaker's use of formal language, or the linguistic code.

It is worth spending a moment with the concept that a circular relationship exists between our linguistic code and our view of the world. Because of the limitations of our nature we can never experience the fullness of reality. More exactly, we can never make contact with the total "reality" of potential stimuli because of the conceptual needs and limitations of our neuromuscular system. By means of our senses, usually automatically and unconsciously, we select those fragments to which we shall attend. Then, by means of our central neurological processing, we organize the impressions drawn from these fragments, joining them into conceptual wholes.

The culmination of this process of perceiving is *categorizations*. After selecting what we will perceive, after interpreting what we perceive, we begin to apply labels, to form categories. To speak, to use language, to think is to classify. The process of classification enables us to organize the confusing complexity of the external world into some kind of order or continuity. These categories constitute our symbolic "reality." Once formed, categories tend to become rigid mental compartments that help to determine what we select to perceive, as well as how we interpret and classify what we perceive. All of this is exceedingly important to the process of communication. What we communicate about—what we talk about—is our perception of what the world is like. Thus, language is a major factor in producing our perceptions, our judgments, and our knowledge. Language is the chief medium through which we organize "reality" and make sense out of it. The process of perceiving directly affects the values and character of our language. The reverse is also true. The values and character of our language also affect our perceiving process. Our language, with its omnipresent categories, helps direct the way we perceive and the way we symbolize what we perceive.

To clarify better the process of symbolization, let us turn to the nonverbal world of the baby. Unable to use words, the baby communicates his feelings as best he can by crying, screaming, or cooing. Later on, he depends largely upon the visual code for communication—fondling and exhibiting his new toy for approval, pointing to the food he wants, nodding his head in assent, turning away in rejection, and "showing off" to gain attention. In time, the baby learns to associate certain sounds with particular objects, ideas, and desires, much as his parents do; thus, he eventually refers to the object that contains milk by saying "bottle"—his communicative powers are no longer limited to a mere pointing to it. The word *bottle* has come to "stand for" the container that holds his milk; the child believes that his parents have the same association when they hear or speak this word. He will soon discover, however, that "bottle" does not always mean milk. For example, "$bottle_1$" may refer to "bottle of milk," "$bottle_2$" to "bottle of vitamin pills," "$bottle_3$" to "bottle of Coke," and so forth. Furthermore, he discovers that not only liquids are "bottled"; traffic may be "bottled," emotions may be "bottled," and a football team's attack may be "bottled." In such cases, the word *bottle* denotes "restraint" or "encompassment," a somewhat broader concept. As the child becomes older and his language facility increases, he finds the problem of symbolization much more complex when dealing with words more abstract than "bottle," "baby," "toy," "book," and "dog." He experiences great difficulty in understanding the precise meaning of a word such as *democracy*. To tell him that this term indicates the form of government we have in the United States will mean little to him, especially if does not know what is meant by "form of government." Additional confusion arises when he finds that Soviet Russia labels herself a "democracy" and calls the United States a "dictatorship," whereas the United States claims the exact reverse! Eventually he may discover that highly abstract words such as *democracy* may have a wide spectrum of denotative and connotative meanings.

From the foregoing, it should be apparent that if "words are only symbols," they possess relative, not absolute meanings and, furthermore, that *language has meaning only in terms of the associations established by individuals between the verbal symbol and the object or concept to which it refers.* Partly because such associations are personalized responses growing out of the individual's experiences and partly because the referent possesses an almost limitless periphery of associated meanings, *a symbol never tells everything about the object or concept to which it refers.* Ten thousand words would be insufficient to reveal all that could be said about the chair in which you may now be sitting. When the noted historian Hans Buchheim completed his biography of former Chancellor Konrad Adenauer, his years of research and writing did not produce the full Adenauer story. His treatise inevitably was an abridgement. To cover *all*, the biography would have to cover in total detail the full periphery of meaning associated with Adenauer: the history of modern Germany—because Adenauer was a product of his times; all that occurred during his administration; the history of Germany yet unborn—because its development was partially the result of Adenauer's influence; the story of Adenauer's family and friends—because they were part of his life; Adenauer's influence upon the rest of the world; what might have happened if he had not become chancellor; and on and on, the full story impossible of completion.

When the Adenauer manuscript was completed, translators set busily to work converting the German form into English. The reason for translation is obvious: to provide a means of communication that would enable those who speak only English to read the volume. The necessity to translate the Adenauer manuscript illustrates the principle: *thought cannot be "transmitted"; it can only be stirred up in the listener or reader.* This same principle applies, of course, whenever you speak or write. When you say the word *honor,* your vocal mechanism sets up a series of sound waves. These sound waves, when they impinge upon the hearer's neuromuscular system, stir up meanings. The nature of these meanings, however, depends largely upon his previously developed associations concerning the word *honor.* The meaning of *honor* is not in the word itself, but in the listener's semantic reactions. Everything that has been said earlier in this book concerning audience-focused communication is centered in the concept of semantic habits. "Our reaction patterns" according to S. I. Hayakawa, "are the internal and most important residue of whatever years of education or miseducation we may have received from our parents' conduct toward us in childhood as well as their teachings, from the formal education we may have had, from all the sermons and lectures we have listened to, from the radio programs and the movies and television shows we have experienced, from all the books and newspapers and comic strips we have read, from the conversations we have had with friends and associates, and from all our experiences." Perhaps now you can appreciate more fully that when you speak to an individual, you are attempting to communicate with his self-system, that is, with his complex neuromuscular system that responds in terms of its physical and psychological environment, its inner state of feelings, and its memories of relevant thoughts and emotions.

Constant changes in denotative and connotative word meanings further complicate the process of communication. Admittedly, English of today is different from that of Shakespeare, even more different from that of Chaucer, and still more different from the Anglo-Saxon of the Venerable Bede. Nevertheless, in contrast to changes in meaning, the changes in the words of the language occur at a snail's crawl. For instance, in Samuel Johnson's *Dictionary* of 1755, *monsieur* meant "a term of reproach for a Frenchman," *wallop* meant "to boil," *barnacle* meant "a bird like a goose," and *wife* meant "a woman of low employment." What you presently believe to be "morally right" may differ in important respects from what your older brother, parents, or grandparents endorse, and their conceptions may resemble only faintly what was considered "moral" in the eighteenth century. Possibly your concept of morality has undergone change within the past year—or past week. Thirty years ago an airplane that attained a speed of 400 mph was "fast"; twenty years ago a speed of 700 mph was "fast"; today a plane is not really "fast" unless it flies at more than three times the speed of sound. Furthermore, manned capsules that repeatedly circle the globe at 17,500 mph are not considered "fast" any more; the greater speed of other rockets makes the earth-orbiting rockets seem almost "slow." An age of fifty years was considered "old" in 1900; today the half-century mark indicates the beginning of middle age. With every object, idea, or principle constantly in the process of change, *no arbitrary, timeless meaning can be ascribed to any verbal symbol.* Thus, the changing nature of meaning further complicates the problem of oral communication.

A sensitive awareness of the nature of language can help you to develop an effective oral style. The knowledge that "the word is not the thing" should remind you to choose words that express as specifically, clearly, and faithfully as possible the concepts you have in mind. In addition, the appreciation that meaning can never be "transmitted" should help you to adjust your use of language to the intelligence, experience, background, and language skills of your auditors.

Specific Guides for the Effective Use of Language

The following suggestions may provide the basis for your self-help program to develop an effective oral style.

Language Should Be Chosen for Its Oral Qualities; It Is Primarily Meant to Be Heard, Not Read

Language meant to be heard possesses certain characteristics.

(1) *Oral language should be personal and direct.* Whereas the writer usually aims at a comparatively indefinite and scattered audience, the speaker talks to a specific, well-defined group. The speaker is closer to his audience both physically and mentally than the writer; even the television and radio audience keenly feels the personality and—particularly the television audience—the physical presence of the speaker. To achieve directness, make extended use of personal pronouns such as "I," "me," "we," "you," "mine," "ours," and "yours." Be conversational rather than formal. Employ short sentences, contractions, and appropriate idi-

oms to promote directness and to personalize your style. Moreover, use direct and rhetorical questions. The direct question is answered by the speaker. For example, the question "Do you know how many teenage dope addicts were arrested last month in Chicago?" would be followed by an answer provided by the speaker. The rhetorical question allows the audience to provide an answer, one that is usually obvious and represents commonly held belief. For example, Ronald Reagan closed his 1980 televised debate with former President Carter—as well as some of his other campaign speeches—by asking his listeners these rhetorical questions:

> All of you will go to the polls. You'll stand there in the polling place and make a decision. I think when you make that decision it might be well if you ask yourself: Are you better off than you were four years ago? Is it easier for you to go and buy things in the stores than it was four years ago? Is there more or less unemployment in the country than there was four years ago? Is America as respected throughout the world as it was? Do you feel that our security is as safe? That we're as strong as we were four years ago?

Some political experts believe that Reagan's strategy of eliciting silent answers to these questions caused many of his listeners to conclude that Mr. Carter's administration had been disastrous.

(2) *Oral language should provide for instant comprehension of meaning.* Whereas the reader who does not fully understand a sentence or paragraph may reread it, the listener obviously does not have the opportunity to listen again to what the speaker said. Instead, new words and sentences strike his ear while he is trying to comprehend what has been said previously. If bombarded with a series of concepts that are not clear, he soon becomes hopelessly lost, and may give up listening altogether. The speaker must phrase his ideas in such a way that they will be immediately understood. Speed of comprehension will be enhanced by developing these language habits: use concrete words to express abstract ideas; employ active rather than passive verb forms; let short simple sentences predominate (The simplest basic sentence construction in English is the subject-verb-object sequence. The modification of this core sequence or the intrusion of supplementary details or qualifications may add variety or impressiveness and, therefore, may be stylistically desirable. Nevertheless, any such alterations necessarily slow the comprehension of meaning.); avoid unusually long, involved constructions; repeat and restate important ideas to ensure their comprehension and retention.

Language Should Be Adapted to Your Own Personality, Your Audience, and the Occasion

Your language usage should fit reasonably well your speaker image: your particular personality, interests, attitudes, reputation, position, and background. A freshman student should not attempt to impress his instructor with a large assortment of polysyllabic words that he scarcely understands and that do not fit his personality, background, or his subject; a middle-aged woman should not couch her ideas in current collegiate slang. Do not attempt to copy closely the style of some well-known speaker; probably it will not fit your personality or background. (However, the study of the speeches of successful speakers will help you to develop your individual style.)

Careful analysis of the audience will enable you to adjust your language patterns to fit the intelligence, backgrounds, attitudes, and interests of your auditors. On the basis of such an analysis, together with your knowledge of the occasion, decide the degree of formality to be used, the extent to which certain technical terms might be understood, the type of idiomatic usage you might include, how much and what type of humor might be effective, the degree and kind of emotional appeal acceptable, and so on.

Language Should Possess Clarity

From Cicero and Quintilian to the present, responsible speechmakers have agreed that "clearness is the first virtue of eloquence." (This is not to deny that sometimes a partisan will deliberately cloud meaning. Because his argument will not stand close scrutiny, a politician, a diplomat, or an advertiser may at times wish to muddy rather than to clarify thought. For instance, according to David S. Broder, as a presidential candidate, Jimmy Carter used language "with extraordinary precision of effect—but not to clarify meaning." Columnist Broder argues that candidate Carter employed "the principles of selective perception and reinforcement" acquired through the study of psychology and learning techniques to wrap a cocoon "of words around the hard realities of choice," "each strand of words spelling reassurance to part of the audience." Even so-called objective scientists may designedly use obscure language. According to Edwin Newman, when resources are tight, "money is more likely to be forthcoming if whatever the money is wanted for can be made to sound abstruse and important." Nevertheless, open, honest, and responsible speaking stresses clarity. Listeners ought to demand as the first requisite of communication that language be clear.) Clarity is that attribute of language that facilitates close correspondence between the speaker's meaning and that stirred up in the minds of his auditors. Clarity will be fostered if language is (1) accurate, (2) simple, and (3) concrete.

(1) To be clear, language should be *accurate*. To select words that "say what they mean," you must first understand clearly the concept that you wish to express. Then you must choose words that correspond closely to that concept *and* that will convey the desired meaning to the listeners.

The purpose of your language, as for all other aspects of speechmaking, is to evoke a particular audience response. Conceivably your language could accurately represent your ideas but could fail to communicate those ideas to the listeners. As an obvious example, a newspaper item reports, "A young housewife was telling another young housewife about taking the car to the garage. 'The man said I needed some motor work done,' she said. 'He said I had a missing valve.' Yep, that's right, she said it: 'And I've looked all over, and can't find it.'"

Sometimes, technical jargon, foreign terms, slang, or uncommon words will confuse meaning. According to the International News Service, this public statement was made by a psychologist in defending a psychological report against charges of ambiguity made by an engineer: "The accusations are undoubtedly the manifestation of a fundamentally dichotomous role-status position in which the out-groups project their ambivalent affectual status against super-oriented members of a prestige structure which seems to threaten their affect and basic ego constellation." We sometimes hear the gobbledygook expression of *contact comfort* instead of *physical cuddling, shaving system* instead of *razor, law enforcement center* instead of *jail, microcluster of role expectations* instead of *family, motorized attendance modules* instead of *school buses, this point in time* instead of *now, terminate with extreme prejudice* instead of *kill,* and so on. In addressing the public, use with caution such terms as (1) from philosophy: *Hegelianism, panologism, logical positivism;* (2) from medicine and nursing: *DOA, I* and *D, T* and *A, gone out, colostomy;* (3) from college life: *GPA, lower division, UDC, prelims, comps, rush tea;* (4) from football: *red dog, safety dog, slot back, post pattern, live color;* (5) from slang: *carbon monkeys, admish, cuffo, chirper, wrinkle, tame, juicer, slander matchstick, bomber;* (6) from criminology: *fuzz, biscuit, boff man, Mr. Bates, sneez, schmecker, on the stride.*

Inaccuracy may also result from the careless use of everyday words with multiple meanings. Many speakers recklessly use abstract words and phrases such as *love, honor, right, wrong, big business, the moneyed interests, socialism, the American way, the farmer's needs, subsidies, plain talk, conservatism, brutality, opportunism,* and *wasteful* without definition and without recognizing that these words may have many meanings. Be certain to clarify words with multiple meanings so that your listeners understand in which sense you use them. Then stick to that definition.

(2) To be clear, language should be sufficiently *simple.* The concept of simplicity is closely related to that of accuracy. Fight the temptation to use a pretentious polysyllabic word when a simple and universally understood word will do as well or better. Use *stop would-be thieves* instead of *dissuade potential individuals with larcenous intent, evidence* instead of *evidentiary data, spanking* instead of *practical negative reinforcement, fire* instead of *conflagration, uneducated* instead of *functional*

illiterates, and *fight* instead of *highly volatile altercation.* When asked if creativity can be identified through tests, two scholars should have answered *yes,* instead of saying: "Our thesis is simple: Contrary to some literature that frees creativity from the terra firma of past experience and seems to base it on a metaphysic of ideational free-wheeling and transempirical dealing, we believe that creativity is cognitively based." When asked to report on a college experimental degree project, the committee should have stated, "Our objective should be to increase the sensitivities of adult students," instead of: "The team is considering such aims and objects as the development of intellectual consistency, the creation of aesthetic awareness, the liberation of the personality, the awakening of nonverbal and nonrational sensibilities to amplify adult experience, and the structure of an insight into the eternality of human aspiration and frustration." It is unnecessary to go to the extreme of emulating the advertiser who converted the simple, "If headaches persist or recur frequently," into the "simplest," "If headaches hang on too long or keep coming back." Nevertheless, in public speaking you should use the simple, straightforward, informal wording of intelligent, spontaneous conversation, not the stiff, involved, or abstruse style of some textbooks or scientific treatises.

(3) To be clear, language should be *concrete.* As mentioned repeatedly in previous pages, concreteness contributes to clarity by substituting particularization and specificity for generalization and abstraction. Concrete language is replete with names, dates, figures, examples, comparisons, contrasts, and qualifying adjectives and adverbs. For instance, the abstract sentence, "We spend a lot of money each year on national defense," would be much more meaningful if you specified the sum expended on defense for the current year. Even this specific figure would have relatively little meaning for most people, however; to be concrete, the statistic would have to be translated into concepts having specific meanings for the listeners. As journalist Clarence Petersen puts it,

> Unless you have something to compare it to, no measure of distance, speed, area, volume, mass, weight, temperature, time, quantity, hardness or noisiness makes much sense. It's just a number pulled out of a size 7¼ hat. You can't understand how small bacteria are, for example, until you compare one to, say, an amoeba, visible under an ordinary microscope. One way to do that: If an amoeba were the size of an elephant, a bacterium would be the size of a flea.

Language Should Be Sufficiently Objective

Objective language is grounded in fact and comparatively undistorted by emotionalism. Emotionalism in language is exemplified in the slogans, stereotypes, and "hidden persuasion" of those who wish to manipulate others. As we have seen previously, such a style attempts to bypass cerebral action by appealing to the emotional predispositions of the listeners. In persuasive speaking, you are attempting to influence belief, feeling, and/or action. To do this, you may designedly help your listeners to identify your points with their values and feelings. Thus, you may stir up appropriate emotions by means of words that, to your listeners, are rich in appropriate connotative meanings. This does not mean, however, that you should use emotive language as a substitute for sound evidence and argument. In informative speaking, your topic is noncontroversial and your purpose is to promote knowledge and understanding. Therefore, except to indicate your enthusiasm for the subject and to help the listeners to relate the subject to their wants, interests, and needs, your language should be free of bias and prejudice.

In the following inset, compare each of the inflammatory terms with the more objective usage appearing opposite to it. Notice that the inflammatory terms represent the language of conflict; they encourage emotionalism and make rational thinking difficult, if not impossible; they are typically used by persuaders who wish to bypass the listeners' cerebral processes and to evoke deep-seated emotional prejudgments.

Inflammatory	*Comparatively Objective*
fanatical rightists	followers of Ronald Reagan
socialized or political medicine	compulsory health insurance
radicals	those who belong to the Democratic party
reactionaries	those who belong to the Republican party
communists	Supreme Court justices who voted against Bible reading in the public schools
bigots	those who oppose busing
bureaucrats	those who hold positions in government
racketeer	one who has been sentenced to jail for gambling
the welfare state	a government that provides Social Security, old-age pensions, unemployment insurance, and so forth

Objective language need not be dull, lifeless, and colorless. All words, except for prepositions and the like, call forth some emotional response, and colorful words heighten interest. The use of emotional language, however, should be tempered by a respect for adequate evidence and valid reasoning.

Language Should Be Vivid and Impressive

Language possessing clarity will be understood; but if language is to hold attention, maintain interest, and create a lasting impression it must also be vivid and impressive. As discussed in Chapter 8, vividness in part results from words and phrases that arouse sense imagery in the listener.

Impressions of our environment are received through the senses—sight, hearing, taste, smell, and touch. Language imagery may evoke a particular sensory response vicariously. Thus, evocative language—or thinking, which is basically subvocal language—may cause us to remember how good the sirloin steak tasted last night, the beautiful coloring of a sunset in the Sierra Nevada Mountains, the loosely rhythmical calypso music at last week's artist series performance, or the aching muscles following an intramural wrestling match. Complex combinations of imagery resulting in new concepts beyond the scope of past experience may be called imagination. Imagery and imagination may be stimulated by words. Coupled with visual aids, physical delivery, and the speaking voice, language helps the listener to relive old experiences and to create new ones through imagination.

Vividness, like clarity, is dependent upon concreteness. Perhaps the following inset will demonstrate that specificity may produce vividness.[1]

> There is probably no culture extant today which owes more than 10 per cent of its total elements to inventions made by members of its own society....
>
> Our solid American citizen awakens in a bed built on a pattern which originated in the Near East but which was modified in Northern Europe before it was transmitted to America.... He takes off his pajamas, a garment invented in India, and washes with soap invented by the ancient Gauls....
>
> Before going out for breakfast he glances through the window, made of glass invented in Egypt, and if it is raining puts on overshoes made of rubber discovered by the Central American Indians and takes an umbrella, invented in Southeastern Asia....
>
> On his way to breakfast he stops to buy a paper, paying for it with coins, an ancient Lydian invention.... His knife is of steel, an alloy first made in southern India, his fork a medieval Italian invention, and his spoon a derivative of the Roman original....
>
> When our friend has finished eating, he settles back to smoke, an American Indian habit, consuming a plant domesticated in Brazil.... While smoking he reads the news of the day, imprinted in characters invented by the ancient Semites upon a material invented in China by a process invented in Germany. As he absorbs the accounts of foreign troubles, he will, if he is a good conservative citizen, thank a Hebrew deity in an Indo-European language that he is 100 per cent American.

Vividness also may be achieved by the use of figures of speech. Probably the most commonly used figures are the *simile* and the *metaphor*. Both are devices to compare objects or concepts basically unlike; each

[1]Ralph Linton, *The Study of Man: An Introduction* (New York: Appleton-Century-Crofts, 1936), pp. 325–27.

calls forth sharp, vivid imagery that clarifies and emphasizes (Chapter 7 contains a discussion of comparison as a form of support). A simile states a likeness between two objects of different classes and connects the two with the word *like*. For example: "The old man stood before us, gaunt and weatherbeaten, like a gnarled oak"; "She appeared fragile and unreal, like a china doll." A metaphor also compares two objects or ideas that are fundamentally different, but does so by a direct identification of the two on the basis of a common likeness. Thus, a *sharp-tongued woman* "is" a *cat; highways* "are" *arteries*, an *initial speech in a campaign* "is" the *opening gun; establishing a basis for promoting communism* "is" *sowing the seeds of communism;* and *flames spreading to the second story of a building* "are" *tongues of flame licking at the second story*. Many metaphorical expressions like the foregoing have become so universal in use that they have lost much of their power to create imagery. Choose figures that are fresh and unusual if you wish to stimulate the most vivid imagery. Be especially careful to avoid mixed figures, such as the following, which were encountered by Lawrence Harrison: "Now we've got to flush out the skeleton"; "He threw a cold shoulder on that idea"; "He deals out of both ends of his mouth"; "Let's do it and listen to how the shoe pinches"; "A study is under foot"; "The project is going to pot in a hand basket"; "We're breaking previrgin territory"; "He got off on a sour foot"; "They treated him as if he had Blue Bonnet plague"; "The issue is on the back burner in a holding pattern"; "It was a case of the tail biting the dog"; "The scientists," so stated Edward E. David, Jr., a former White House adviser, "were using science as a sledgehammer to grind their political axes."

Another useful figure is *personification*, in which ideas or inanimate objects are given certain characteristics of living beings. *Time marches on* is a commonly used example of personification. The previously cited figure, *tongues of flame licking at the second story,* utilizes personification as well as metaphor.

Vividness is closely related to impressiveness. Vivid language may elicit an intellectual-emotional response sufficiently strong to provide a lasting impression. Impressiveness also may be secured by means of the following: striking facts, statistics that are interpreted according to the experiences of the listeners, pithy quotations and epigrams, sharply etched descriptions, antitheses, parallel language structure, graphic illustrations, and the techniques of surprise, climax, suspense, and conflict.

Originality in the choice of words also lends force and impressiveness. Most of us are addicted to the use of trite phrases; in extemporizing, these expressions usually come to mind first. Unfortunately, listeners have become inured to them. Your efforts to develop fresh, original usages will be rewarded by attentive and retentive listening. The following quotations are examples of the sprightly style.

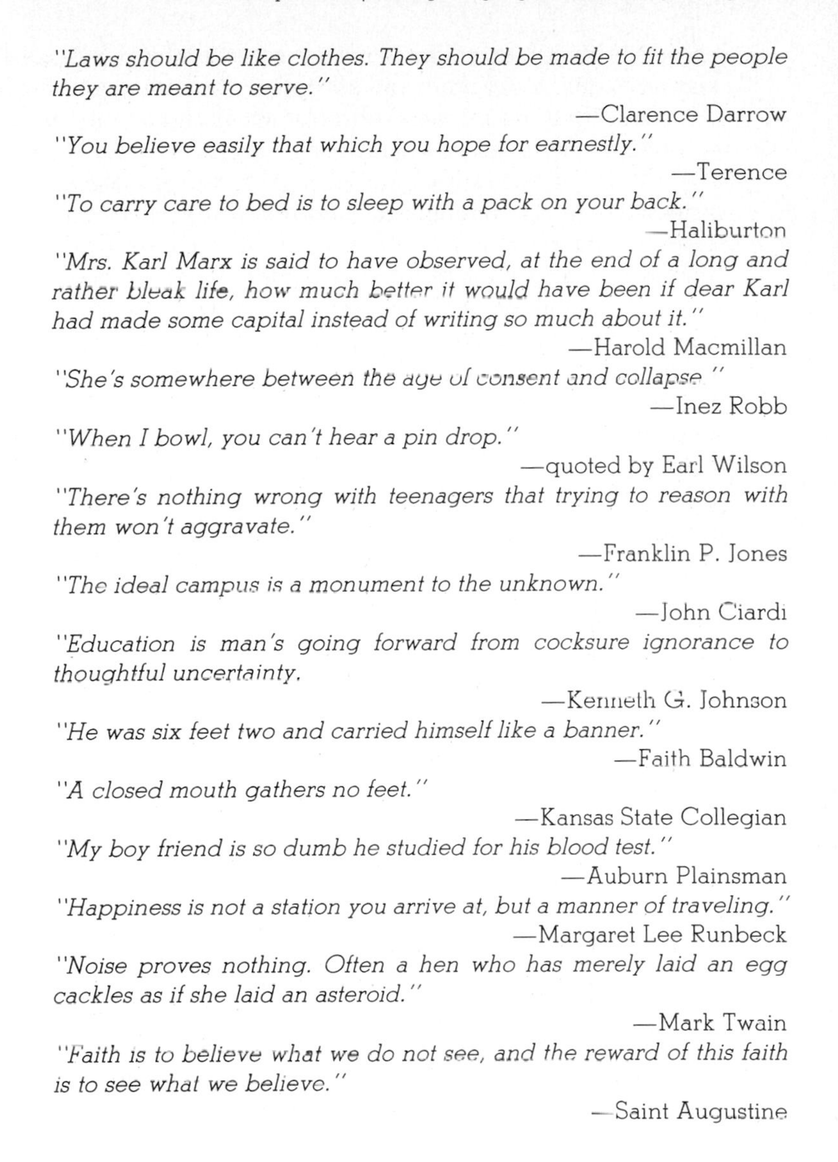

"*Laws should be like clothes. They should be made to fit the people they are meant to serve.*"

—Clarence Darrow

"*You believe easily that which you hope for earnestly.*"

—Terence

"*To carry care to bed is to sleep with a pack on your back.*"

—Haliburton

"*Mrs. Karl Marx is said to have observed, at the end of a long and rather bleak life, how much better it would have been if dear Karl had made some capital instead of writing so much about it.*"

—Harold Macmillan

"*She's somewhere between the age of consent and collapse.*"

—Inez Robb

"*When I bowl, you can't hear a pin drop.*"

—quoted by Earl Wilson

"*There's nothing wrong with teenagers that trying to reason with them won't aggravate.*"

—Franklin P. Jones

"*The ideal campus is a monument to the unknown.*"

—John Ciardi

"*Education is man's going forward from cocksure ignorance to thoughtful uncertainty.*

—Kenneth G. Johnson

"*He was six feet two and carried himself like a banner.*"

—Faith Baldwin

"*A closed mouth gathers no feet.*"

—Kansas State Collegian

"*My boy friend is so dumb he studied for his blood test.*"

—Auburn Plainsman

"*Happiness is not a station you arrive at, but a manner of traveling.*"

—Margaret Lee Runbeck

"*Noise proves nothing. Often a hen who has merely laid an egg cackles as if she laid an asteroid.*"

—Mark Twain

"*Faith is to believe what we do not see, and the reward of this faith is to see what we believe.*"

—Saint Augustine

Language Should Include an Abundant Stock of Connective and Transitional Words and Phrases

In the words of Lou Sarett, "Like coupling pins that link freight cars together, connectives insure coherence, interlock all parts, and make the sequence of ideas easy to remember." Although seemingly well-prepared, the beginning speaker frequently finds that his language effectiveness breaks down perceptibly when moving from one point to another. Even the experienced extemporizer with considerable language facility often connects ideas awkwardly and abruptly. Therefore, you should "stock up" on connective words and phrases so that transitions can be made smoothly, clearly, and with variety.

Many speakers are limited to the use of only a few connectives. Among the most common are *another thing, now, my second point is, also, for example,* and *in other words.* To achieve freshness, the speaker should have ready for instant use a wide variety of connective words and phrases, including *furthermore, moreover, meanwhile, nevertheless, whereas, on the contrary, in consequence, at the same time, in contrast to, inasmuch as,* and *on the other hand.* To promote clarity and unity, employ connective words and phrases that clearly indicate the relationship among ideas and that help to tie the ideas to the Specific Speech Purpose. Here are some examples: "The third reason why our organization should go on record as being opposed to the increase in student activity fees is. . . ."; "Now that we have established the practicality of using nuclear energy for industrial purposes, let us examine the safety aspects. . . ."; "In addition to resisting arrest and assaulting the sergeant at the desk, the defendant continued throughout the night to create a disturbance. . . ."; "As soon as the copyedited manuscript has been returned by the author, it is sent to the compositor by whom it will be set in type. . . ."

Language Should Be Arranged into Clear and Varied Sentences

Unlike the writer who may rework a sentence until it is polished to his satisfaction, in facing an audience the extemporaneous speaker has only one opportunity to compose a given sentence. "On the spot" construction frequently results in the stringing together of distantly related ideas in abstruse, complex-compound sentences; faulty syntax, producing ambiguity; and inflexible sentence structure, resulting in monotony.

The essence of the extempore mode is that words and sentences are for the most part improvised at the moment of utterance. During the speech, you are necessarily so occupied with other aspects of communication that you have little, if any, opportunity to consider principles of sentence structure. You are compelled to depend primarily upon the nearly automatic functioning of well-established habits of effective expression. The following suggestions, then, concern your long-term efforts to develop an effective oral style.

As for any other facet of oral style, the first step in improving the clarity and variety of sentences is to become actively and continuously interested in oral language. At every opportunity, listen analytically to the sentence structure used by effective speakers on radio, television, and the platform. Especially by listening repeatedly to the same speaker, such as a news commentator, you can become sensitively attuned to his style. Study printed speeches, especially those given under informal circumstances. (Those delivered at formal occasions, such as the State of the Union Message or a governor's inaugural address, may use a formality of language usage and sentence structure that is unsuitable to your purposes.) Practice writing speeches that you can read orally and deliver extemporaneously in your room. Record such practice speeches and (if the procedure does not make you self-conscious) your class speeches on tape; play back the tape to observe your sentence structure.

In your self-help program, keep in mind the following suggestions:

(1) Sentences should be relatively short, probably under a dozen words on the average. Short sentences are usually more easily understood.

(2) Occasionally, use longer sentences (thirty words or more) to help provide variety and avoid choppiness and lack of rhythm.

(3) Secure freshness and interest by employing a variety of sentence types. Whereas the majority of your sentences will begin with the subject and end with the predicate, do not neglect the periodic structure, in which the order is reversed, with the conditional elements appearing first. For example, the following construction is loose: "Inflation could be curbed if every citizen would buy only what he needs, avoid excessive installment buying, and invest in government bonds." The occasional inversion of such a sentence provides greater interest and suspense: "If every citizen would buy only what he needs, avoid excessive installment buying, and invest in government bonds, inflation could be curbed." Another type, the balanced sentence, sometimes uses antithesis for emphasis. To illustrate, "If I go to a movie, I'll fail the exam; if I stay home and study, I'll pass."

(4) Make liberal use of interrogative, exclamatory, and imperative sentences to add balance, variety, and persuasiveness. Although declarative sentences predominate in a written style, interrogative, exclamatory, and imperative sentences appear in great numbers in an effective oral style. Direct and rhetorical questions have been discussed earlier in this chapter. Exclamatory sentences may also enliven style. For example, a speaker at a Republican rally might say, "Some nostalgic Democrats still think that Senator Kennedy's promises will lead to the promised land. Well, we know better! The Democrats' promised land is just that: a land of empty promises!" Listeners sometimes react strongly to the exhortation of imperative sentences, such as "Don't forget! Be here on time!"; "Open your hearts and your minds!"; "Vote out the reformers!"; "Look out for snakes."

Language Should Be Chosen from a Constantly Increasing Speaking Vocabulary

Since all the foregoing advice for developing an effective oral style basically depends upon your choice of individual words, the final suggestion is to build a consistently larger *speaking* vocabulary. Although dictionaries list hundreds of thousands of words, most of us are fortunate if we can count 35,000 of these in our reading vocabularies. Our writing and listening vocabularies are much smaller, and our stock of words available for facile use in extempore speaking is much smaller yet.

Although one should constantly work to stretch his basic vocabulary by wide reading, by a close familiarity with a good dictionary and thesaurus, and by developing "word consciousness" and "word interest," of even greater importance to the speaker is the growth of his active speaking vocabulary. Your primary effort, therefore, should be directed toward the consistent transfer of words from your reading and writing vocabularies to your active speaking vocabulary. An increased word supply should help you in expressing thought clearly, simply, vividly, and impressively.

Summary

Keep these general principles in mind in developing an oral style: (1) words are symbols having meaning only in terms of associations established between symbols and the objects or concepts to which they refer; (2) words never represent completely the objects or ideas they symbolize; (3) meaning cannot be "transmitted"; it can only be stirred up in the listener; and (4) word meanings are constantly changing.

The following principles should guide the speaker in developing an effective oral style: (1) language should be designed primarily to be heard, not to be read; (2) it should be adapted to the speaker's personality, audience, and occasion; (3) it should be clear; (4) it should be reasonably objective; (5) it should be vivid and impressive; (6) it should include a variety of connective and transitional words and phrases; (7) it should be arranged into clear and varied sentences; and (8) it should be chosen from a constantly increasing *speaking* vocabulary.

Exercises and Assignments

1. Examine carefully the language used in a published essay, a theme you have written for English composition class, or a newspaper article. Is the language better adapted to reading or listening? Rewrite the selection to conform more closely to the requisites of oral style. Hand to your instructor the original and your rewritten version.

2. List ten words whose meaning have undergone considerable change in the last fifty years. Trace each change by a series of short written definitions.

3. Make a list of the hackneyed words and phrases used in a debate, discussion, or on a radio or television panel show. Opposite each word or phrase written on your paper write a more original usage.

4. Evaluate the language in a printed speech (consult *Vital Speeches,* a bimonthly publication, or look under the subject "speeches" in the library file catalogs) for (1) clarity, (2) objectivity, and (3) vividness and impressiveness. Support your judgments with examples from the text of the speech. Give an oral report of your findings to the class.

5. Rewrite a speech made by a public official or a faculty member. Attempt to make the style more informal and idiomatic.

6. Examine for the use of loaded words the language used in several newspaper, radio, or television advertisements, or in a political address. Have these words or phrases been used to mask faulty reasoning? Rewrite, substituting a more objective term for each loaded word. Does this weaken the persuasive power of the advertisement? Discuss in class.

7. Bring to class a written list of ten unusual figures of speech. A student committee may be appointed to combine the individual lists into one large one, which may be Xeroxed for distribution to the class. Attempt to use several of these figures in your remaining class speeches. Save the list for future use.

8. In your next speech, attempt through careful word choice to arouse vivid sense imagery involving at least two of the senses.

9. Record a three-minute extemporaneous speech. Listen carefully to the playback for (1) a rough estimate of average sentence length, (2) the possible predominance of one type of sentence structure at the expense of others, (3) long, involved sentences, (4) an excessive number of short, choppy sentences occurring in succession, (5) needless repetition of some words and phrases, and (6) an insufficient variety of connective and transitional words and phrases. It may be necessary to listen to the playback several times in order to complete these observations. Take notes rather than to rely on memory. Attempt to improve your extemporaneous style on the basis of this analysis.

10. Make a list of one hundred words whose meanings you know, but which you rarely if ever use in extemporaneous speaking. Attempt to include at least three of them in your next speech. Add several others from the list to each future speech until you have used each at least once and preferably several times before the end of the course.

SECTION V

Adapting Basic Techniques to Special Forms of Speaking

Essential Purpose of Section V: to enable the reader to apply basic principles in preparing and delivering speeches of special types

CHAPTER 16

Speeches of Special Types

The Impromptu Speech

Almost everyone is called upon at some time to face an audience without opportunity for preparation. In fact, the more widely known a speaker becomes the more often he will be asked "to say a few words." Conceivably, when a preceding discussion has been stimulating and the speaker has been called upon to discuss briefly a familiar subject, his speaking may exhibit a spontaneity and fluency not characteristic of his prepared talks. Such effectiveness depends primarily upon a favorable combination of circumstances. The inexperienced speaker who has felt a pleasurable glow as the result of having spoken impromptu with success or even brilliance should not be misled into a reliance upon inspirations of the moment. Impromptu speaking is usually unsatisfactory, especially when more than a few remarks are required. Many a speaker who is thoroughly competent when he has had an opportunity to plan and rehearse, finds that the task of thinking through a full-length speech while on his feet is difficult if not impossible.

As was indicated in Chapter 12, there are suggestions that will help the average speaker to meet successfully an impromptu situation. First, if you suspect that you might be called upon, pay close attention to the discussion from the floor and from the platform. If you can do so unobtrusively, jot down a few salient notations of the proceedings. Observe that you disagree with a point some speaker has made, that an erroneous conclusion has been drawn, or that obvious arguments are being overlooked. In this way, you are gathering speech materials and are organizing your thinking.

Second, utilize the brief interim between the call to speak and your first words to control your emotions and to plan what you are going to say. Do not waste emotional energy with feelings of fear or despair. Recognize that a rush of adrenalin into the bloodstream is inevitable. Such is nature's way of preparing the body for an emergency. Be grateful that you are so stimulated; without such motive power you probably could not meet the occasion adequately. Control this surge of energy. Relax by taking several deep breaths and by making a conscious effort to ease muscular tension. Rise to your feet calmly. If you are expected to speak from a podium, walk deliberately without hesitation or undue haste. Before beginning your impromptu talk, look at the audience, ordinarily address the chairman, take a full breath, and start to speak.

At the same time that you are preparing yourself physically, you should also be planning what you are going to say. Almost any impromptu speech can be organized according to the following plan:

I. POINT Step (Tell the audience in a clear statement what you will attempt to establish in your speech.)
II. Reason Step (State a reason why your POINT is valid.)
III. Evidence Step (Support your reason by means of illustration, comparison, quotation, or statistic.)
IV. Restatement of POINT Step

This schematic organizational plan represents the minimum demands upon the impromptu speaker. Ordinarily, you should be able to think of *more than one reason* why the audience might accept the POINT you are attempting to make. Actually, this simple outline represents nothing new to the reader. According to the tripartite method of development (Introduction, Body, and Conclusion), such a plan would have the following heads:

Introduction:
I. State the POINT of your speech
Body:
I. Give a reason why your POINT is valid
A. Offer some evidence to support your reason
Conclusion:
I. Summarize the gist of the speech by restating the POINT

Now, let us see how this plan would operate under various circumstances.

(1) Upon being asked a question, you might repeat the interrogation and then answer it in one sentence. Your answer, of course, is the POINT of your talk. Give a reason or reasons why you have answered the question as you have. Back up your reason(s) with supporting evidence. In conclusion, restate your answer.

(2) If you believe that an important argument has been omitted in the earlier discussion, state as your POINT that the particular argument has been overlooked. Tell why you think this new point of view is important or germane. Support your reason(s). Then, as a summary, say that you feel the argument merits the consideration of the group because of the reasons given.

(3) To persuade your listeners that a particular proposal should be rejected, state as your POINT that you believe the argument to be invalid. Point out as your reason(s) that those who have supported the measure have used faulty reasoning, misleading statistics, untrustworthy testimony, or atypical examples; explain and support your reason(s); and restate your POINT.

(4) A careful study of the elements of problem solving, discussed in Chapter 6, will be of considerable aid in meeting many impromptu situations. For instance, if the seriousness of a problem under discussion has been exaggerated, state as your POINT that you feel the problem is not as severe as has been presented. Give reasons with evidence why this is so. Then restate your POINT. Follow this basic procedure when you believe that important causes of a problem have been overlooked or distorted, and when it seems evident that the proposed solution would not solve the problem, could not be put into effect, would create additional severe problems, or is not the best solution.

The Manuscript Speech

Many persons in business, government, and the professions choose to read the majority of their speeches rather than to deliver them extemporaneously. Several factors may account for the frequent use of the manuscript speech. If a speech is broadcast or telecast, it must be timed very carefully; furthermore, stations may ask to examine the test of a speaker's remarks prior to the broadcast. The possibility that an address may be quoted in whole or in part prompts many speakers to read rather than extemporize in order to assure exactness in language. Many who are faced with frequent speaking obligations have had little if any training or experience in extemporizing from notes, and are too busy to undertake a program to develop this skill. Distrusting their ability to extemporize, they choose to read from a manuscript, particularly if the speaking occasion is an important one.

Is it a wise decision to read rather than to talk? Many speech teachers advise students not to read from a manuscript, except in situations where exactness in language or timing is mandatory. Such teachers offer two primary objections to the manuscript speech. The first of these is that a manuscript imposes severe limitations upon flexibility, with the result that adjustments to the audience and occasion are difficult to make during the presentation of the speech. When reading a manuscript, the speaker may find it difficult, if not impossible, to make changes in word choice, phrasing, or content. If the manuscript speech is to be broadcast or telecast, straying from the written words invites trouble in concluding the speech on time. Only the experienced speaker dares take such liberties with a radio or television speech. In defense of the manuscript speech, however, it should be pointed out that if the situation permits and the speaker is sufficiently skilled, considerable flexibility may be achieved by omissions, extemporaneous insertions, and word substitutions.

The second common objection to reading a speech is that it often results in ineffective oral and physical delivery. Such a criticism is undoubtedly based upon the valid observation that most persons are unskilled at oral reading. It does not follow, however, that because the majority of us do not read aloud with skill the manuscript speech is to be avoided; by such reasoning, another large group of speakers who lack the ability to extemporize well would be advised to avoid the extemporaneous mode!

The position of this text is that it is unrealistic to expect experienced speakers to shun the manuscript speech. Many who extemporize with skill deliberately choose to read their speeches on frequent occasions. They do so because they recognize certain advantages to be enjoyed by the speaker who can read well. One advantage is the polish in style attainable in a carefully prepared manuscript. A well-written speech possesses clarity, conciseness, vividness, impressiveness, and other language attributes to a degree that can be equaled only by a few extremely effective extemporizers. Not only does such a polished style evoke favorable audience response but it also permits the speech to stand the scrutiny of those who may later study and analyze a published text of the remarks.

Effective manuscript reading, while posing some genuine problems, offers certain advantages to the skilled speaker. By acquiring skill in both reading and extemporizing, one is free to choose the mode that seems better adapted to a given situation.

The remainder of this section discusses the ways in which the fundamental principles of speech preparation and delivery (Chapters 1–13) may be adapted to facilitate the effective composition, rehearsal, and presentation of the manuscript speech.

Preparing the Manuscript Speech

It should be made clear at the outset that the manuscript speech cannot be classified as a *special type,* in the same sense as most other types of speeches treated in this chapter. A manuscript speech may seek to inform, persuade, or entertain. With the exception of the impromptu speech, the special types discussed in this chapter may on occasion be read, although some of them are usually more effective when extemporized. The manuscript speech may not be characterized, therefore, on the basis of general or specific purpose; rather, it is differentiated from other types of speeches essentially by certain characteristics of preparation, rehearsal, and delivery.

In preparing the manuscript speech, the following sequence may be helpful: (1) *Develop your outline;* (2) *write the first draft of your manuscript;* (3) *revise your first draft;* and (4) *prepare your final copy.*

Develop Your Outline. The initial phase in your preparation should be identical with that of the extemporized speech. You should choose your subject, gather materials, and develop an outline containing an Introduction, Body, and Conclusion. Although some experienced speakers plan only a very rough preliminary outline of what they wish to say, the novice should develop a detailed outline before attempting to write the first draft.

Write the First Draft of Your Manuscript. Before beginning to write, possibly you should re-examine Chapter 15 ("Using Language in Delivering the Speech") to remind yourself of the characteristics of good oral style. In particular, be aware of the necessity of choosing words which are clear, objective, vivid, and impressive. Avoid long, complicated sentence structure, and exercise economy in the use of words. *Do not write an essay.* Make certain that your manuscript is written in language meant primarily to be heard, rather than to be read. It may help to dictate to a secretary, if one is available; by so doing, your composition may acquire more of the qualities of oral style.

Keep your outline constantly before you to guide the organization and development of your speech. A complete, well-developed outline may simplify the task of writing.

Revise Your First Draft. When you have finished the first draft, read it aloud to check the overall timing and the degree of ease with which the individual words and combinations of words lend themselves to oral reading. The extent of revision necessary will obviously depend upon how closely the first draft adheres to time limits, and to what extent it reflects the previously noted attributes of effective oral language.

Strict timing must be achieved if the speech is to be broadcast or telecast. If the manuscript is too long, delete words, phrases, and sentences until it is no more than one-half minute longer or shorter than the prescribed time. It is safer to be too short than too long. Although timing need not be as precise in face-to-face speaking, do not vary significantly from the time allotted you. Careful revision should enable you to adhere closely to time limits.

Revision should also be guided by your knowledge of the principles of effective language. Do you find awkward and complicated sentences? Break them up into shorter, simpler units. Does your language seem wordy? Cut out unnecessary words and phrases, or restate entire portions more concisely. Does every word clearly express the meaning you intend? Eliminate vague and inaccurate terms. Are important points adequately developed? Amplify ideas that seem to need further emphasis. Have you made liberal use of appropriate figures of speech, parallel structure, and other techniques for achieving vividness and impressiveness? Take the time needed to develop these language attributes during revision. Are you guilty of too frequent use of favorite words and phrases? Find substitutes to break up excessive repetition.

Occasionally, revision may turn a speech into an essay. In attempting to polish the first draft, do not sacrifice those qualities of language that tend to establish a direct and personal relationship between speaker and audience, and which provide for instant comprehension of meaning.

Most of the changes you decide upon may be made on the copy of the first draft. However, if deleted portions, crossed-out words, and written-in sections are abundant on certain pages, retype or rewrite them at once (unless you plan to begin the final draft without delay); later on, such pages may be incomprehensible.

Prepare Your Final Copy. The concluding step in preparing the manuscript speech is to write the final copy for use in delivery. *Do not practice delivery with the marked-up revision; only the final copy should be used for rehearsal.* In order to promote maximum audience contact and to facilitate rapid comprehension when glancing at your manuscript, you should become familiar with the particular copy you intend to use in delivery.

Observe these rules when preparing the final copy:

(1) *Use reasonably stiff paper.* Paper without sufficient body may curl when placed on a lectern or table, or may be difficult to control when held in the speaker's hands. Heavy bond paper or note cards will prove to be better choices.

(2) *Use paper or cards of the proper size.* For most persons, paper of the popular 8½″ by 11″ size is slightly too large to permit easy holding of the manuscript and turning of the pages. More usable is the 8½″ by 5½″ size derived from cutting the former size page horizontally in half. If you prefer, use note-cards instead of paper.

(3) *Use only one side of the paper.* To use both sides of a card or sheet of paper may confuse you during delivery; you may not always be sure whether you are reading the first or second side of a given sheet of paper.

(4) *Number your pages.* Numbering will facilitate rapid rearrangement if an improper sequence is discovered during delivery. The number should appear in the same place on each page—probably the upper right-hand corner is most convenient.

(5) *Type your manuscript with double or triple spacing.* Unless your handwriting is unusually legible, have your speech typed to ensure easy reading. Exclusive use of capital letters will aid those who find small letters difficult to see. Double or triple spacing between the lines tends to prevent confusing one line with another during delivery.

(6) *Arrange your material into short paragraphs.* Short paragraphs are easier for the eye to encompass, and facilitate keeping one's place on the page.

(7) *Maintain neatness.* Unless absolutely necessary, avoid such last-minute changes as crossed-out passages, interlinear insertions, and erasures. If your final copy is to possess maximum readability, it must be clean and neat.

Rehearsing the Manuscript Speech

The primary purpose of rehearsing the manuscript speech is to establish such familiarity with the ideas, phrasing, and wording that you can read it with maximum spontaneity, meaning, directness, and enthusiasm. Effective delivery may be accomplished by observing the following sequence of procedures.

(1) Read the speech aloud a number of times, keeping your eyes on the manuscript as much as necessary.

(2) If you find the procedure helpful, mark your script to indicate emphasis, pauses, and vocal phrases. Although some speakers find that such markings make them excessively word-conscious and tend to destroy spontaneous delivery, others rate these markings as unusually helpful. During rehearsal you might experiment with script markings and compare the results with those obtained with an unmarked script. If you decide to use markings, underline words that should receive special emphasis; use a diagonal line (/) to designate points at which a short pause would be

appropriate, and a double diagonal line (//) to indicate the need for an extended pause.

(3) By acquiring close familiarity with the script, as previously discussed, you will reduce dependence upon it; by practicing to increase the number of words you can encompass in a glance, the frequency with which you need to glance at your paper will be reduced. First, look at the page and concentrate; then, deliver as many as words as possible without looking down; finally, consult the page again and repeat the procedure. By rehearsing, you will gradually increase your visual span until you can grasp long phrases and sentences in a short glance and deliver them without hesitation or looking down. However, when you take a manuscript to the stand, you should read from it rather than recite most of the speech from memory.

(4) Practice to acquire ease in handling the manuscript. Placing it on the speaker's stand, as is usually recommended, will free your hands for gesturing, but will tie you closely to the lectern. Holding the papers in your hands will permit unrestricted movement about the platform, but will limit hand gestures, will attract attention to the manuscript, and will pose special problems in handling the manuscript. During rehearsal, if you decide to hold the script, keep it at the proper level; you should not be compelled to bend your head down, nor should the pages conceal your face from the audience; when you have completed the reading of a page, move it easily to one side and place it under the pile.

Delivering the Manuscript Speech

In addition to observing the fundamental principles of good delivery, consider the following suggestions.

(1) Endeavor to *rethink* and *recreate* the speech at the time of presentation. Whereas the extemporaneous speaker is forced to think of his ideas in order to choose his words, the manuscript speaker is seemingly relieved of this necessity to think—his words are before him. To neglect thinking of ideas, however, makes the speaker word-conscious, and usually results in a monotonous presentation. Concentrate on meanings, therefore, rather than words, if you are to speak with appropriate emphasis, proper phrasing, and enthusiasm.

(2) Be particularly conscious of rate. Although you may have established an appropriate rate in rehearsal, the tendency during delivery is to accelerate perceptibly. Relieved of the necessity of "finding" words to express your ideas, you may be tempted to increase your rate, particularly if tense and anxious to finish. Excessive speed is frequently accompanied by inadequate emphasis, slurring, and mumbling.

(3) Do not attempt to conceal your manuscript or apologize for the fact that you are reading.

If you follow suitable procedures in preparing the manuscript and in rehearsing, and if you endeavor to recreate the speech while reading it, your presentation of the manuscript speech should be successful.

The After-Dinner Speech

The after-dinner speech is one of the most common of the various types of occasional speeches. Probably all civilized and barbaric peoples engage in after-dinner speaking, Once, following a meal of roast pig, the famed explorer, Frank Buck, sat around the campfire in interior Africa with his native hosts. After Buck had solicited their aid in the preparation of a motion picture, several natives offered constructive suggestions. There, in the wilderness a program of after-dinner speaking was taking place. From Fairbanks to Cape Town and from Archangel to Brisbane, men and women engage in public speech over dining tables.

Despite its frequent occurrence, the after-dinner speech is the most difficult to define of all the types of occasional speeches. Almost any original oral communication lasting long enough to be considered a speech, and taking place after some meal, may be termed an after-dinner speech. Other writers have pointed out that the after-dinner speech is not actually a *type,* but rather a *class,* of speeches. A talk following a dinner might range from a serious, dignified presentation of a problem to a hilarious selection of anecdotes.

The Serious After-Dinner Speech

A majority of after-dinner speeches are basically serious. Dinners, lunches, suppers, and even breakfasts often serve as the occasion for serious speaking. Top-drawer executives frequently engage in policy determination over the table cloth; Community Fund committees meet at dinners to plan campaigns; fraternities pay tribute at banquets to the founders of their orders; representatives of labor and management gather in dining rooms to discuss the probable effects of some recent federal legislation. Speeches delivered at such occasions might seek to inform, convince, stimulate, or actuate.

In preparing the serious after-dinner speech you should follow the suggestions given in earlier chapters; essential principles remain the same, whether the speech is presented in a restaurant or in a labor hall. In some respects the after-dinner audience may be easier to please. Inasmuch as the auditors have eaten together in pleasant surroundings and have engaged in congenial conversation, they may tend to feel comfortable and relaxed. The occasion itself has produced a friendly in-group feeling. In other ways, of course, such an audience presents a more difficult challenge. Everyone tends to experience a "logy" sensation immediately after eating, with a corresponding decline in mental and physical efficiency. If serious speeches are in order, they should be developed in a vivid, sparkling, interesting manner. Long chains of logical reasoning, detailed arguments, dull statistics, and the like will drug most after-dinner audiences into sluggish apathy. Do not let your speech drag; possibly make greater use of illustrations and analogies than usual; use a liberal sprinkling of relevant humor; speak with animation and warmth; let your manner reflect congeniality and sincerity. Do not permit your speech to become heavy or otherwise unpalatable.

The Entertaining After-Dinner Speech

Fortunately, the after-dinner audience is in a mood to be entertained. Relatively little stiffness or unyielding dignity is present in most situations where entertaining speeches are appropriate. Your speech is expected to be consistent with the general mood of relaxation and congeniality. Since the format of the typical entertaining after-dinner speech is based upon humor, review the rules prescribed in Chapter 8 for the satisfactory use of humor, that is, recall that humor should be relevant, appropriate, fresh, compact, and pointed. A diverting after-dinner speech needs to be planned as carefully as a serious one. However, you should keep your organization sufficiently fluid to be able to make on-the-spot adaptations to the speaking situation. Listen carefully to the conversations at your table during the meal and to the other speakers. Frequently, some chance remark or unusual happening, when incorporated into the speech in the appropriate place, can serve as an extremely effective source of humor. When the chairman introduces you, listen thoughtfully with the expectation of tying in your speech with some facetious comment he may have made. Once a petite woman was introduced by a jovial six-foot toastmaster with the remark that the speaker was so small he could put her in his pocket. Upon arising, the woman won a terrific response from the audience by her saucy retort: "In that case, Mr. Toastmaster, you'd have more brains in your pocket than you have in your head." Such repartee, though perhaps appropriate in a jocular situation, might be out of place at a more dignified occasion. Like all humor, playful digs at the chairman should always be in good taste.

In order to be effective the entertaining after-dinner speech must be well planned and rehearsed, be appropriate to the speaker, the audience, and the occasion, and must possess charm in content and presentation.

The Speech of Goodwill

The extensive growth of public relations departments in business and industry in recent years reflects a growing sensitivity to public opinion. Modern advertising promotes friendship as well as sales. The United States Steel Corporation, for example, appears almost as interested in promoting goodwill as in selling steel. Interest in securing the goodwill of the public is evidenced also by nonprofit organizations, community projects, pressure groups, educational and religious institutions, and governmental agencies.

Most public and private institutions are aware of the power of the spoken word as one means of achieving successful public relations. Many of these groups encourage their officers and administrative personnel to appear publicly on behalf of the company; some have organized speakers' bureaus to arrange public speaking engagements for employees; still others schedule company-sponsored courses in effective speaking for interested personnel.

If you presently hold, or someday hope to secure, a responsible position in business or government, or if you are reasonably active in volunteer work in your community, you will probably be asked to prepare and deliver speeches of goodwill on behalf of your organization.

While any speech seeks a favorable attitude toward the speaker and his subject, the goodwill speech has as its primary goal the winning of friends for the speaker's organization, project, or cause. Ultimately, this friendship may result in money for a project, increased patronage, favorable legislation, or votes. The *apparent* purpose of the speech of goodwill is to inform the audience about the speaker's organization or cause and to indicate how it performs valuable services for the listeners and their community; the *implicit* purpose is to persuade the audience to lend its friendship and support to the organization.

The persuasive techniques employed to achieve the implicit purpose must be *unobtrusive* and *direct.* Overt persuasive devices have no place in the speech of goodwill; using them puts an audience "on its guard." If you openly exhort your audience to give money, buy products, or vote for a candidate, your primary purpose is to secure action, not to seek goodwill; if you plead for belief in a principle or directly attack your opposition, your primary purpose is to convince rather than to secure goodwill. Thus, a speech of goodwill on the subject of the Red Cross might trace its history, outline its functions, and offer its services, but would not include an open plea for financial support. A speech on behalf of the Central Power and Lighting Company might review its superior service record, offer its special free consulting service for proper indoor illumination, and conclude with a demonstration of new lighting techniques. Omitted, however, would be any derogatory reference to public ownership of utilities or any overt plea for support of legislation favorable to private utilities.

Among the most common occasions for the speech of goodwill are luncheon meetings, service and social club gatherings, school and college assemblies, and convention programs.

With some adaptations, the following formula for the development of the goodwill speech should fit any subject and occasion:

I. *Your Introduction should arouse curiosity about the institution or cause you represent.*
(You may open by referring to the importance of this opportunity to speak, by complimenting the audience or by using any of the other attention-getting devices discussed in Chapter 10. To arouse curiosity, you might present a few unusual, startling, or novel facts concerning your organization, such as its amazing growth, volume of business, service record, and so on.)

II. *Explain how your organization is designed to meet the needs of the community.*
(Here you may need to explain something of the background, development, and organization of your cause. These facts should be as novel and interesting as possible. Since you are an employee or representative of your institution, you may be in a position to reveal information not commonly known. Your audience will appreciate hearing the "inside story." Stress the services your group offers to the community. Do not boast about its financial success, its nationwide reputation, or its superiority to competitors or similar organizations. Do not ask for approval or argue for support. Assume that your audience is already favorable to your group.)

III. *Indicate in what way your organization can directly benefit your listeners.*
(Your speech of goodwill may conclude by your offering special services to the audience. Obviously, the specific method used will depend upon the nature of the service. You may demonstrate a model of an ideal kitchen; you might pass out literature or distribute coupons entitling the signer to visit the company's plant or attend a demonstration; or you may explain precisely where and when your organization makes its services available, and what steps may be taken to secure them. Be sure that your offer of services is specific as to *time, place,* and *nature.* Avoid leaving your listeners with the vague impression that somewhere and sometimes you hope to be able to serve them. Do not conclude with obvious pleas for sympathy, understanding, patronage, contributions, votes, or membership. Your conclusion should stress what your organization can do for the audience, not what the audience can do for your organization.)

The fundamental principles of effective delivery for all speaking occasions apply in presenting the speech of goodwill. The following characteristics of speech personality are particularly important: (1) Be *genial.* Avoid seeming overzealous and polemic. A friendly, easygoing approach is essential. (2) Be *enthusiastic* and *lively.* Without overdoing it, demonstrate that you are "sold" on your organization or cause, and that you are pleased to discuss its functions and services. Your audience may catch some of your spirit. (3) Be *modest.* Do not let your enthusiasm for your cause lead you to adopt a superior, arrogant manner. Beware of overselling yourself or your organization. (4) Be *tolerant.* Your manner, as well as the content of your speech, should show tolerance and magnanimity, particularly toward competing organizations. Should reference be made to competitors in a question period following your speech, your attitude should be one of politeness and diplomacy.

The Speeches of Courtesy

The Speech of Introduction

If you are reasonably active in the social and civic affairs of your community, undoubtedly you will be asked some time to present a speaker to an audience. At first glance such an assignment would seem exceedingly simple. Unfortunately, far more ineffectual speeches of introduction are given than good ones. With inexcusable frequency speeches of introduction say too much or too little, are too long or too brief, embarrass the guest speaker with flattery, or deaden audience anticipation with hackneyed, insipid comments. The following discussion may help you to avoid these typical errors and to deliver a speech of introduction with felicity and ease.

The basic purpose of the speech of introduction is to stimulate a favorable attitude toward the speaker and his subject. You are a salesman in the limited sense that you are exciting a feeling of anticipation, a desire to hear this particular speaker on this particular subject. Here are five suggestions to help you prepare an introductory speech.

Analyze the Audience, Occasion, the Guest Speaker, and the Nature of His Speech. Your introduction should be skillfully adjusted to the nature and mood of your audience, the character and purpose of the meeting, the personality and status of the guest speaker, and the general tenor of his speech. When possible, you should consult the speaker himself to ascertain what *he* would like to have you say or, equally important, what he might prefer your *not* saying. Check the accuracy of the data you plan to use with the speaker himself.

Be Brief but Adequate. As a general rule, the speech of introduction should last at least twenty seconds, but should not exceed two minutes. Ordinarily, the better known the speaker is, the shorter the necessary introduction. In 1915, Shailer Mathews set the prototype for future presentations of the nation's chief executive by this concise introduction of Woodrow Wilson: "Ladies and gentlemen, the President." For most situations, however, such an introduction would be abrupt, almost to the point of rudeness. In most cases you should help arouse interest in the speaker's subject and in the speaker himself.

Exercise Good Taste. (1) Subordinate yourself and your speech in order to focus proper attention upon the speaker and his address. Any unnecessary discussion about yourself or your ideas on the subject helps defeat the purpose of your speech. Remember that you are not competing for attention with the main speaker. On the contrary, the more attention you steal, the poorer is your introduction.

(2) Do not embarrass the speaker by extravagant praise. Tell only enough of his exploits to establish him as a person of character and stature, and to stimulate audience anticipation. Do not compliment him so profusely that he will be unable to live up to expectations. On the other hand, be certain to do him justice. Indicate that there is much that you could say if time permitted. Avoid such unflattering remarks as: "I don't know very much about this man," or "Our speaker has been somewhat successful in business." The anticipation of hearing a personnel expert was diminished instead of increased for one audience because of this discouraging introduction: "The next speaker is a former schoolteacher who quit his job because he got tired of teaching. It seems like teachers and farmers are chronically dissatisfied. After he quit teaching he got a job in our personnel department. To be truthful, I don't know what he does. I talked to a couple of people in the personnel office this afternoon and asked them—and they didn't know either. However, let's hear a few words from him. OK, Doctor———, that's your cue."

(3) Do not make the speaker's mission more difficult by calling attention to his speaking ability. A chairman once mentioned to Robert Ingersoll, one of the finest speakers in the history of American public address, that he intended to introduce him as the world's greatest orator. Ingersoll is said to have exploded that he would rather be presented as an atheist than as an orator. He did not want the attention of the audience distracted from his message to his techniques of delivery.

(4) Provided it is used in good taste, humor is unexcelled for producing an atmosphere of congeniality. It serves to put both the speaker and the audience at ease. But humor must fit the speaking situation, the speaker you are introducing, and his speech. It is always poor form to make a goat of the speaker or to belittle either his subject or the occasion.

(5) Good taste demands that you avoid trite expressions such as: "Our speaker needs no introduction," "It is an honor and a privilege," "We are indeed fortunate to have with us," or "A person who is an outstanding pillar of society."

Plan Your Comments in a Climactic Order. With some variations, the following organization will fit most speeches of introduction:

I. *Address the audience*
(If the audience is unusually large or distinguished, if it has endured inclement weather to attend, if it is especially enthusiastic, and so on, you might make an appropriate compliment. If suitable, you might make a brief reference to the occasion or purpose of the meeting.)

II. *Direct favorable attention toward the speaker*
(Tell briefly and modestly of the background of the speaker which qualifies him to speak on the subject. Build a friendly feeling toward him and stimulate a desire to hear him speak.)

III. *Direct favorable attention toward the speaker's subject*
(Mention briefly the significance and the appropriateness of the subject. Do not say too much because you might infringe upon the speaker's address. Attempt to arouse an interest in the subject so as to make the speaker's task less difficult.)

IV. *Announce the speaker by name*
(Probably you should withhold the name of the speaker until the final sentences. With a slight increase in force and volume, make a formal presentation in some such phrase as: "It is with pleasure that I present to you, Dr. Edward B. Hopkins. Dr. Hopkins"; "I give you the Honorable Robert L. Warner. Senator Warner"; or "Here he is, ladies and gentlemen—the greatest football coach in America—Tom Landry.")

Speak Sincerely and Enthusiastically in the Extemporaneous Mode. As in most other types of occasional speaking, avoid obviously reading the speech of introduction. Also, since such speeches place a high premium upon spontaneity, verbatim memorization probably should be avoided. If you use the organizational pattern suggested in the preceding paragraphs, and if you rehearse adequately, you should have little difficulty remembering what you wish to say. Your delivery should be adapted to the dignity or informality of the occasion. Use adequate volume and projection to ensure easy audibility for all listeners. Address the audience rather than the speaker. Reduce your rate of utterance somewhat from that of ordinary speaking. Enunciate clearly, especially when announcing the speaker's name and his topic. Let your manner indicate that *you* are awaiting the speech with pleasant anticipation.

The Speech of Presentation

Many organizations utilize public observances to present awards, gifts, and memorials. Industrial concerns award diamond stickpins to employees with thirty years of service; Boy Scout troops give waterproof matchboxes to the boys who sell the most tickets to the annual jamboree; universities distribute scholarships on honor days and bestow honorary degrees at commencement programs to prominent citizens; sportswriters present trophies to outstanding athletes; civic groups present statues to the community. At each such event appropriate speeches must accompany the awarding of the gift. Such presentations should be well suited to the audience, the donor, the purpose of the meeting, the recipient of the gift, the gift itself, and to you as the speaker. Your talk should be brief, usually under five minutes. Carefully prepare your speech to accomplish the following points.

I. *Tell why the presentation is being made*
(Direct attention to the achievements, services, or qualities of the recipient that warrant the presentation. If a contest was held to determine the winner, such as a popularity poll or a beauty contest, explain the nature of the contest briefly. In the case of a memorial, tell something of the character and qualities of the person or group of persons being honored. Praise should always be genuine and sincere, without straining for effect. If the recipient has been selected to accept a gift as a symbol for a group, praise the ideals, purposes, or services of the group as well as those of the recipient.)

II. *Express the satisfaction felt by the donor in making the presentation*
(Identify the donor, if different from the group in attendance. Express the sincere sentiments with which the gift is presented. Let the recipient realize that the donor considers it an honor to be able to offer the present. If the gift has intrinsic merits, it might be advisable to point them out. However, you should indicate that the gift is basically a symbol of the esteem in which the donor regards the recipient.)

III. *Make the actual presentation*
(Save the actual presentation until the last. Up to this point you have been speaking to the audience, but now turn toward the donee and address him directly. With sufficient volume for all to hear make a formal presentation in some such way as the following: "It is with a deep sense of appreciation that the Alpha chapter of Phi Kappa Tau presents to you this silver vase. We shall never forget your loyal, devoted service as our faculty adviser.")

The Speech of Acceptance

When a person receives a gift in a public presentation, he is expected to express appropriately his appreciation. Such speeches are called those of acceptance. They follow and grow out of addresses of presentation. The acceptance speech must be well adapted not only to the audience, occasion, donor of the gift (if different from the audience), and the gift but also *to the preceding speech of presentation.* The subject matter as well as the mood is suggested, if not determined, by the speech of presentation. If the manner of the presenting speaker has been solemn and dignified, your remarks in acceptance must be likewise sober. If the presenter has been especially congenial, however, you must respond in an appropriate vein. The length of such a speech varies somewhat in different circumstances, but is usually short. Whereas a mere "thank you" is sufficient in some cases, a twenty-minute address might be expected from the speaker who accepts a monument for a community. It is difficult to give advice on the preparation of the speech of acceptance; often much of such a talk necessarily is an impromptu adaptation to the total speaking situation. However, by using the following sequence you will be able to plan, at least tentatively, what you are going to say.

I. *Express appreciation for the gift*
(Express genuine sentiment to indicate that you appreciate the gift for its own value and because it serves as a symbol of the group's regard. Refer specifically to the gift. Be simple and direct, without straining for effect.)

II. *Minimize your own services and magnify the services of your associates*
(Be modest but not self-depreciating. Pay sincere tribute to those who have helped you achieve your success. For example, a halfback receiving a trophy as the conference leader in total yardage gained might state that he never forgot that he had ten men blocking for him and that most of his long gains were the result of key blocks by teammates. He might even relate the story told of Knute Rockne, who once became disturbed by the egocentric attitude of his famous backfield of the Four Horsemen. Wishing to teach his ball carriers a lesson, Rockne asked his varsity to vote on the question: "Which is more important to a football team, a backfield or a line?" The result was, of course, 7–4, with the linemen all voting against the backfield. To deflate the ego of his Four Horsemen still further, Rockne let the regular linemen warm the bench while a line composed of substitutes blocked for the Horsemen. After consistently failing to gain, the backfield learned the lesson that a ball carrier is only as effective as his line permits him to be.)

III. *Pay tribute to the donor*
(Express your recognition of the merits of the group awarding the gift. As an example, if a representative of a civic committee for traffic safety has awarded you a loving cup at a public dinner for being the safest driver in Trenton, you should in your acceptance direct deserved attention to the outstanding work of the committee. Usually such people serve faithfully as a civic duty, with little or no compensation. Briefly indicate how much you and other citizens appreciate their efforts to reduce the maimings and fatalities caused by accidents.)

IV. *Conclude by accepting the gift*
(You may tie your speech together and attain a climax by saving a formal acceptance of the gift until the close of your talk. During your comments of formal acceptance you should probably look at the gift, turn toward it, pick it up, or in some way give recognition of its presence. A professor who had completed a series of lectures to the graduate students of another university was presented with an expensive set of books. The formal acceptance portion of her speech went something like this: "Let me thank you again for solving most of my recreational problems for the next few months. This beautiful two-volume set of *The Letters of Virginia Woolf* will be my evening companion for weeks to come. Every time I pull a volume out of its box,

I will remember this and many other expressions of your kindness during my week's sojourn with you.")

The Speech of Welcome

The reception of a distinguished visitor, group, or convention at a public occasion necessitates an appropriate address of welcome. The speech of welcome must extend a sincere greeting which makes the recipient feel appreciated and at ease. Such speeches should be short, well planned, cordial, gracious, and in good taste. Unlike the speech of introduction which serves to present *a guest speaker and his speech,* the speech of welcome is concerned only with welcoming a *newcomer* to the organization or to the community. Because of the wide variety of possible types of speaking situations, only general suggestions can be offered for the organization of such a speech. However, with some alterations the following sequence should be satisfactory for most circumstances.

I. *Identify the group extending the welcome and the recipient of the welcome*
(Here are some sample opening sentences: "The City of Rochester is honored to welcome home its Olympic gold medal winner and native son, Thomas Higgins." "The University of Houston is pleased to welcome to this campus the eminent physicist, Dr. John Sievers." "This evening the Baptist Training Union has the unusual opportunity of experiencing the fellowship of our state director, Bess Frockton.")

II. *Make complimentary remarks about the individual or group you are welcoming*
(Mention some of the outstanding accomplishments or services rendered by the visitor(s). If you are welcoming a convention, call attention to the significance of the meeting, and to the purpose, importance, and history of the group.)

III. *Explain the reason for the visit*
(Tell why the guest(s) is (are) visiting the organization or community, for example, for scientific investigation, relaxing at the beach, engaging in athletic competition, or visiting relatives. If you are welcoming a convention that has selected your locality for particular reasons, you might mention such reasons.)

IV. *Mention the mutual benefits that will occur through the association*
(Sometimes it is fitting to direct attention to the contributions the guest(s) will make to the welcoming organization, or to society at large. Perhaps your community or welcoming organization will be able to aid the recipient in various ways. For instance, when welcoming a new member into a fraternal organization you might show briefly the mutual benefits of this new association.)

V. *Conclude by specifically extending the welcome*
(Only one or two sentences are needed to sum up the gist of the entire speech

in a congenial expression of appreciation at being able to extend the welcome. For instance, a representative of the Los Angeles Chamber of Commerce might close a welcome to a visiting dignitary in this way: "And so, Mr. Ambassador, the city of Los Angeles and the entire State of California extend a most cordial welcome. We hope that you will stay with us for many weeks, and that the California sun, beach, and surf will offer you relaxation and pleasure.")

The Speech of Response to a Welcome

Usually some remarks of appreciation must follow a speech of welcome. If a convention is being welcomed to a community, some representative of the group will make an appropriate response. If an individual is so honored, he will be expected to say a few words. Such a speech of response should be brief and well adapted to the speaking situation and to the preceding speech of welcome. Like the speech accepting a gift, the speech of response sometimes must of necessity be largely impromptu. However, if you know you will be called upon to make such a speech, you can plan your remarks under the following main heads.

I. *Identify for whom and to whom you are speaking*
(If responding to a speech of welcome as the representative of an organization or convention, you should mention the group by name. Recognize immediately the source which has accorded you the honor. A Rotarian visiting a lunch meeting of that organization in another state might begin his remarks of response in this way: "I appreciate this opportunity to visit the Denver Rotary Club. . . .")

II. *Express genuine appreciation for being so honored*
(Sometimes, as the Rotarian did in the preceding paragraph, a simple statement of appreciation is sufficient. If a signal honor has been accorded, however, it might be well to explain why you value the courtesy. An astronaut just returned from a space flight might, upon being welcomed by a public reception, explain his gratitude for such a demonstration.)

III. *Make complimentary remarks about the group or agency extending the welcome*
(For instance, if you are the spokesman for a convention being welcomed to a city, refer briefly to the cultural, scenic, industrial, or historical significance of the community. If a particular organization has welcomed you as a guest, you might indicate that you are aware of the reputation, exploits, or services of the organization. Be gracious, tactful, and sincere.)

IV. *Mention that you are looking forward to pleasant experiences*
(If you or the group you represent are to be the guests of a community for a period, you could say that you are looking forward to an enjoyable and enriching visit. If you are a guest at a meeting, you might express an expectation of enjoying the proceedings.)

The Speech of Farewell

When a person leaves the employ of a company, moves to another locality, or goes into retirement, he may wish to express publicly his regrets about leaving. Frequently, such speeches take place at farewell dinners or parties, and are preceded by the awarding of a "going-away" present. In such a case, the speaker must thank the group for the gift, in addition to saying good-bye. The typical valedictory speech should cover the following points:

I. *Express genuine regrets about leaving*
(Tell why you are reluctant to leave. Say that you have enjoyed your work, and tell why. Dwell briefly on your pleasant associations with the members of the group. Reminisce over previous happy experiences. Indicate that you will take with you many happy memories. Plan this heading carefully to avoid aimless rambling about past happenings.)

II. *Indicate that you hold the group in high esteem*
(Express genuine regard for the merit and quality of the group. Reveal that you have profited much from the association.)

III. *Predict future cordial relations*
(Express the hope that although you are leaving, you will still experience the friendship of the group and will enjoy many future contacts. If you are moving to another locality, tell your listeners that you anticipate seeing them at, let us say, the national sales convention, or invite them to call upon you in case they visit your new community. If you are planning a tour of Europe before retiring to Florida, you might promise to send postcards to the members of the group and, upon your return, to tell them of your experiences.)

IV. *Conclude by wishing the group farewell*
(Make this step short. Avoid dragging out a final expression of good-bye. If you can think of nothing else to say, you can rely on the often-used: "Good-bye and God bless you.")

The Radio and Television Speech

With radio and television blanketing the entire nation, today's speaker should be prepared to use these media when the opportunity or obligation to do so arises. In the following section, we note significant similarities and differences between speaking to the face-to-face audience and to the broadcast or telecast audience. Although the differences necessitate certain adaptations, the basic procedures for effective speech preparation and delivery, discussed earlier in this book, are essentially applicable to radio-television speaking.

Your purpose in speaking to the air audience is basically the same as in any face-to-face situation. Whether facing a live audience, a microphone, or a camera, speakers seek to inform, entertain, or persuade their listeners; they discuss and debate, introduce other speakers, pay tribute, and say farewell; they must choose subjects, find materials, organize and support ideas, and deliver them effectively.

Understanding the Radio and Television Audience

In keeping with our consistent emphasis on the audience as the focal point in speechmaking, we turn now to an analysis of the air audience as the first step in understanding the adaptations of speech content and delivery to the mass media.

The Air Audience Is Potentially Universal and Almost Certain to Be More Heterogeneous than the Face-to-Face Audience. The ticket to an air performance is access to a radio or television set. Thus, an audience may include individuals of various races, creeds, political beliefs, ages, occupations, and intellectual capacities. Their attitudes toward you and your subject may range from the strongly favorable to the strongly opposed. Members of the face-to-face audience, on the other hand, are likely to have more in common. Attending a speech requires considerably more effort than tuning in a radio or television receiver; in the former case, you must go to the speaker, whereas the mass media speaker comes to you. Attending a speech involves travel time, possibly unpleasant weather, and some expense. The inconvenience of attending a face-to-face speech tends to limit the audience to those who are already interested or who feel an obligation to appear. Moreover, a "live" speech is often restricted to members of a particular organization and their guests. These factors tend to provide considerable audience homogeneity.

The potential universality of an air audience is, of course, limited by *interest and opportunity.* Although anyone within range may sample your speech if he wishes, only those who are sufficiently interested in you and/or your topic will linger until the end. Your audience will also be limited by the availability of listeners or viewers. During the daytime hours, the audience is composed predominantly of homemakers and shut-ins. Children clamor for their favorite programs in late afternoons and early evenings. The man of the house is likely to be in the audience only during evening hours on work days, although he is more generally available on weekends. Another limitation on the universality of the audience is that some stations obviously point toward specialized groups. Small urban stations may cater to farmers' interests; some stations woo music lovers with programs of "good music"; and college-owned outlets specialize in educational offerings.

The Radio and Television Audience Is Composed of Many Small, Intimate Groups and Single Individuals. When the President talks to 100 million or more people via radio and television, he is entering the privacy of, say, 35 million living rooms, automobiles, club rooms, and the like. Listeners and viewers in small groups are sufficiently influenced by their surroundings to expect a warm, informal, and conversational approach by the speaker; they will tolerate excessively vigorous projection and a formal speaker manner only if they know that the speech is being broadcast before a face-to-face audience.

No Circular Response Is Possible with the Air Audience. Unless a visible audience is present, the radio-television speaker has no way of discovering during his speech what response he is evoking from his listeners. Without audience feedback, the speaker may experience difficulty in developing a lively sense of communication, in converting ideas into extemporized expression, and in using voice and body with maximum effectiveness. Later, we consider methods of compensating for a lack of feedback in broadcast speaking.

The Air Audience Is More Difficult to Hold. Members of an actual audience are reluctant to distract a speaker and audience by leaving while a speech is in progress. Furthermore, attendance is usually prompted by interest in the speech, the speaker, or the occasion, and possibly all three. The radio-television listener, however, is subject to no embarrassment if, by turning his dial, he abandons a speaker in the middle of his speech. Other programs compete for his attention: the speech may be in competition with a variety show, a comedian, or an intersectional football game. Also, distractions in his environment may make his attention difficult to retain. Crying babies, the clamorous play of young children, ringing telephones, buzzing doorbells, and the conversation of companions may bid strongly for his attention.

In the light of this discussion of the nature of the air audience, we turn now to those adaptations in preparation and delivery that will enhance the effectiveness of the broadcast speech.

Preparing the Radio and Television Speech

In adapting basic principles of speech preparation to the mass media, certain guides should be observed.

Content and Organization. Although you may be primarily interested in reaching a limited segment of the air audience, remember that your actual audience may include many kinds of people, possessing differing interests, backgrounds, and intelligence. Consider also that your air time is more limited than in most face-to-face speaking situations and that the air audience has no opportunity to ask questions for clarification and amplification. Because of these factors, observe the following guides:

(1) A simple, very clear pattern of organization should be used.

(2) Supporting materials should be as universal in appeal as possible, easy to follow, and concrete. The typical air audience will not follow you through abstract explanations or complicated reasoning.

(3) The difficulty in holding the air audience requires that special utilization be made of such interest factors as proximity, vivid concreteness, significance, variety, and humor.

(4) Because of the rigid time demands of the media, you may be cut off the air if your speech is more than fifteen seconds too long. Keep in mind that the opening and closing, station identification, announcements, and commercials will typically consume two or three minutes of a fifteen-minute period. Determine the exact amount of time that is available to you and tailor your speech accordingly.

Language. Language should be simple and concrete, yet alive and colorful. Avoid pedantic and hackneyed expressions. Use provincialisms sparingly, particularly on a network presentation. Sentence structure should be varied, but complicated periodic structures should rarely be used. Simple, reasonably short, sentences should predominate. Move from one idea to the next with informal, varied, clear transitions. Above all, be certain that the speech sounds like a speech and not like an essay.

Preparing Manuscripts and Outlines. Most radio and television speeches are probably read or extemporized from manuscript. Until you gain experience, you probably should plan to use a manuscript when using the mass media. In addition to the advice given earlier in this chapter for preparing the speech manuscript, consider the following suggestions. Because time limits are strictly enforced, write and rewrite until maximum clarity and conciseness is achieved. Make allowance for the possibility that nervous tension may cause you to speak more rapidly than in rehearsal. Planned flexibility may be achieved by bracketing near the end of the speech an optional section that can be retained or deleted as time permits. Obviously, the bracketed material should not be crucial to your speech.

If you wish, place markings on the typescript to aid in emphasis and vocal phrasing (see pp. 359–360). Since you will not be concerned with eye contact in the *radio speech,* unless an actual audience is present, you will be free to give full attention to your manuscript. It should be typewritten and double or triple spaced. If your eyes demand slightly larger print, type exclusively in capital letters. Instead of bond paper and onion skin, both of which tend to crackle noisily, perhaps use cheaper, pulplike paper, which is relatively quiet when handled.

If your manuscript speech is to be *telecast,* two additional suggestions should be heeded in your preparation. Visual aids are particularly helpful in television, where close-up shots reveal minute details. For example, although useless in an actual audience situation, words in a newspaper clipping held in the speaker's hand are clearly readable in a close-up shot. Visual aids also relieve the audience of the probable monotony of looking at the speaker for extended periods. Before preparing visual aids, however, consult the broadcast studio for technical advice. A second suggestion is to become so familiar with the speech that you reduce to the barest minimum your dependence upon the manuscript. Occasional glances at your text should be sufficient to keep you on track. Of course, while the camera is trained upon a visual aid rather than upon you, you may read from your manuscript. Rather than to use a manuscript, some speakers prefer to use large sign cards or a mechanical prompting device from which a televised speech may be read.

From the manuscript speech, we turn now to a discussion of the extemporaneous speech delivered from an outline. This method of preparation and delivery is not customarily used in radio. Most extemporizing on radio is done in discussions, debates, and interview programs. When a speech is to be extemporized on radio or television, rehearse sufficiently to ensure that you know precisely the sequence of the ideas you wish to present and that you will be able to express your ideas fluently. During your practice, resolve that in the actual speech you will not add impromptu material. Although the seasoned speaker may safely do this, knowing that he will be forced to cut or telescope some material near the end, the novice should plan to adhere closely to his outline. A helpful device in timing is to record in the margin of the outline at various places the minutes that should have elapsed by the time you get to that point in the speech.

Delivering the Radio Speech

Shortly before the actual broadcast, you probably will be asked to do a brief audition on the microphone. This usually consists of speaking for a few moments into the microphone while the control operator checks your volume and your position and distance in relation to the mike. In a large station, you may be assigned a studio and a producer for rehearsal. If possible, rehearse the entire speech. It will give you an opportunity to check your timing and to profit from the professional advice of the producer.

It is important for the beginning speaker to realize that a normal conversational level provides sufficient volume for radio transmission and that he has considerable freedom of physical movement, so long as he stays within the pickup range of the microphone. He should be careful, however, to avoid extraneous noise. The sensitive microphone picks up the noise of drumming fingertips, smacking lips, heavy breathing, rustling papers, an accidental bumping of the microphone, and so forth.

Delivery must also take into account the absence of the visual code. Emphasis, pause, vocal phrasing, pitch, inflection, quality or timbre, and vocal animation must be used to best advantage if one's voice is to compensate for the lack of visual stimuli. Your listeners want you to sound like a relaxed, animated conversationalist sitting in the same room with them. Although gestures and facial expression will not reach your listeners, do not hesitate to use them, if you wish. Often their use aids the voice in getting across meaning.

If an audience is present during your radio talk, as in the case of a public forum, delivery should be very much like that used in any actual audience situation. When a radio speech is directed primarily at an actual audience, radio listeners do not expect an intimate, subdued delivery, and seem content to be "overhearing" a live-audience speaking situation.

We have noted the need to adjust speech length to time limits. Continue this time-consciousness in delivering your speech. Check the passage of time periodically by looking at the studio clock or at the producer, who will give you time signals and can also communicate by prearranged signals other pertinent information about the progress of your talk.

A word might be said at this point about stage fright. To some speakers, microphones and insulated studios are frightening. Although such fear usually is alleviated by time and experience, the beginner can help relieve his trepidations by ignoring the microphone, except for the physical and vocal adjustments previously mentioned, by thinking of some friend and speaking directly to him. Do not be upset if your voice sounds "different" to you; the cause is the construction of the studio: to prevent reverberation the walls absorb rather than reflect much of the sound. You will probably become accustomed to this acoustical condition during the audition and rehearsal period.

Delivering the Television Speech

In respect to the auditory aspects of communication, television speaking is much like radio speaking. In both cases, sound is picked up by microphone. One difference in microphone adaptation should be noted, however. Whereas the radio microphone usually is stationary, the sound pickup in television is made by a lavaliere mike (a small instrument that may be suspended from a cord around your neck or clipped to your tie or lapel) or by a microphone attached to a boom, which can be moved around the studio during a program, if necessary. Adjustments in the directional pickup also can be made by the operator of the boom. This makes it possible for the microphone to follow the speaker and adjust to his movements. The television speaker, therefore, does not have to be as particular about his distance and position in relation to the microphone.

Television speaking allows the use of movement, gesture, and facial expression to help make ideas meaningful, much as in addressing the face-to-face audience. The face-to-face listener, however, maintains a constant position and views you from a single angle and distance. The television audience, on the other hand, may see you from a distance of forty feet directly in front, from an angle at a distance of ten feet, a profile view at five feet, or a close-up which brings you "near enough to touch." Furthermore, almost nothing escapes the close-up lens. The intimacy with which your audience sees you makes facial expression, movement, dress, and personality extremely important.

You will probably be asked to rehearse your television presentation in much the same way that a radio speech is auditioned. The rehearsal period will serve to check camera locations, the placement of lights, your voice level, and any movements that you intend to make in the course of your speech. Find out how far you may move in any direction and still be in camera range, and where you are to sit; check on arrangements for the placement of visual aids and the cues to be used for training the camera on them. In order to make the most of your audition follow closely the suggestions and guidance of your producer. He is familiar with the equipment and facilities of his station; it is his job to see that your program goes off well.

Make the Most of the Visual Aspects of Delivery. (1) Without overdoing it, try to be expressive facially; avoid being a "dead pan." Let your face reflect the meaning and emotion you hope to convey. (2) If your televised speech is being presented to an actual audience, employ movement and gesture in the usual animated way described in Chapters 12–14. If speaking exclusively to the television audience, you probably will be seated at a desk or in an easy chair. Perhaps your only movement would consist of moving to another seat or going to and from some visual aid. Gestures may be plentiful, but should not be too sweeping or too rapid. (3) Mannerisms are distracting, especially in close-up pictures. Try to avoid needless physical movements. (4) If your televised speech is presented to an actual audience, keep your eyes on them; if no audience is present, look at the camera. If more than one camera is in use, the one that is "taking the picture" may be identified by a glowing red light on its face. By "following the red light" you will always keep eye contact with your viewers. Transfer of your gaze from one camera to another should not be sudden and jerky; when a camera light goes out, turn your head easily and relatively slowly toward the newly activated camera and look at the lense. If powerful floodlights and spotlights cause difficulty in seeing the lense, fix your eyes upon the red light, which is always easily seen. (5) Dress and appearance are of obvious concern to the television speaker. Color television necessitates carefully chosen color combinations. Pronounced plaids and extravagantly figured or striped designs create a "busy" effect. Be cautious about wearing tie clasps, metal bracelets, and other accessories that sparkle or shine. Careful grooming is essential, of course. Makeup may be necessary to soften facial lines, cover shiny noses and circles under the eyes, or to eliminate the unkempt look that heavily bearded men find difficult to avoid, even when freshly shaven.

Adjust Vocal Delivery. The suggestions given for vocal delivery in radio speaking also apply to television speaking. Two differences, however, should be noted: in television vocal delivery is supplemented by visual aids, facial expression, movement and gesture; extended pauses, which leave "dead air" on radio, may seem entirely natural in the television speech, particularly when a chart or demonstration is the center of attention. As in radio, the television speaker should avoid "high pressure," overly emphatic delivery. Animation, vitality, and enthusiasm can be projected without bombast.

Summary

The successful use of the information contained in this chapter depends upon a proper application of the fundamental principles discussed in the first thirteen chapters. This chapter has presented particular factors to be considered in presenting speeches of special types.

Exercises and Assignments

1. Write a manuscript speech, utilizing the advice given in this chapter. Read it to the class. Hand in the manuscript to your instructor for comments and criticism.

2. Deliver a goodwill speech concerning your university to a high school assembly program or to some other off-campus meeting. Report your experiences to the class.

3. Give an impromptu talk upon a topic selected for you by some member of the class or by the instructor. After studying this chapter, you should be able to think on your feet more effectively than previously.

4. Give an entertaining after-dinner speech based on the current political scene, international diplomacy, life in a college dormitory, scenes in the coffee shop, peculiar people, and so forth. If possible, this set of speeches by you and

your classmates should be given in the college cafeteria or in some eating establishment off campus.

5. During the final week of the semester give a brief speech of farewell to the class.

6. Bring a visitor to class, introduce him, and welcome him to the group.

7. In the next series of speeches, introduce a member of the class and his speech.

8. In a short talk present an imaginary award to a classmate.

9. (In conjunction with Exercise 8): Accept appropriately an imaginary award presented to you by a member of the class.

10. Either as individuals or as a group, arrange to visit a local radio or television station when live programs are being produced. Pay close attention to the microphone and camera work, particularly as it is being planned in the audition and rehearsal periods. The next class meeting may be used for discussing what you have learned from the visit and how it may help you in future radio and television speaking performances.

11. Carefully analyze a radio or television performance by some well-known speaker. Give particular attention to (1) his adaptations to his potential audience in terms of organizational pattern, Forms of Support (including visual aids, if on television) and language; to (2) his vocal delivery if on radio, and his use of both vocal and physical delivery, if on television. In class, compare your evaluation with those of others who listened.

Appendix

You may find helpful these suggestions concerning exercises and possible speech topics.

1. Prepare a five- to ten-minute speech involving a "how to do it," "how it operates," "how it is done," or "how it is produced" type of process. Develop the Body according to two to five main temporal steps or stages. This sequence is called a Time Pattern. Here are some possible subjects, many of which welcome the use of visual aids.

Operating an electronic telescope
Preparing transparencies for overhead projectors
Drawing contour maps
Making ceramics
Organizing a political club
Doing finger painting
Making a hooked rug
Learning how to relax
Preparing for a job interview
Making fishing flies
Making simple plumbing repairs
Preparing gazpacho
Treating a snake bite
How plywood is made
Converting an attic into a playroom
Conducting a business meeting
Making slipcovers
Making a time and motion study
Planning a marketing survey
How the Union forces won the Battle of Gettysburg
How the space shuttle system works
How genetic engineering operates
How false teeth are made
How a feature article is prepared for *Time* magazine
How a case is handled by the United States Supreme Court
How sugar cane is harvested

2. Deliver a five- to ten-minute talk in which you use a Spatial Pattern to describe the physical appearance of something. Examples of "how it looks" topics:

A missile gantry
A formal garden
A window display
The Milky Way
The White House
A famous golf course
A dude ranch
Carlsbad Caverns
Fisherman's Wharf, San Francisco
An historical home
Royal Gorge
Colonial Williamsburg
A giant wheat elevator
A jai alai court
A stained-glass window in a church
Kezar Stadium or Soldier Field
The Abraham Lincoln Memorial in Washington, D.C.
The Pentagon building
A tobacco warehouse
French Quarters, New Orleans
Mont-Saint-Michel
A famous bridge
The main geographical features of Mars

3. Make a five- to ten-minute speech using a Topical Pattern. Possible subjects:

Offensive and defensive football formations
Contributions of the Kiwanis clubs
Openings in government service for college graduates
The business cycle
Being a good listener
New methods for treatment of the mentally ill
Interesting customs of the Chinese
Changes recommended in the summer curriculum
Ways in which card sharks cheat
Methods by which manufacturing can be stimulated in the state
Evils of the present farm subsidy system
Advantages of proper training for policemen
Safety in the home
Types of fallacies used by politicians
Methods of improving parking facilities on campus
Benefits derived from active participation in intramural programs

4. Prepare a seven- to ten-minute speech using either the Problem-Solution or the Topical Pattern. Possible topics:

Fee splitting among physicians should be made a criminal offense
One-year jail sentences should be made mandatory for all those convicted of carrying a gun without a permit
The jury system should be abolished for all except criminal cases
Off-track betting should be legalized
All drivers should be required to pass physical examinations every three years
The United States should abandon the policy of détente with Russia
The United States should adopt a national system of public defenders
The use of marijuana should be decriminalized
The federal government should guarantee a minimum yearly income to all citizens
Fraternities and sororities should be abolished at the university
All victimless crimes should be decriminalized

The United States should underwrite a national system of crime insurance
All abortions should be made illegal
The federal government should initiate a program providing full employment
Government employees below cabinet rank should be deprived of chauffeured limousines
All candidates for the presidency should be compelled to take a rigid health examination
The present electoral system in voting for president and vice-president should be abolished in favor of direct popular vote

5. Prepare a seven- to ten-minute speech using the Criteria-Matching Pattern. Sample topics:

The commuter tax is necessary to save cities from bankruptcy
The manned bomber is obsolete
Milk is dangerous to the health
Blue laws are against the best interests of religion
The Western alliance suffers from a lack of mutual confidence
Haiti is a land of fear and misery
The CIA is a potential threat to legislative prerogatives concerning war and peace
The mistakes of the present administration have damaged American prestige abroad
The use of police decoys is immoral
The FDA is lax in supporting the public interest
Much foreign missionary work is alien to the true spirit of religion
Government offers unusual opportunities for lawyers
The local transit system is inefficient
The UN is no longer an effective instrument for international understanding
American cultural standards are declining
The present speed limit on interstate highways is unrealistic

6. Prepare a seven- to ten-minute speech in which you take the opposite side of one of the topics listed in Exercises 10 and 11.

7. Prepare a five- to ten-minute speech using a Cause-and-Effect Pattern. Some possible topics:

Inflation
Credibility gap in government
Public apathy toward the political process
Drug culture
Secrecy in government
Hospital costs
Jobless youth
Nervous tension
Crime in large cities
Affirmative action
Heart attacks
The present crisis in the UN
The racial situation in South Africa
Spirit at the university (or at our factory)

8. Prepare a five- to ten-minute talk involving the use of some visual aid. Possible topics:

Making a pair of beach sandals from a pair of old shoes
Holding a baseball for different types of pitches

Applying stage makeup
Skinning game
Docking procedures of satellites in orbit
Making a dress
Cleaning a carburetor
Making puppets
Removing a fossil from its place of discovery
The operation of a fire extinguisher
Different kinds of knots
Man-to-man and zone defenses in basketball
The seige of Vicksburg
Genetic engineering
How a submarine submerges and resurfaces
The topography of Mars
Simple plumbing repairs
The circulatory system of a human being
Some sights of Paris
A nuclear power plant
The Colorado's water system
The Kremlin
The Vatican
Westminster Abbey
The Berkeley Gardens
The Alaskan pipeline

Index